Destiny's HAND

Volume Two

WRITTEN BY
NUNZIO DEFILIPPIS
AND CHRISTINA WEIR

ILLUSTRATED BY
MELVIN CALINGO

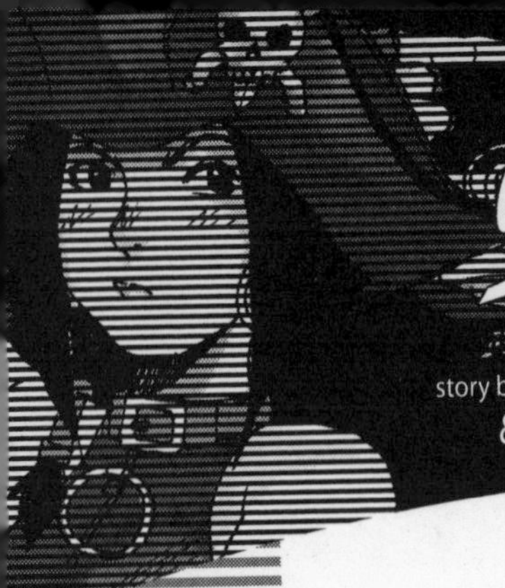

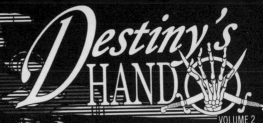

Destiny's HAND

VOLUME 2

story by Nunzio DeFilippis & Christina Weir art by Melvin Calingo

STAFF CREDITS

toning	Ludwig Sacramento
lettering & graphic design	Jon Zamar
cover design	Nicky Lim
assistant editor	Adam Arnold
editor	Jason DeAngelis
publisher	Seven Seas Entertainment

This is a work of fiction. Names, characters, places, and incidents are the products of the author's imagination or are used fictitiously. Any resemblance to actual events, locales, or persons, living or dead, is entirely coincidental.

Visit us online at www.gomanga.com.

Seven Seas

ISBN 978-1-933164-52-6

Printed in Canada

First printing: September, 2007

10 9 8 7 6 5 4 3 2 1

Destiny's HAND
Volume 2

Contents

SPECIAL FEATURES

OUR TALE SO FAR...

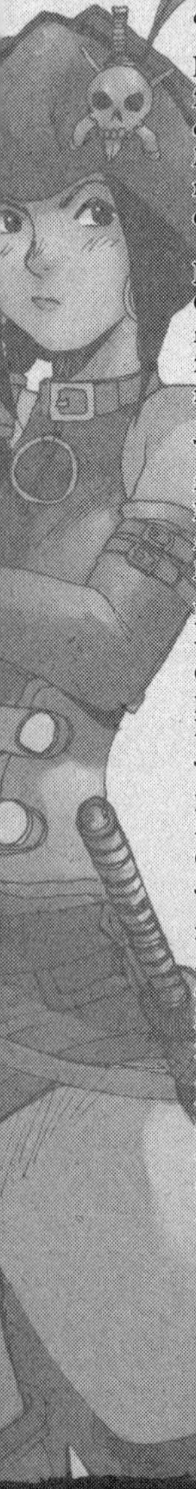

In all the seas, there is no pirate ship quite like DESTINY'S HAND.

Captained by SEBASTIAN BLAINE, the gentleman pirate, the crew of Destiny's Hand do not kill their prey. If you surrender your cargo without a fight, the crew promises your safety. Not only that, your ship is under their protection all the way to port, and they'll tell you pirate tales to boot!

But Blaine is the last of an era. The new breed of pirates are typified by LARS MULGREW, Captain of the KRAKEN, as cut-throat and vile a lot as ever set sail. They take no prisoners, leave no-one or nothing unharmed and unspoiled. More and more pirates follow this brutal new path, and this is bringing an end to the era of pirates.

But this is not the only thing that makes Destiny's Hand unique. Given magical protection by a lost love of Blaine's, the ship is nigh unsinkable. Though its magical protection does not extend to the people aboard the vessel, it makes the ship one of the most respected in the seas.

Three years ago, Captain Blaine took on a young runaway named OLIVIA SOLDANA. She has since become a member of his crew, despite the objections of some of the men aboard. She not only has Blaine's protection, but is in many ways heir to his legacy.

Repeated run-ins with Mulgrew have left Blaine wounded, and when he suffers another serious blow in combat, he confides in Olivia and a handful of crew members that he is dying. Before he dies,
he wants them to help him find the greatest treasure of all.

The Devil's Eye is said to be a magical artifact of great power hidden on the lost Isle du Diablo. Blaine made a promise to his lost love to one day find it and keep it out of the hands of truly evil pirates like Mulgrew.

The crew has one piece of the map to Isle du Diablo, but finding the treasure will require someone who speaks Priscus, the language of the ancients. The son of Blaine's lost love has such an education, and Blaine tells the crew this boy, Elias Houghton, is his son. They bring the boy to the ship, but must kidnap him to do so.

Elias was raised as the son of Governor Houghton of St. Vickensburg, the most anti-pirate port in the seas. When he arrives on the ship, he refuses to believe he is the son of a pirate. He grabs one of Olivia's guns, and prepares to execute Captain Blaine!

OLIVIA SOLDANA

Olivia is the daughter of a shipping tycoon who, when she was 13, made plans to marry her off to an up and coming naval student from a noble family on Valroux. Their ship was waylaid by Destiny's Hand, and her father behaved treacherously towards the gentleman pirate. Olivia defended her father's life, but having impressed Captain Blaine with her skill and spirit, left her parents to start a life of piracy. Now 16 years old, she is running the ship while Blaine lies dying, pretending all her orders come from him.

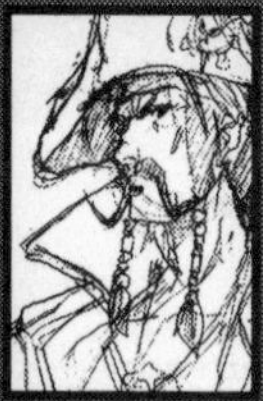

Sebastian Blaine

The Gentleman Pirate, who honors all surrenders and will not kill unless there is no other choice. He represents the old breed of pirate, more honor than savagery, and sees that way dying with him. Mortally injured by a truly evil pirate, he now asks his crew to race in order to honor the promise he made his lost love: find the Devil's Eye and keep it out of the wrong hands.

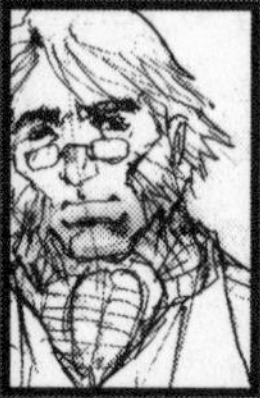

Frederick Matthau

Right hand man to Blaine, he is an old hand at the sea, and was a veteran sailor when Blaine was a young man. He is unflinchingly loyal to Blaine, and will do anything to help honor Blaine's last wish. He is Olivia's main advisor, and knows the truth about everything on the ship.

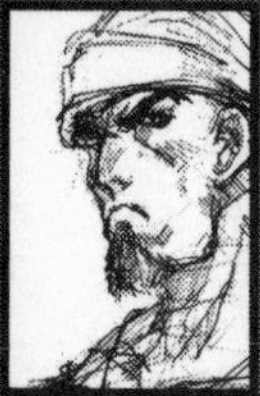

Diego Basteon

The boatswain (bosun) of Destiny's Hand, he is in charge of discipline and order. He is fiery, and seemingly tired of the surrenders and fight-free pirate existence. He is unaware that Blaine is dying, but is becoming suspicious. He resents Olivia's presence on the ship, and resents her giving the orders even more.

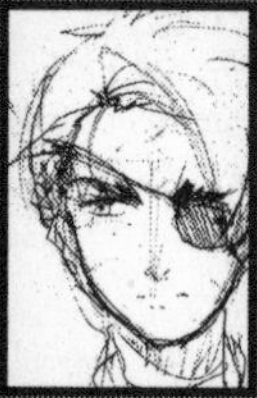

Owen Galviston

Owen is a scribe, and a biographer, on the ship to write a biography of Captain Blaine. He's been with the crew for so long, he acts like he's one of them, and some doubt he'll ever write that biography. No one knows how he got the eyepatch, as he's not really a combat kind of crewman. He doesn't know the truth about the Captain, but is also starting to get suspicious and feel left out.

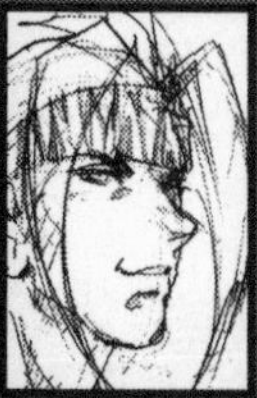

Lars Mulgrew

Mulgrew is the face of the new breed of piracy. Brutal, selfish, and with no sense of honor. He's matched up with Olivia at least once, and wants another shot at the little 'minx.' He's the one who injured Blaine, but doesn't know yet that his work has left the Gentleman Pirate dying. He was after the same ship Blaine was, the one that had the first map piece, but it's unclear at this time if he knows anything about the Devil's Eye.

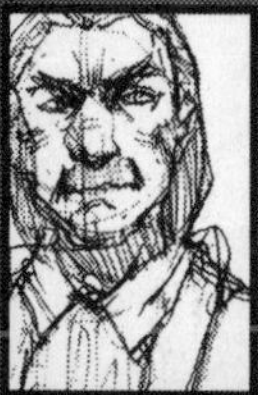

Thomas Houghton

Governor of St. Vickensburg, Houghton was promised to marry Katherine Marsh, when she ran off and had an affair with Sebastian Blaine. She returned to him and they were married, and he has convinced himself she was kidnapped by the vile Blaine. They had a son, and Houghton always convinced himself that son was his. His hatred for pirates has always been fueled by his knowledge that Katherine was in love with Blaine until the day she died.

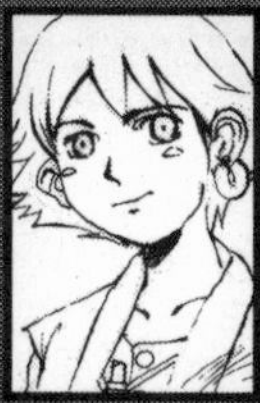

Wyatt

A young urchin who found his way onto the ship and is lookout for Destiny's Hand. He overheard the truth about Blaine, and thought this meant he could be considered part of the core crew who helped find the Devil's Eye. But his laziness and general lack of responsibility on the ship kept Blaine from making him a key crew member. This hurt young Wyatt's feelings, and he's been sulking around the ship ever since.

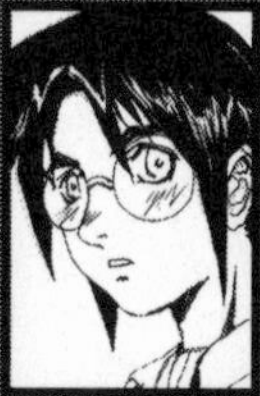

Elias Houghton

Raised by a very anti-pirate governor, Elias never knew that this was not his real father, and that he was actually the son of Sebastian Blaine. He has been educated in a manner befitting a governor's son, and is something of a young genius. He has mastered the long dead language of the ancients, Priscus, which means the crew of Destiny's Hand needs him to help them find the treasure. His hatred of pirates has prevented him from accepting the facts about his mother that he, deep down, knows to be true. He was very intrigued by Olivia, even after learning she was a pirate.

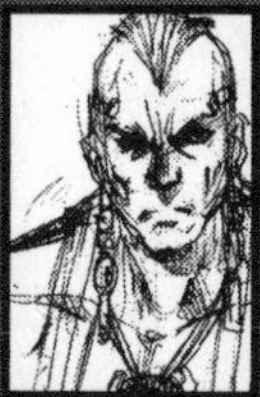

Badru

An island native who is wiser and better educated than most will give him credit for, Badru's loyalty is to Blaine. But he is very protective of Olivia. He knows the Captain is dying, and is willing to cover this up to help the crew get used to having Olivia in charge.

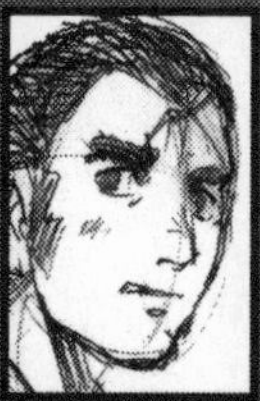

Michel Langrisse

Captain of Le Sabre Argenté, flagship of the Valroux fleet, Michel is from a noble Valroux family. He was the young man who the 13-year-old Olivia was supposed to marry. He has admiration for the crew of Destiny's Hand, and deep affection for Olivia. But he has warned Olivia that his governor is under pressure to close Valroux's port to even the most gentlemanly of pirates.

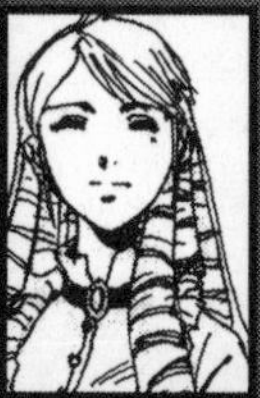

Katherine Houghton / Lady Kate

Katherine Marsh ran off to avoid marrying Thomas Houghton, and fell in love with a young Sebastian Blaine. Skilled in the magical arts, she foresaw the future, and saw a day when Blaine's crew would be the last of the noble pirates and the powerful Devil's Eye would be pursued by those with evil in their hearts. Pregnant with Blaine's child, she knew that their son would need a classical education to decipher the clues to the Devil's Eye, so she left Blaine to return to Houghton. To protect Blaine, she left a piece of her magical soul within the ship's figurehead. Katherine died in childbirth. But the figurehead, Lady Kate, is the magical protector of the ship. She influences luck and chance to favor the ship and keep it from sinking. The extent of Lady Kate's power and her true nature are unknown.

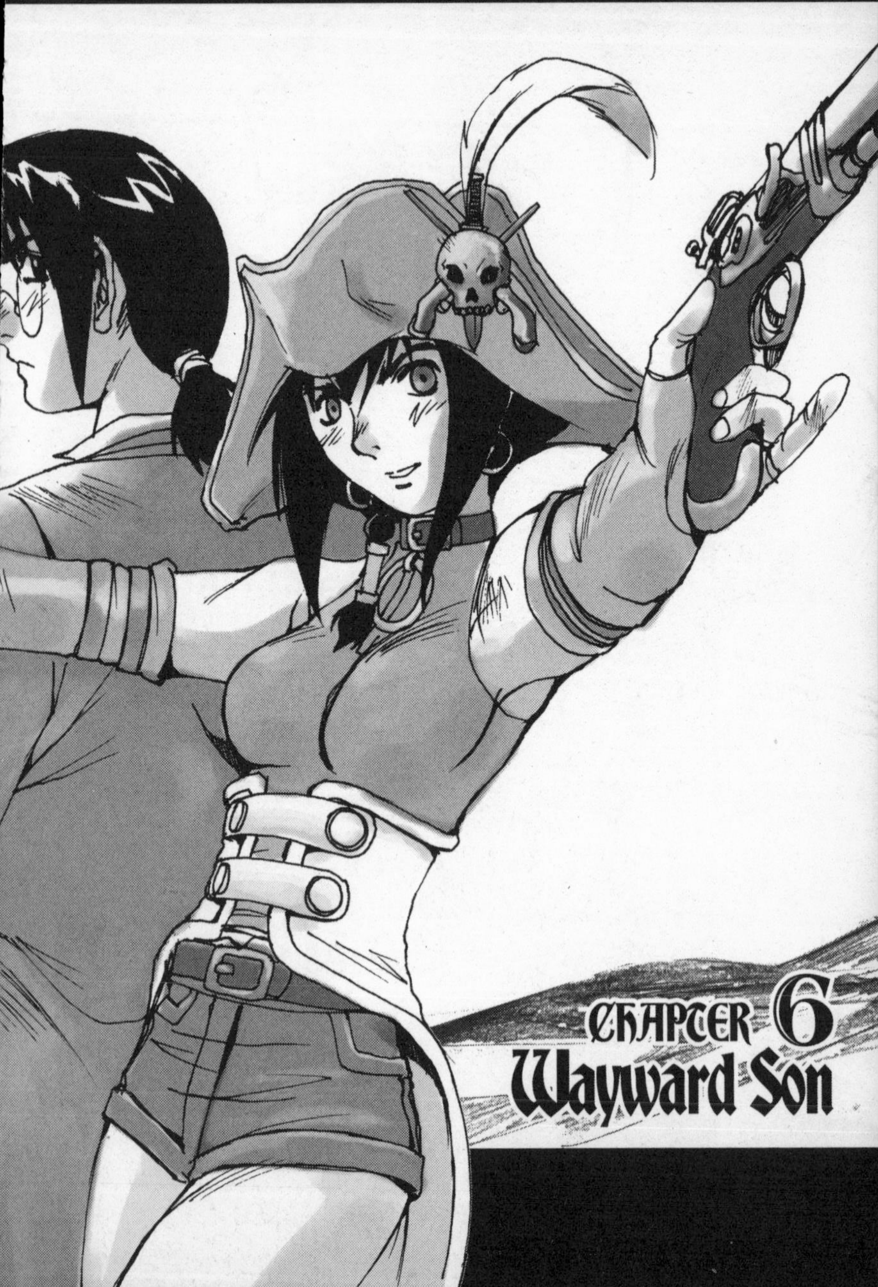
CHAPTER 6
Wayward Son

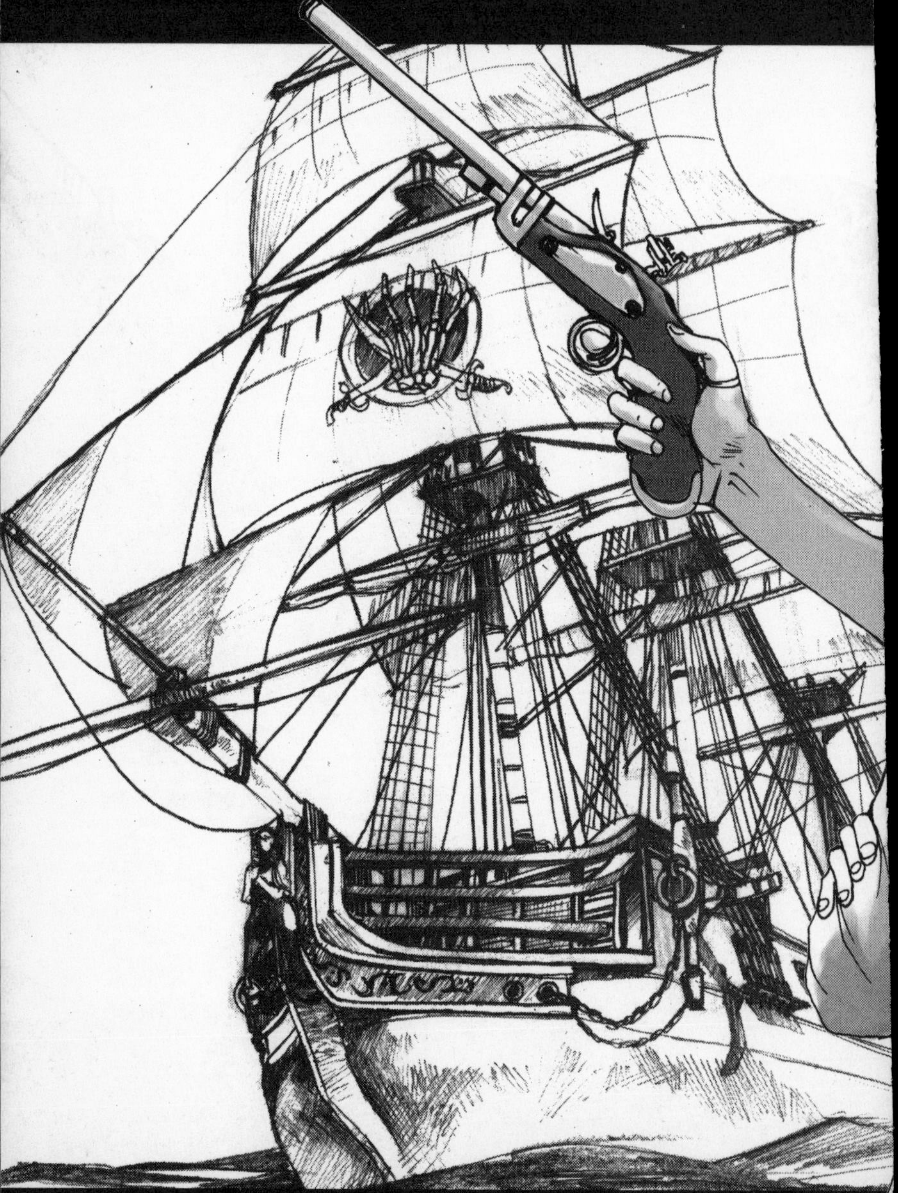

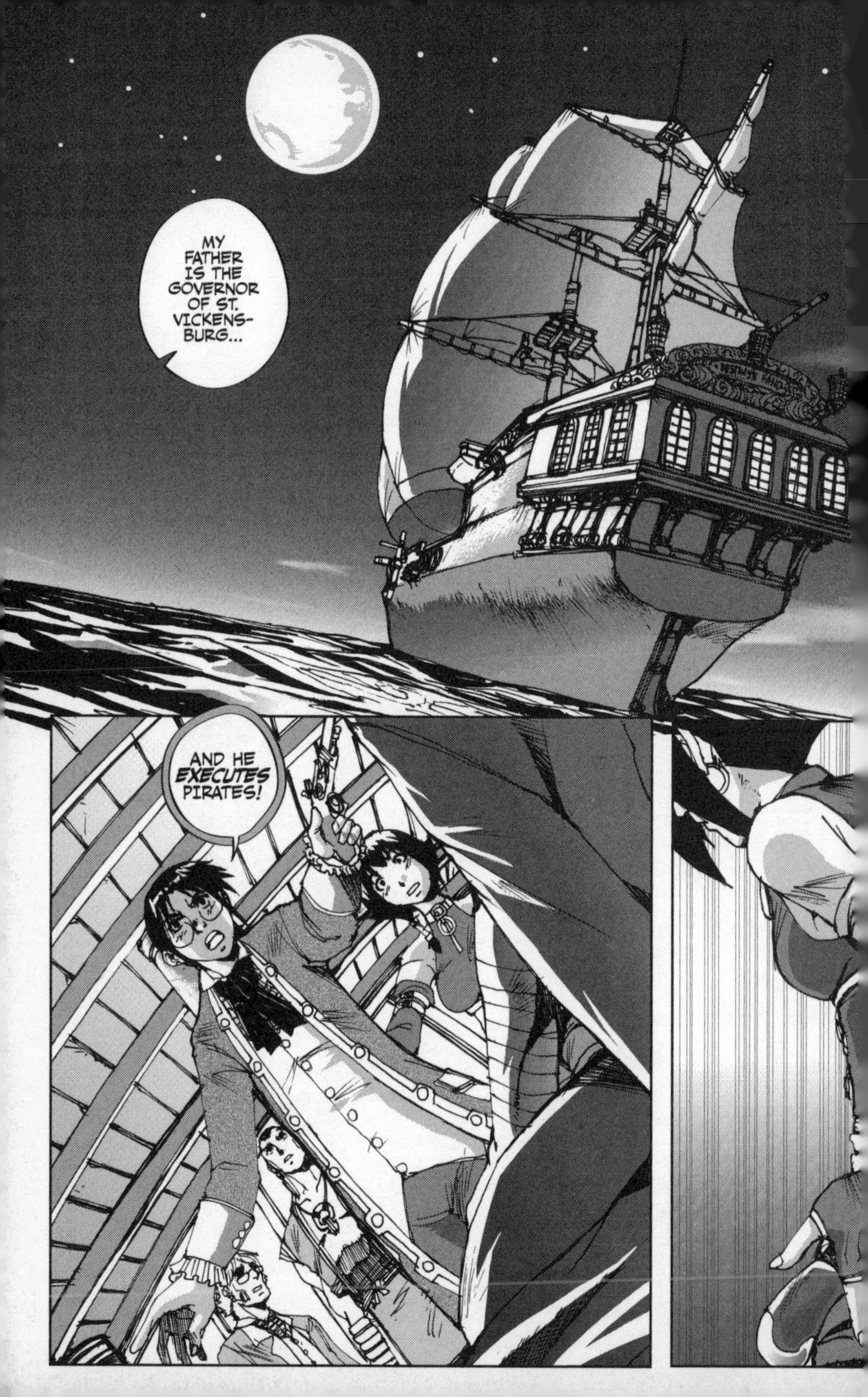
MY FATHER IS THE GOVERNOR OF ST. VICKENSBURG...
AND HE *EXECUTES* PIRATES!

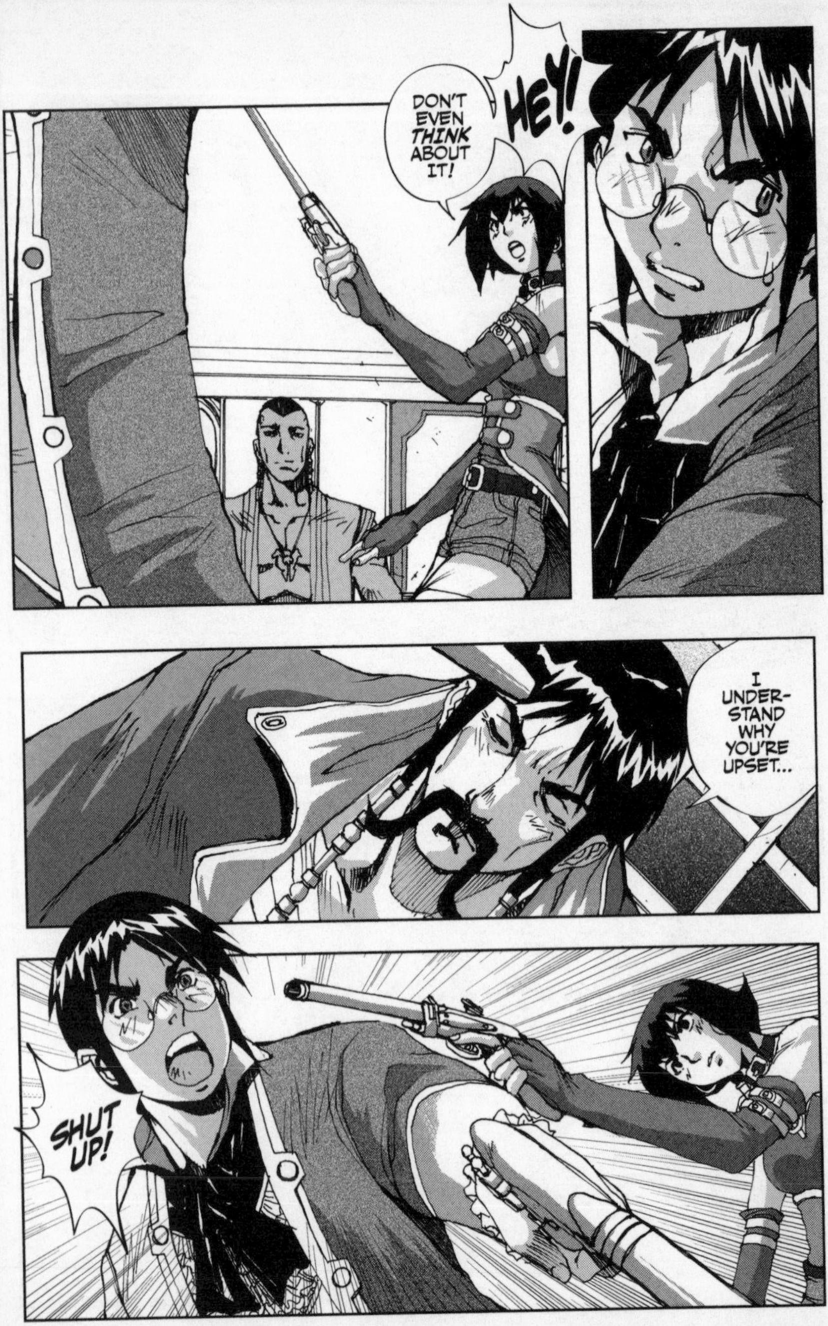
HEY!
DON'T EVEN *THINK* ABOUT IT!
I UNDER-STAND WHY YOU'RE UPSET...
SHUT UP!

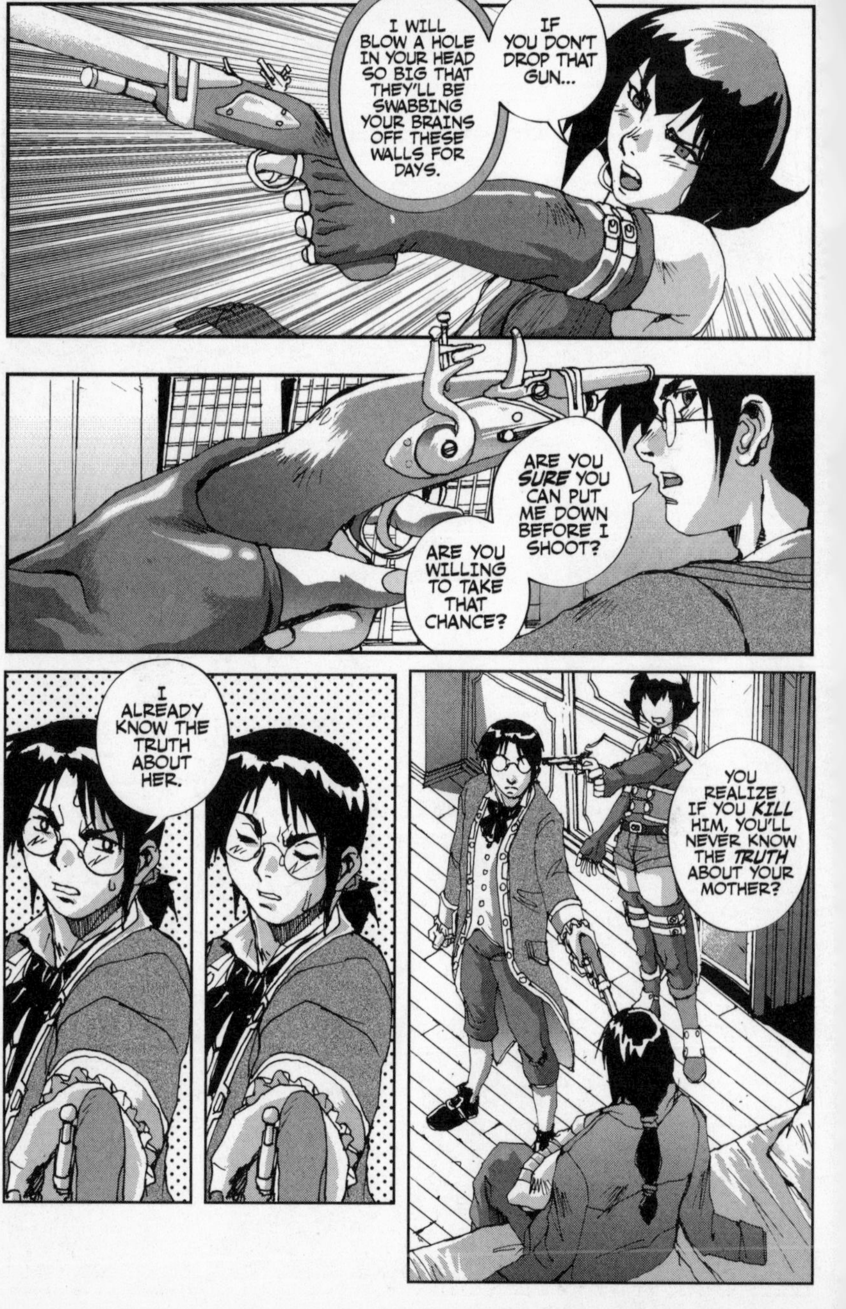
IF YOU DON'T DROP THAT GUN...
I WILL BLOW A HOLE IN YOUR HEAD SO BIG THAT THEY'LL BE SWABBING YOUR BRAINS OFF THESE WALLS FOR DAYS.
ARE YOU SURE YOU CAN PUT ME DOWN BEFORE I SHOOT?
ARE YOU WILLING TO TAKE THAT CHANCE?
YOU REALIZE IF YOU KILL HIM, YOU'LL NEVER KNOW THE TRUTH ABOUT YOUR MOTHER?
I ALREADY KNOW THE TRUTH ABOUT HER.

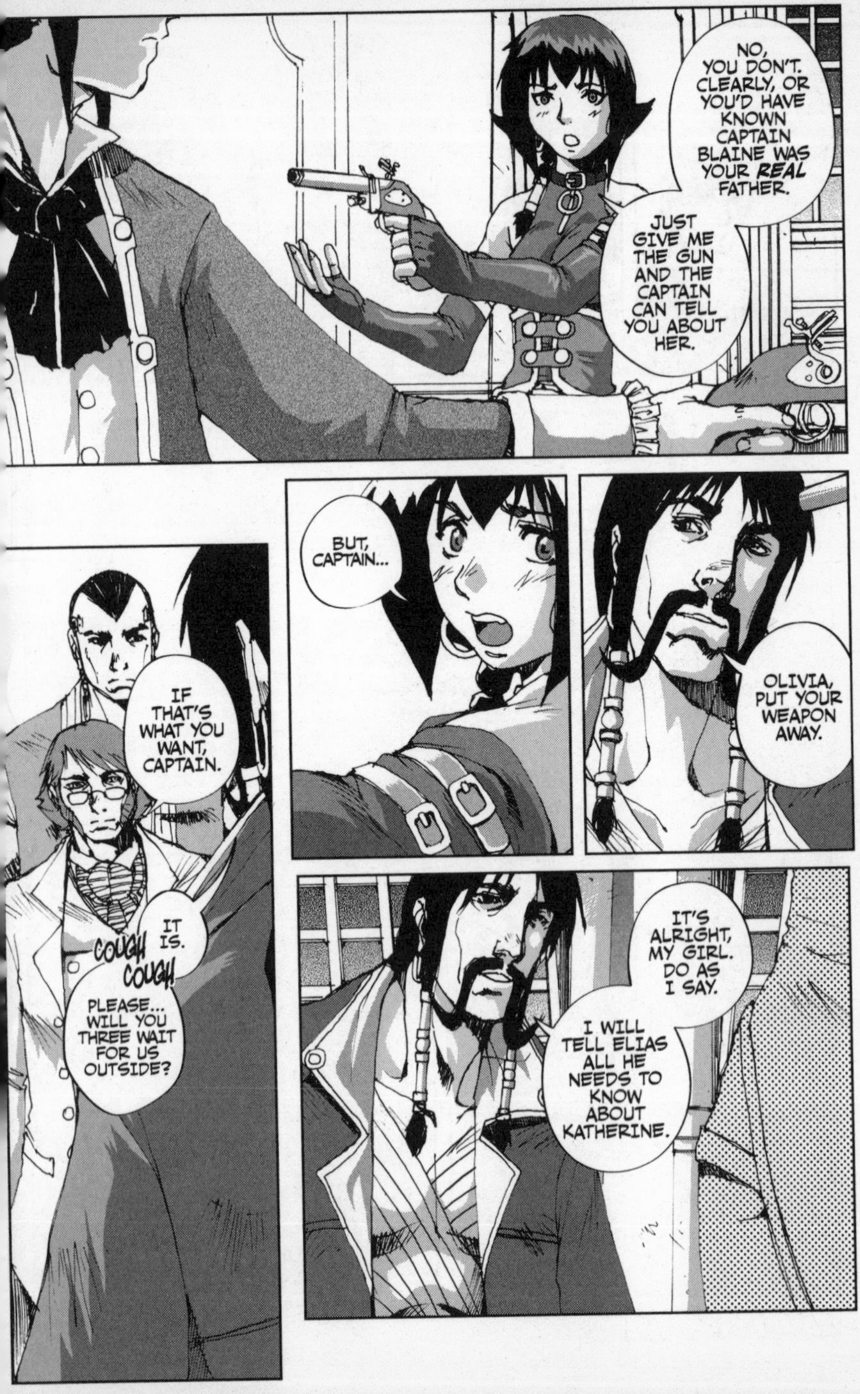
NO, YOU DON'T. CLEARLY, OR YOU'D HAVE KNOWN CAPTAIN BLAINE WAS YOUR REAL FATHER.
JUST GIVE ME THE GUN AND THE CAPTAIN CAN TELL YOU ABOUT HER.
OLIVIA, PUT YOUR WEAPON AWAY.
BUT, CAPTAIN...
IT'S ALRIGHT, MY GIRL. DO AS I SAY.
I WILL TELL ELIAS ALL HE NEEDS TO KNOW ABOUT KATHERINE.
IF THAT'S WHAT YOU WANT, CAPTAIN.
IT IS.
COUGH COUGH
PLEASE... WILL YOU THREE WAIT FOR US OUTSIDE?

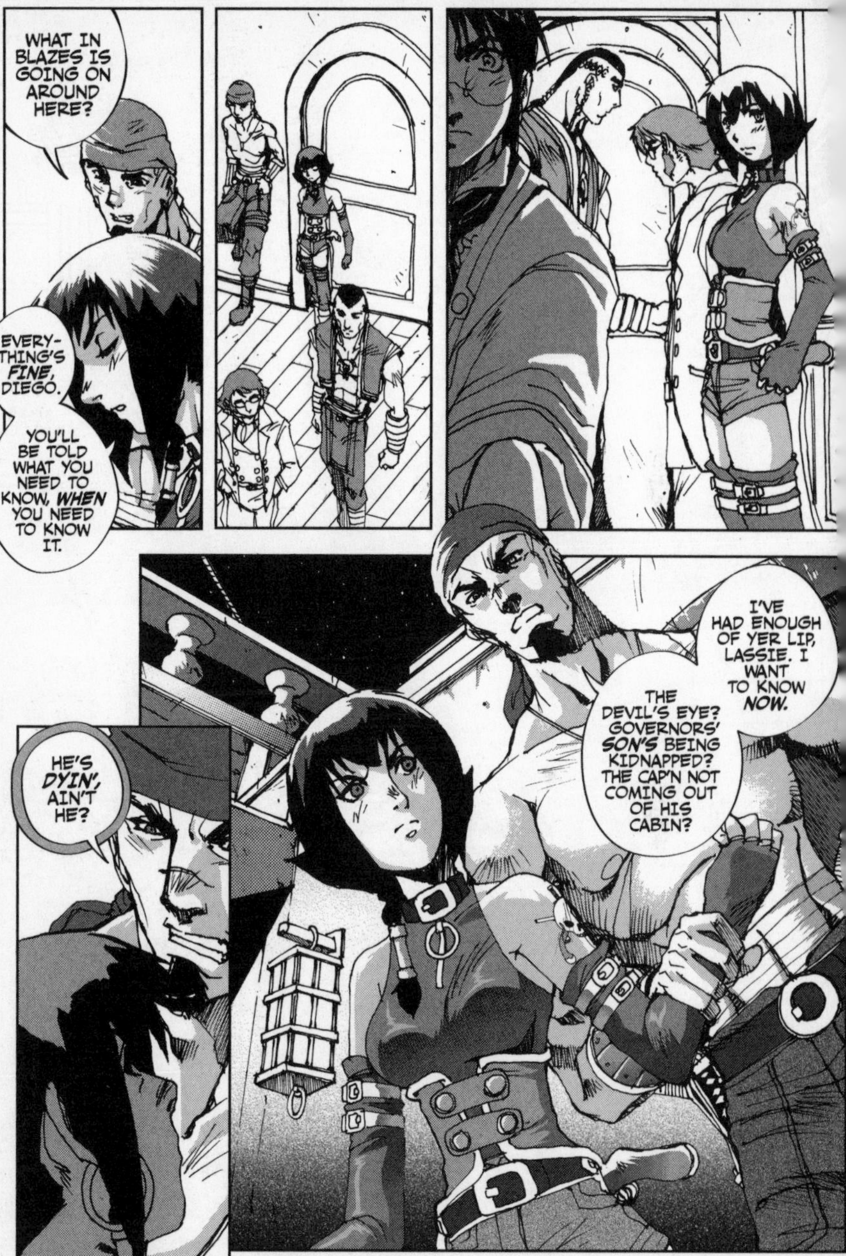
WHAT IN BLAZES IS GOING ON AROUND HERE?
EVERYTHING'S *FINE*, DIEGO.
YOU'LL BE TOLD WHAT YOU NEED TO KNOW, *WHEN* YOU NEED TO KNOW IT.
I'VE HAD ENOUGH OF YER LIP, LASSIE. I WANT TO KNOW *NOW.*
THE DEVIL'S EYE? GOVERNORS' *SON'S* BEING KIDNAPPED? THE CAP'N NOT COMING OUT OF HIS CABIN?
HE'S *DYIN'*, AIN'T HE?

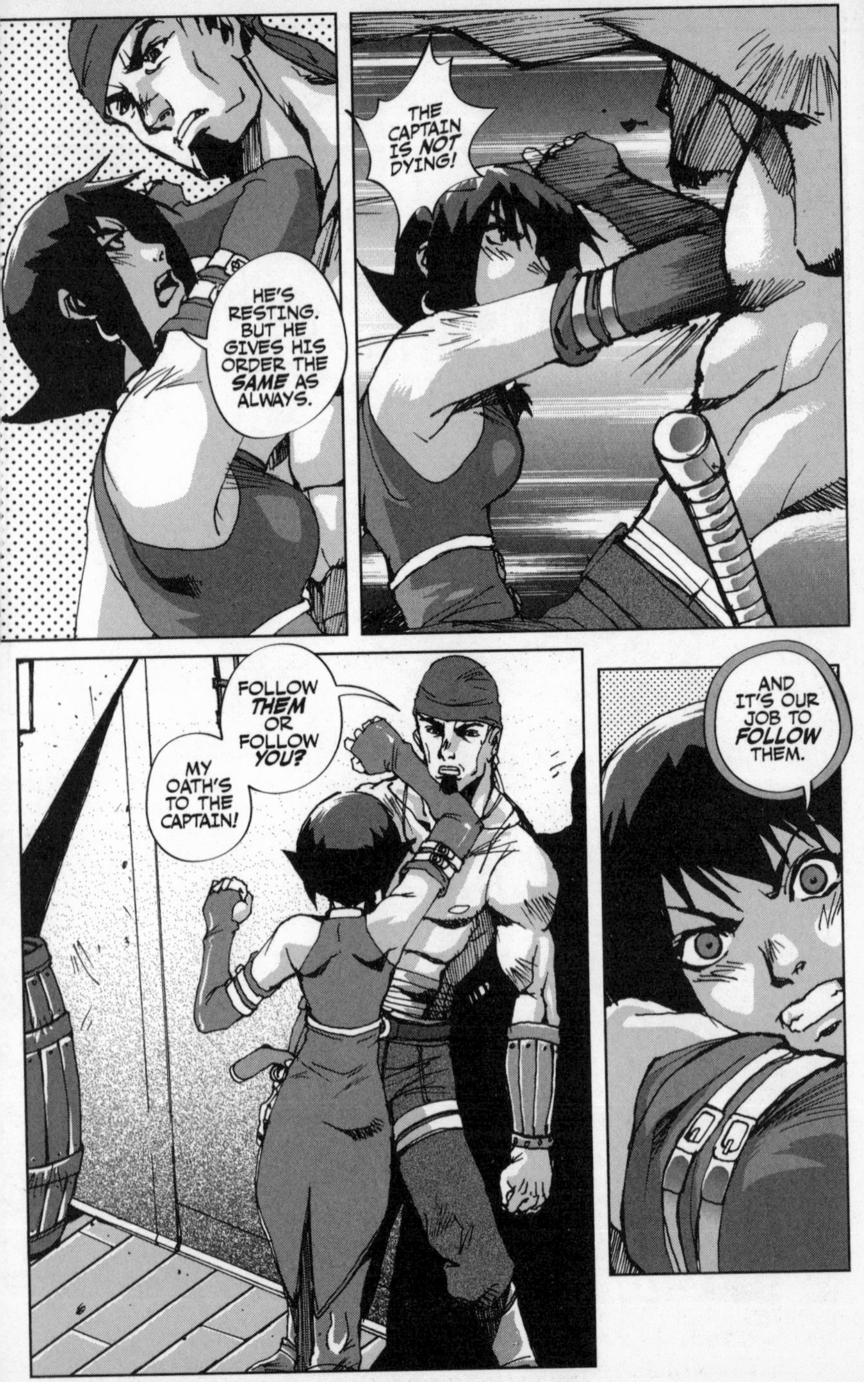
THE CAPTAIN IS *NOT* DYING!
HE'S RESTING. BUT HE GIVES HIS ORDER THE *SAME* AS ALWAYS.
AND IT'S OUR JOB TO *FOLLOW* THEM.
FOLLOW *THEM* OR FOLLOW *YOU?*
MY OATH'S TO THE CAPTAIN!

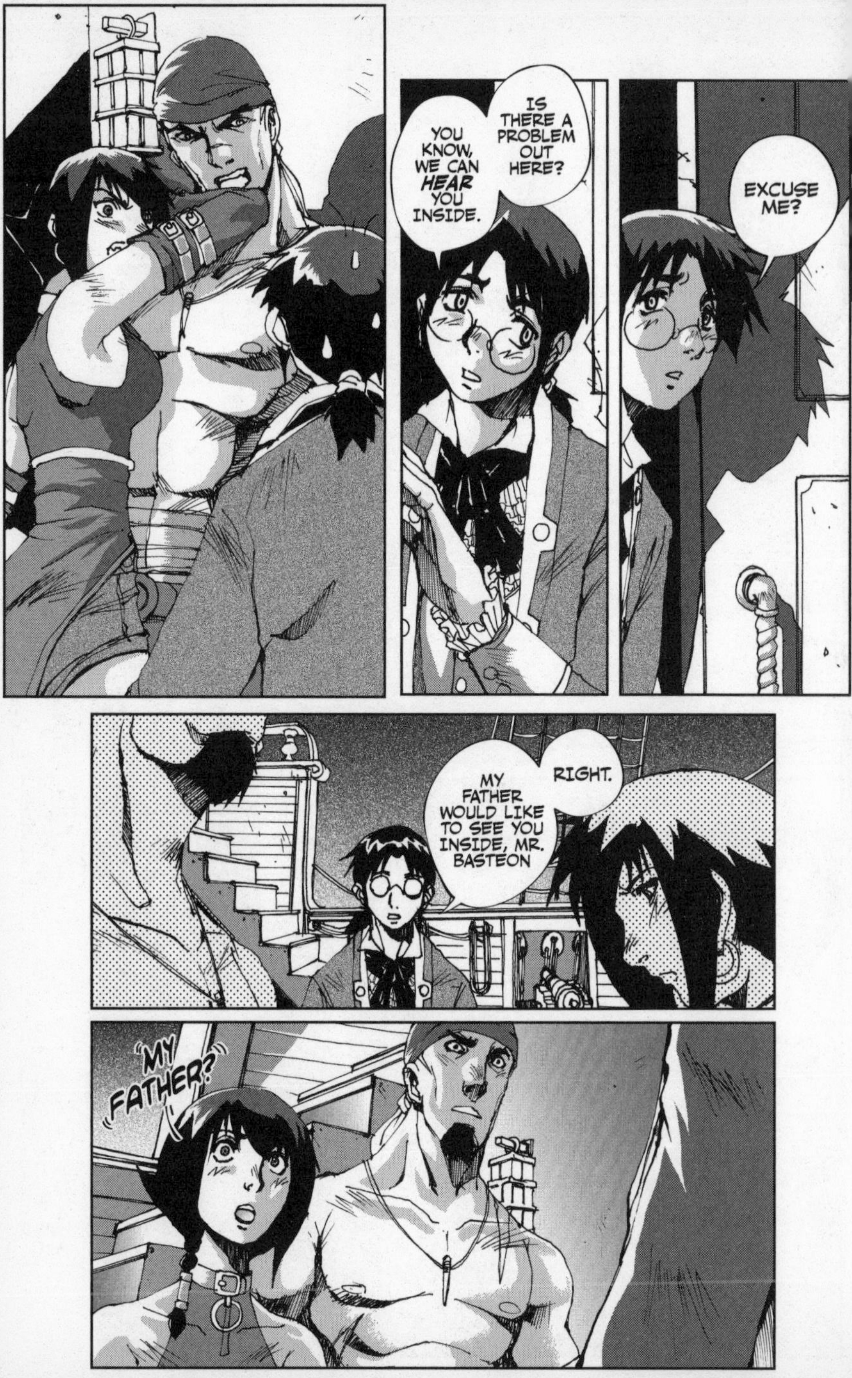
EXCUSE ME?
IS THERE A PROBLEM OUT HERE?
YOU KNOW, WE CAN HEAR YOU INSIDE.
RIGHT.
MY FATHER WOULD LIKE TO SEE YOU INSIDE, MR. BASTEON
"MY FATHER?"

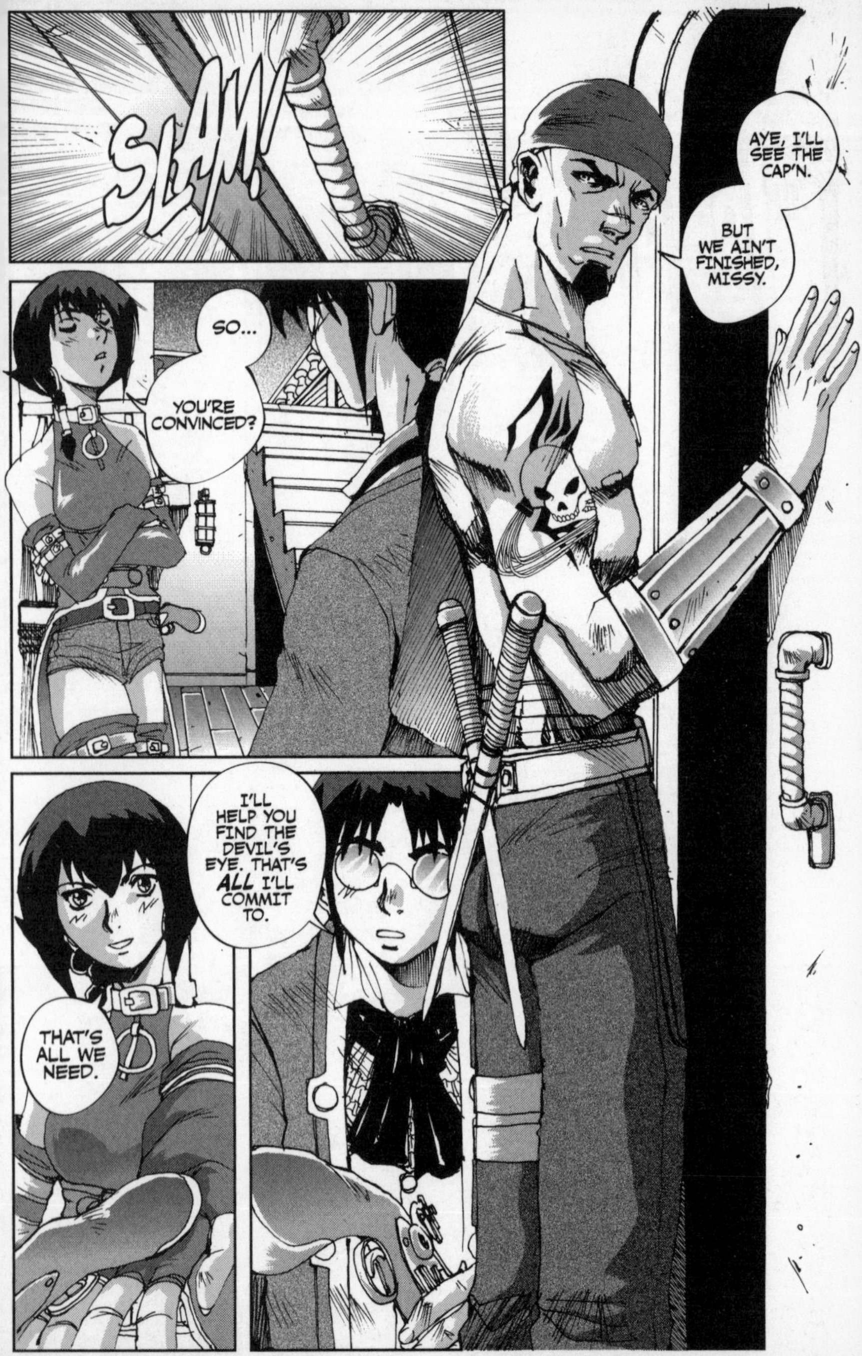
AYE, I'LL SEE THE CAP'N.
BUT WE AIN'T FINISHED, MISSY.
SLAM!
SO...
YOU'RE CONVINCED?
I'LL HELP YOU FIND THE DEVIL'S EYE. THAT'S **ALL** I'LL COMMIT TO.
THAT'S ALL WE NEED.

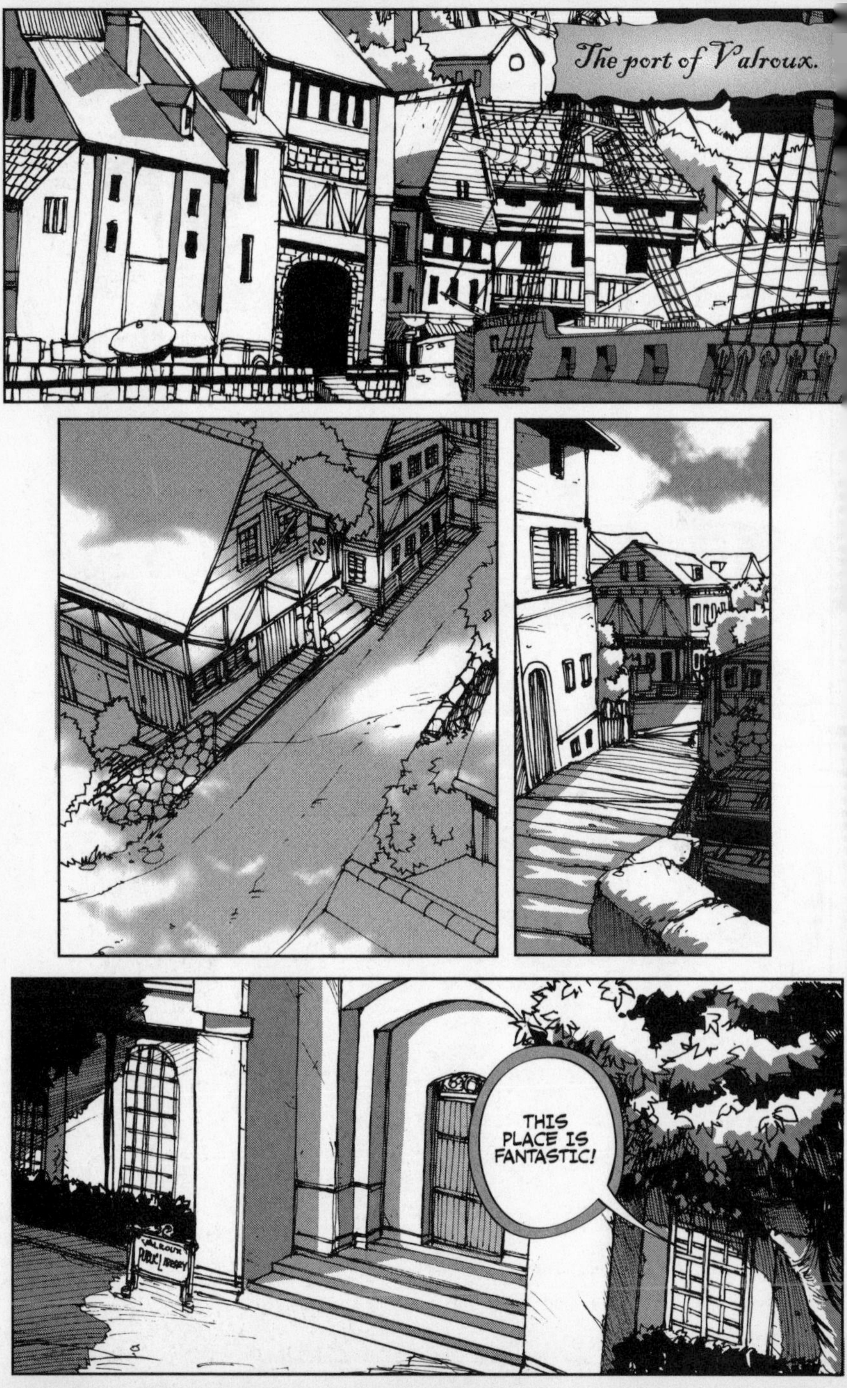
The port of Valroux.
THIS PLACE IS FANTASTIC!
VALROUX PUBLIC LIBRARY

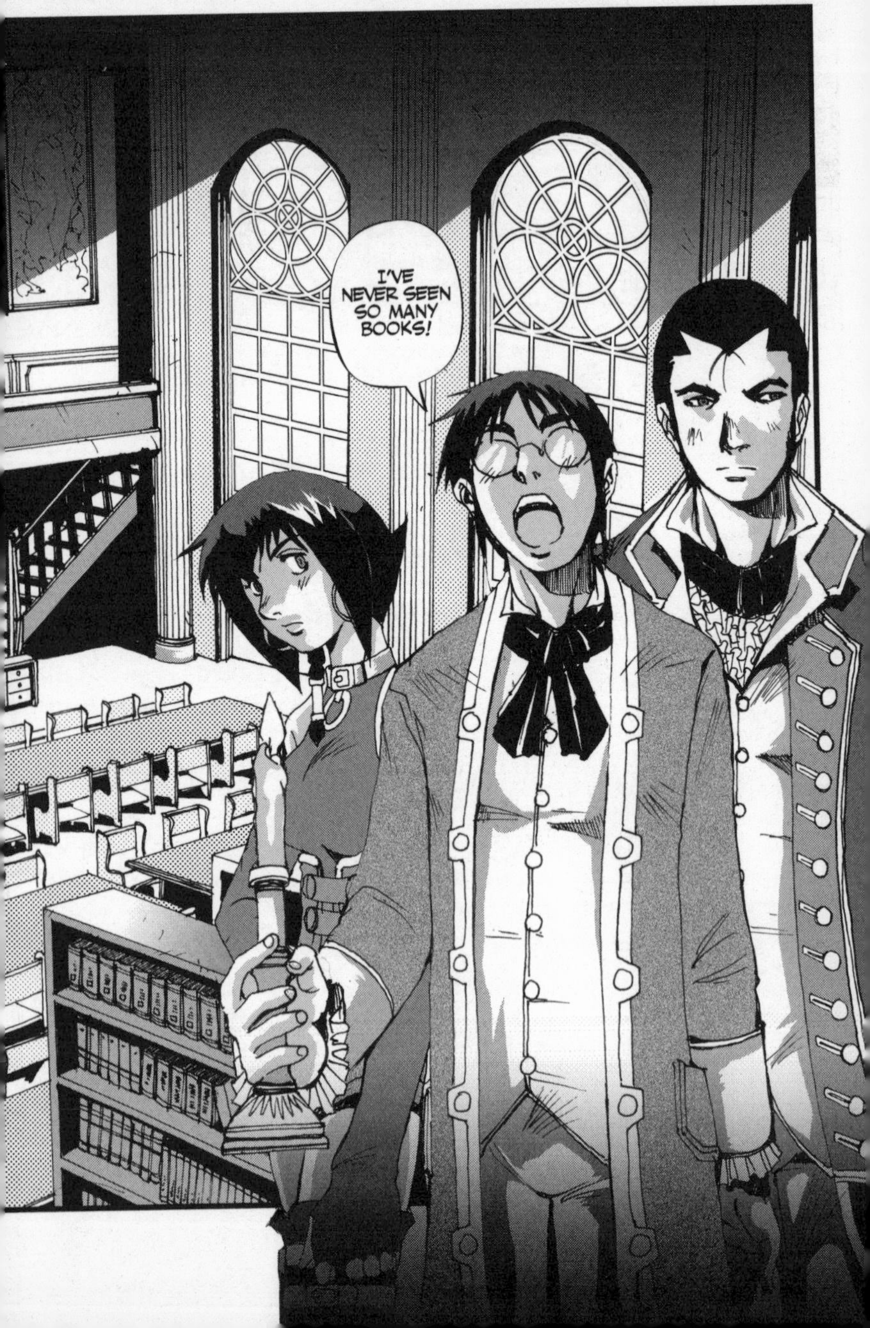
I'VE NEVER SEEN SO MANY BOOKS!

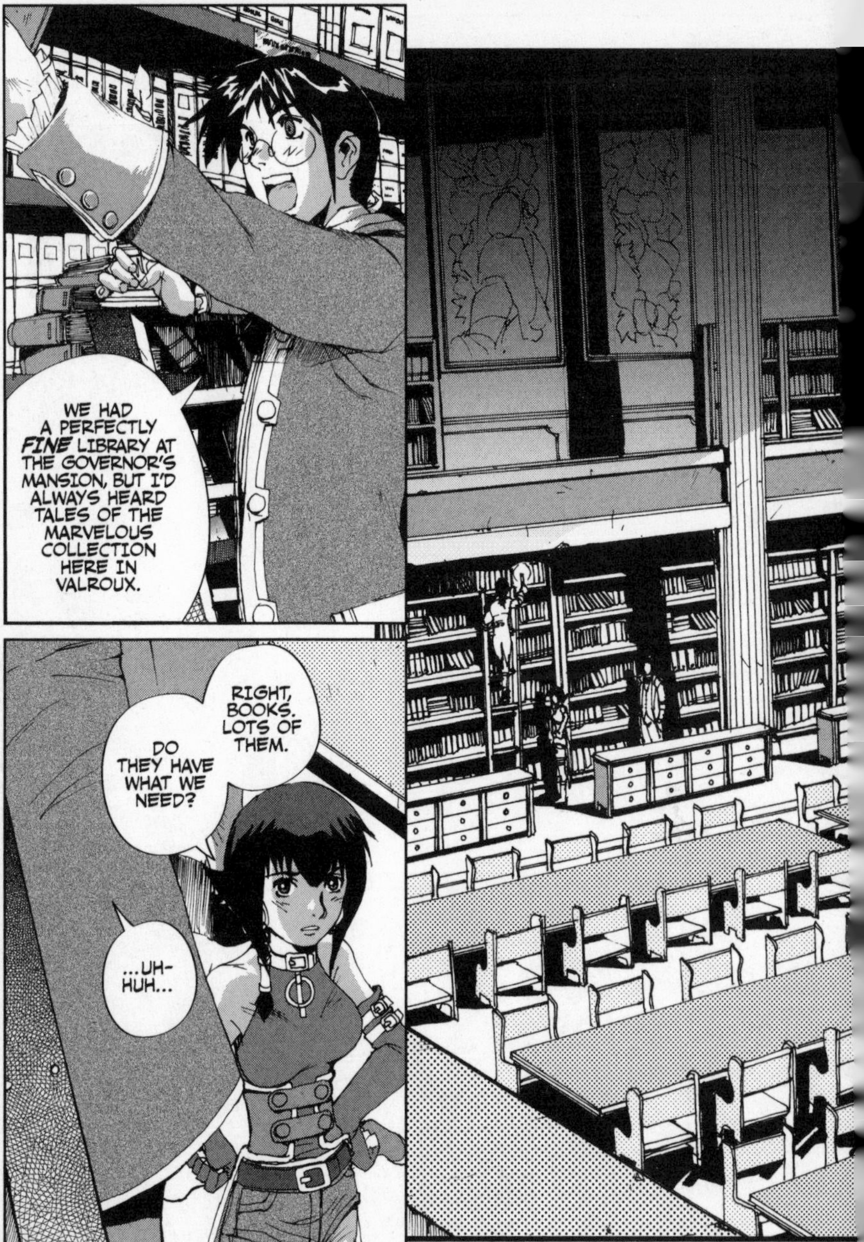
WE HAD A PERFECTLY *FINE* LIBRARY AT THE GOVERNOR'S MANSION, BUT I'D ALWAYS HEARD TALES OF THE MARVELOUS COLLECTION HERE IN VALROUX.
RIGHT, BOOKS. LOTS OF THEM.
DO THEY HAVE WHAT WE NEED?
...UH-HUH...

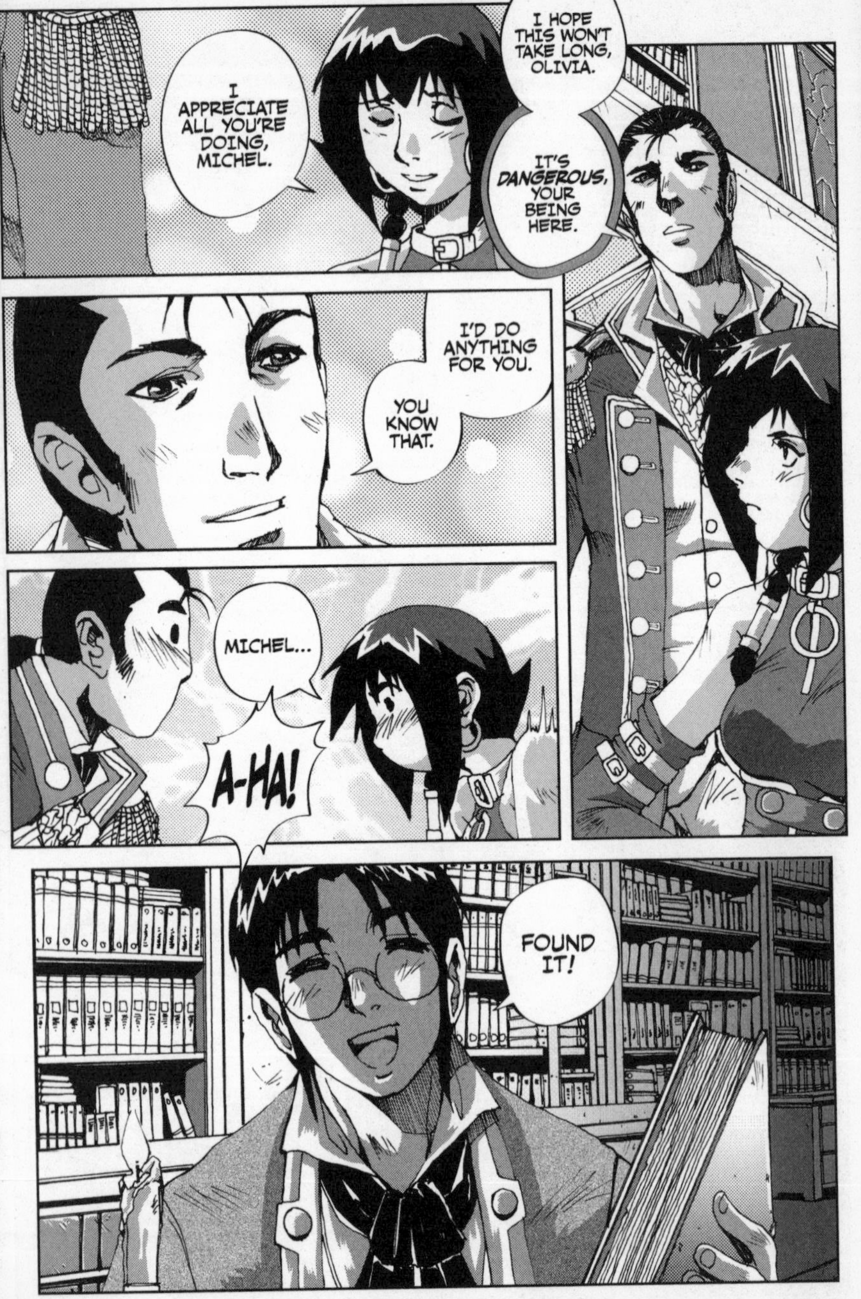
I HOPE THIS WON'T TAKE LONG, OLIVIA.
IT'S *DANGEROUS*, YOUR BEING HERE.
I APPRECIATE ALL YOU'RE DOING, MICHEL.
I'D DO ANYTHING FOR YOU.
YOU KNOW THAT.
MICHEL...
A-HA!
FOUND IT!

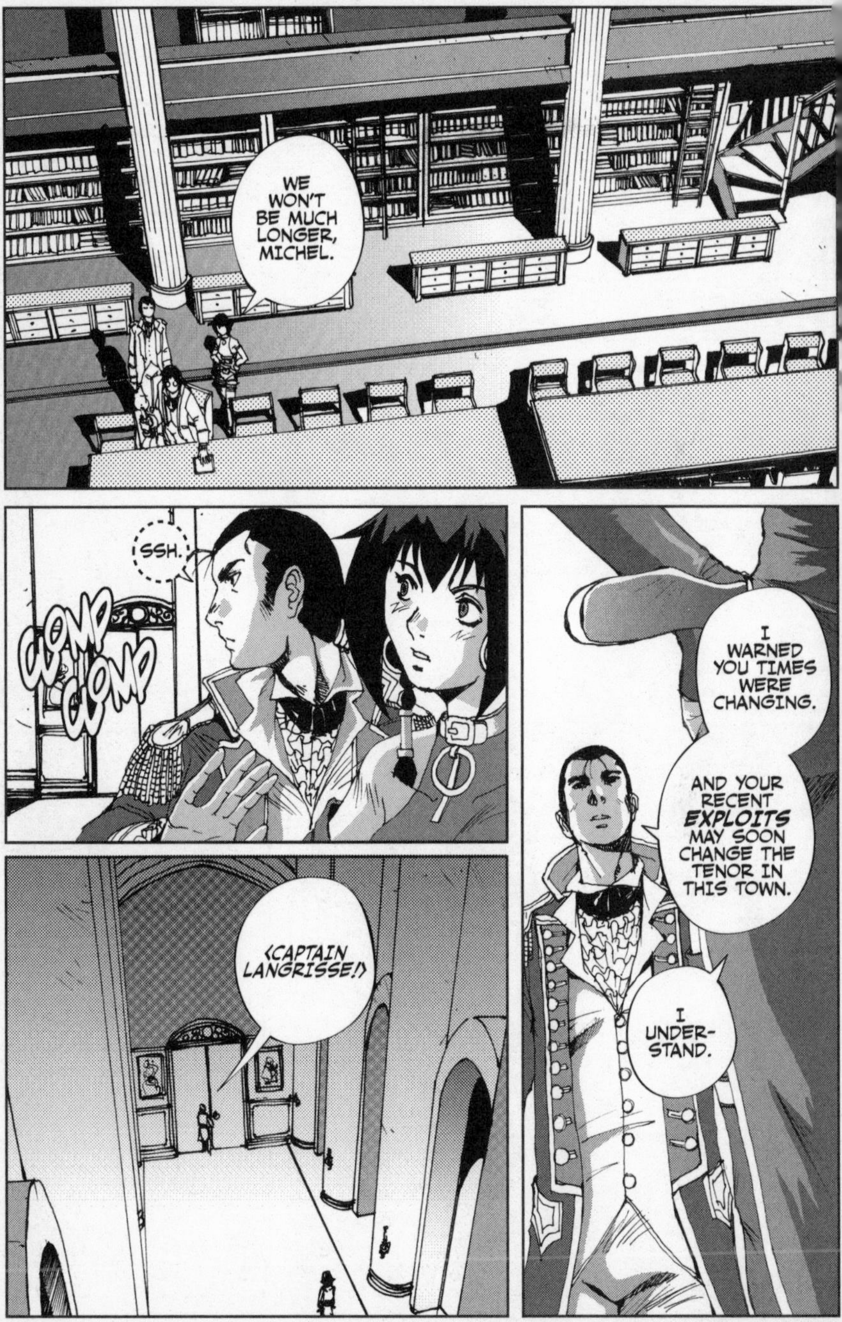
WE WON'T BE MUCH LONGER, MICHEL.
I WARNED YOU TIMES WERE CHANGING.
AND YOUR RECENT ***EXPLOITS*** MAY SOON CHANGE THE TENOR IN THIS TOWN.
I UNDER-STAND.
SSH.
CLOMP CLOMP
‹CAPTAIN LANGRISSE!›

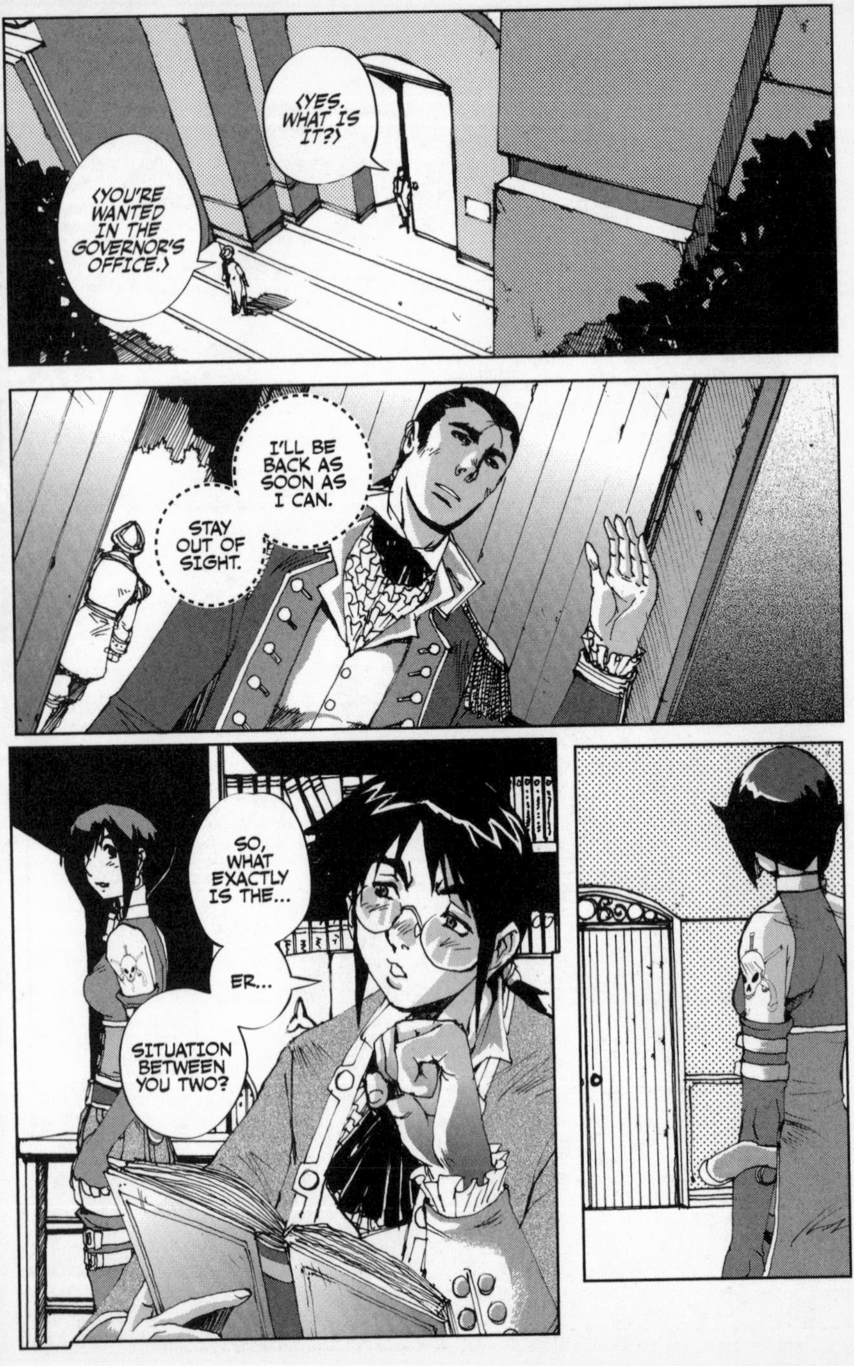
‹YES. WHAT IS IT?›
‹YOU'RE WANTED IN THE GOVERNOR'S OFFICE.›
I'LL BE BACK AS SOON AS I CAN.
STAY OUT OF SIGHT.
SO, WHAT EXACTLY IS THE...
ER...
SITUATION BETWEEN YOU TWO?

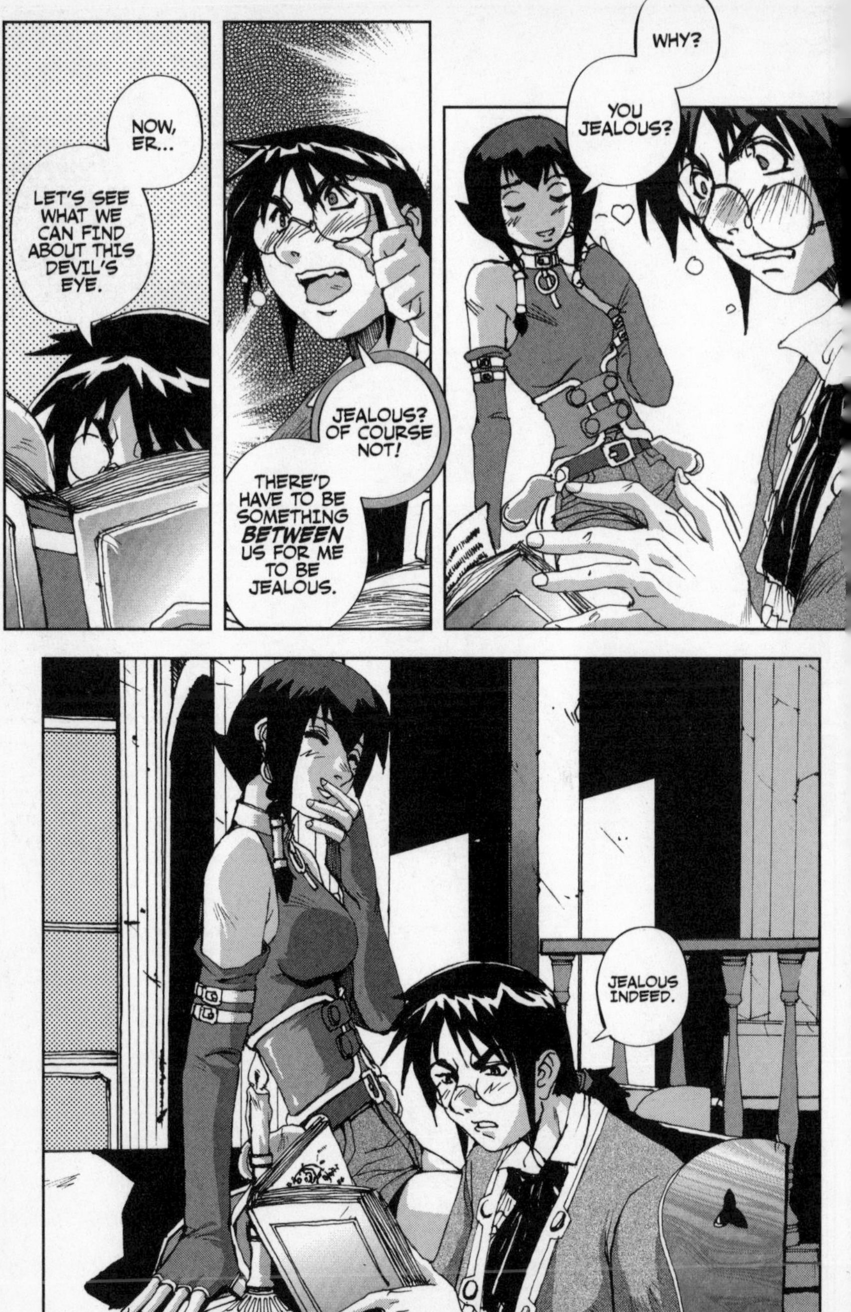
WHY?
YOU JEALOUS?
JEALOUS? OF COURSE NOT!
THERE'D HAVE TO BE SOMETHING ***BETWEEN*** US FOR ME TO BE JEALOUS.
NOW, ER...
LET'S SEE WHAT WE CAN FIND ABOUT THIS DEVIL'S EYE.
JEALOUS INDEED.

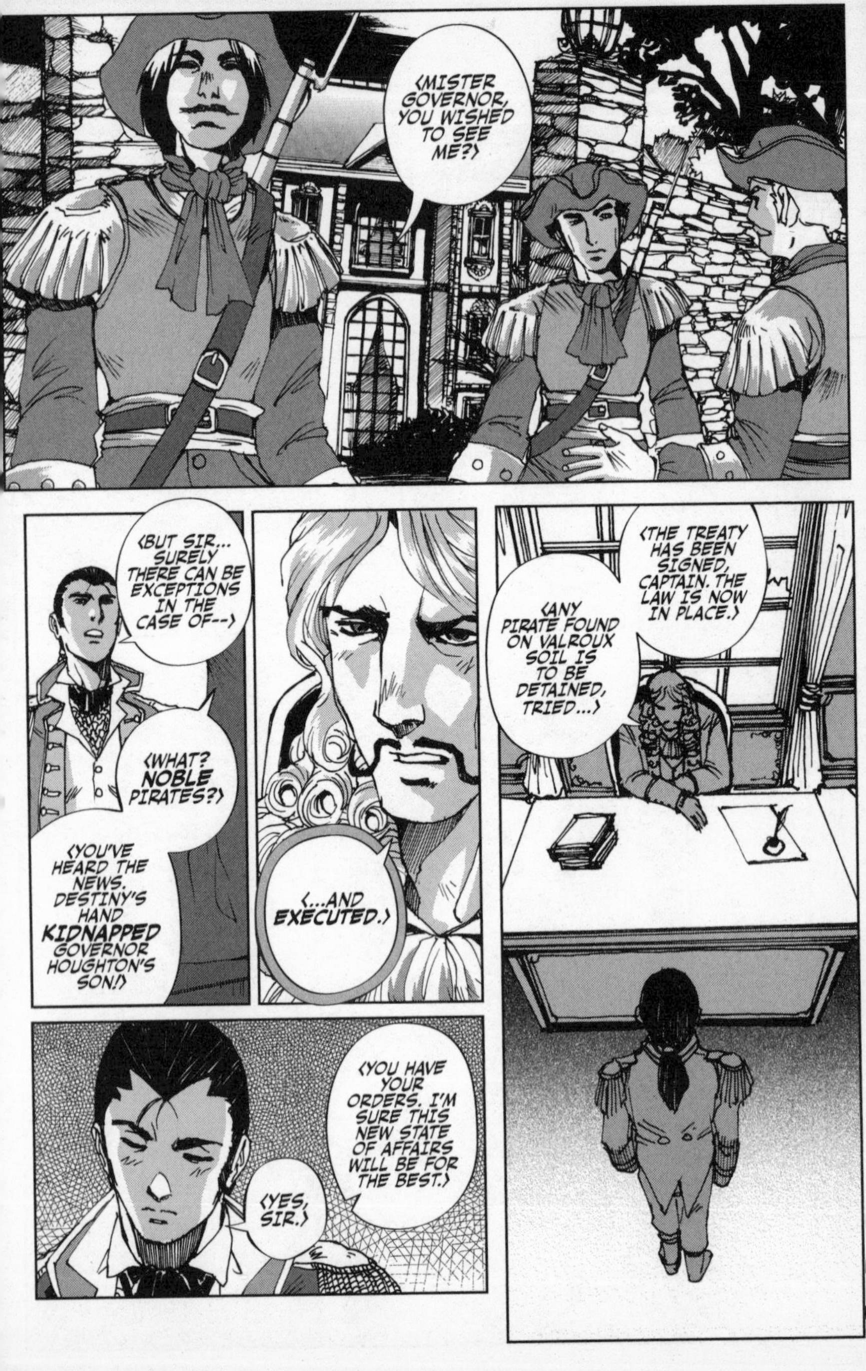
‹MISTER GOVERNOR, YOU WISHED TO SEE ME?›
‹THE TREATY HAS BEEN SIGNED, CAPTAIN. THE LAW IS NOW IN PLACE.›
‹ANY PIRATE FOUND ON VALROUX SOIL IS TO BE DETAINED, TRIED...›
‹...AND **EXECUTED**.›
‹BUT SIR... SURELY THERE CAN BE EXCEPTIONS IN THE CASE OF--›
‹WHAT? **NOBLE** PIRATES?›
‹YOU'VE HEARD THE NEWS. DESTINY'S HAND **KIDNAPPED** GOVERNOR HOUGHTON'S SON!›
‹YOU HAVE YOUR ORDERS. I'M SURE THIS NEW STATE OF AFFAIRS WILL BE FOR THE BEST.›
‹YES, SIR.›

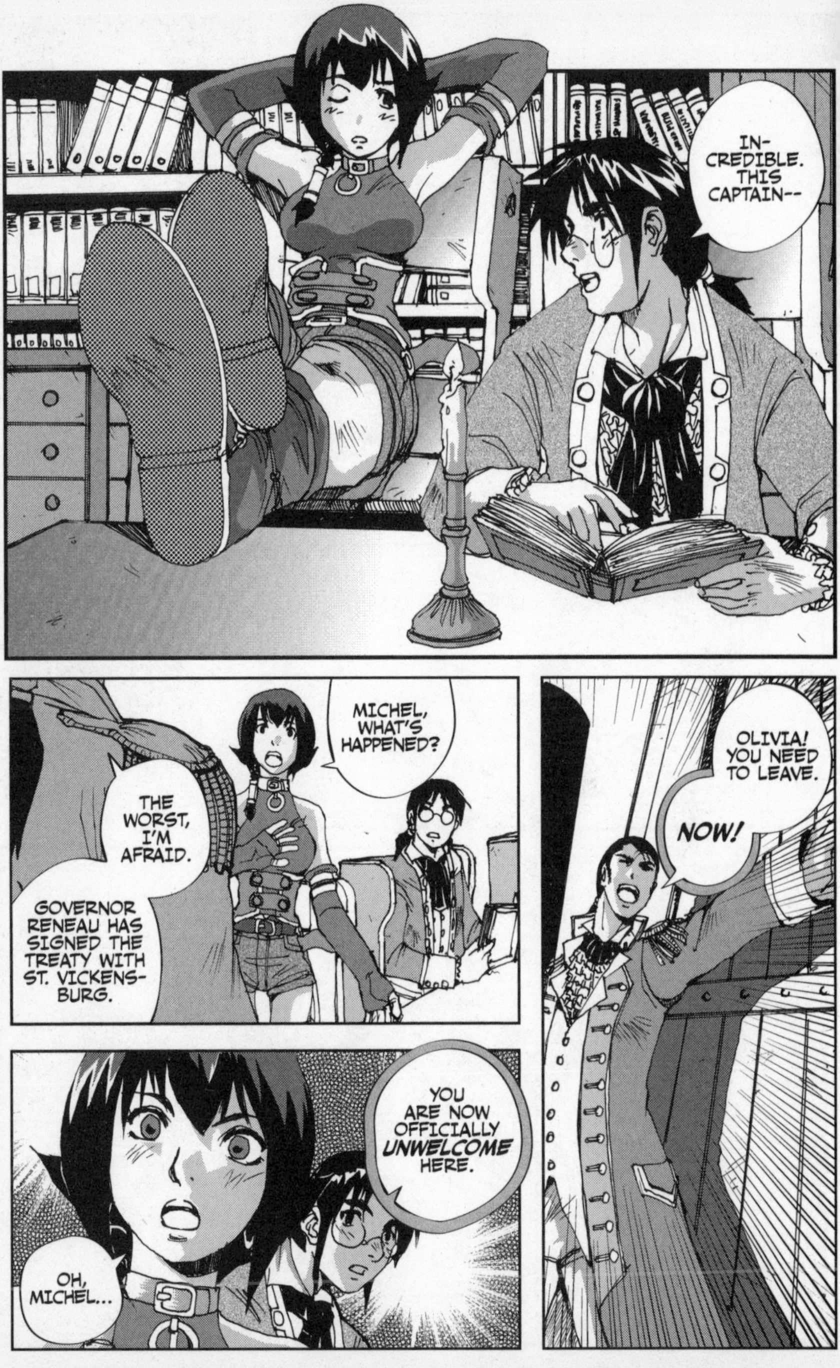
IN-CREDIBLE. THIS CAPTAIN--
OLIVIA! YOU NEED TO LEAVE.
NOW!
MICHEL, WHAT'S HAPPENED?
THE WORST, I'M AFRAID.
GOVERNOR RENEAU HAS SIGNED THE TREATY WITH ST. VICKENSBURG.
YOU ARE NOW OFFICIALLY *UNWELCOME* HERE.
OH, MICHEL...

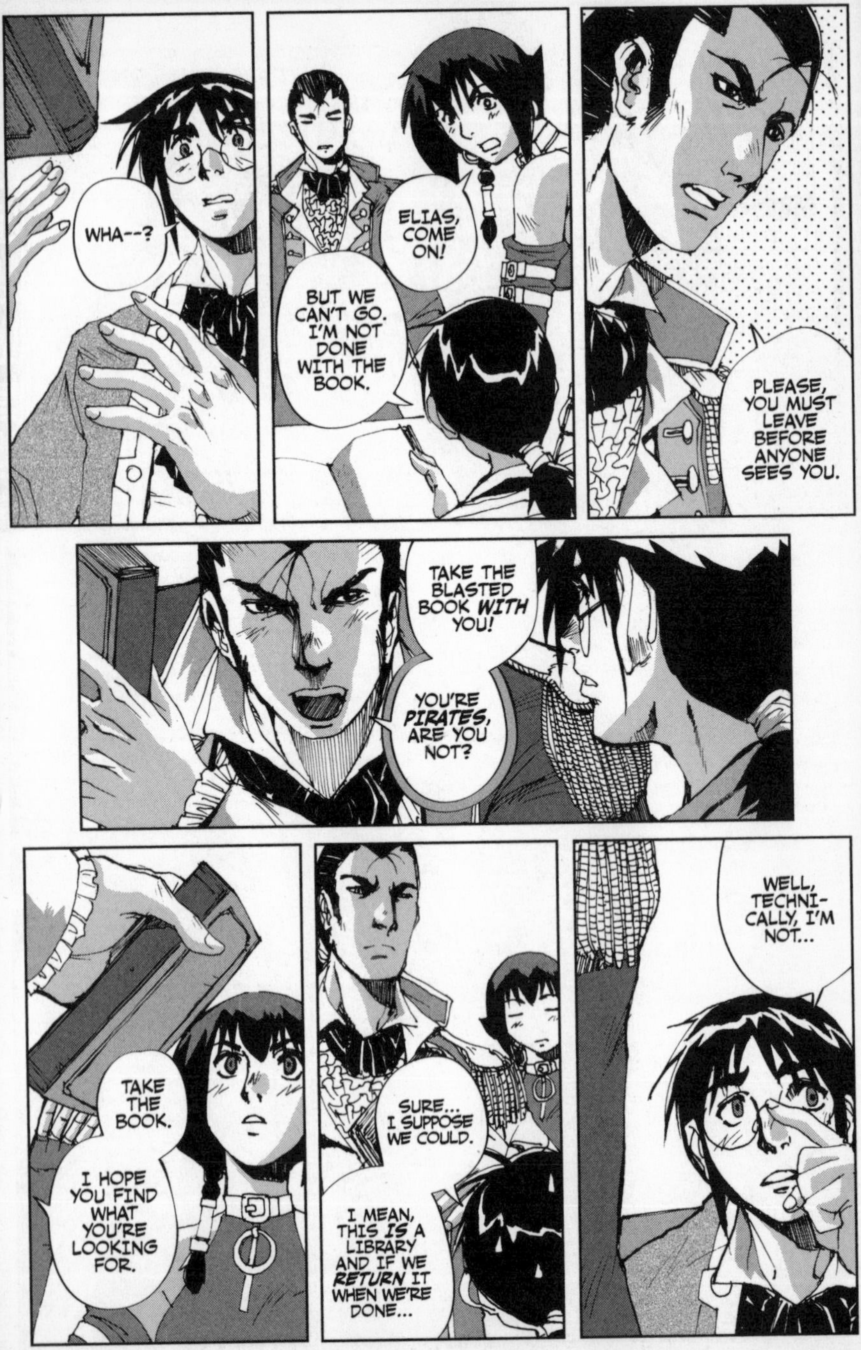
PLEASE, YOU MUST LEAVE BEFORE ANYONE SEES YOU.
ELIAS, COME ON!
BUT WE CAN'T GO. I'M NOT DONE WITH THE BOOK.
WHA--?
TAKE THE BLASTED BOOK *WITH* YOU!
YOU'RE *PIRATES*, ARE YOU NOT?
WELL, TECHNI-CALLY, I'M NOT...
SURE... I SUPPOSE WE COULD.
I MEAN, THIS *IS* A LIBRARY AND IF WE *RETURN* IT WHEN WE'RE DONE...
TAKE THE BOOK.
I HOPE YOU FIND WHAT YOU'RE LOOKING FOR.

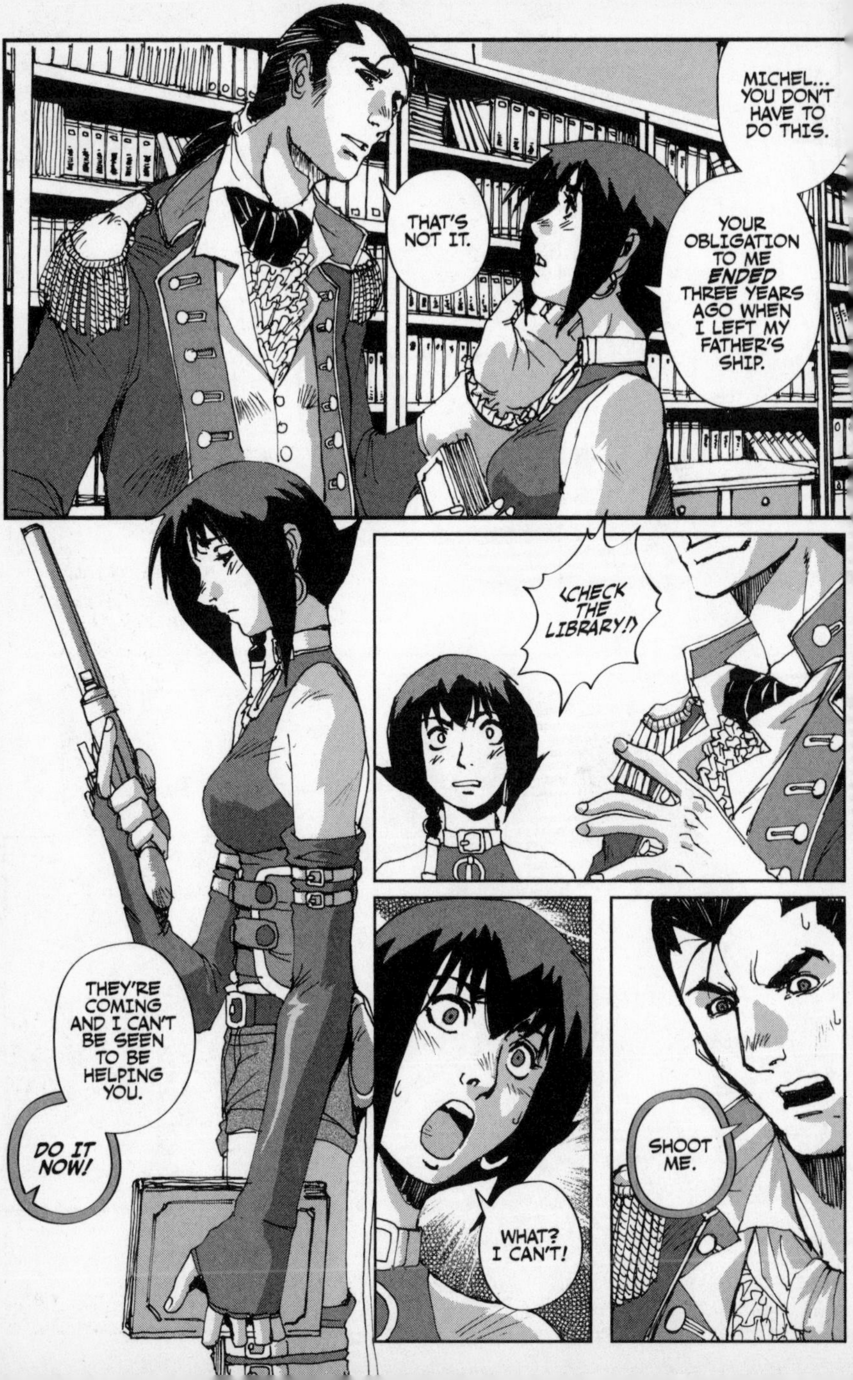
MICHEL... YOU DON'T HAVE TO DO THIS.
YOUR OBLIGATION TO ME *ENDED* THREE YEARS AGO WHEN I LEFT MY FATHER'S SHIP.
THAT'S NOT IT.
‹CHECK THE LIBRARY!›
SHOOT ME.
WHAT? I CAN'T!
THEY'RE COMING AND I CAN'T BE SEEN TO BE HELPING YOU.
DO IT NOW!

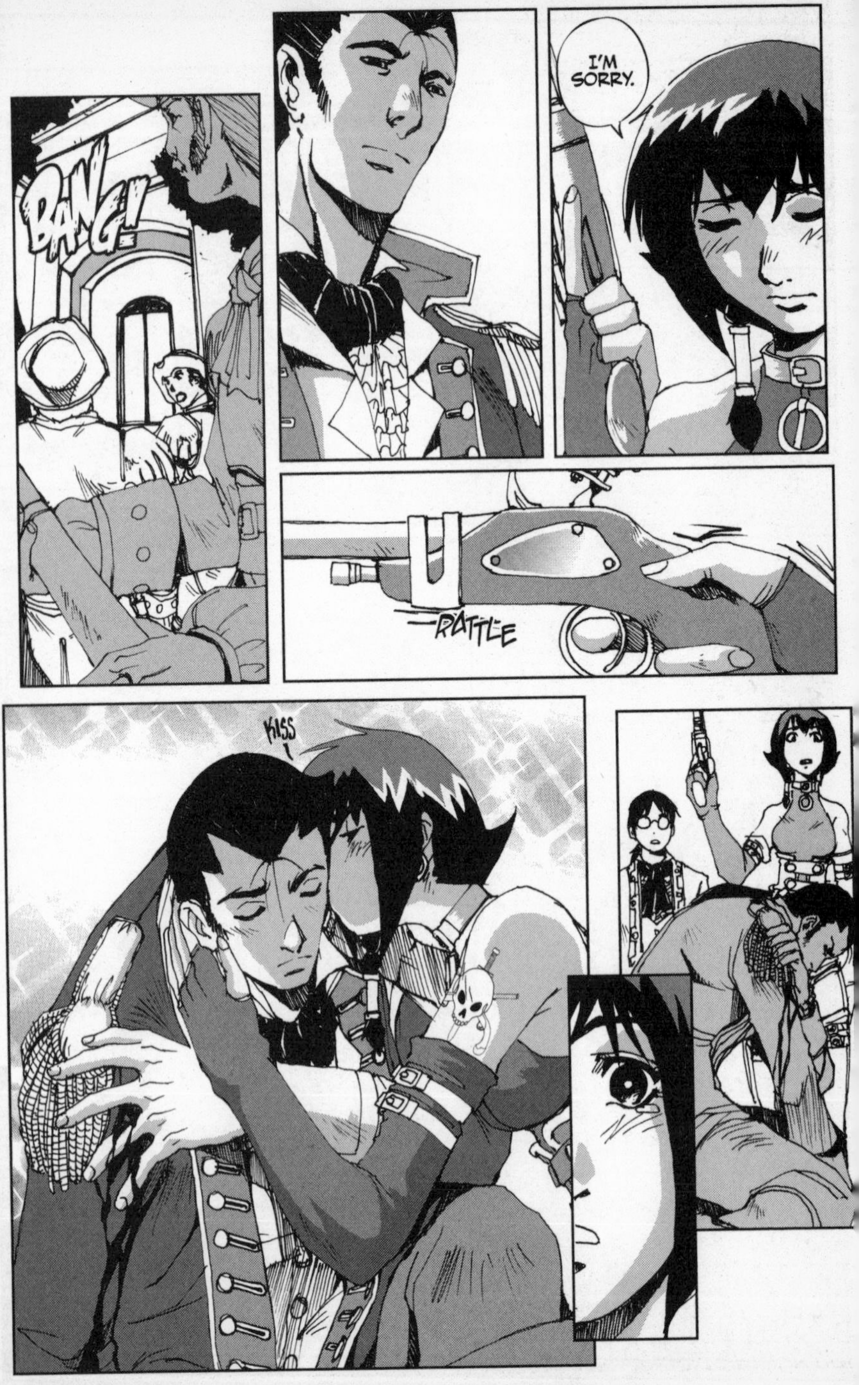
I'M SORRY.
BANG!!
RATTLE
KISS

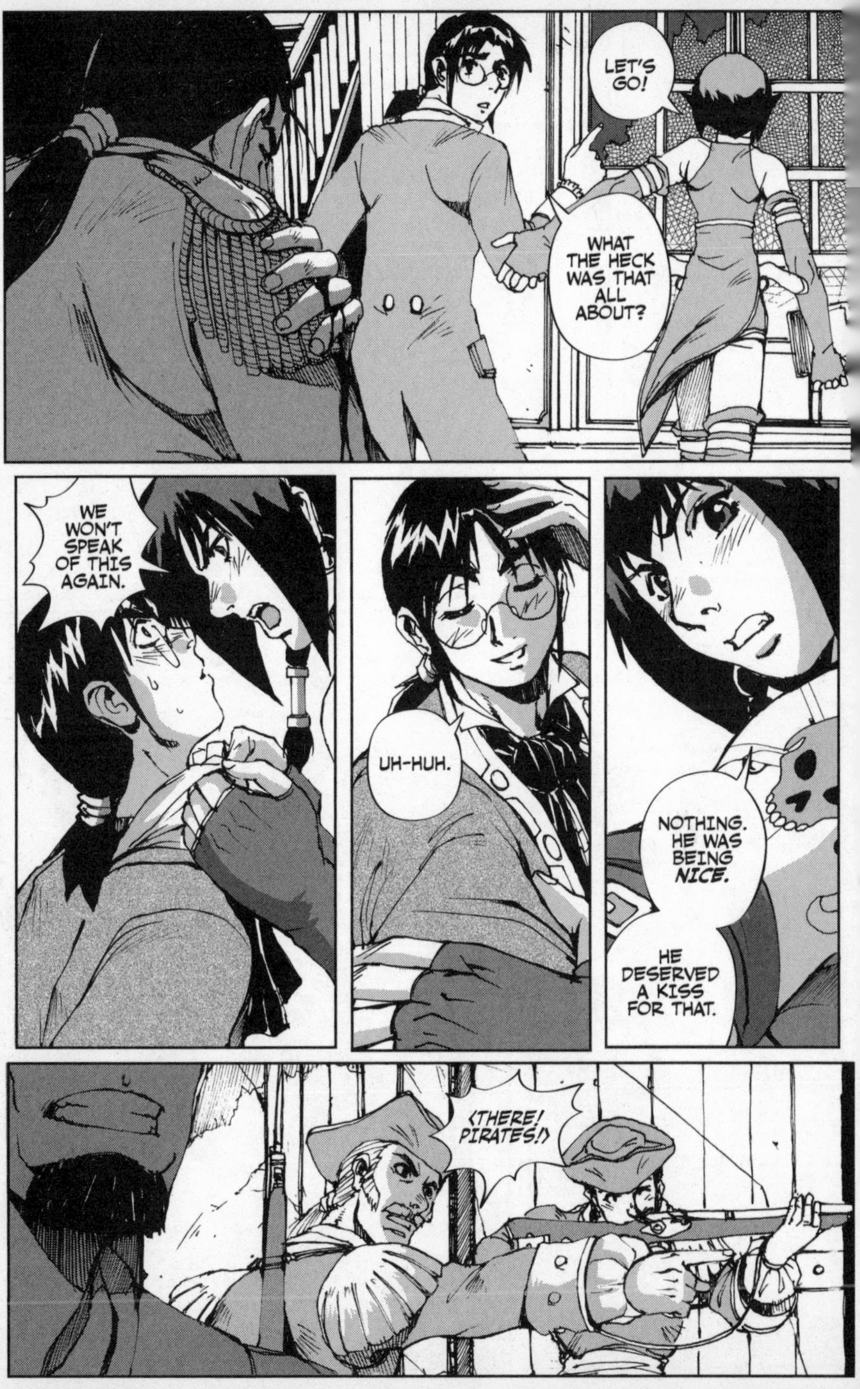
LET'S GO!
WHAT THE HECK WAS THAT ALL ABOUT?
NOTHING. HE WAS BEING *NICE.*
HE DESERVED A KISS FOR THAT.
UH-HUH.
WE WON'T SPEAK OF THIS AGAIN.
<THERE! PIRATES!>

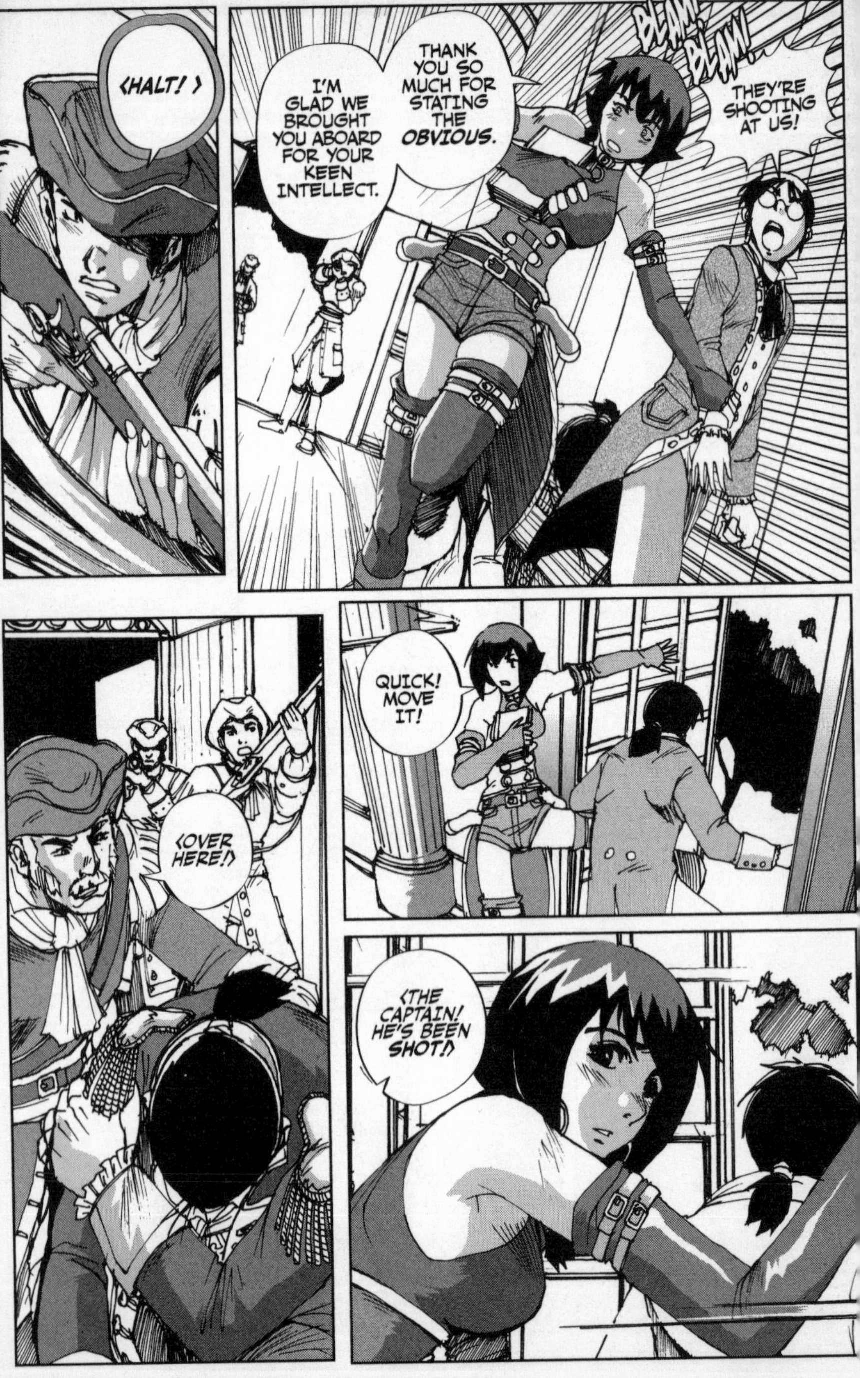
BLAM! BLAM!
THEY'RE SHOOTING AT US!
THANK YOU SO MUCH FOR STATING THE *OBVIOUS*.
I'M GLAD WE BROUGHT YOU ABOARD FOR YOUR KEEN INTELLECT.
‹HALT!›
QUICK! MOVE IT!
‹THE CAPTAIN! HE'S BEEN SHOT!›
‹OVER HERE!›

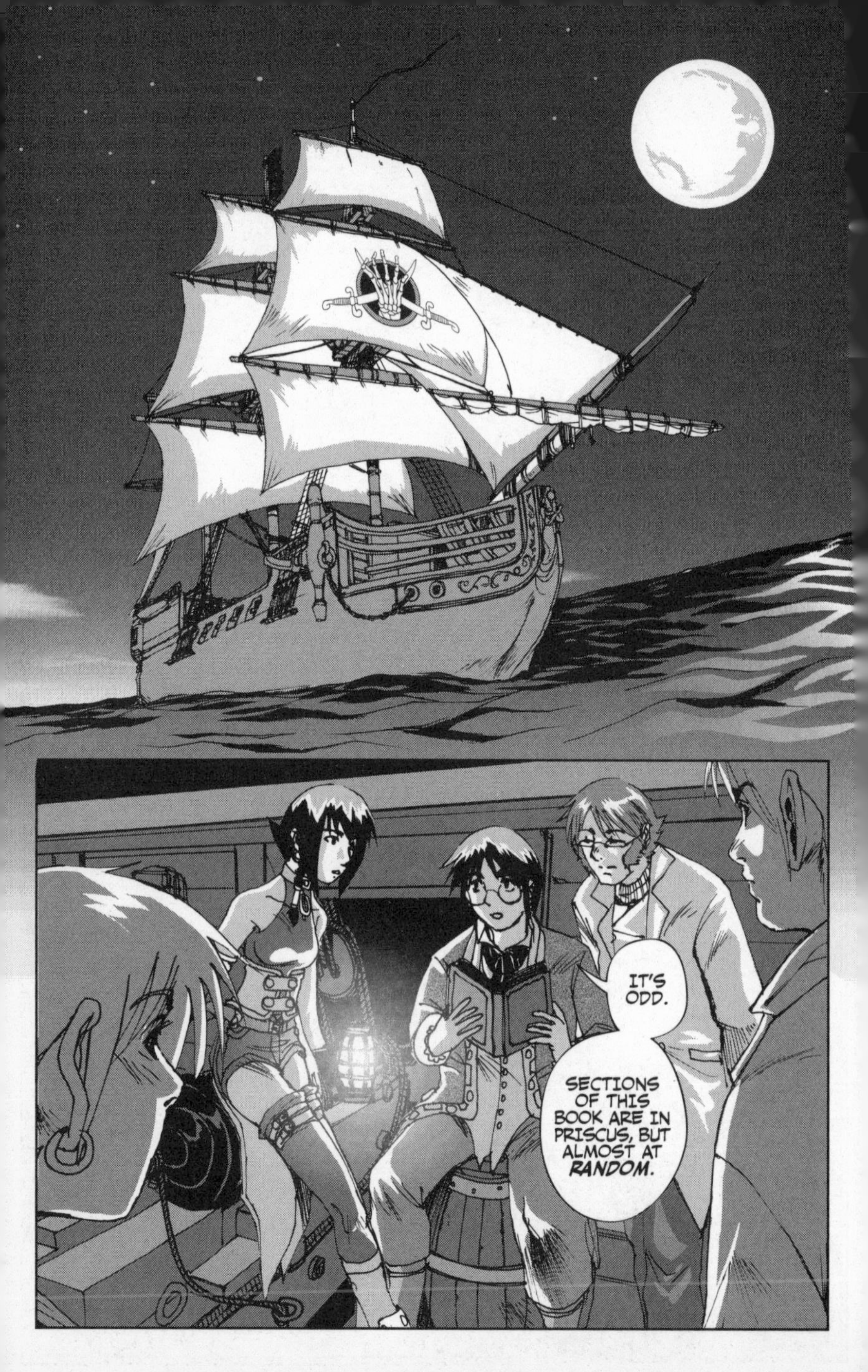
IT'S ODD.
SECTIONS OF THIS BOOK ARE IN PRISCUS, BUT ALMOST AT *RANDOM*.

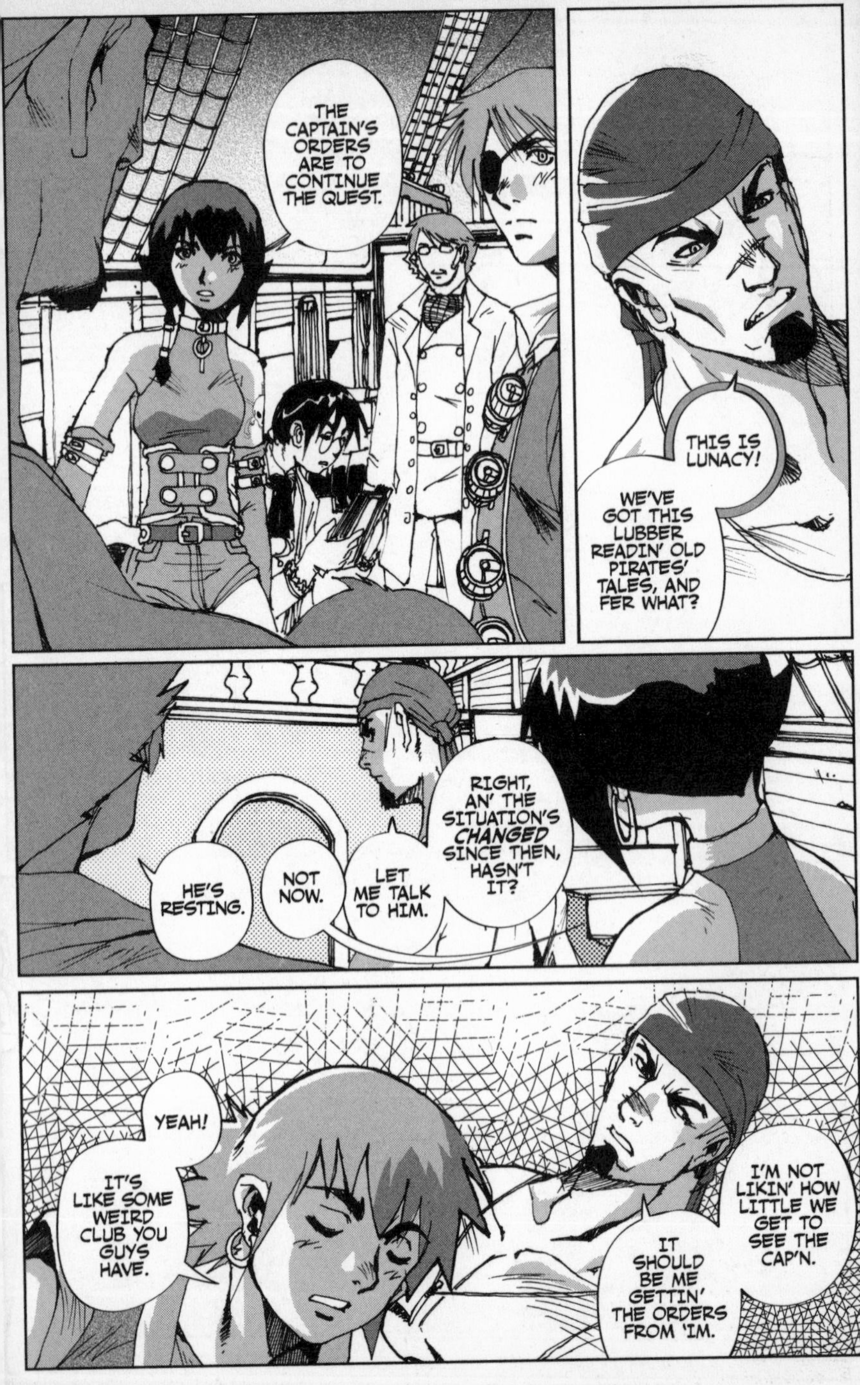
THIS IS LUNACY!
WE'VE GOT THIS LUBBER READIN' OLD PIRATES' TALES, AND FER WHAT?
THE CAPTAIN'S ORDERS ARE TO CONTINUE THE QUEST.
RIGHT, AN' THE SITUATION'S *CHANGED* SINCE THEN, HASN'T IT?
LET ME TALK TO HIM.
NOT NOW.
HE'S RESTING.
I'M NOT LIKIN' HOW LITTLE WE GET TO SEE THE CAP'N.
IT SHOULD BE ME GETTIN' THE ORDERS FROM 'IM.
YEAH!
IT'S LIKE SOME WEIRD CLUB YOU GUYS HAVE.

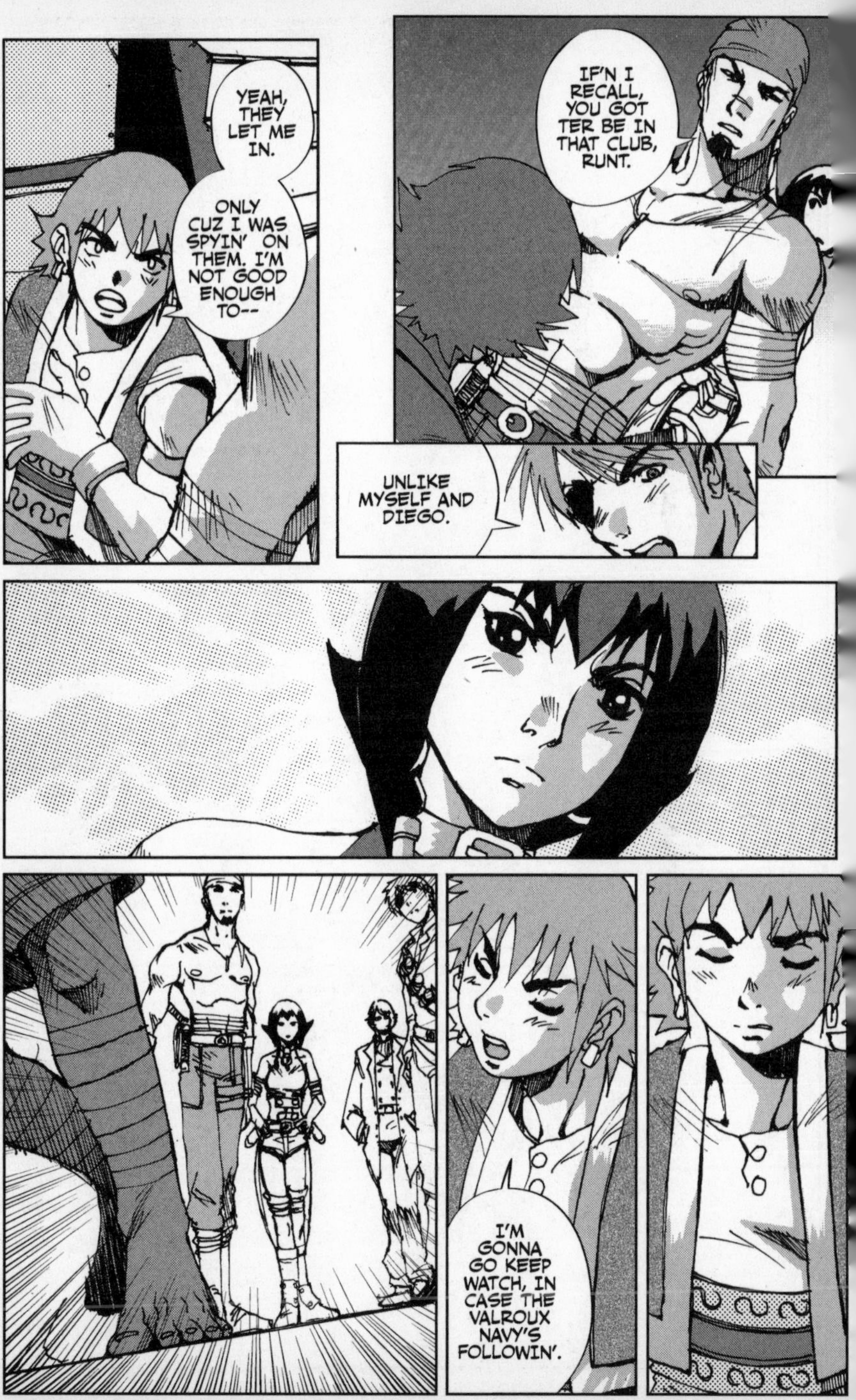
IF'N I RECALL, YOU GOT TER BE IN THAT CLUB, RUNT.
UNLIKE MYSELF AND DIEGO.
YEAH, THEY LET ME IN.
ONLY CUZ I WAS SPYIN' ON THEM. I'M NOT GOOD ENOUGH TO--
I'M GONNA GO KEEP WATCH, IN CASE THE VALROUX NAVY'S FOLLOWIN'.

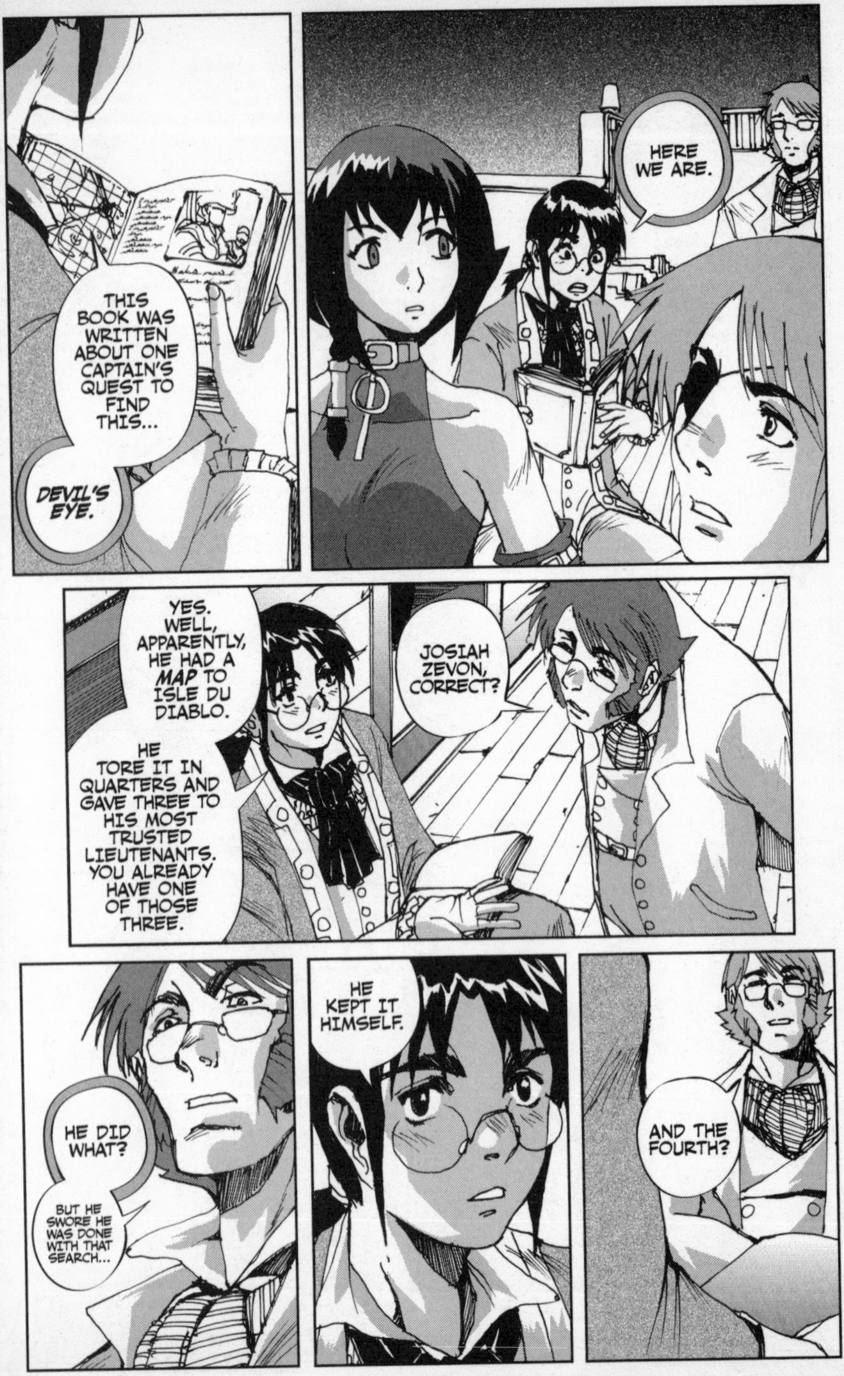
HERE WE ARE.
THIS BOOK WAS WRITTEN ABOUT ONE CAPTAIN'S QUEST TO FIND THIS...
DEVIL'S EYE.
JOSIAH ZEVON, CORRECT?
YES. WELL, APPARENTLY, HE HAD A *MAP* TO ISLE DU DIABLO.
HE TORE IT IN QUARTERS AND GAVE THREE TO HIS MOST TRUSTED LIEUTENANTS. YOU ALREADY HAVE ONE OF THOSE THREE.
AND THE FOURTH?
HE KEPT IT HIMSELF.
HE DID WHAT?
BUT HE SWORE HE WAS DONE WITH THAT SEARCH...

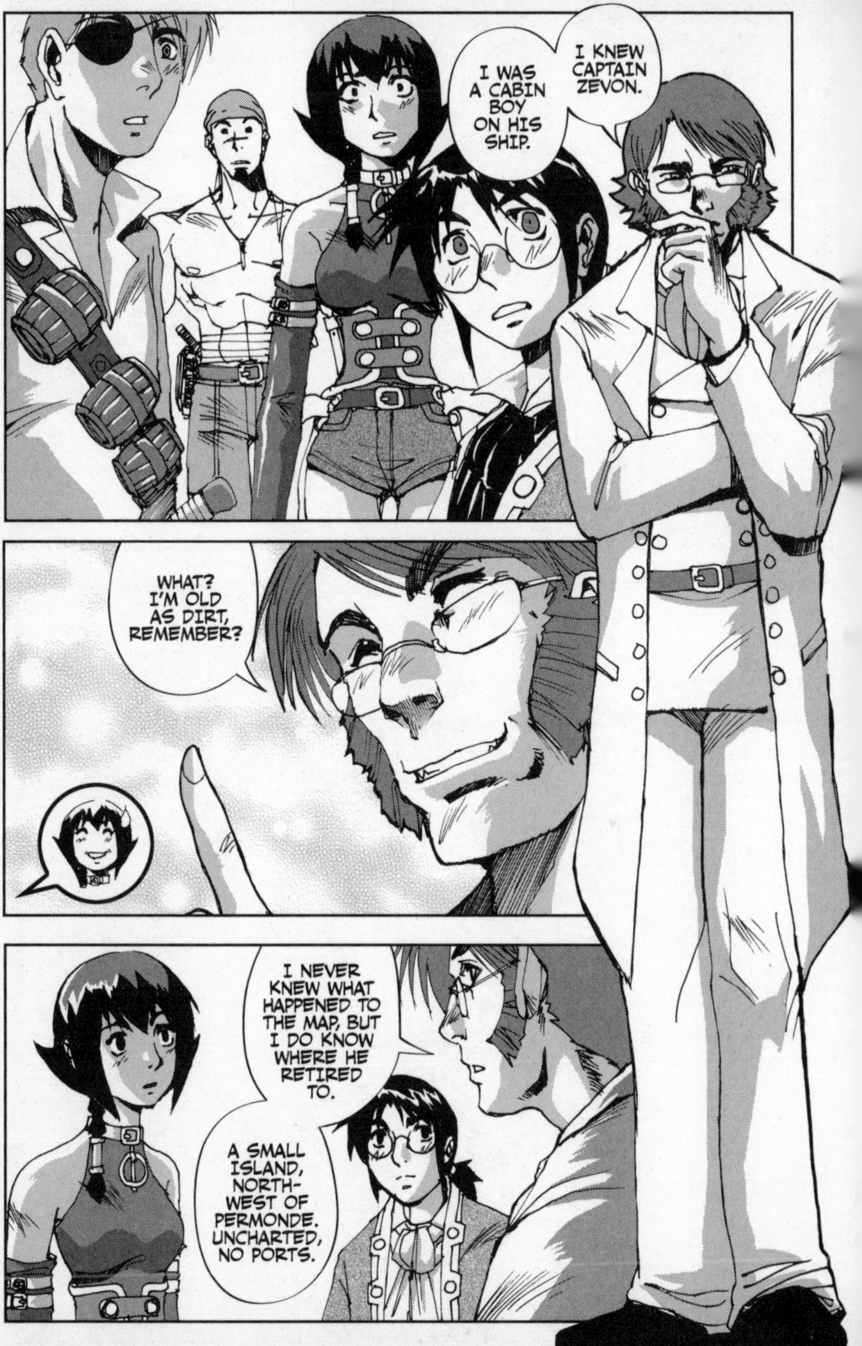
I KNEW CAPTAIN ZEVON.
I WAS A CABIN BOY ON HIS SHIP.
WHAT? I'M OLD AS DIRT, REMEMBER?
I NEVER KNEW WHAT HAPPENED TO THE MAP, BUT I DO KNOW WHERE HE RETIRED TO.
A SMALL ISLAND, NORTH-WEST OF PERMONDE. UNCHARTED, NO PORTS.

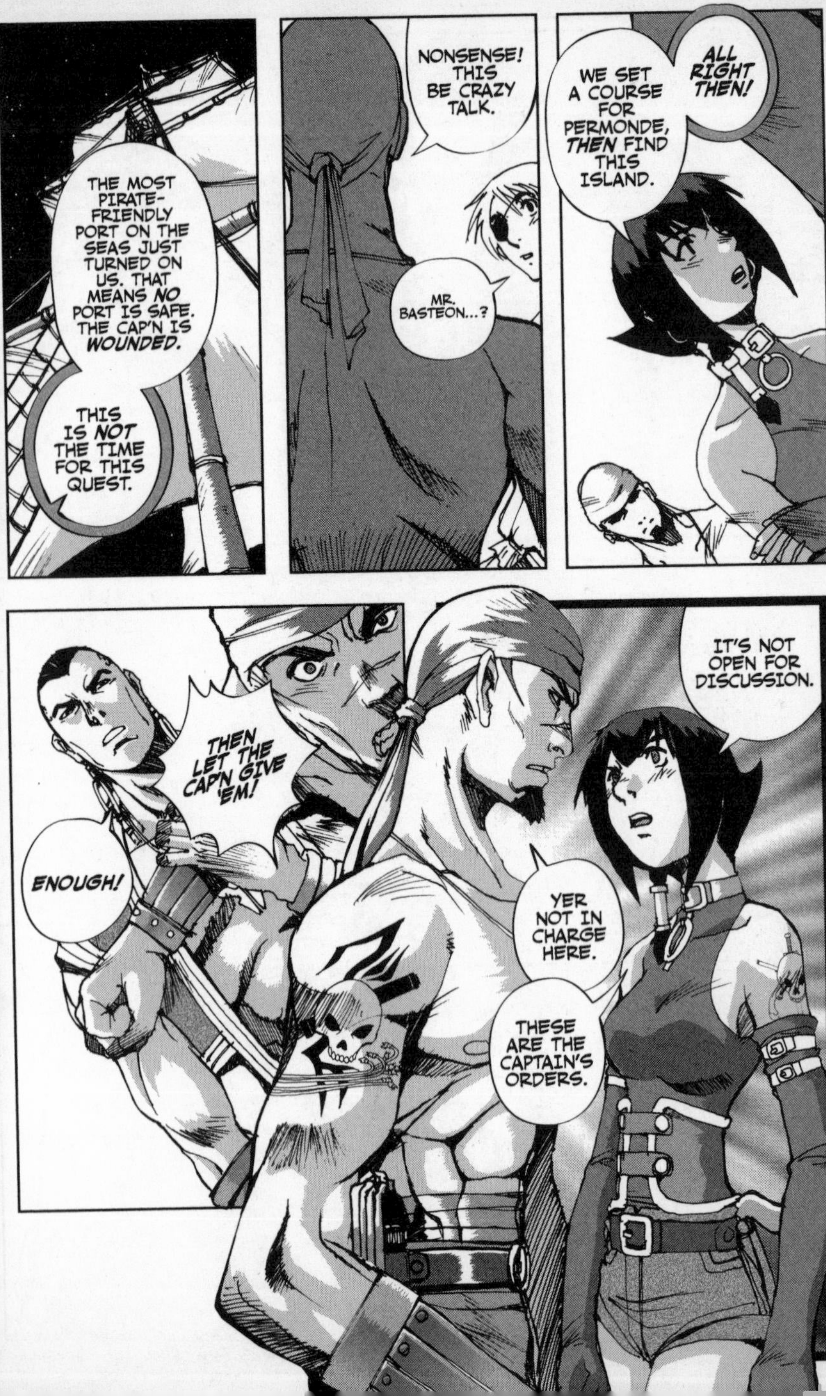
THE MOST PIRATE-FRIENDLY PORT ON THE SEAS JUST TURNED ON US. THAT MEANS NO PORT IS SAFE. THE CAP'N IS WOUNDED.
THIS IS NOT THE TIME FOR THIS QUEST.
NONSENSE! THIS BE CRAZY TALK.
MR. BASTEON...?
ALL RIGHT THEN!
WE SET A COURSE FOR PERMONDE, THEN FIND THIS ISLAND.
IT'S NOT OPEN FOR DISCUSSION.
YER NOT IN CHARGE HERE.
THESE ARE THE CAPTAIN'S ORDERS.
THEN LET THE CAP'N GIVE 'EM!
ENOUGH!

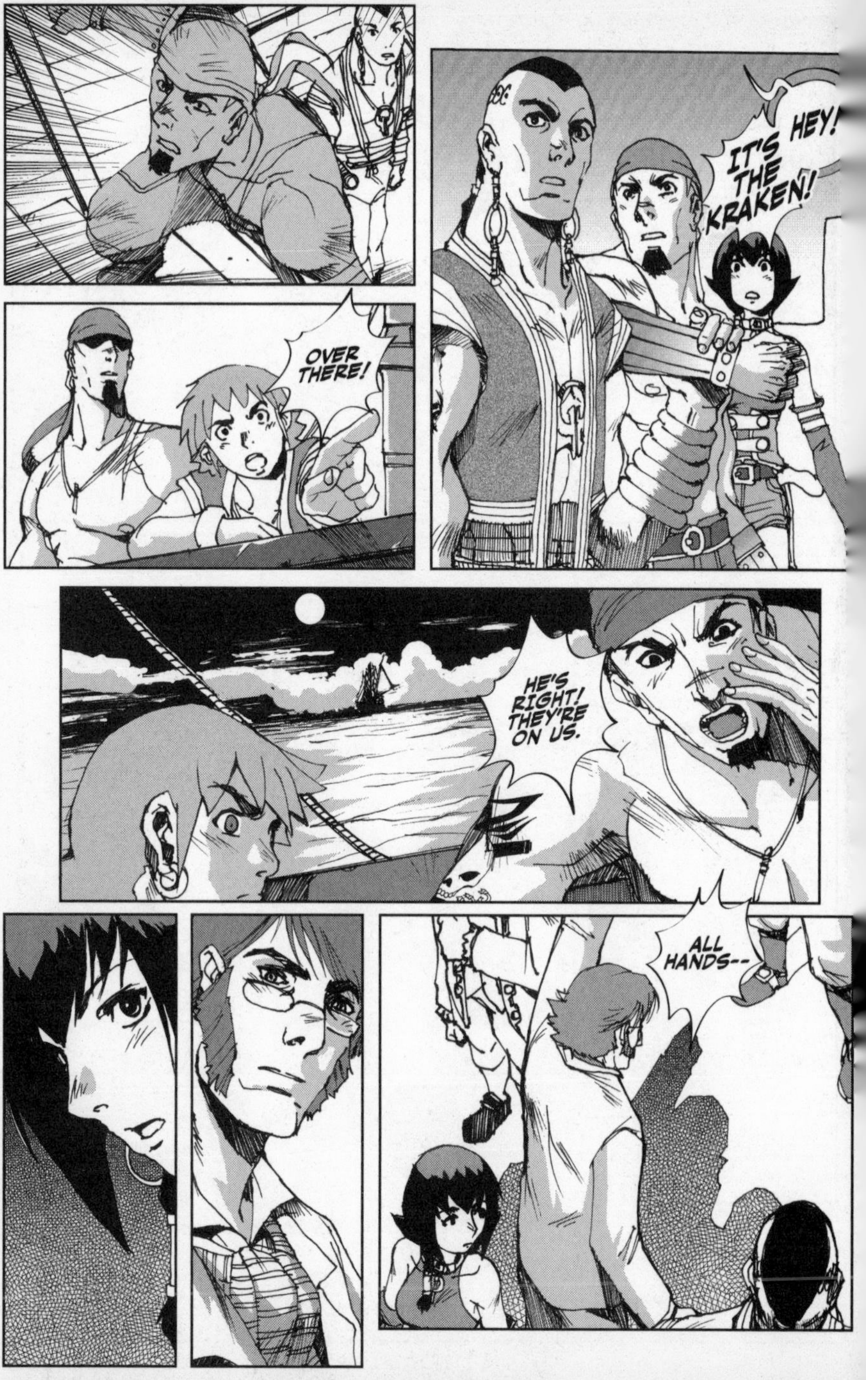
HEY! IT'S THE KRAKEN!
OVER THERE!
HE'S RIGHT! THEY'RE ON US.
ALL HANDS--

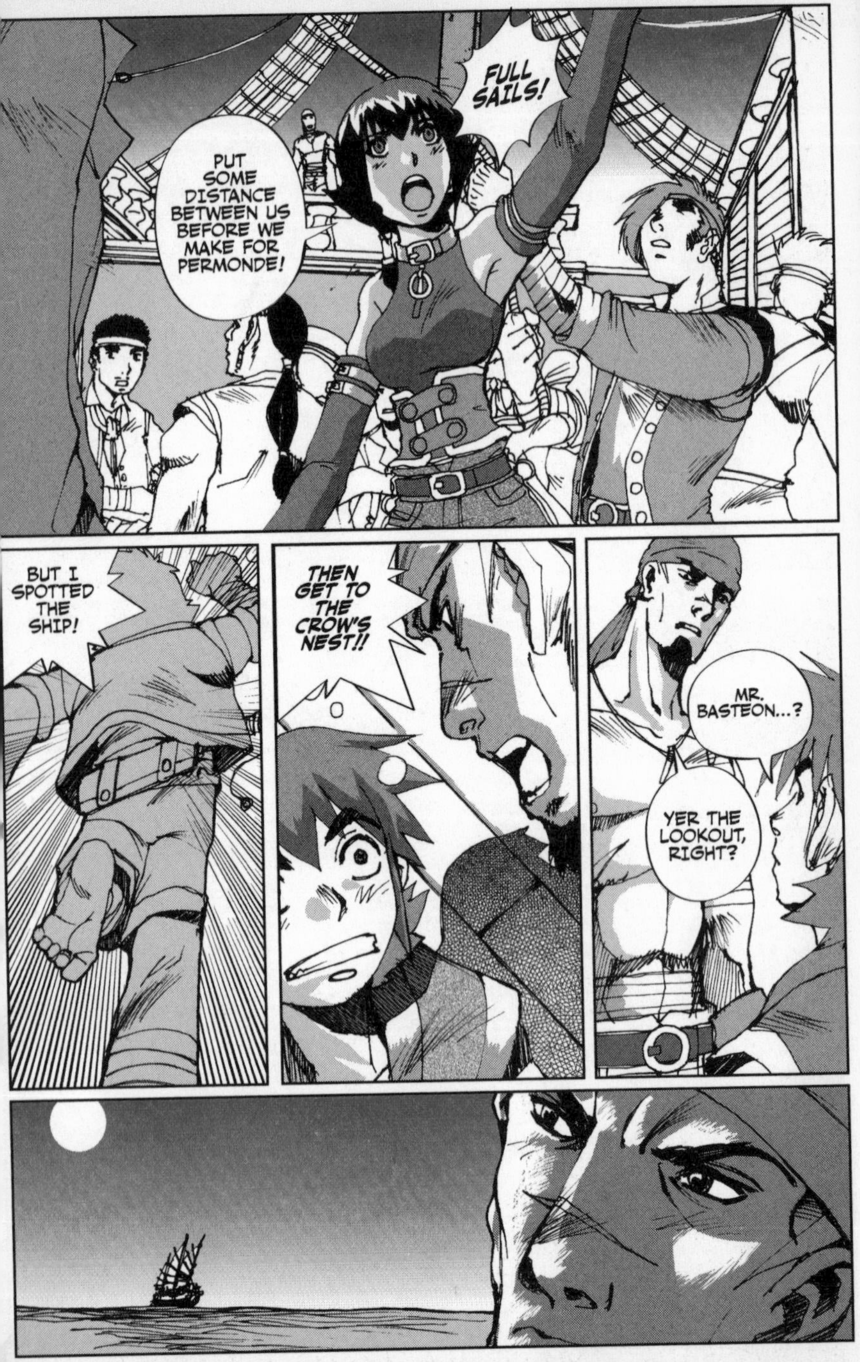
FULL SAILS!
PUT SOME DISTANCE BETWEEN US BEFORE WE MAKE FOR PERMONDE!
MR. BASTEON...?
YER THE LOOKOUT, RIGHT?
THEN GET TO THE CROW'S NEST!!
BUT I SPOTTED THE SHIP!

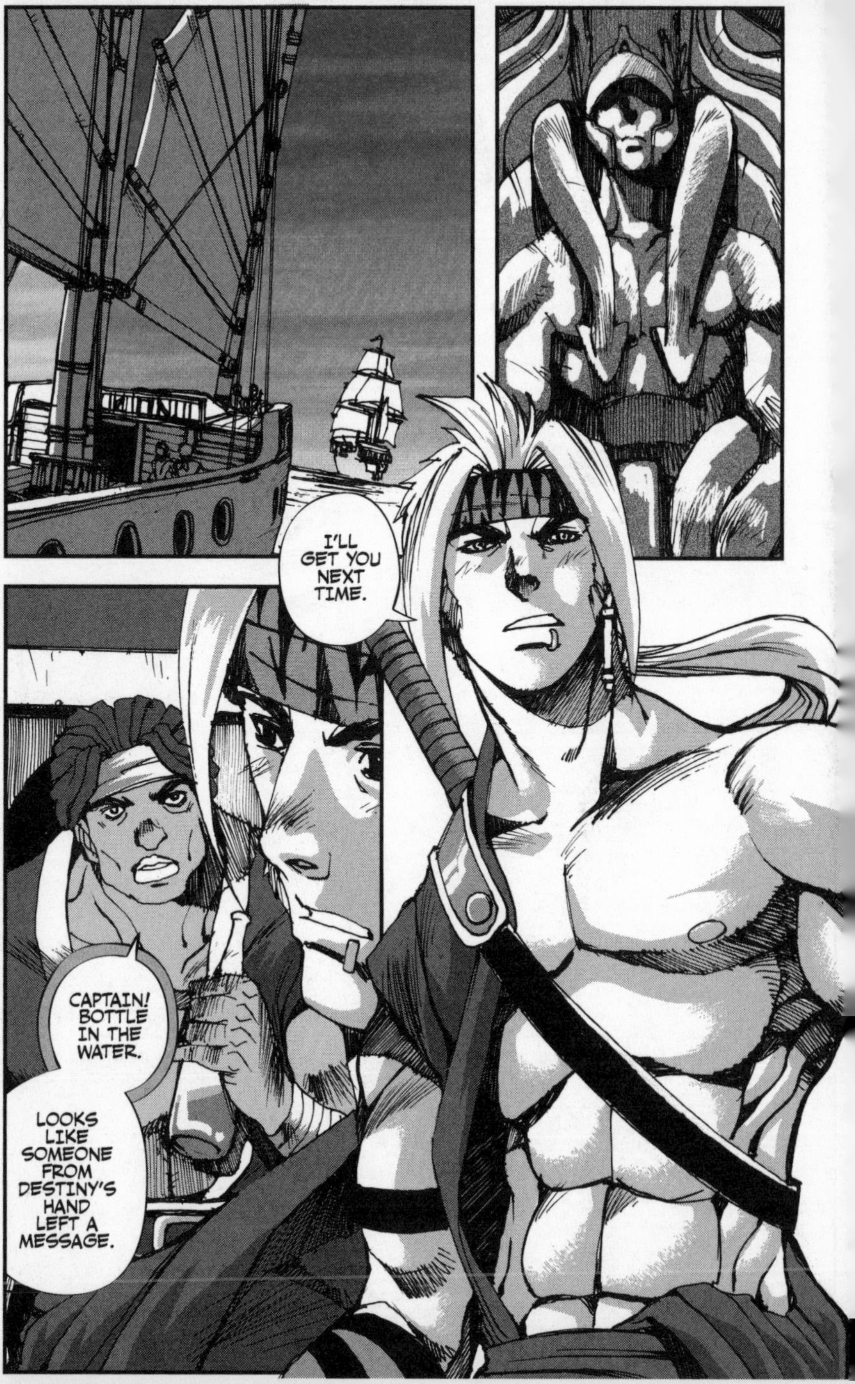

I'LL GET YOU NEXT TIME.
CAPTAIN! BOTTLE IN THE WATER.
LOOKS LIKE SOMEONE FROM DESTINY'S HAND LEFT A MESSAGE.

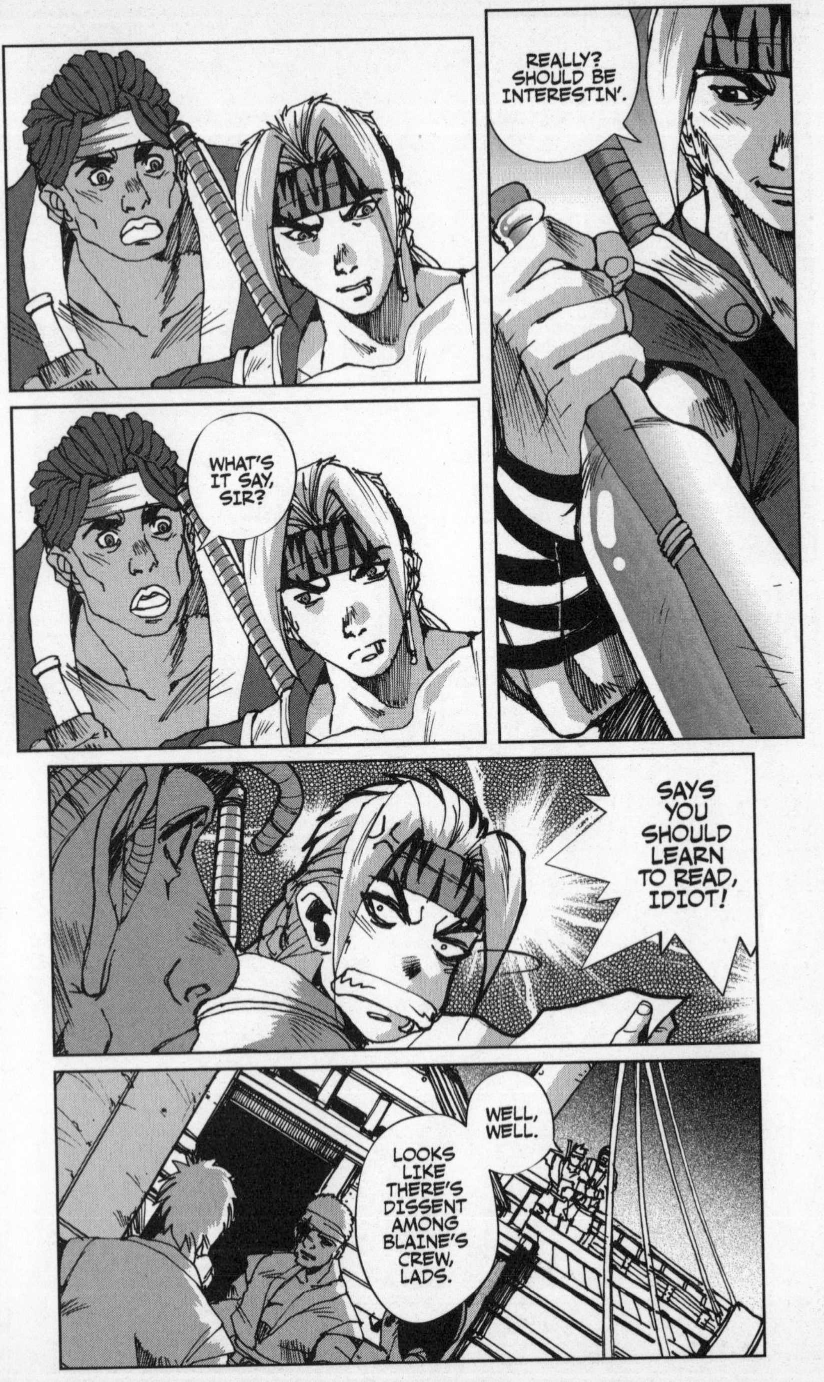
REALLY? SHOULD BE INTERESTIN'.
WHAT'S IT SAY, SIR?
SAYS YOU SHOULD LEARN TO READ, IDIOT!
WELL, WELL.
LOOKS LIKE THERE'S DISSENT AMONG BLAINE'S CREW, LADS.

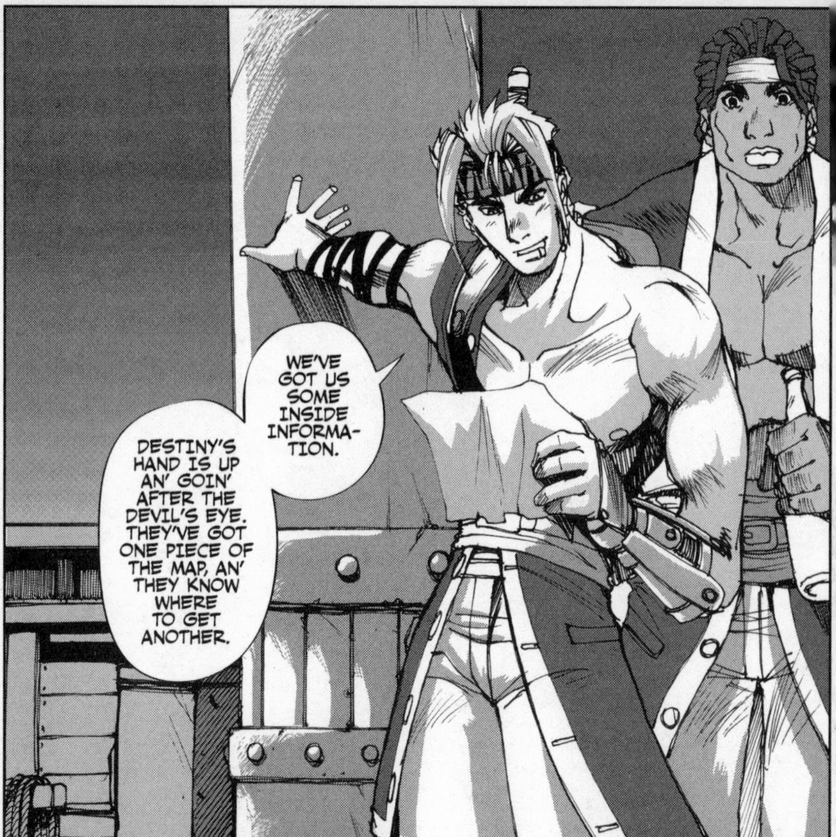
WE'VE GOT US SOME INSIDE INFORMATION.
DESTINY'S HAND IS UP AN' GOIN' AFTER THE DEVIL'S EYE. THEY'VE GOT ONE PIECE OF THE MAP, AN' THEY KNOW WHERE TO GET ANOTHER.
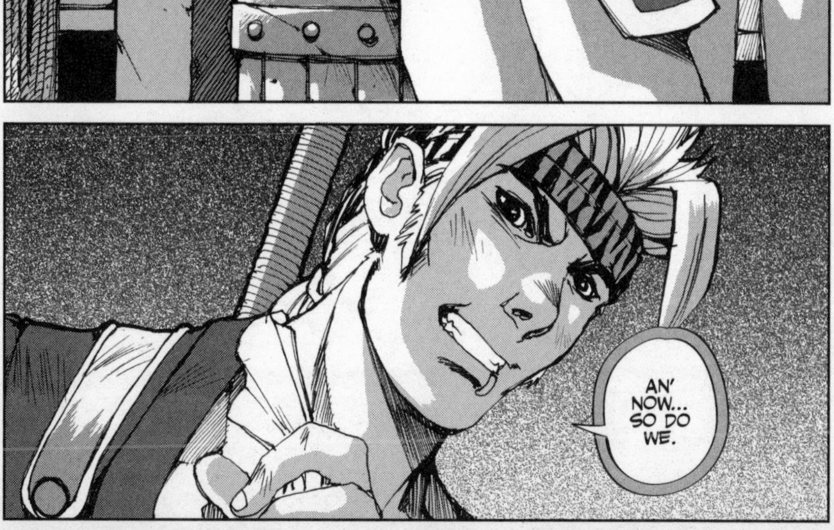
AN' NOW... SO DO WE.

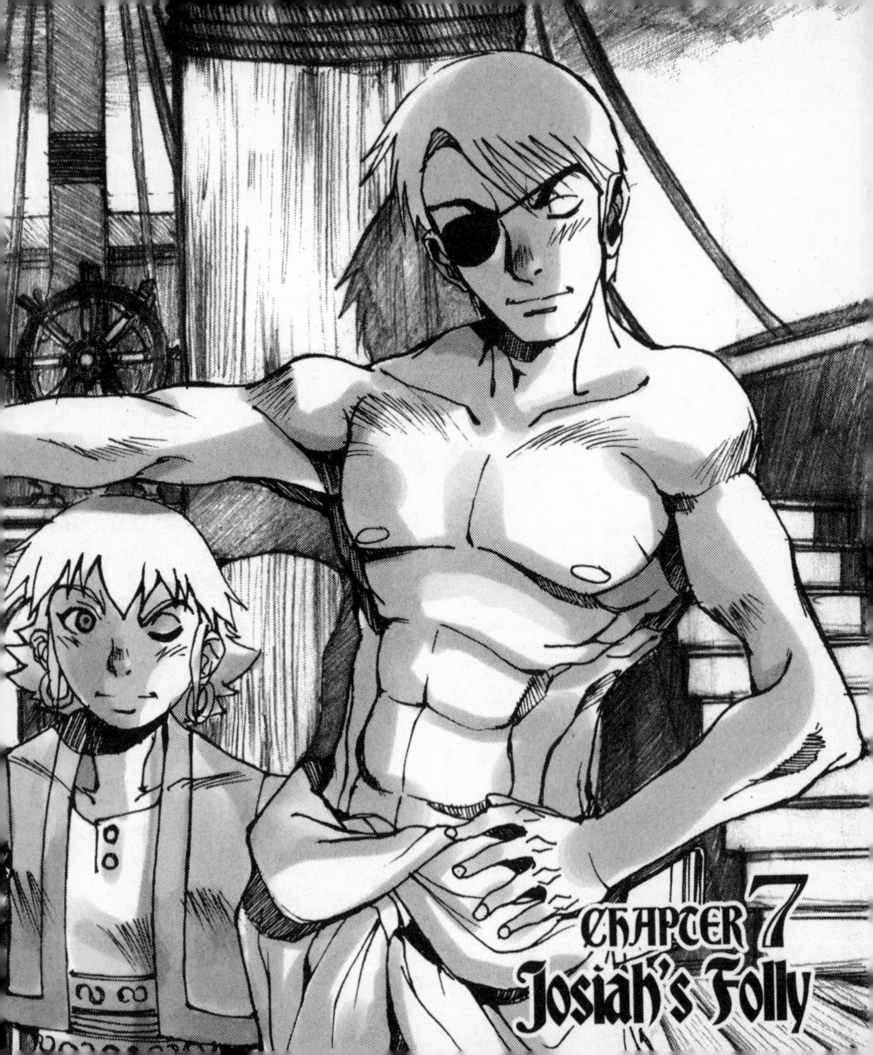
CHAPTER 7
Josiah's Folly

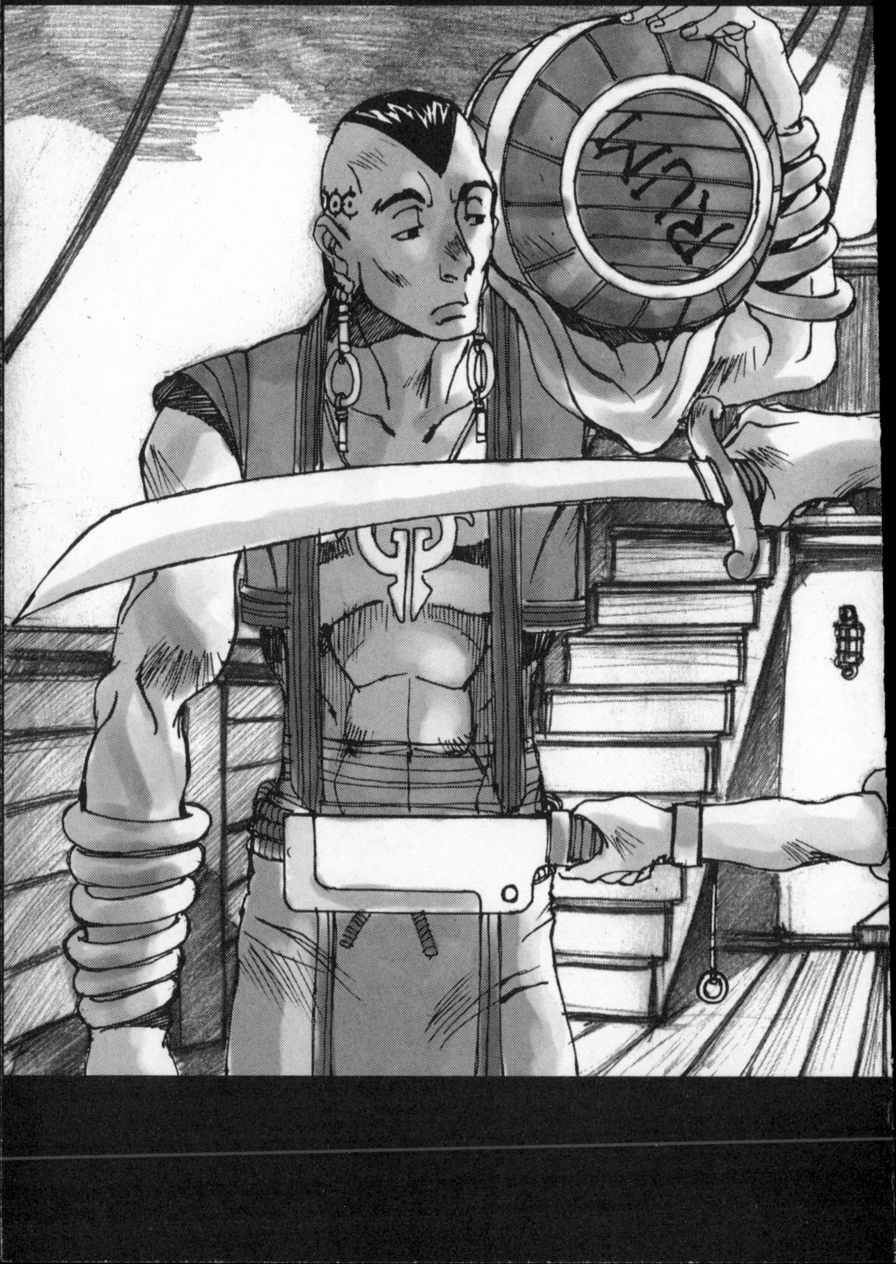

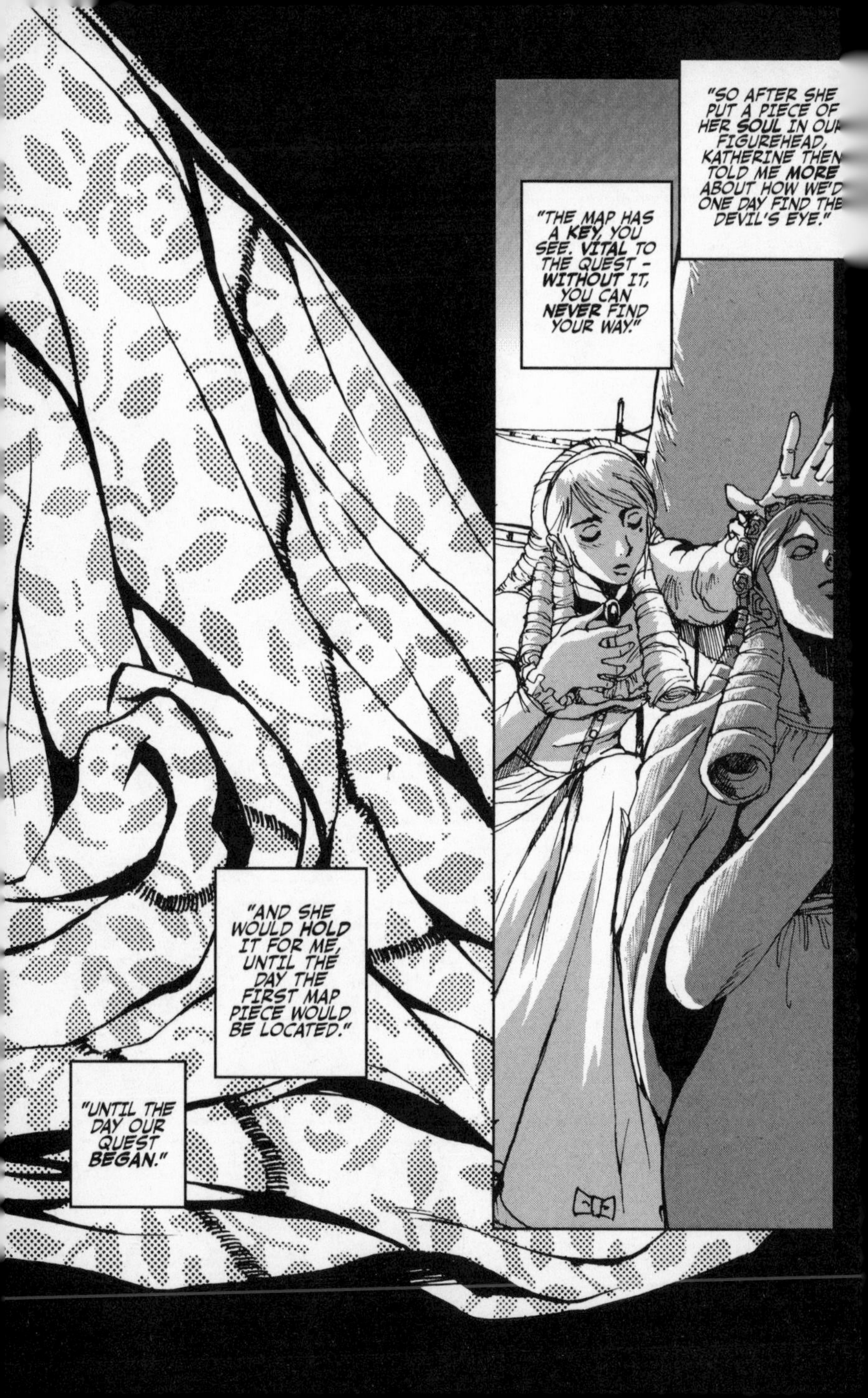
"SO AFTER SHE PUT A PIECE OF HER **SOUL** IN OUR FIGUREHEAD, KATHERINE THEN TOLD ME **MORE** ABOUT HOW WE'D ONE DAY FIND THE DEVIL'S EYE."
"THE MAP HAS A **KEY**, YOU SEE. **VITAL** TO THE QUEST - **WITHOUT** IT, YOU CAN **NEVER** FIND YOUR WAY."
"AND SHE WOULD **HOLD** IT FOR ME, UNTIL THE DAY THE FIRST MAP PIECE WOULD BE LOCATED."
"UNTIL THE DAY OUR QUEST **BEGAN**."

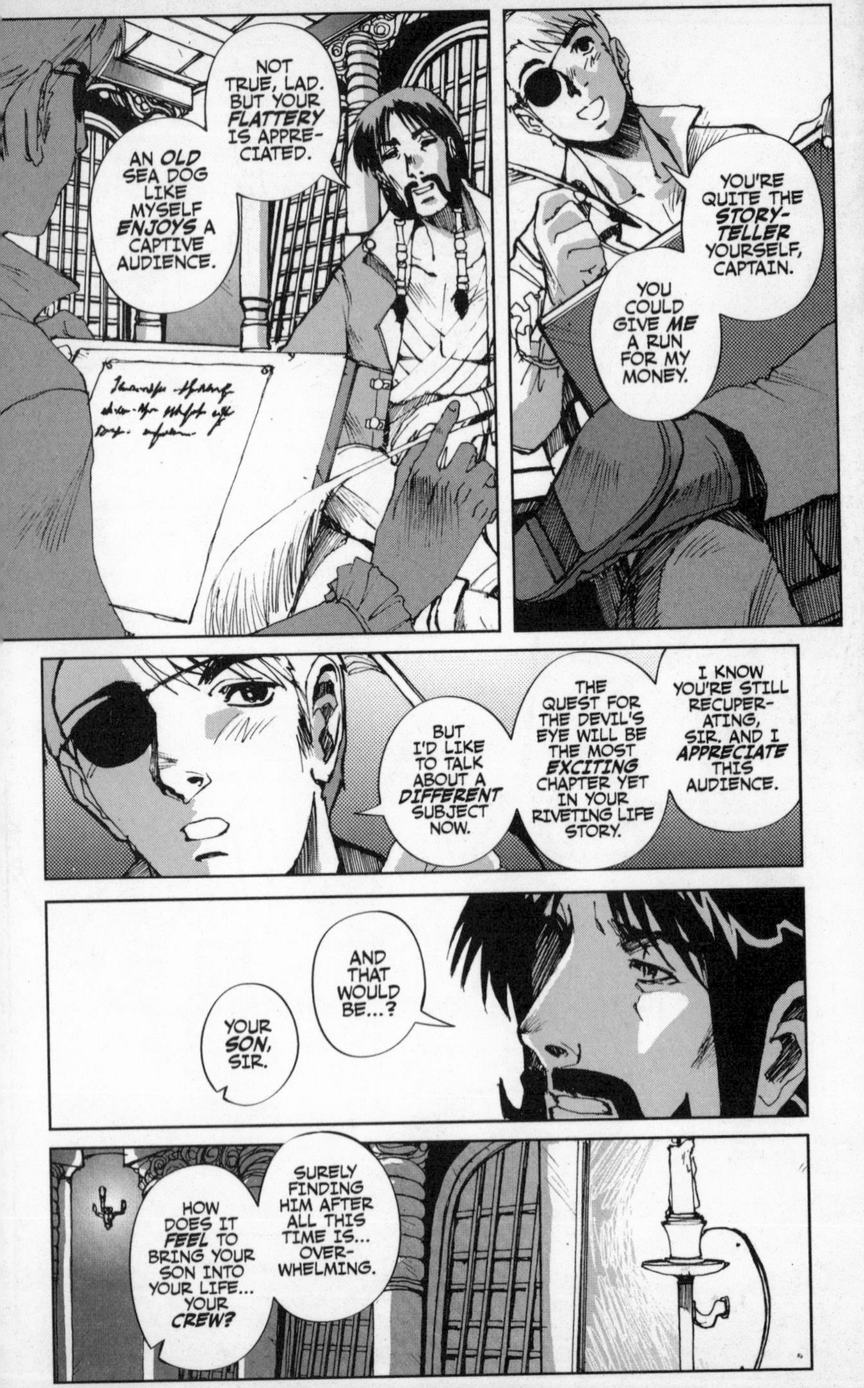
YOU'RE QUITE THE STORY-TELLER YOURSELF, CAPTAIN.
YOU COULD GIVE ME A RUN FOR MY MONEY.
NOT TRUE, LAD. BUT YOUR FLATTERY IS APPRE-CIATED.
AN OLD SEA DOG LIKE MYSELF ENJOYS A CAPTIVE AUDIENCE.
I KNOW YOU'RE STILL RECUPER-ATING, SIR. AND I APPRECIATE THIS AUDIENCE.
THE QUEST FOR THE DEVIL'S EYE WILL BE THE MOST EXCITING CHAPTER YET IN YOUR RIVETING LIFE STORY.
BUT I'D LIKE TO TALK ABOUT A DIFFERENT SUBJECT NOW.
AND THAT WOULD BE...?
YOUR SON, SIR.
SURELY FINDING HIM AFTER ALL THIS TIME IS... OVER-WHELMING.
HOW DOES IT FEEL TO BRING YOUR SON INTO YOUR LIFE... YOUR CREW?

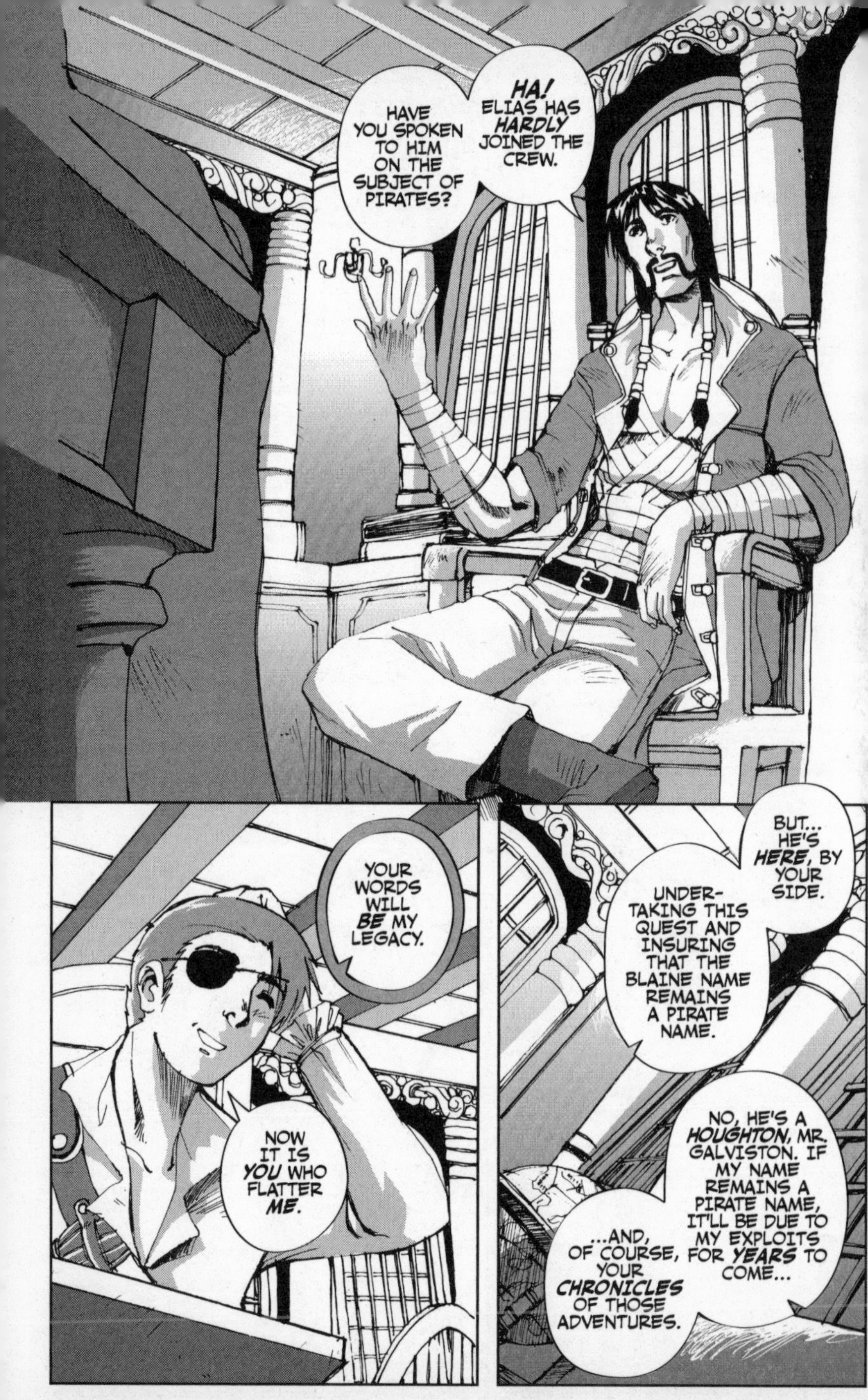
HA! ELIAS HAS *HARDLY* JOINED THE CREW.
HAVE YOU SPOKEN TO HIM ON THE SUBJECT OF PIRATES?
BUT... HE'S *HERE*, BY YOUR SIDE.
UNDER-TAKING THIS QUEST AND INSURING THAT THE BLAINE NAME REMAINS A PIRATE NAME.
NO, HE'S A *HOUGHTON*, MR. GALVISTON. IF MY NAME REMAINS A PIRATE NAME, IT'LL BE DUE TO MY EXPLOITS FOR *YEARS* TO COME...
...AND, OF COURSE, YOUR *CHRONICLES* OF THOSE ADVENTURES.
YOUR WORDS WILL *BE* MY LEGACY.
NOW IT IS *YOU* WHO FLATTER *ME*.

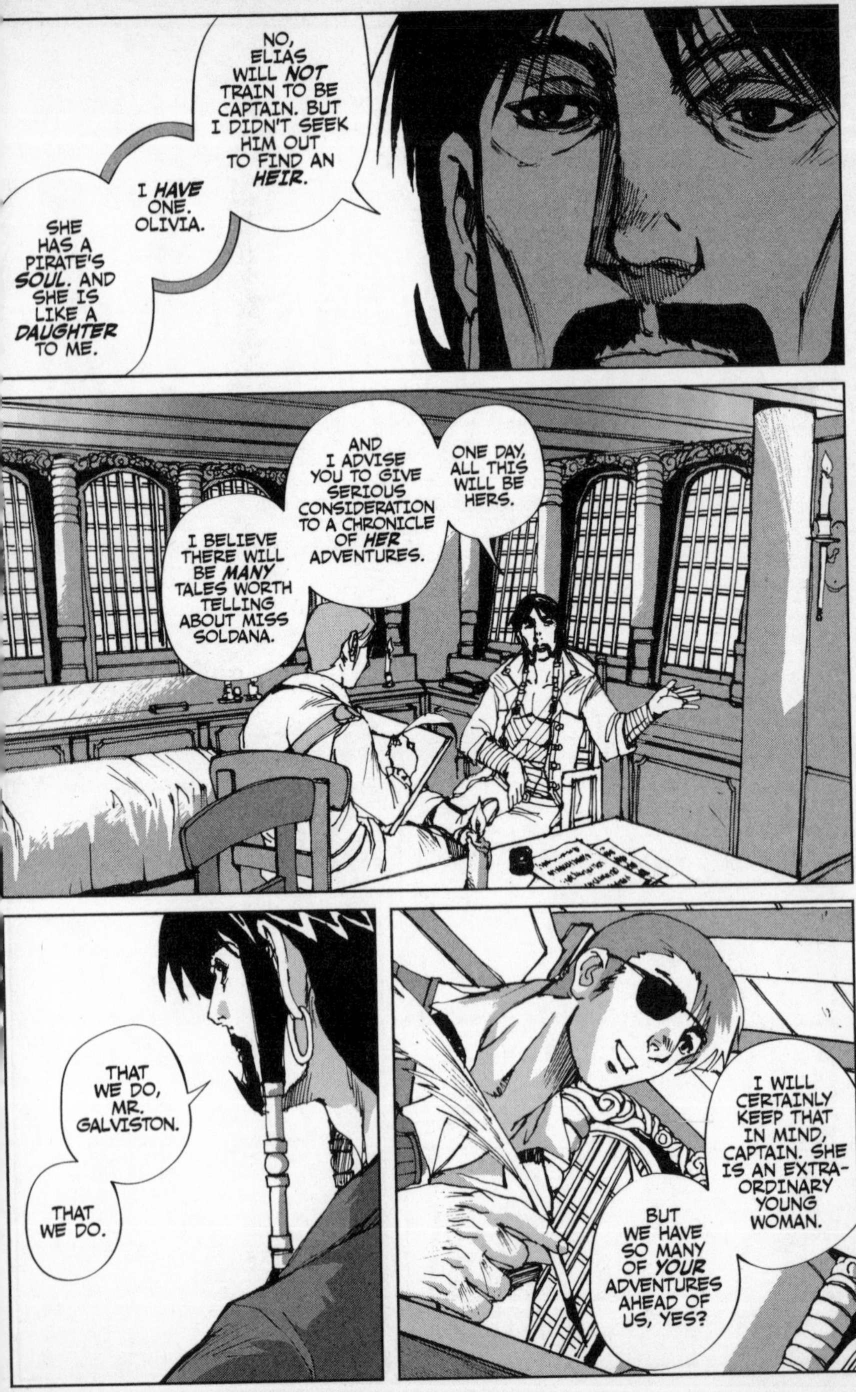
NO, ELIAS WILL *NOT* TRAIN TO BE CAPTAIN. BUT I DIDN'T SEEK HIM OUT TO FIND AN *HEIR*.
I *HAVE* ONE. OLIVIA.
SHE HAS A PIRATE'S *SOUL*. AND SHE IS LIKE A *DAUGHTER* TO ME.
ONE DAY, ALL THIS WILL BE HERS.
AND I ADVISE YOU TO GIVE SERIOUS CONSIDERATION TO A CHRONICLE OF *HER* ADVENTURES.
I BELIEVE THERE WILL BE *MANY* TALES WORTH TELLING ABOUT MISS SOLDANA.
I WILL CERTAINLY KEEP THAT IN MIND, CAPTAIN. SHE IS AN EXTRA-ORDINARY YOUNG WOMAN.
BUT WE HAVE SO MANY OF *YOUR* ADVENTURES AHEAD OF US, YES?
THAT WE DO, MR. GALVISTON.
THAT WE DO.

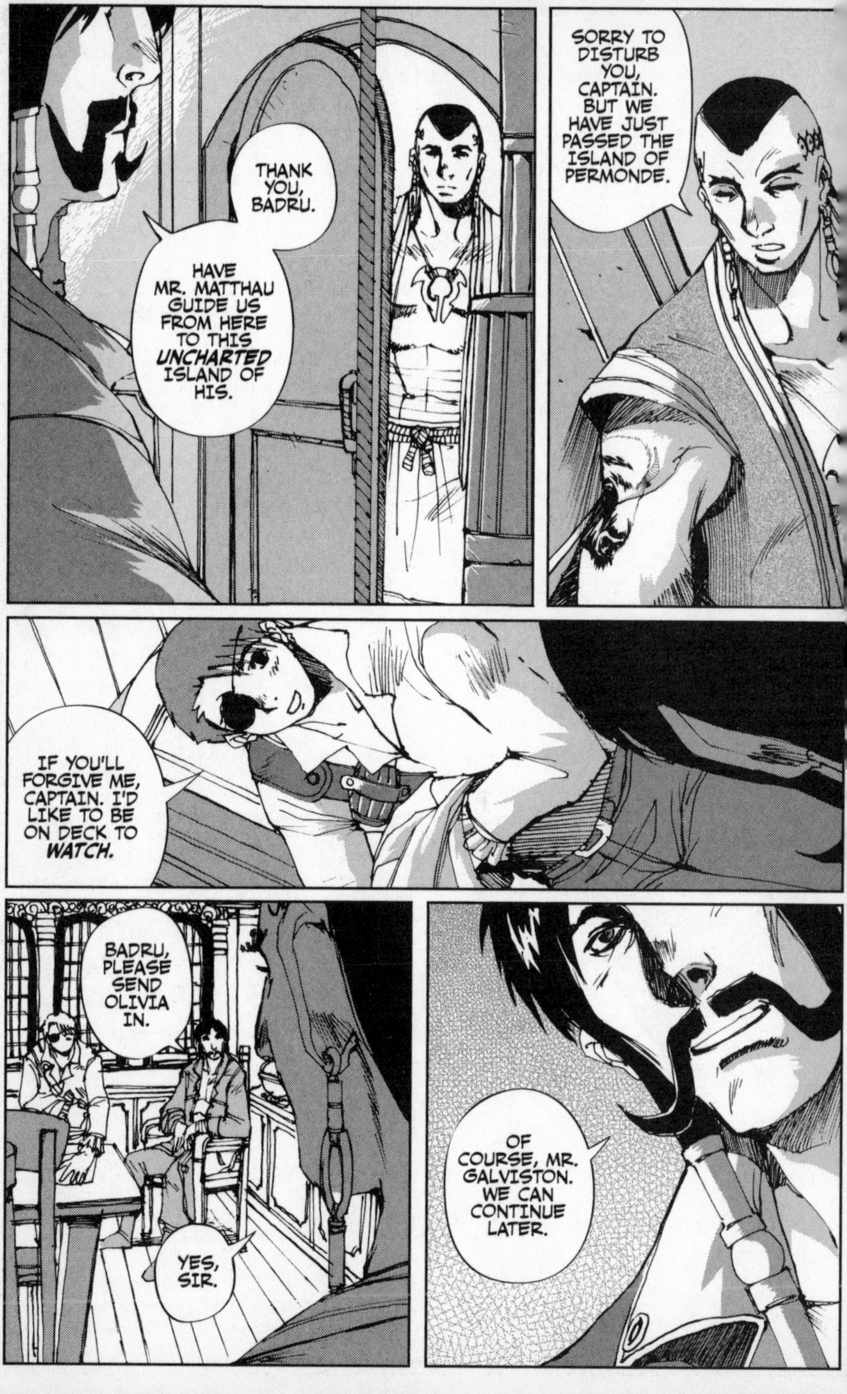
SORRY TO DISTURB YOU, CAPTAIN. BUT WE HAVE JUST PASSED THE ISLAND OF PERMONDE.
THANK YOU, BADRU.
HAVE MR. MATTHAU GUIDE US FROM HERE TO THIS *UNCHARTED* ISLAND OF HIS.
IF YOU'LL FORGIVE ME, CAPTAIN. I'D LIKE TO BE ON DECK TO *WATCH.*
OF COURSE, MR. GALVISTON. WE CAN CONTINUE LATER.
BADRU, PLEASE SEND OLIVIA IN.
YES, SIR.

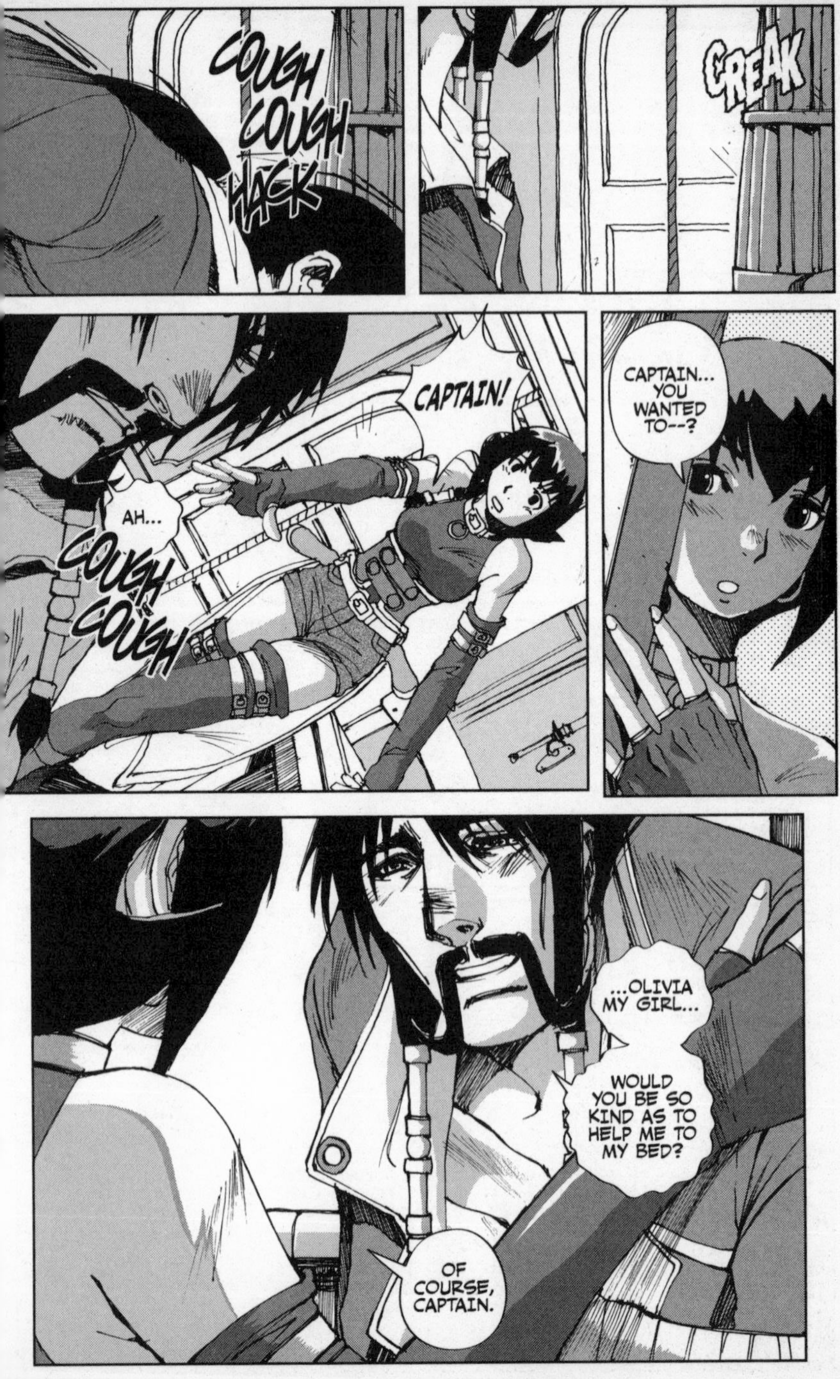
CREAK
COUGH COUGH HACK
CAPTAIN... YOU WANTED TO--?
CAPTAIN!
AH...
COUGH COUGH
...OLIVIA MY GIRL...
WOULD YOU BE SO KIND AS TO HELP ME TO MY BED?
OF COURSE, CAPTAIN.

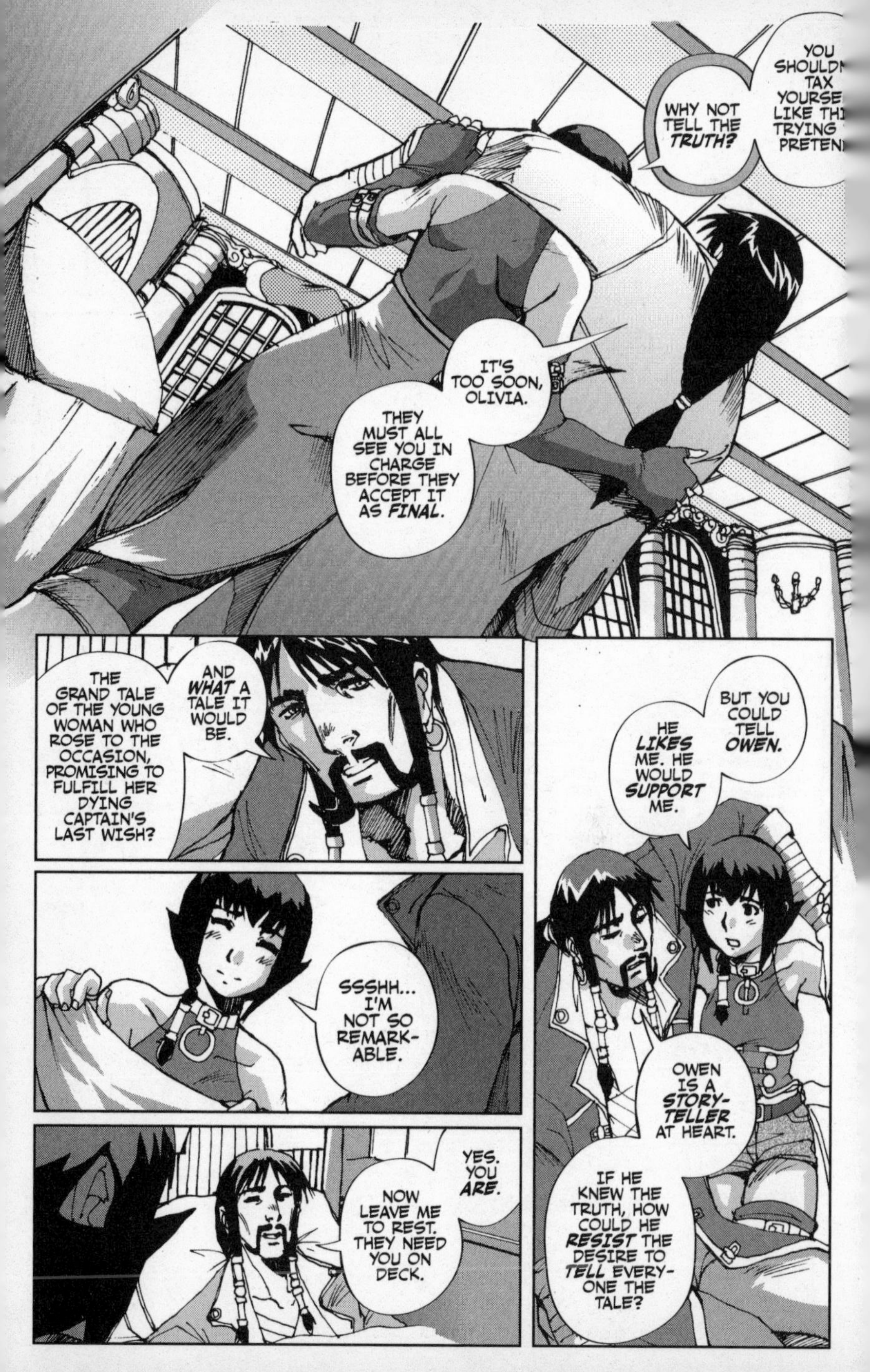
YOU SHOULDN TAX YOURSE LIKE THI TRYING PRETEN
WHY NOT TELL THE *TRUTH?*
IT'S TOO SOON, OLIVIA.
THEY MUST ALL SEE YOU IN CHARGE BEFORE THEY ACCEPT IT AS *FINAL*.
BUT YOU COULD TELL *OWEN.*
HE *LIKES* ME. HE WOULD *SUPPORT* ME.
OWEN IS A *STORY-TELLER* AT HEART.
IF HE KNEW THE TRUTH, HOW COULD HE *RESIST* THE DESIRE TO *TELL* EVERY-ONE THE TALE?
AND *WHAT* A TALE IT WOULD BE.
THE GRAND TALE OF THE YOUNG WOMAN WHO ROSE TO THE OCCASION, PROMISING TO FULFILL HER DYING CAPTAIN'S LAST WISH?
SSSHH... I'M NOT SO REMARK-ABLE.
YES. YOU *ARE*.
NOW LEAVE ME TO REST. THEY NEED YOU ON DECK.

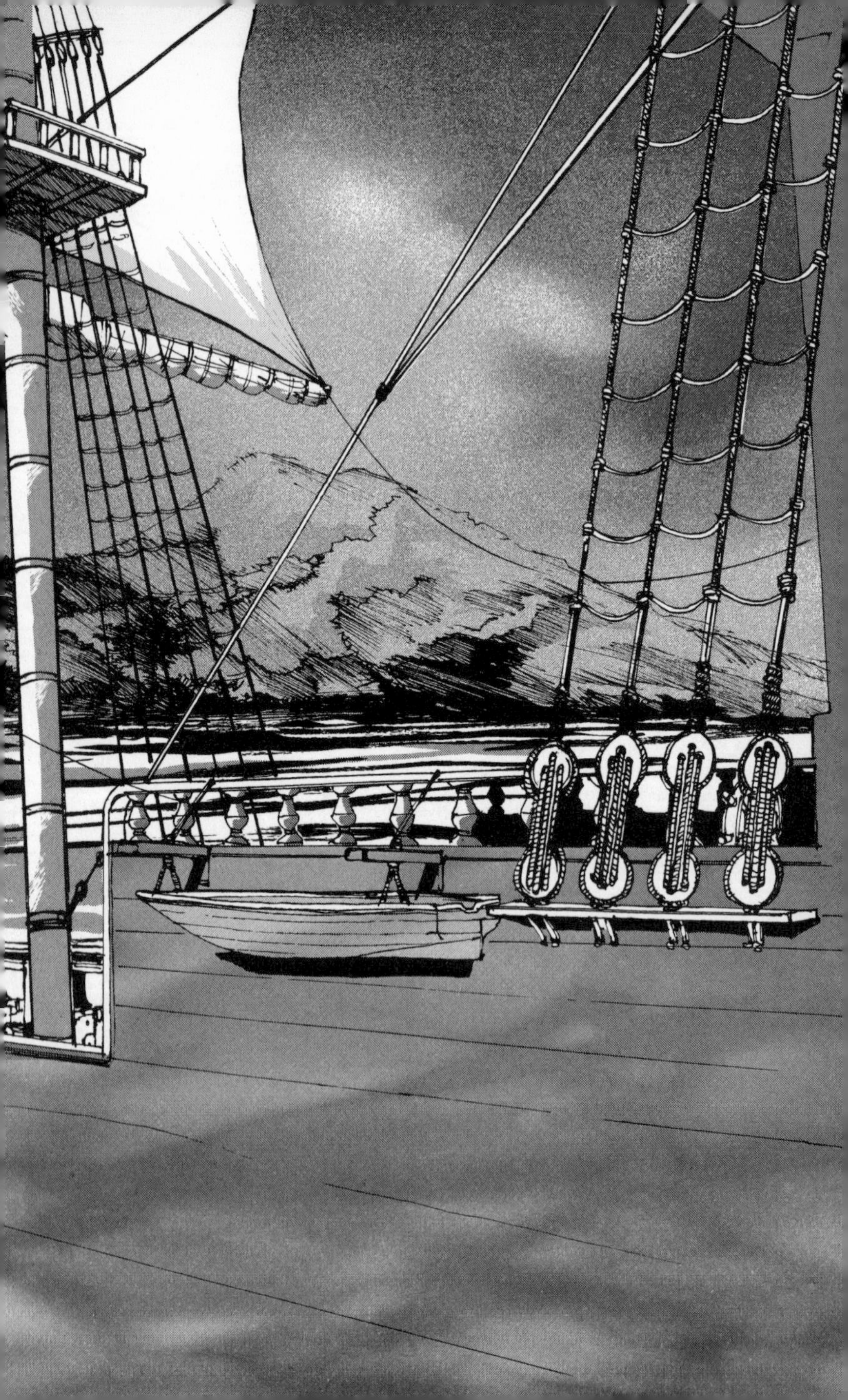

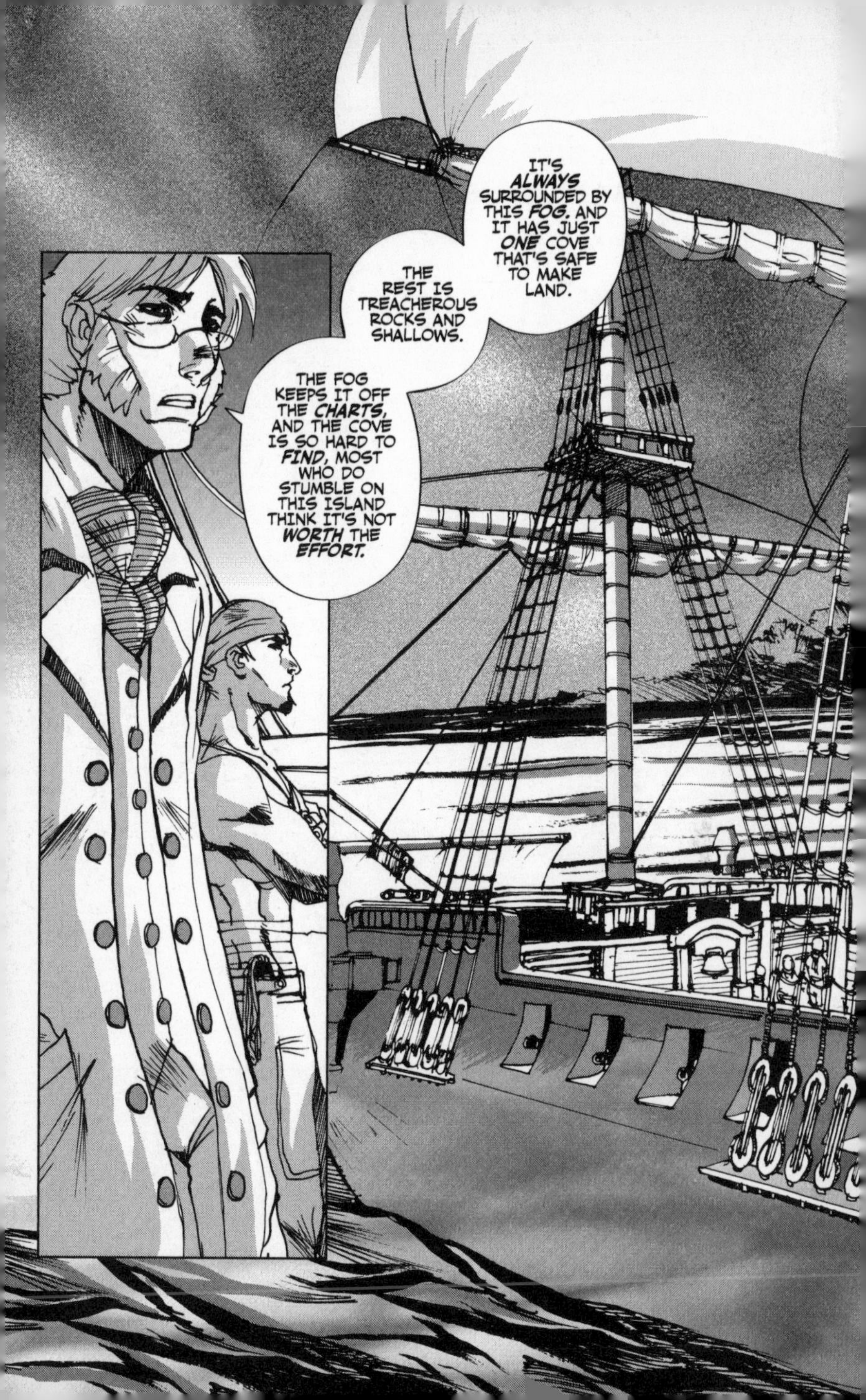
IT'S ALWAYS SURROUNDED BY THIS FOG, AND IT HAS JUST ONE COVE THAT'S SAFE TO MAKE LAND.
THE REST IS TREACHEROUS ROCKS AND SHALLOWS.
THE FOG KEEPS IT OFF THE CHARTS, AND THE COVE IS SO HARD TO FIND, MOST WHO DO STUMBLE ON THIS ISLAND THINK IT'S NOT WORTH THE EFFORT.

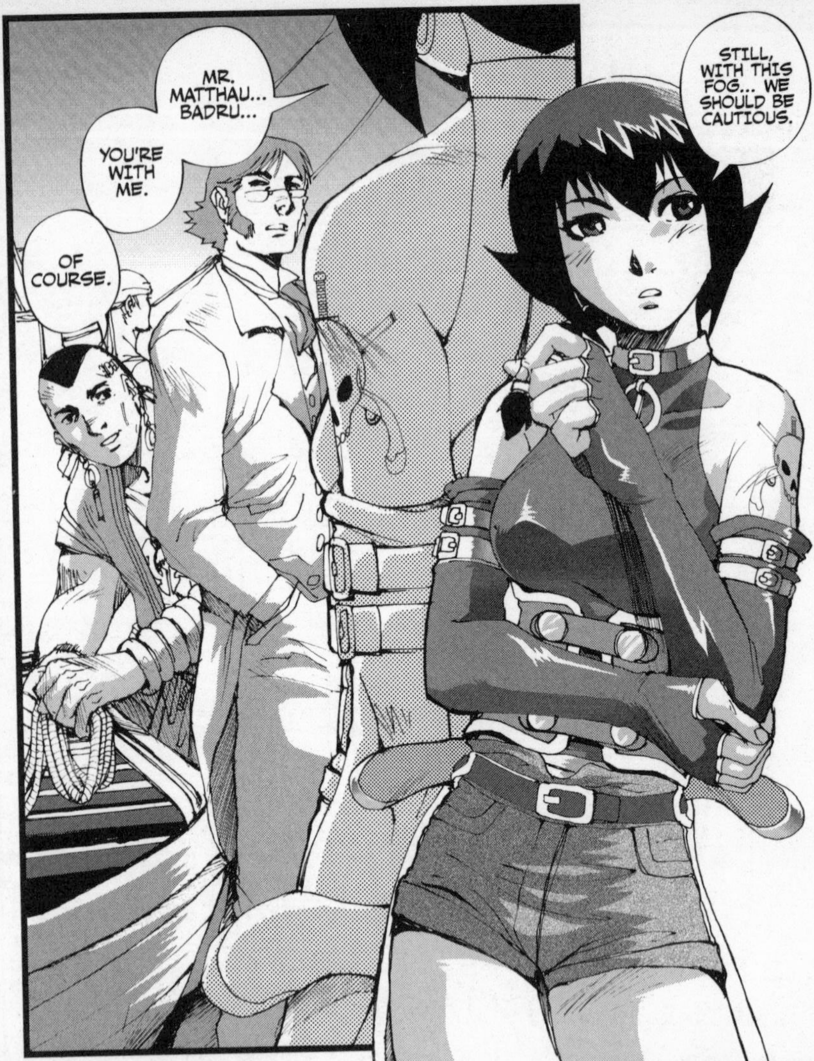
MR. MATTHAU... BADRU...
YOU'RE WITH ME.
OF COURSE.
STILL, WITH THIS FOG... WE SHOULD BE CAUTIOUS.
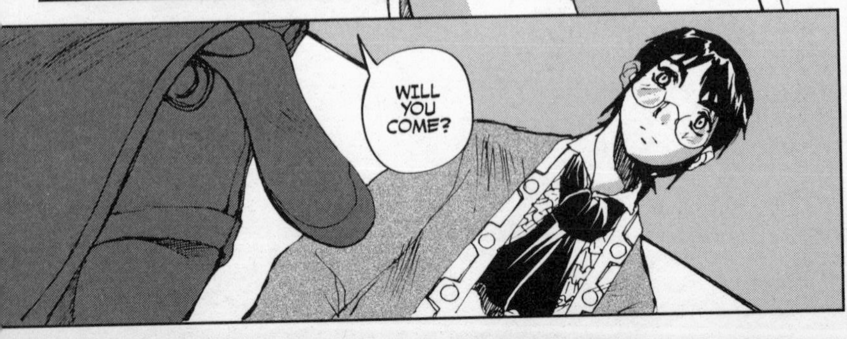
WILL YOU COME?

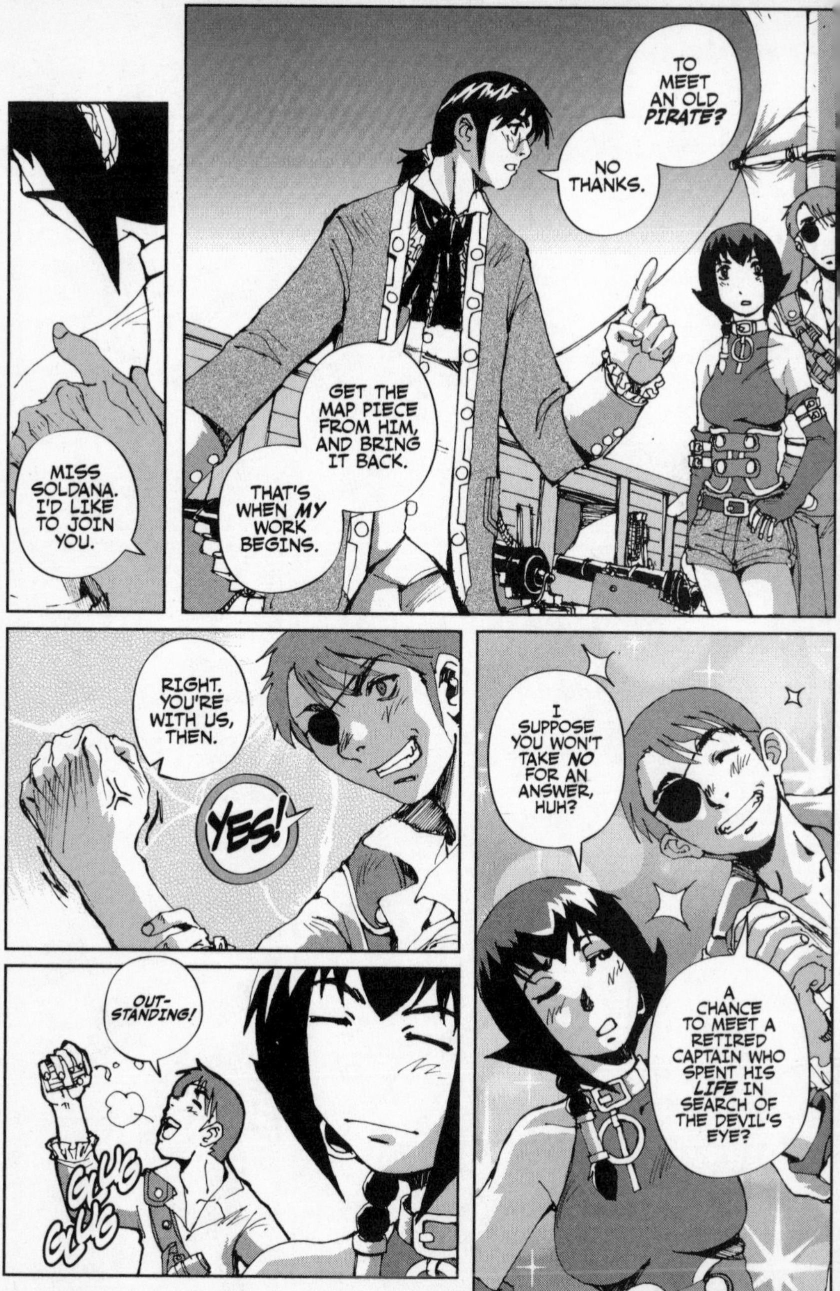
TO MEET AN OLD *PIRATE?*
NO THANKS.
GET THE MAP PIECE FROM HIM, AND BRING IT BACK.
THAT'S WHEN *MY* WORK BEGINS.
MISS SOLDANA. I'D LIKE TO JOIN YOU.
I SUPPOSE YOU WON'T TAKE *NO* FOR AN ANSWER, HUH?
A CHANCE TO MEET A RETIRED CAPTAIN WHO SPENT HIS *LIFE* IN SEARCH OF THE DEVIL'S EYE?
RIGHT. YOU'RE WITH US, THEN.
YES!
OUT-STANDING!
GLUG GLUG

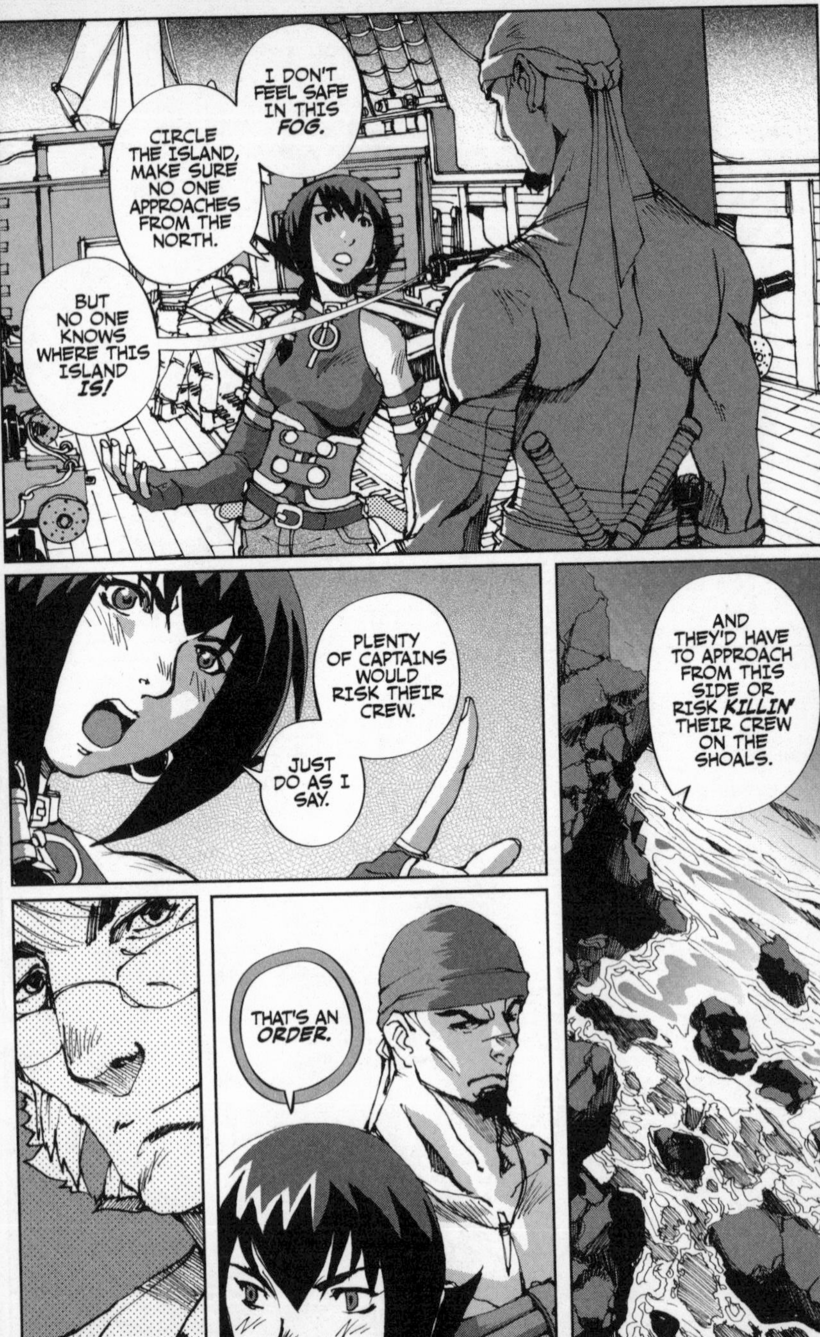
I DON'T FEEL SAFE IN THIS *FOG.*
CIRCLE THE ISLAND, MAKE SURE NO ONE APPROACHES FROM THE NORTH.
BUT NO ONE KNOWS WHERE THIS ISLAND *IS!*
AND THEY'D HAVE TO APPROACH FROM THIS SIDE OR RISK *KILLIN'* THEIR CREW ON THE SHOALS.
PLENTY OF CAPTAINS WOULD RISK THEIR CREW.
JUST DO AS I SAY.
THAT'S AN *ORDER.*

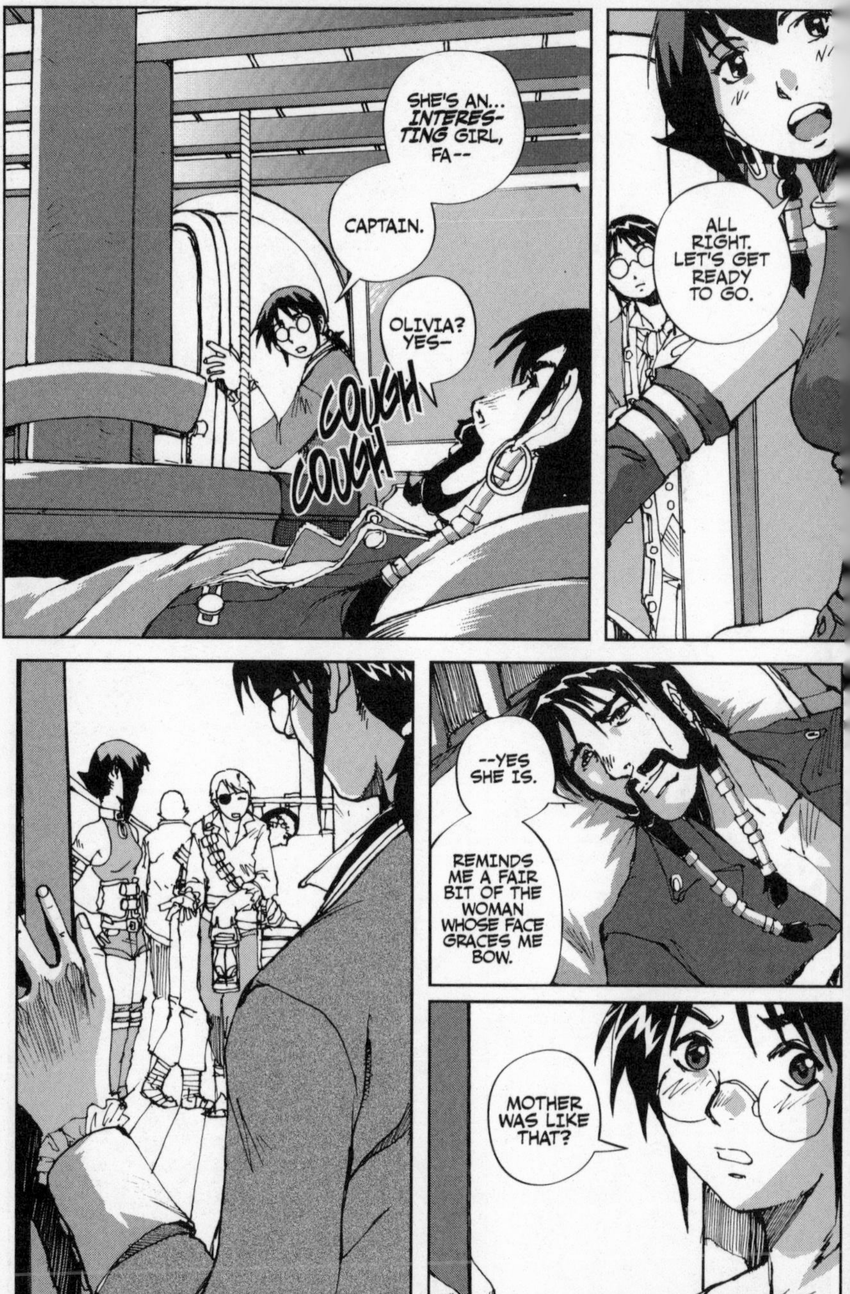
ALL RIGHT. LET'S GET READY TO GO.
SHE'S AN... *INTERESTING* GIRL, FA--
CAPTAIN.
OLIVIA? YES-
COUGH COUGH
--YES SHE IS.
REMINDS ME A FAIR BIT OF THE WOMAN WHOSE FACE GRACES ME BOW.
MOTHER WAS LIKE THAT?

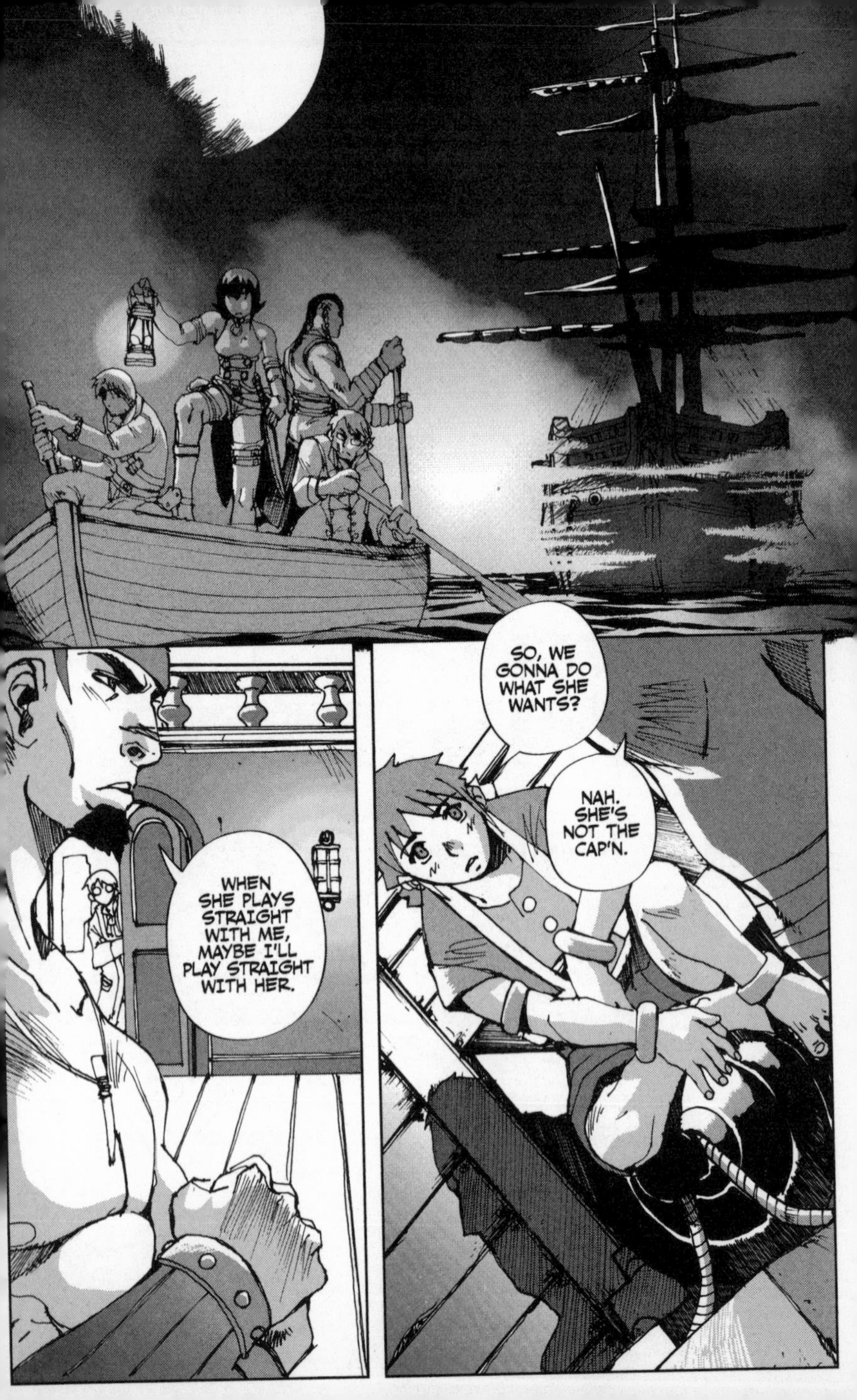
SO, WE GONNA DO WHAT SHE WANTS?
NAH. SHE'S NOT THE CAP'N.
WHEN SHE PLAYS STRAIGHT WITH ME, MAYBE I'LL PLAY STRAIGHT WITH HER.

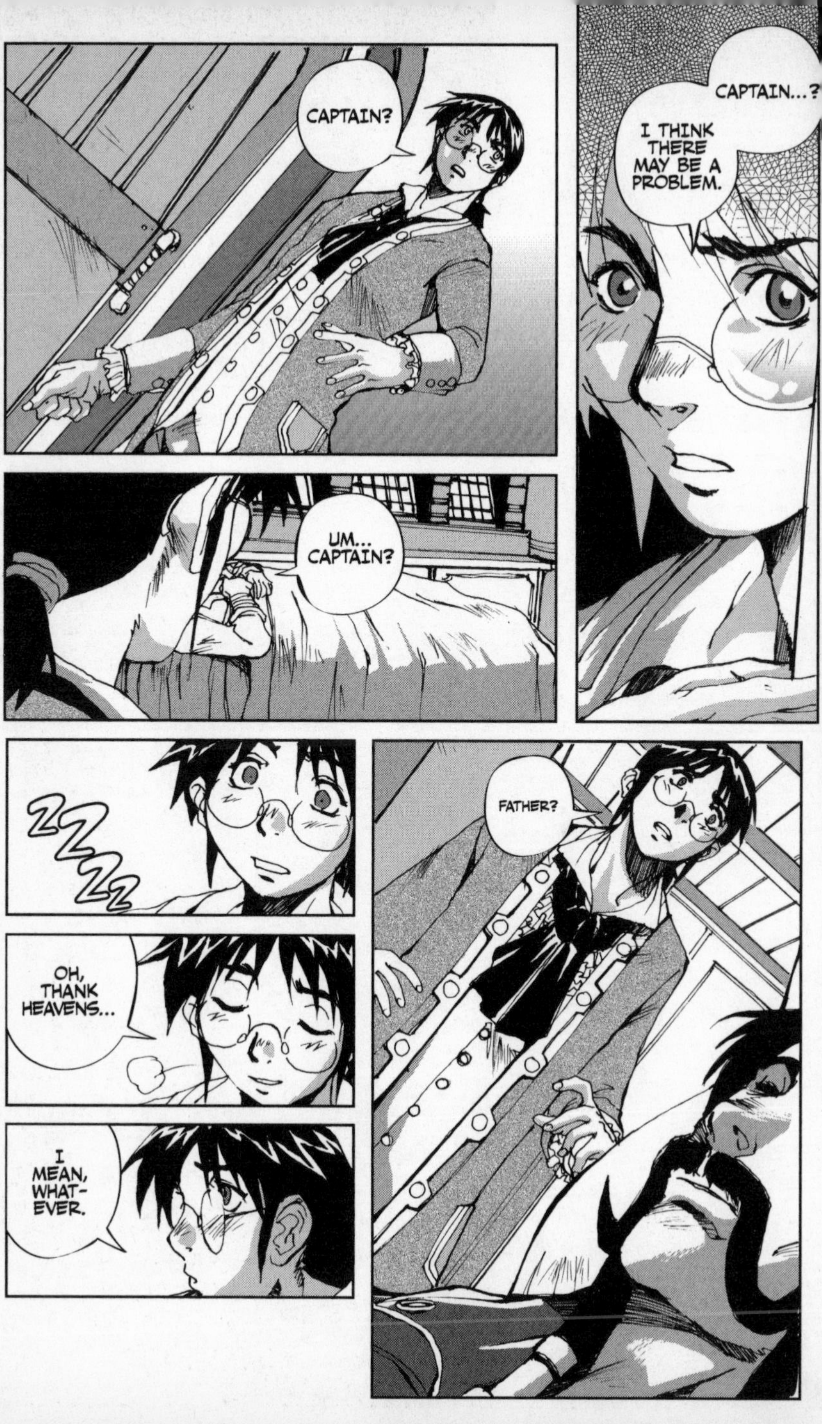
CAPTAIN...?
I THINK THERE MAY BE A PROBLEM.
CAPTAIN?
UM... CAPTAIN?
FATHER?
OH, THANK HEAVENS...
I MEAN, WHAT-EVER.

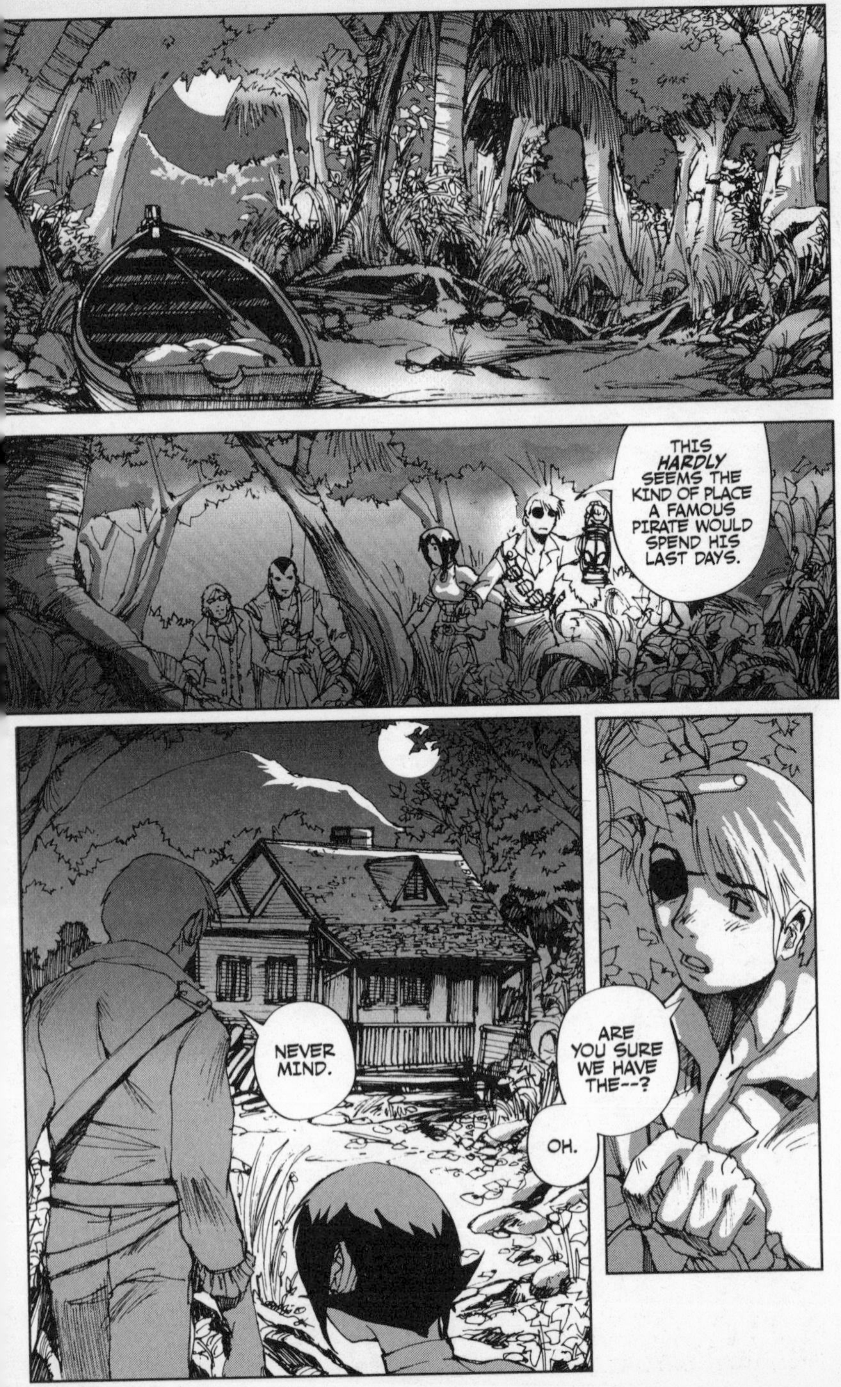
THIS *HARDLY* SEEMS THE KIND OF PLACE A FAMOUS PIRATE WOULD SPEND HIS LAST DAYS.
ARE YOU SURE WE HAVE THE--?
OH.
NEVER MIND.

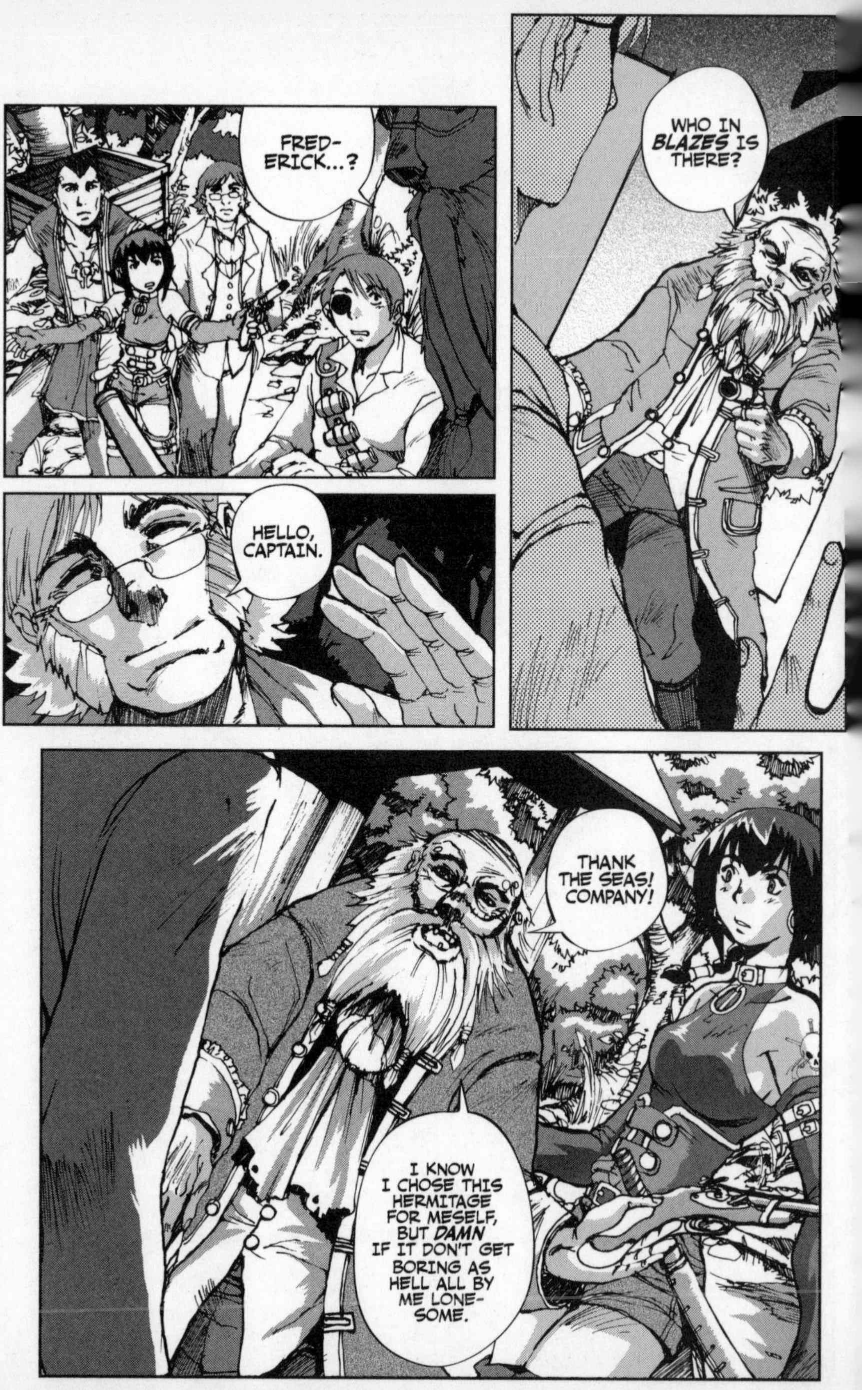
WHO IN *BLAZES* IS THERE?
FRED-ERICK...?
HELLO, CAPTAIN.
THANK THE SEAS! COMPANY!
I KNOW I CHOSE THIS HERMITAGE FOR MESELF, BUT *DAMN* IF IT DON'T GET BORING AS HELL ALL BY ME LONE-SOME.

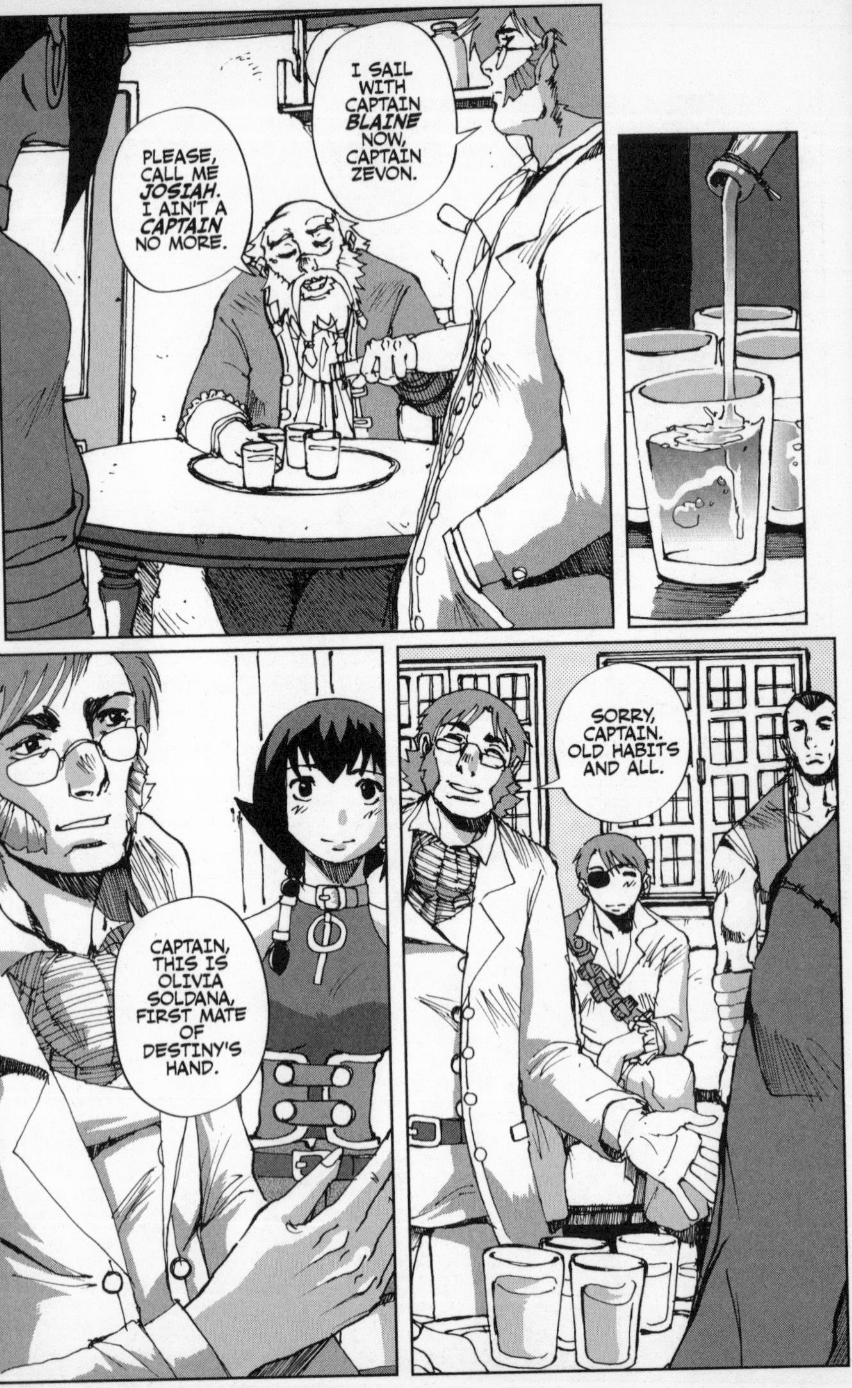
I SAIL WITH CAPTAIN BLAINE NOW, CAPTAIN ZEVON.
PLEASE, CALL ME JOSIAH. I AIN'T A CAPTAIN NO MORE.
SORRY, CAPTAIN. OLD HABITS AND ALL.
CAPTAIN, THIS IS OLIVIA SOLDANA, FIRST MATE OF DESTINY'S HAND.

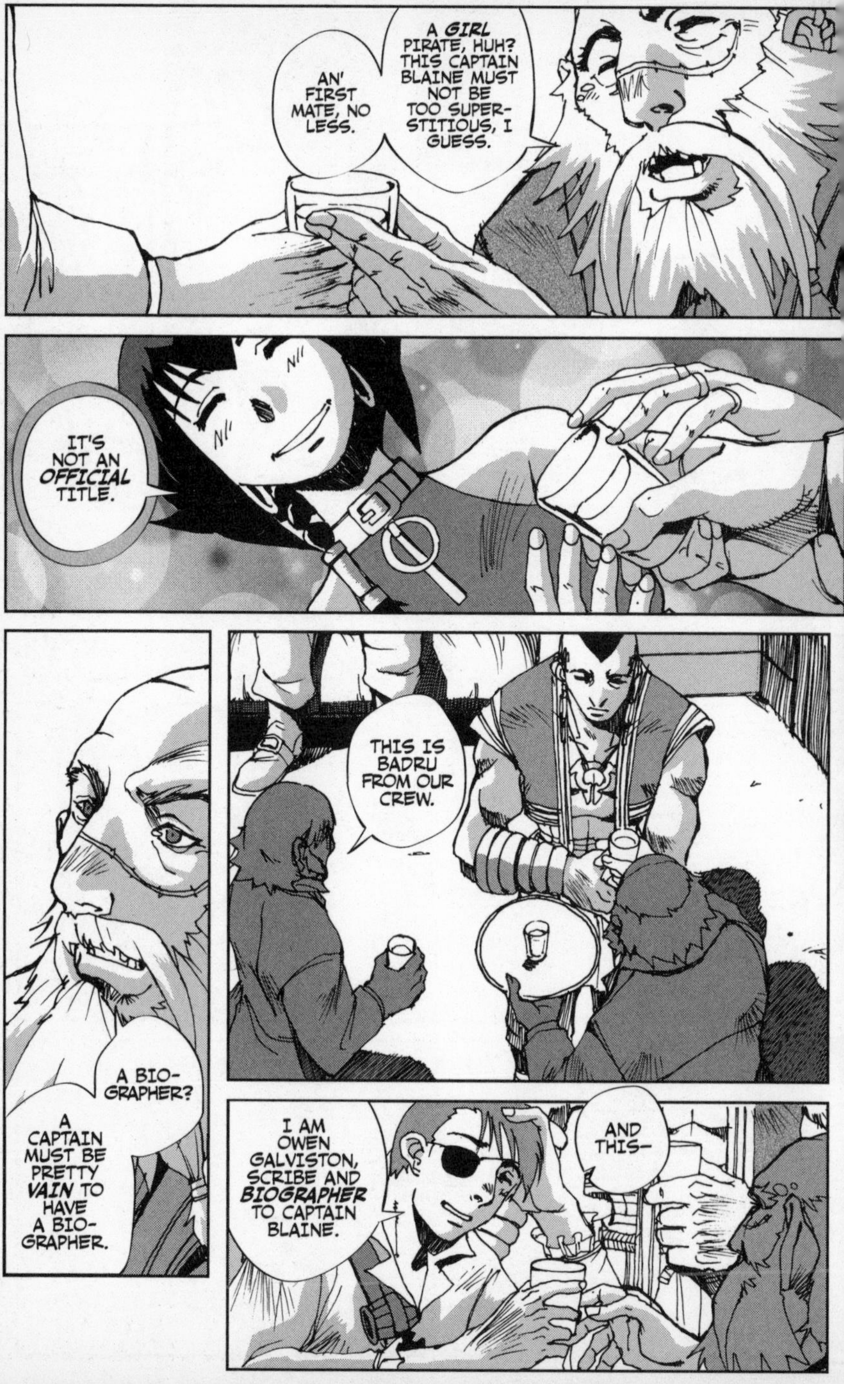
A GIRL PIRATE, HUH? THIS CAPTAIN BLAINE MUST NOT BE TOO SUPER-STITIOUS, I GUESS.
AN' FIRST MATE, NO LESS.
IT'S NOT AN OFFICIAL TITLE.
THIS IS BADRU FROM OUR CREW.
AND THIS—
I AM OWEN GALVISTON, SCRIBE AND BIOGRAPHER TO CAPTAIN BLAINE.
A BIO-GRAPHER?
A CAPTAIN MUST BE PRETTY VAIN TO HAVE A BIO-GRAPHER.

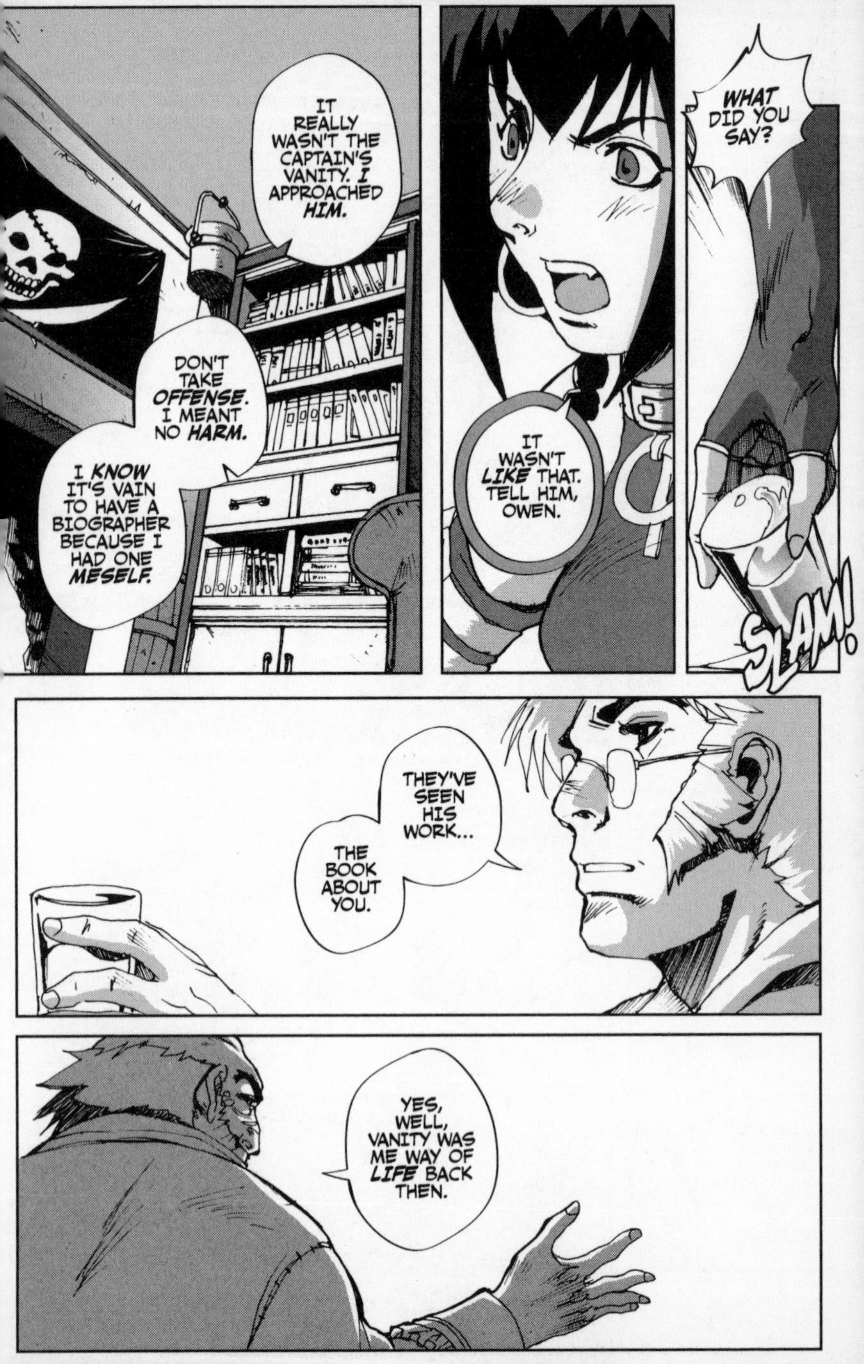
WHAT DID YOU SAY?
SLAM!
IT WASN'T LIKE THAT. TELL HIM, OWEN.
IT REALLY WASN'T THE CAPTAIN'S VANITY. I APPROACHED HIM.
DON'T TAKE OFFENSE. I MEANT NO HARM.
I KNOW IT'S VAIN TO HAVE A BIOGRAPHER BECAUSE I HAD ONE MESELF.
THEY'VE SEEN HIS WORK...
THE BOOK ABOUT YOU.
YES, WELL, VANITY WAS ME WAY OF LIFE BACK THEN.

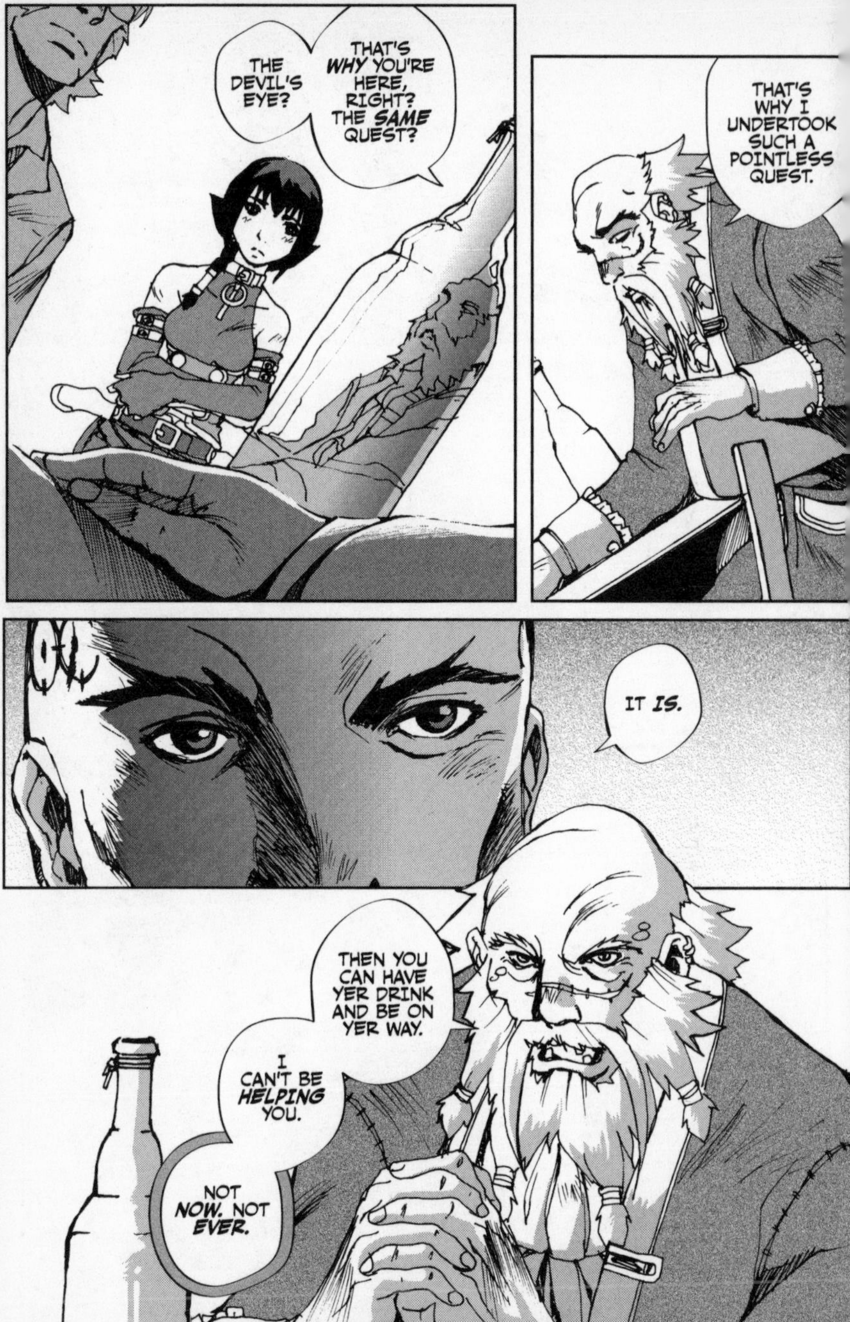
THAT'S WHY I UNDERTOOK SUCH A POINTLESS QUEST.
THAT'S *WHY* YOU'RE HERE, RIGHT? THE *SAME* QUEST?
THE DEVIL'S EYE?
IT *IS.*
THEN YOU CAN HAVE YER DRINK AND BE ON YER WAY.
I CAN'T BE *HELPING* YOU.
NOT *NOW.* NOT *EVER.*

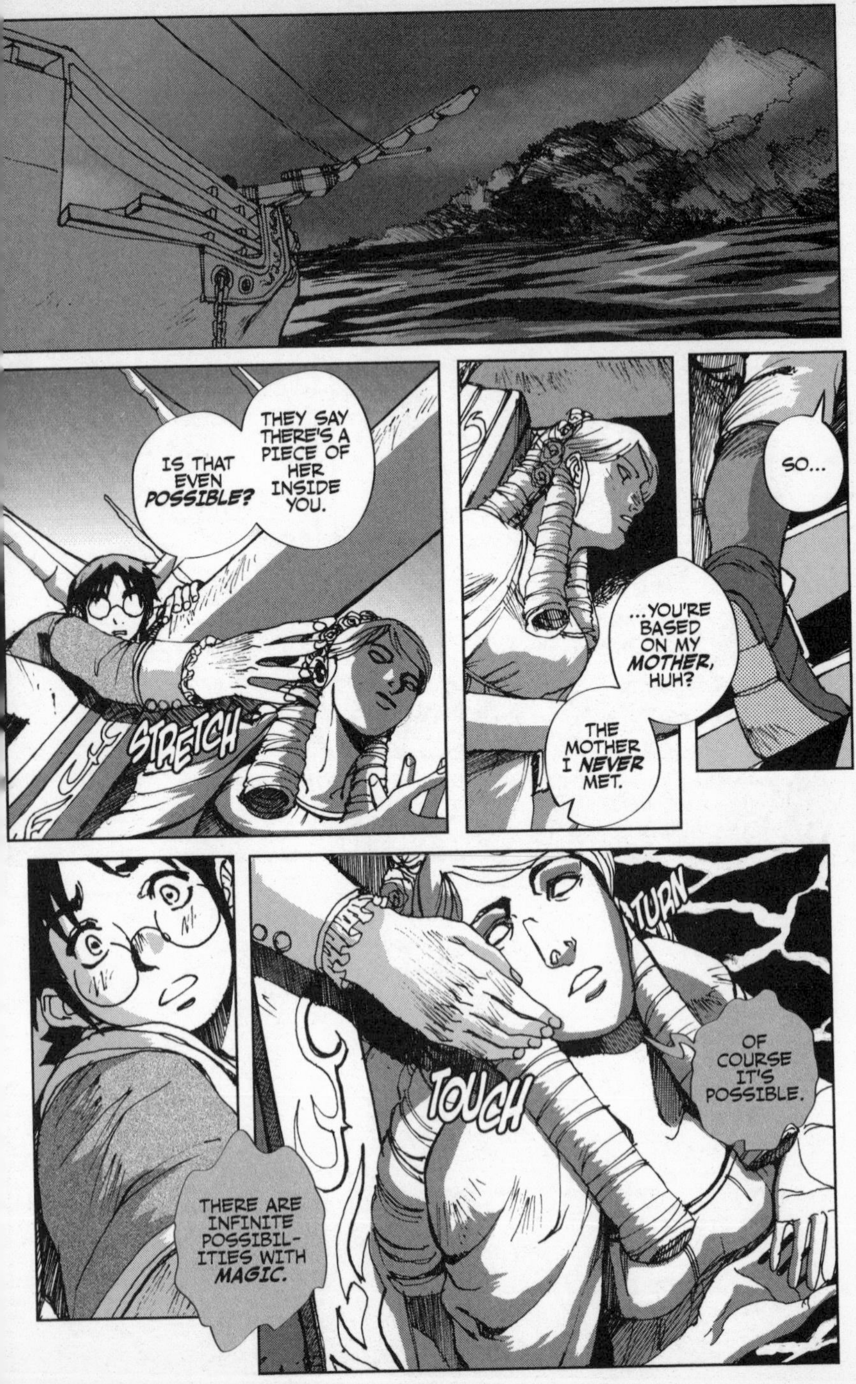
SO...
...YOU'RE BASED ON MY *MOTHER*, HUH?
THE MOTHER I *NEVER* MET.
THEY SAY THERE'S A PIECE OF HER INSIDE YOU.
IS THAT EVEN *POSSIBLE?*
STRETCH
TURN
OF COURSE IT'S POSSIBLE.
TOUCH
THERE ARE INFINITE POSSIBIL-ITIES WITH *MAGIC.*

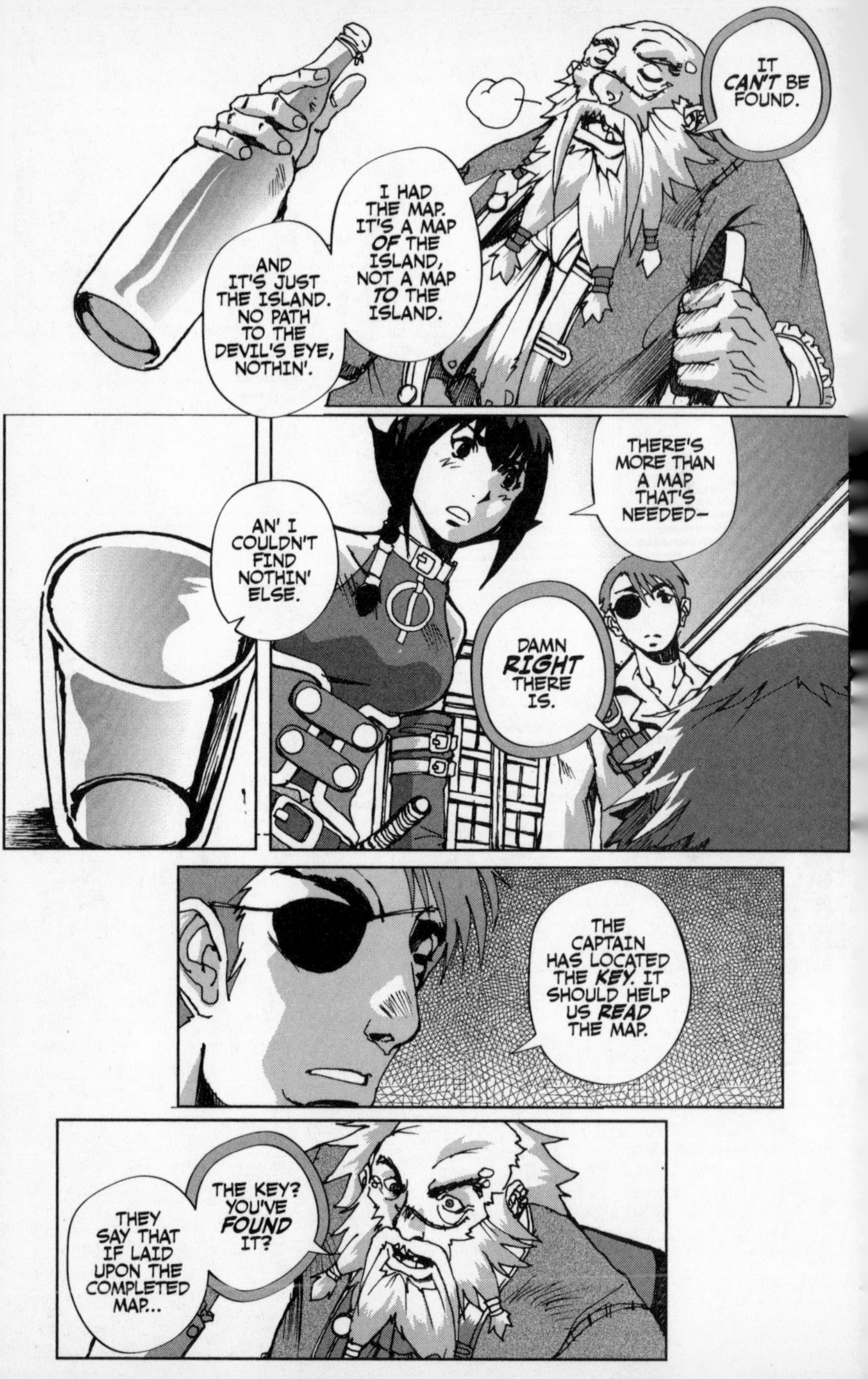
IT CAN'T BE FOUND.
I HAD THE MAP. IT'S A MAP OF THE ISLAND, NOT A MAP TO THE ISLAND.
AND IT'S JUST THE ISLAND. NO PATH TO THE DEVIL'S EYE, NOTHIN'.
AN' I COULDN'T FIND NOTHIN' ELSE.
THERE'S MORE THAN A MAP THAT'S NEEDED—
DAMN RIGHT THERE IS.
THE CAPTAIN HAS LOCATED THE KEY. IT SHOULD HELP US READ THE MAP.
THE KEY? YOU'VE FOUND IT?
THEY SAY THAT IF LAID UPON THE COMPLETED MAP...

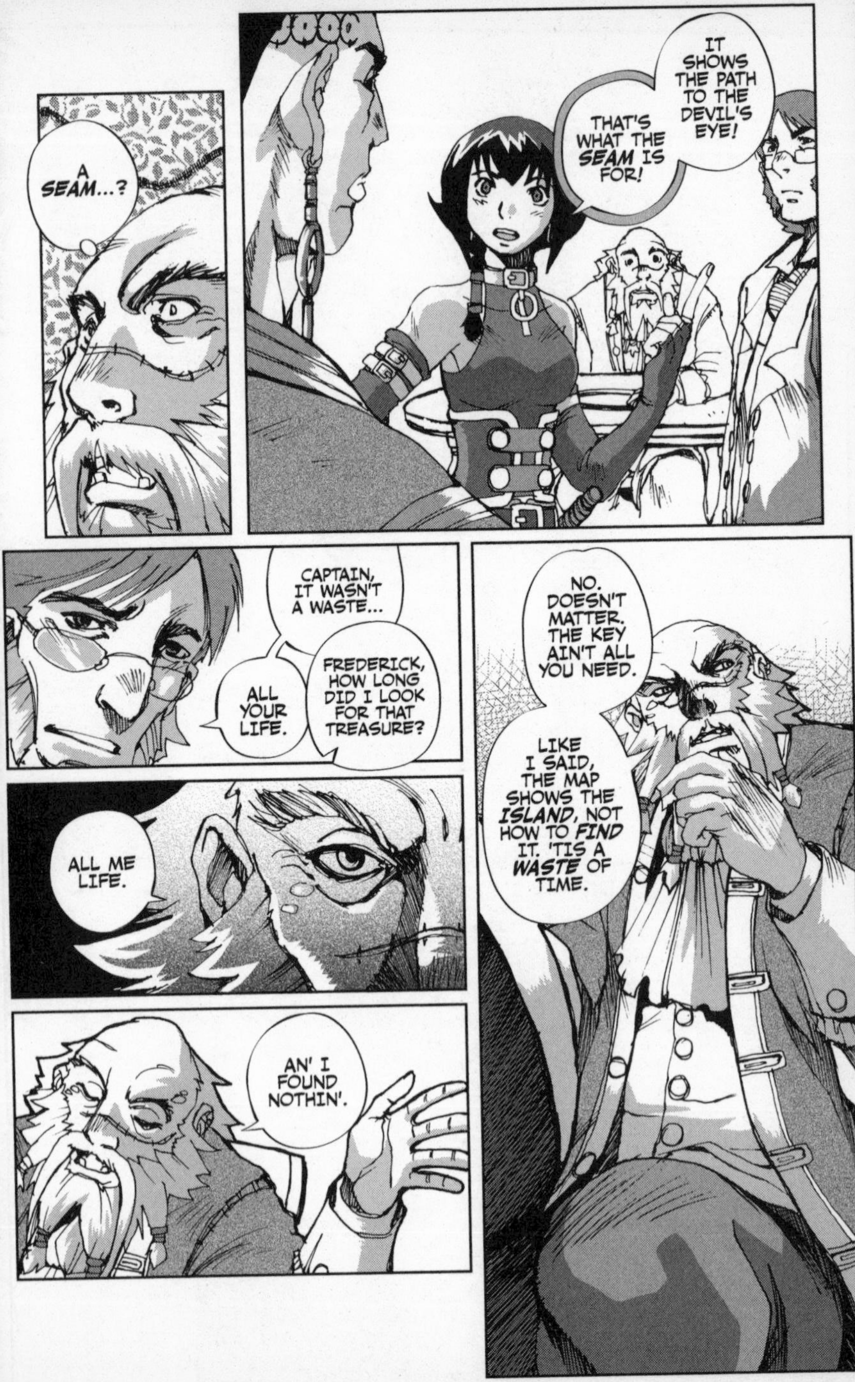
IT SHOWS THE PATH TO THE DEVIL'S EYE!
THAT'S WHAT THE SEAM IS FOR!
A SEAM...?
NO. DOESN'T MATTER. THE KEY AIN'T ALL YOU NEED.
LIKE I SAID, THE MAP SHOWS THE ISLAND, NOT HOW TO FIND IT. 'TIS A WASTE OF TIME.
CAPTAIN, IT WASN'T A WASTE...
FREDERICK, HOW LONG DID I LOOK FOR THAT TREASURE?
ALL YOUR LIFE.
ALL ME LIFE.
AN' I FOUND NOTHIN'.

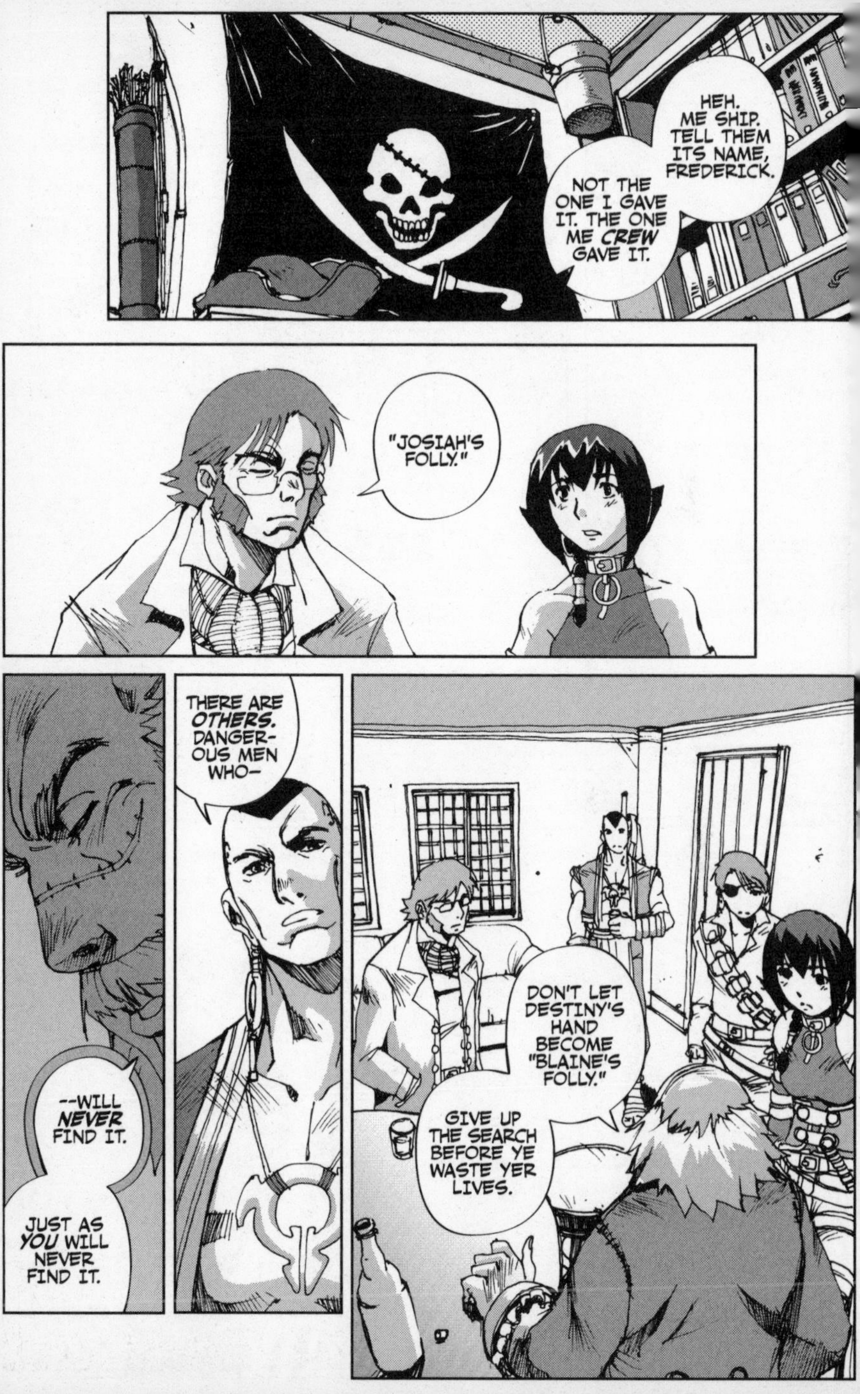
HEH. ME SHIP. TELL THEM ITS NAME, FREDERICK.
NOT THE ONE I GAVE IT. THE ONE ME *CREW* GAVE IT.
"JOSIAH'S FOLLY."
DON'T LET DESTINY'S HAND BECOME "BLAINE'S FOLLY."
GIVE UP THE SEARCH BEFORE YE WASTE YER LIVES.
THERE ARE *OTHERS.* DANGER-OUS MEN WHO–
--WILL *NEVER* FIND IT.
JUST AS *YOU* WILL NEVER FIND IT.

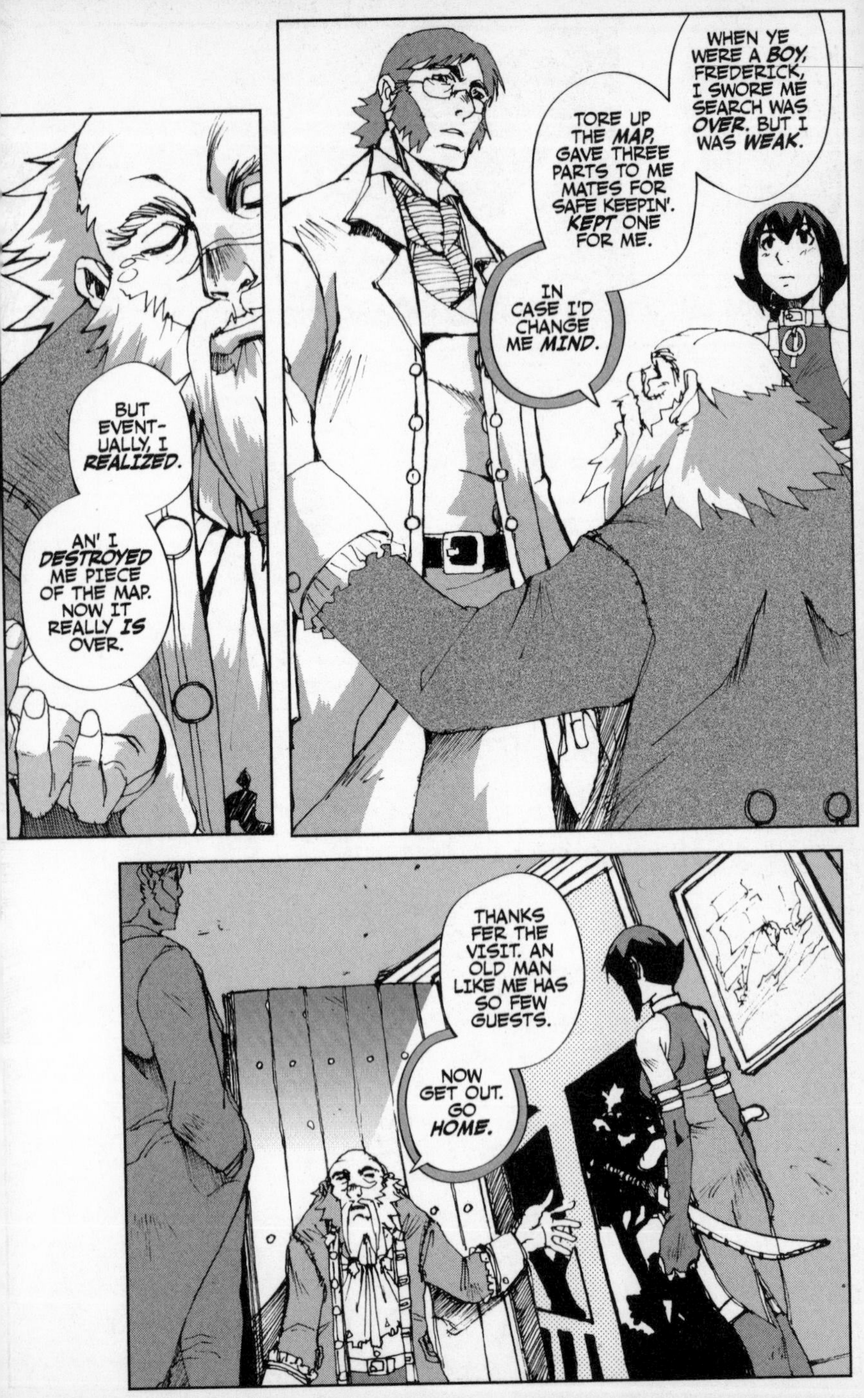
WHEN YE WERE A *BOY*, FREDERICK, I SWORE ME SEARCH WAS *OVER*. BUT I WAS *WEAK*.
TORE UP THE *MAP*, GAVE THREE PARTS TO ME MATES FOR SAFE KEEPIN'. *KEPT* ONE FOR ME.
IN CASE I'D CHANGE ME *MIND*.
BUT EVENT-UALLY, I *REALIZED*.
AN' I *DESTROYED* ME PIECE OF THE MAP. NOW IT REALLY *IS* OVER.
THANKS FER THE VISIT. AN OLD MAN LIKE ME HAS SO FEW GUESTS.
NOW GET OUT. GO *HOME*.

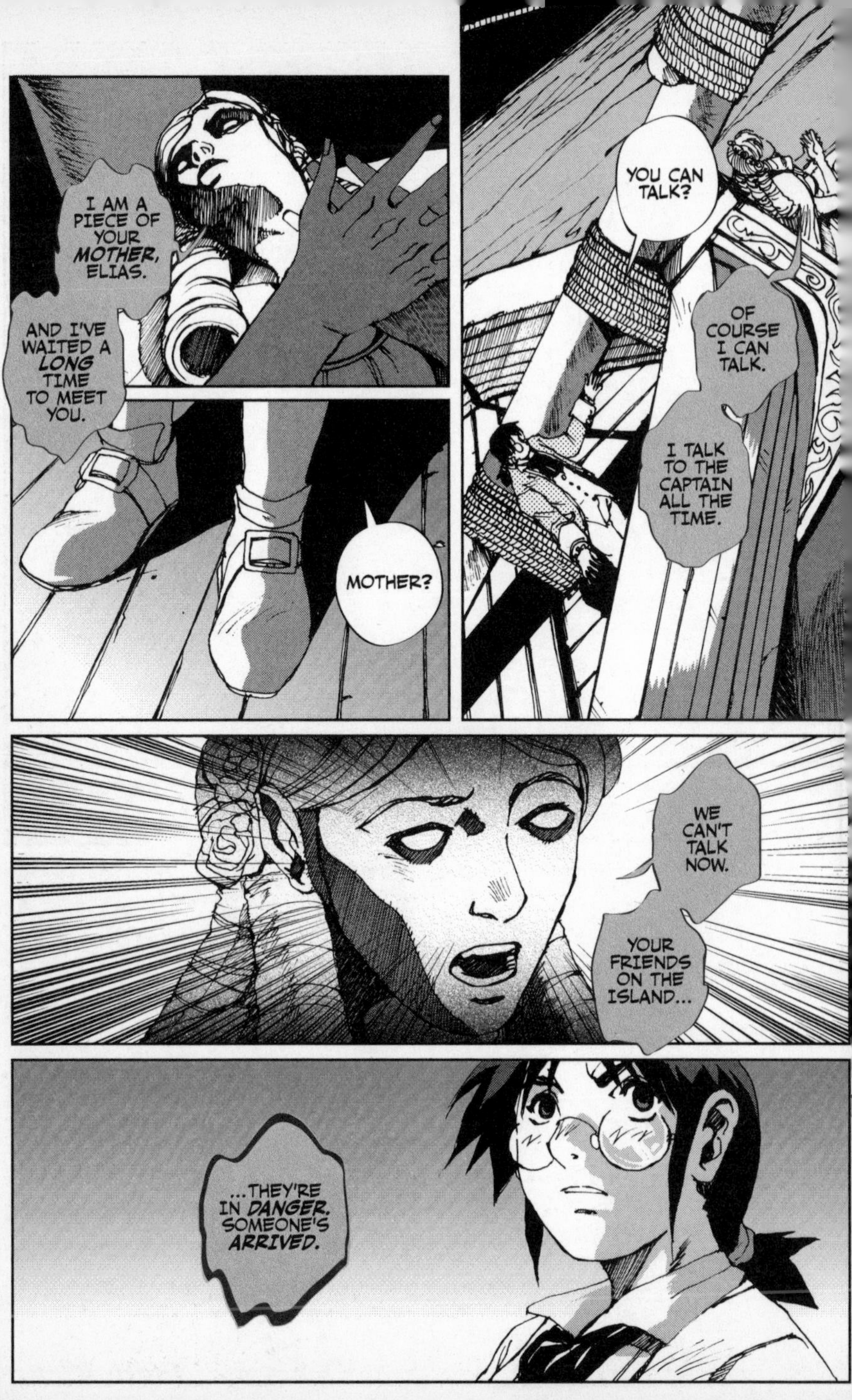
YOU CAN TALK?
OF COURSE I CAN TALK.
I TALK TO THE CAPTAIN ALL THE TIME.
I AM A PIECE OF YOUR MOTHER, ELIAS.
AND I'VE WAITED A LONG TIME TO MEET YOU.
MOTHER?
WE CAN'T TALK NOW.
YOUR FRIENDS ON THE ISLAND...
...THEY'RE IN DANGER. SOMEONE'S ARRIVED.

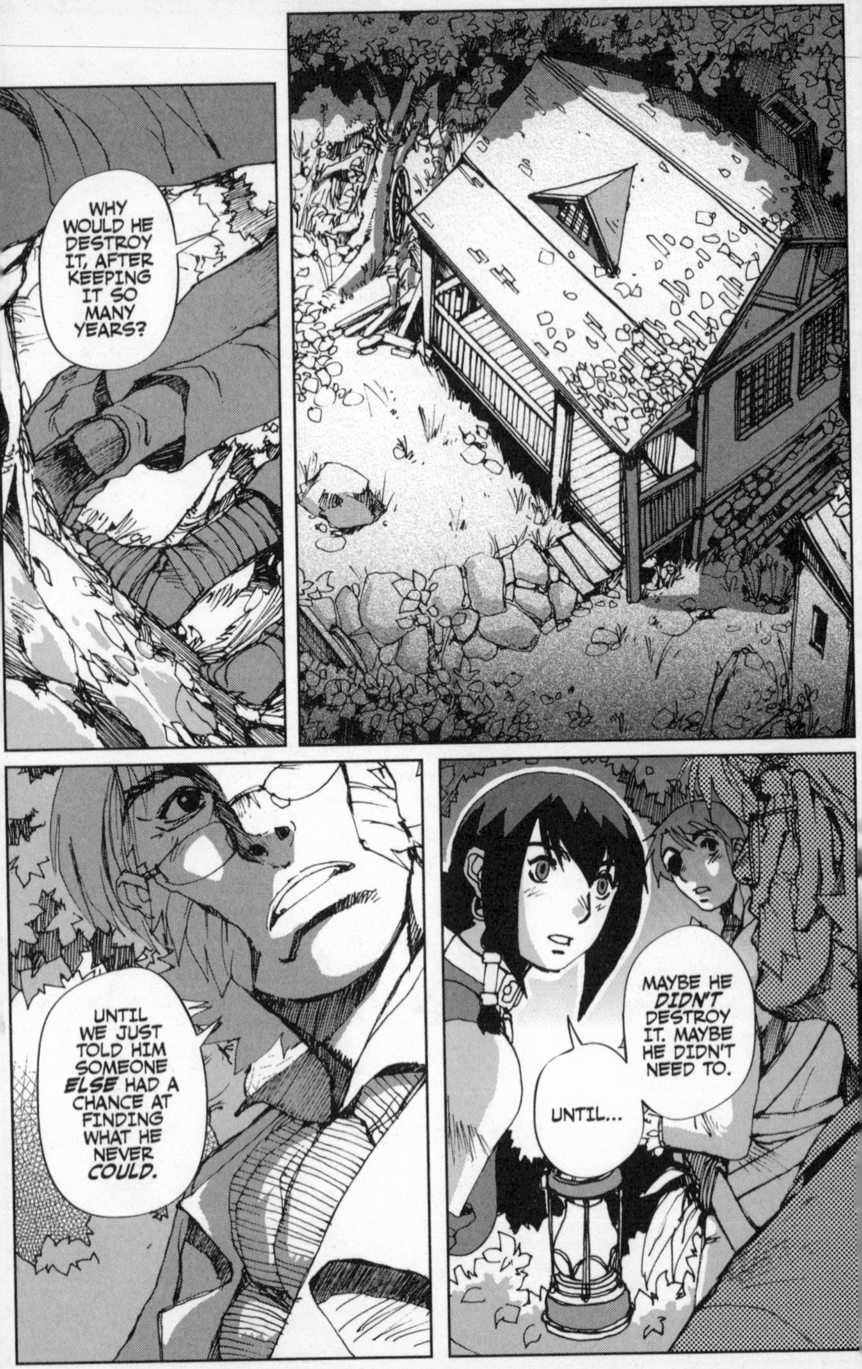
WHY WOULD HE DESTROY IT, AFTER KEEPING IT SO MANY YEARS?
MAYBE HE *DIDN'T* DESTROY IT. MAYBE HE DIDN'T NEED TO.
UNTIL...
UNTIL WE JUST TOLD HIM SOMEONE ***ELSE*** HAD A CHANCE AT FINDING WHAT HE NEVER ***COULD.***

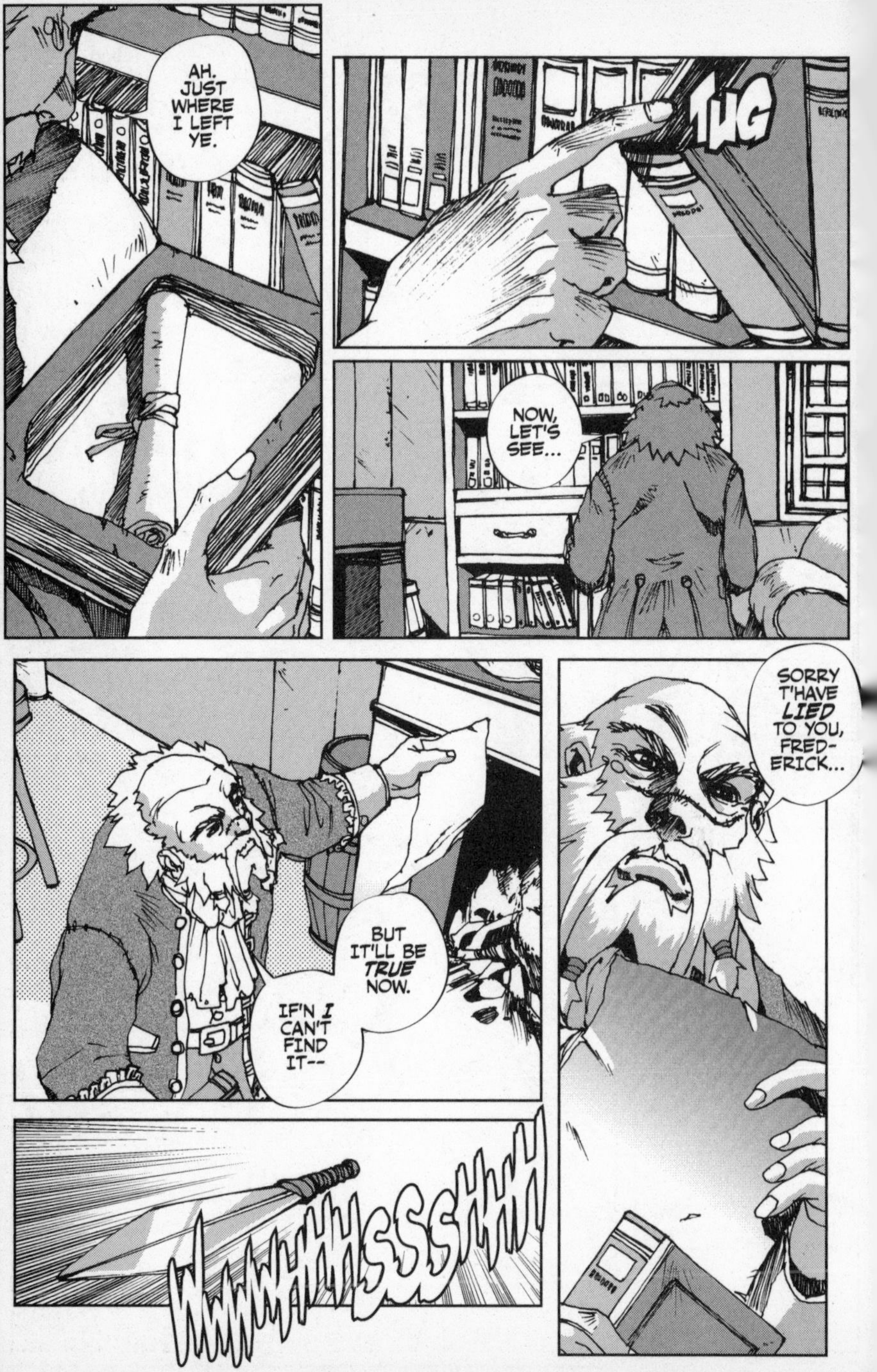
TUG
NOW, LET'S SEE...
AH. JUST WHERE I LEFT YE.
SORRY T'HAVE LIED TO YOU, FRED-ERICK...
BUT IT'LL BE TRUE NOW.
IF'N I CAN'T FIND IT--
WWWHHHSSSSHHH

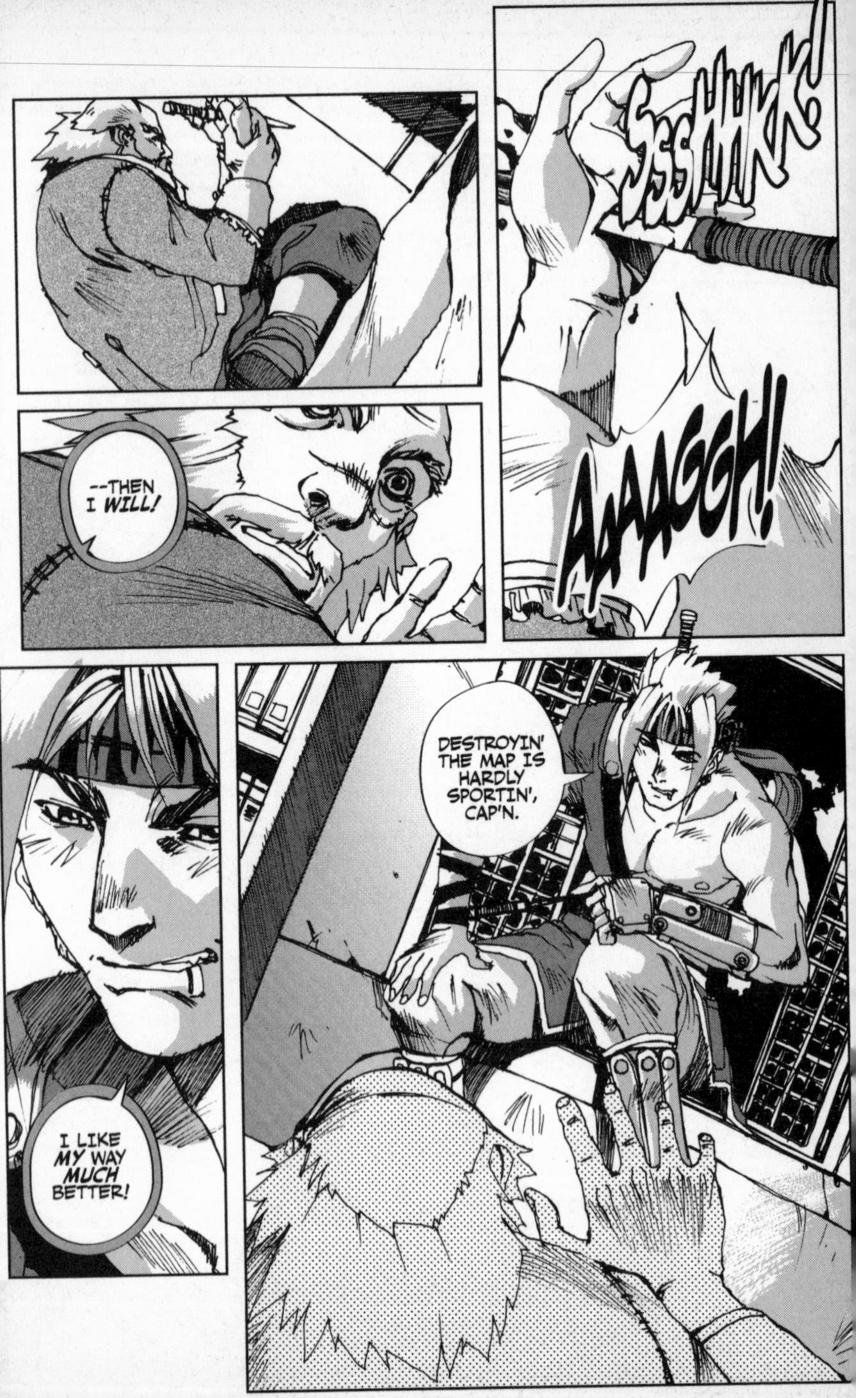
SSSHHKK!
AAAGGH!
--THEN I *WILL!*
DESTROYIN' THE MAP IS HARDLY SPORTIN', CAP'N.
I LIKE *MY WAY MUCH* BETTER!

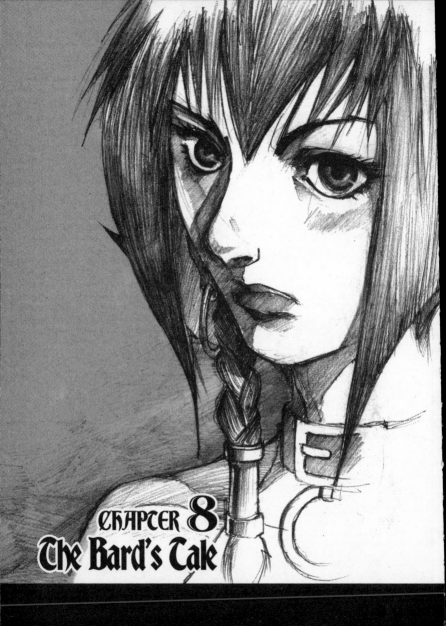

CHAPTER **8**
The Bard's Tale

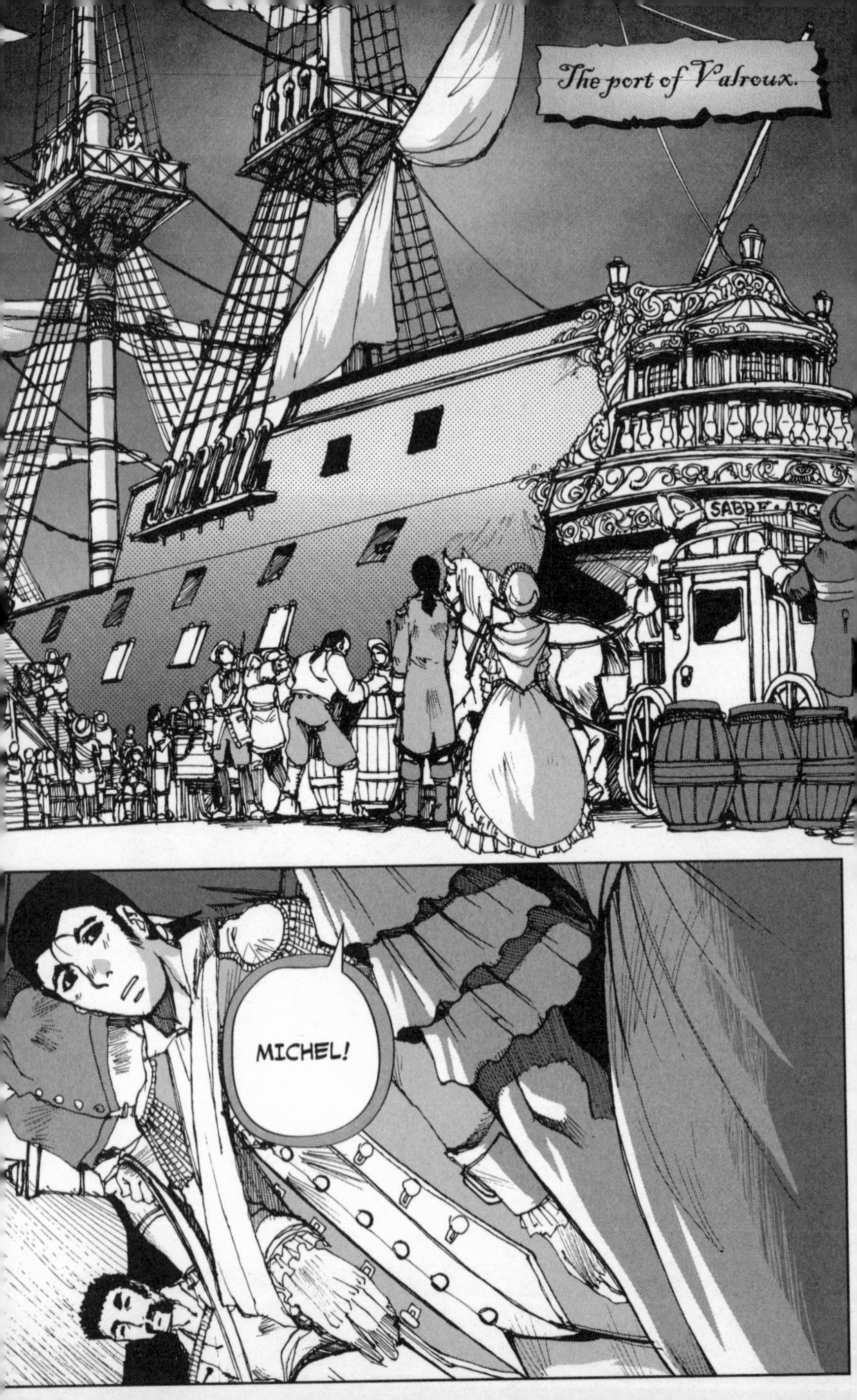
The port of Valroux.
MICHEL!

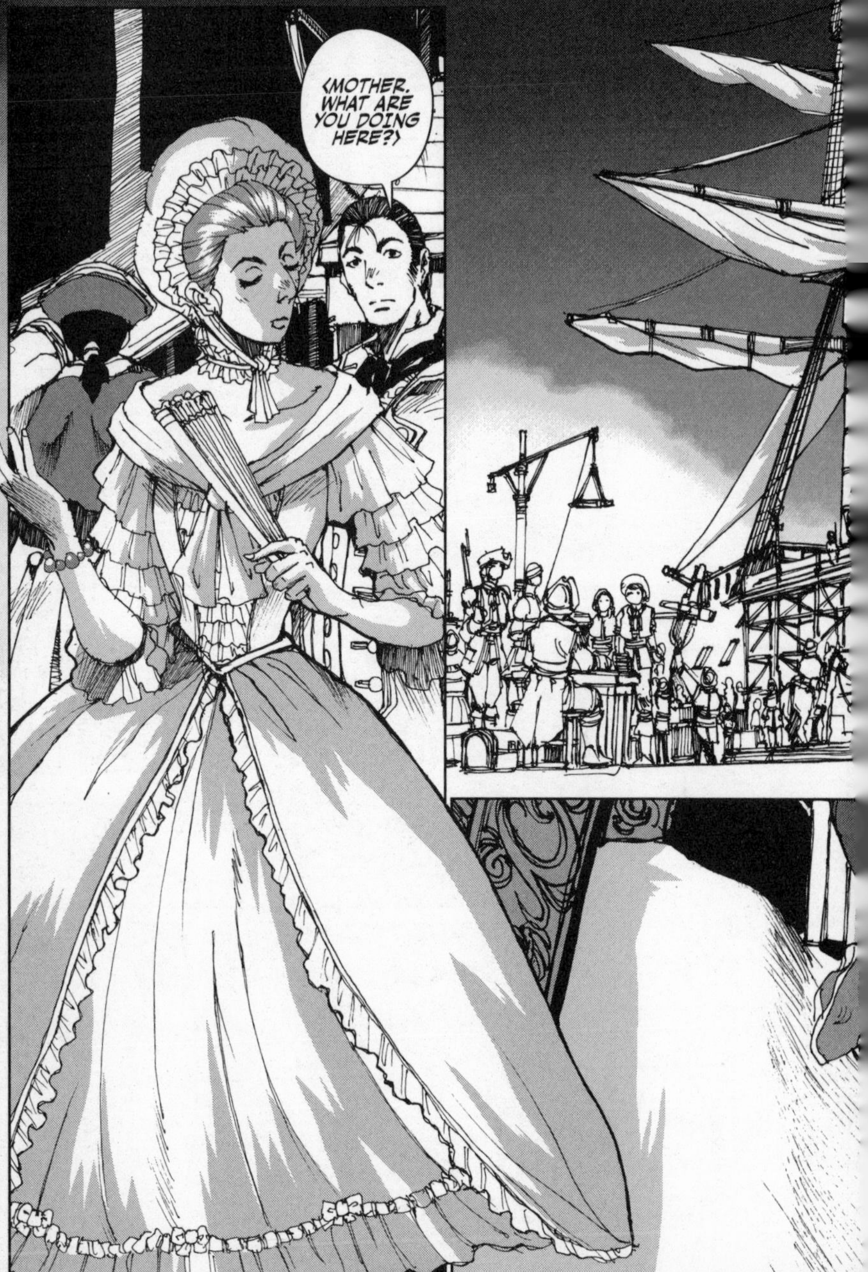
<MOTHER. WHAT ARE YOU DOING HERE?>

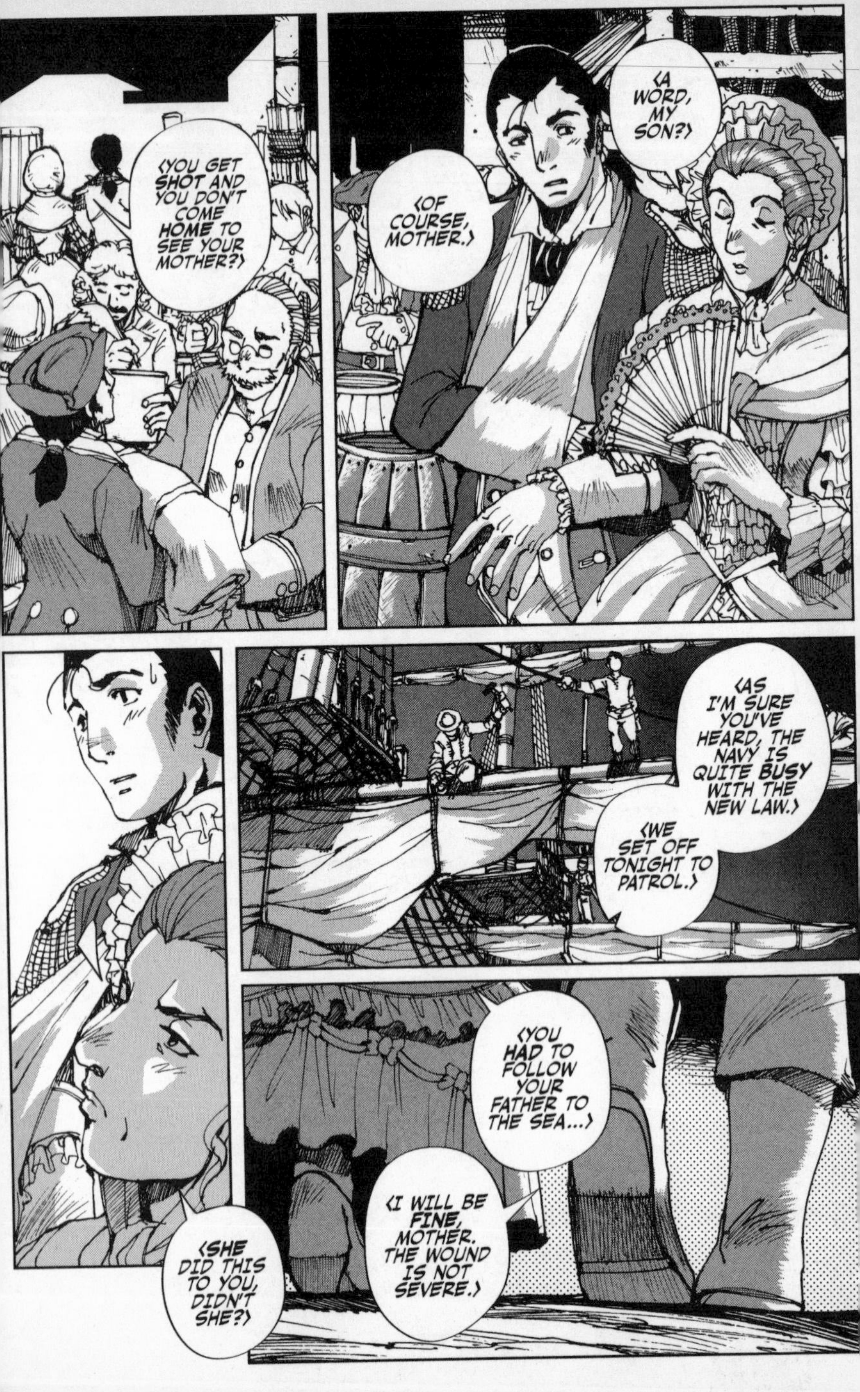
‹A WORD, MY SON?›
‹OF COURSE, MOTHER.›
‹YOU GET SHOT AND YOU DON'T COME HOME TO SEE YOUR MOTHER?›
‹AS I'M SURE YOU'VE HEARD, THE NAVY IS QUITE BUSY WITH THE NEW LAW.›
‹WE SET OFF TONIGHT TO PATROL.›
‹YOU HAD TO FOLLOW YOUR FATHER TO THE SEA...›
‹I WILL BE FINE, MOTHER. THE WOUND IS NOT SEVERE.›
‹SHE DID THIS TO YOU, DIDN'T SHE?›

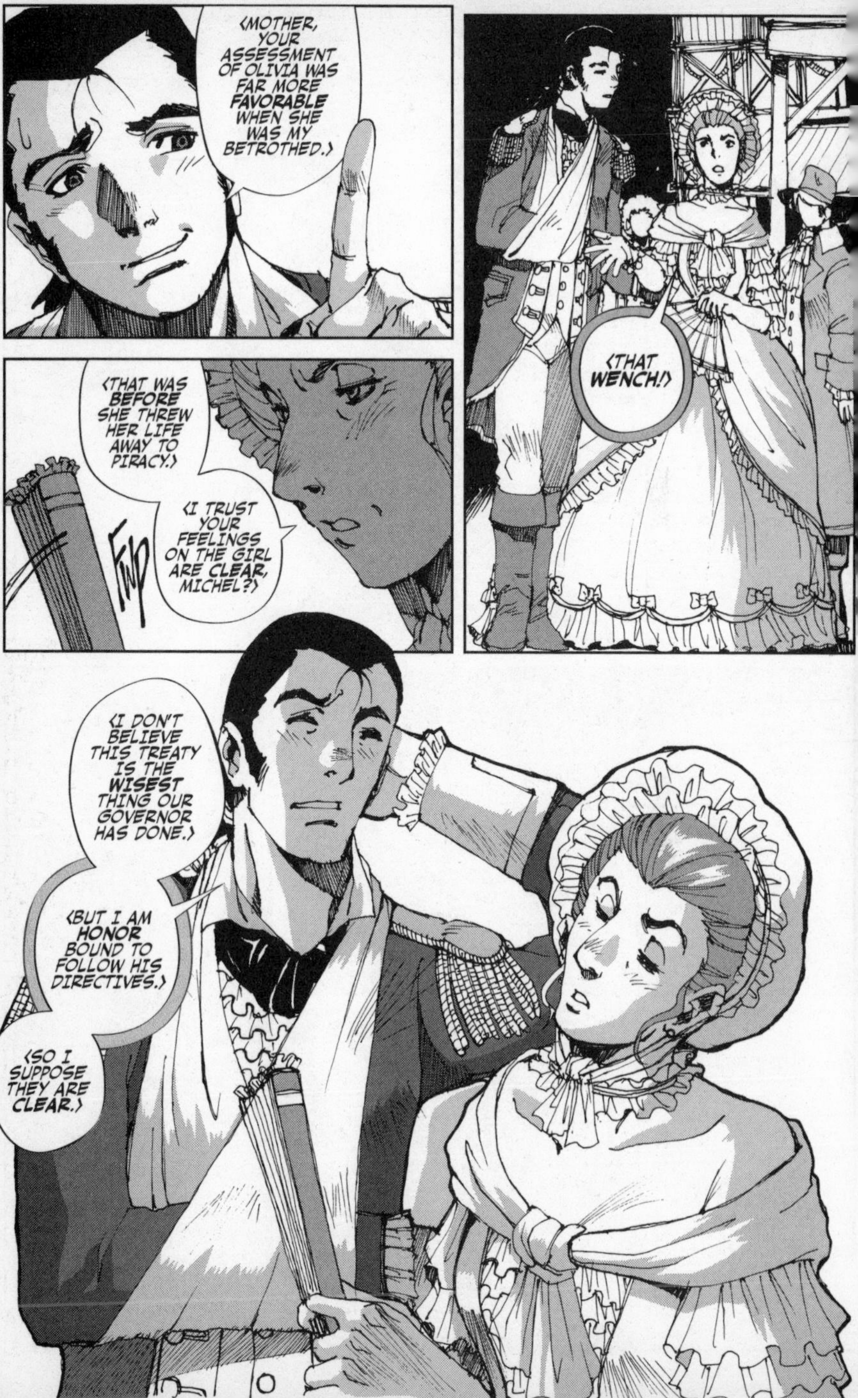
⟨THAT WENCH!⟩
⟨MOTHER, YOUR ASSESSMENT OF OLIVIA WAS FAR MORE FAVORABLE WHEN SHE WAS MY BETROTHED.⟩
⟨THAT WAS BEFORE SHE THREW HER LIFE AWAY TO PIRACY.⟩
⟨I TRUST YOUR FEELINGS ON THE GIRL ARE CLEAR, MICHEL?⟩
FWP
⟨I DON'T BELIEVE THIS TREATY IS THE WISEST THING OUR GOVERNOR HAS DONE.⟩
⟨BUT I AM HONOR BOUND TO FOLLOW HIS DIRECTIVES.⟩
⟨SO I SUPPOSE THEY ARE CLEAR.⟩

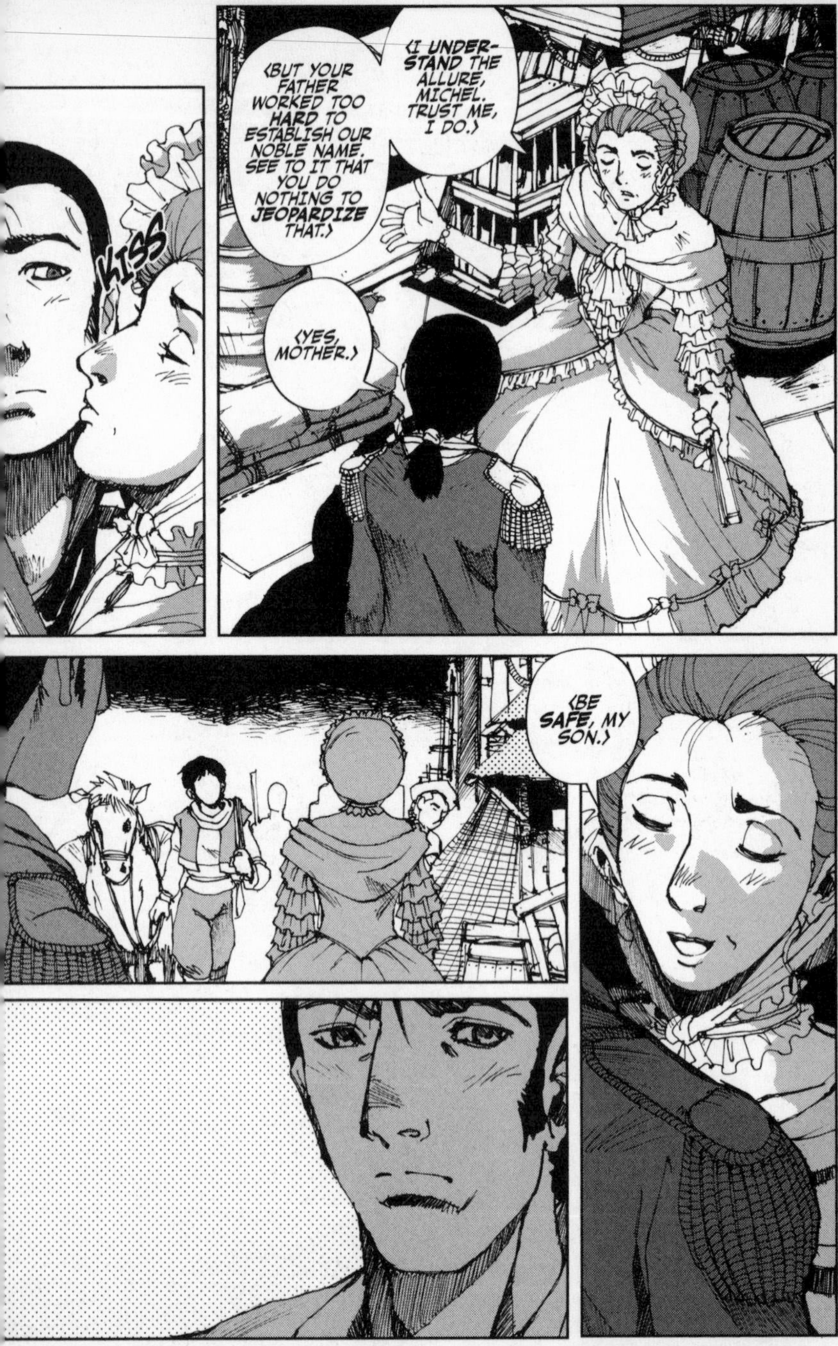
⟨I UNDERSTAND THE ALLURE, MICHEL. TRUST ME, I DO.⟩
⟨BUT YOUR FATHER WORKED TOO HARD TO ESTABLISH OUR NOBLE NAME. SEE TO IT THAT YOU DO NOTHING TO JEOPARDIZE THAT.⟩
⟨YES, MOTHER.⟩
KISS
⟨BE SAFE, MY SON.⟩

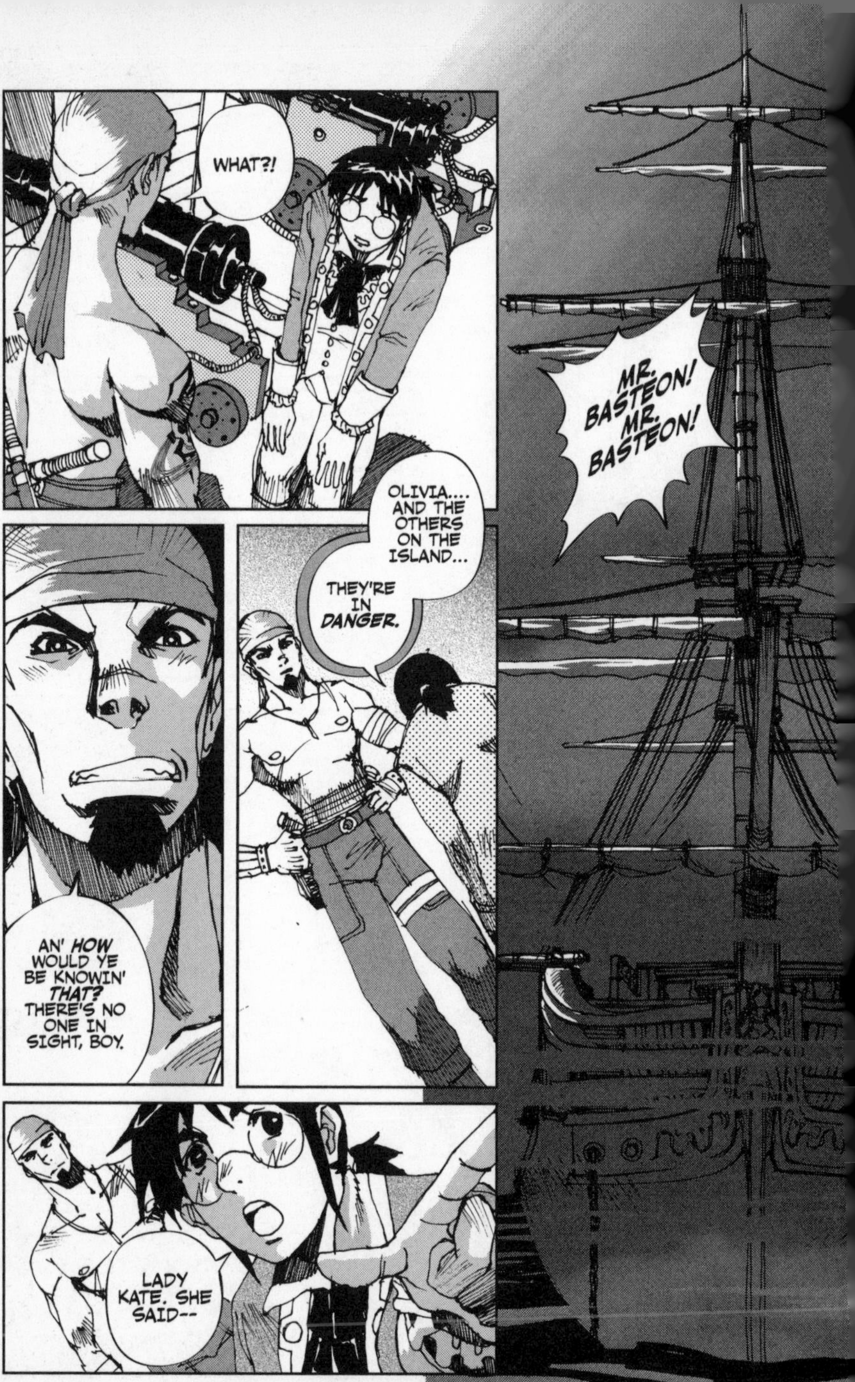
MR. BASTEON! MR. BASTEON!
WHAT?!
OLIVIA.... AND THE OTHERS ON THE ISLAND...
THEY'RE IN *DANGER*.
AN' *HOW* WOULD YE BE KNOWIN' *THAT?* THERE'S NO ONE IN SIGHT, BOY.
LADY KATE. SHE SAID--

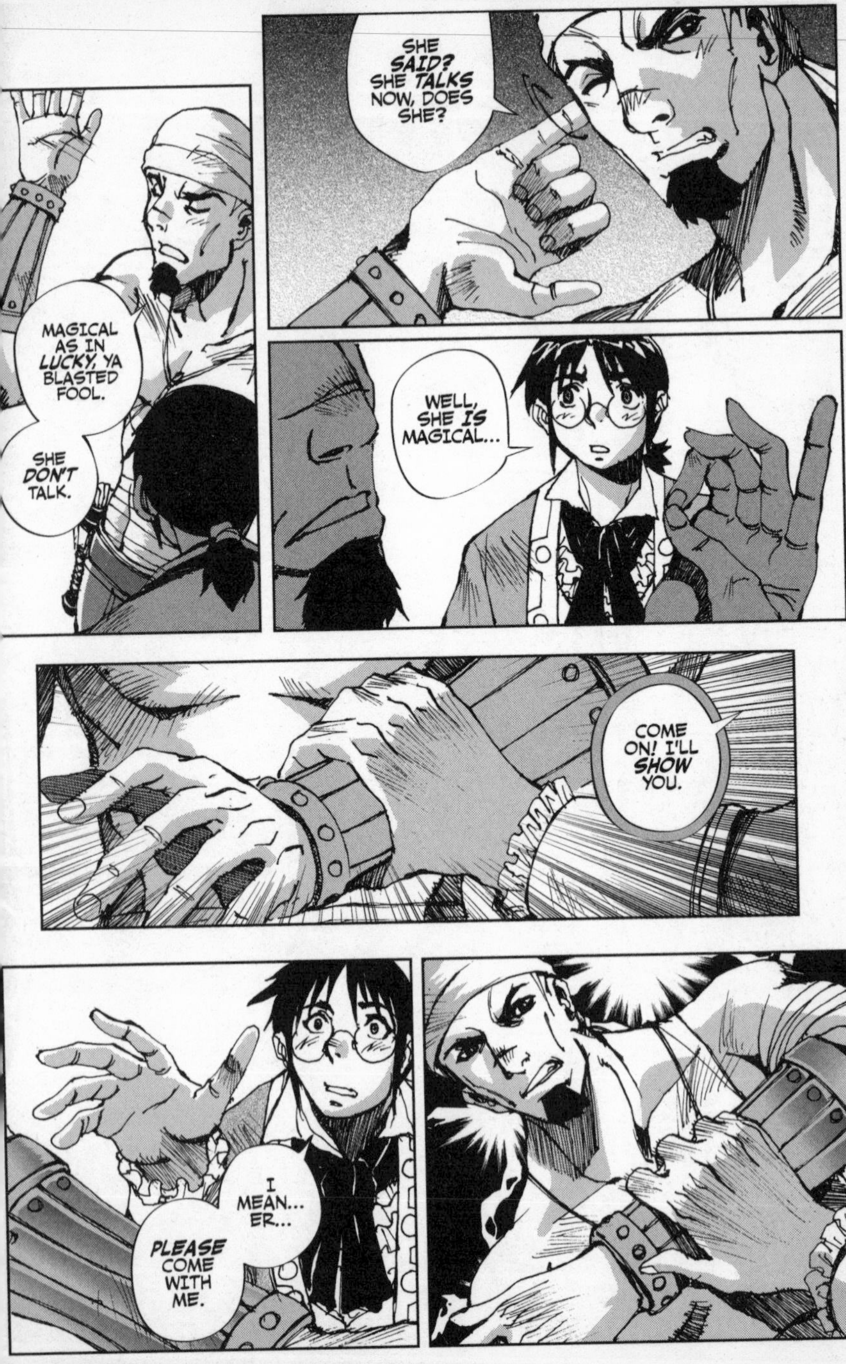
SHE *SAID?* SHE *TALKS* NOW, DOES SHE?
WELL, SHE *IS* MAGICAL...
MAGICAL AS IN *LUCKY*, YA BLASTED FOOL.
SHE *DON'T* TALK.
COME ON! I'LL *SHOW* YOU.
I MEAN... ER...
PLEASE COME WITH ME.

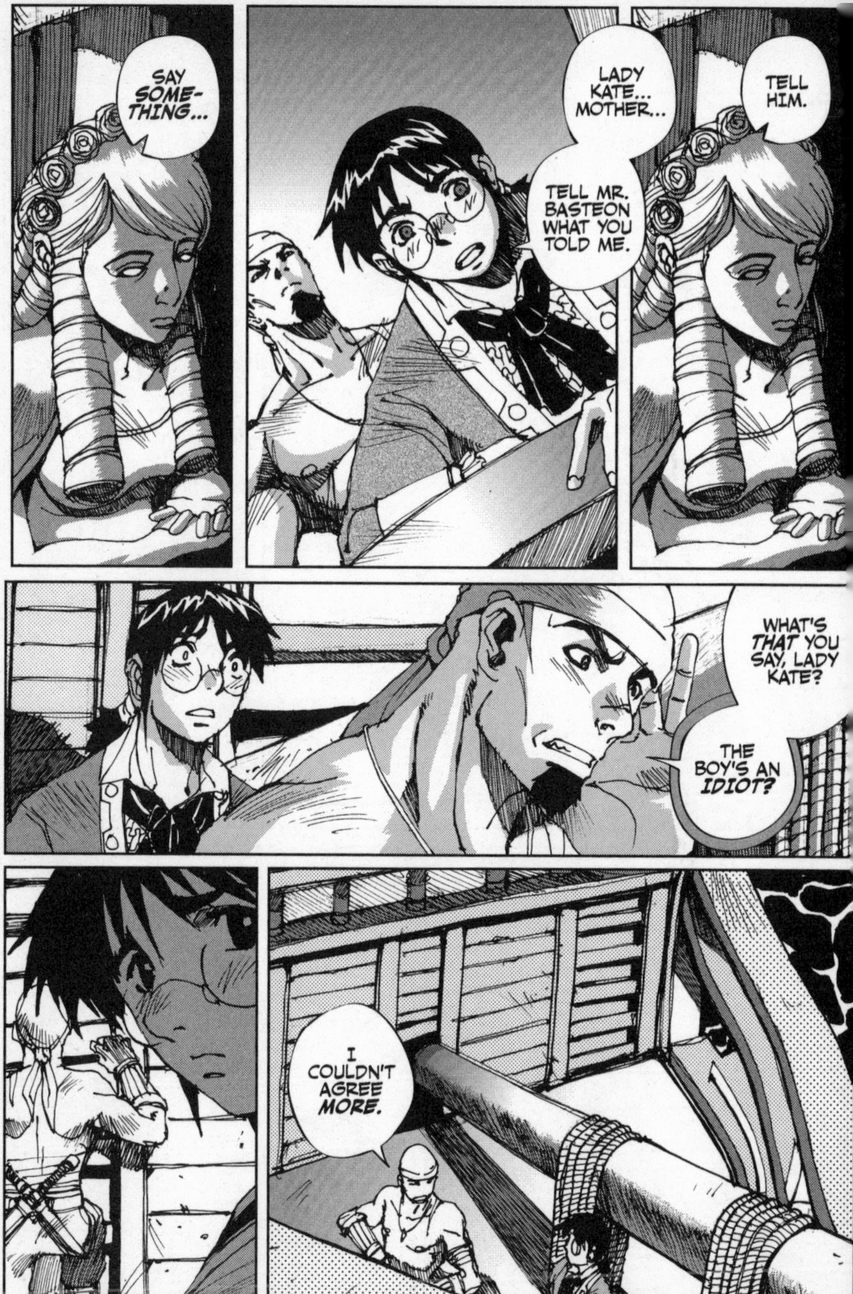
TELL HIM.
LADY KATE... MOTHER...
TELL MR. BASTEON WHAT YOU TOLD ME.
SAY SOME-THING...
WHAT'S THAT YOU SAY, LADY KATE?
THE BOY'S AN IDIOT?
I COULDN'T AGREE MORE.

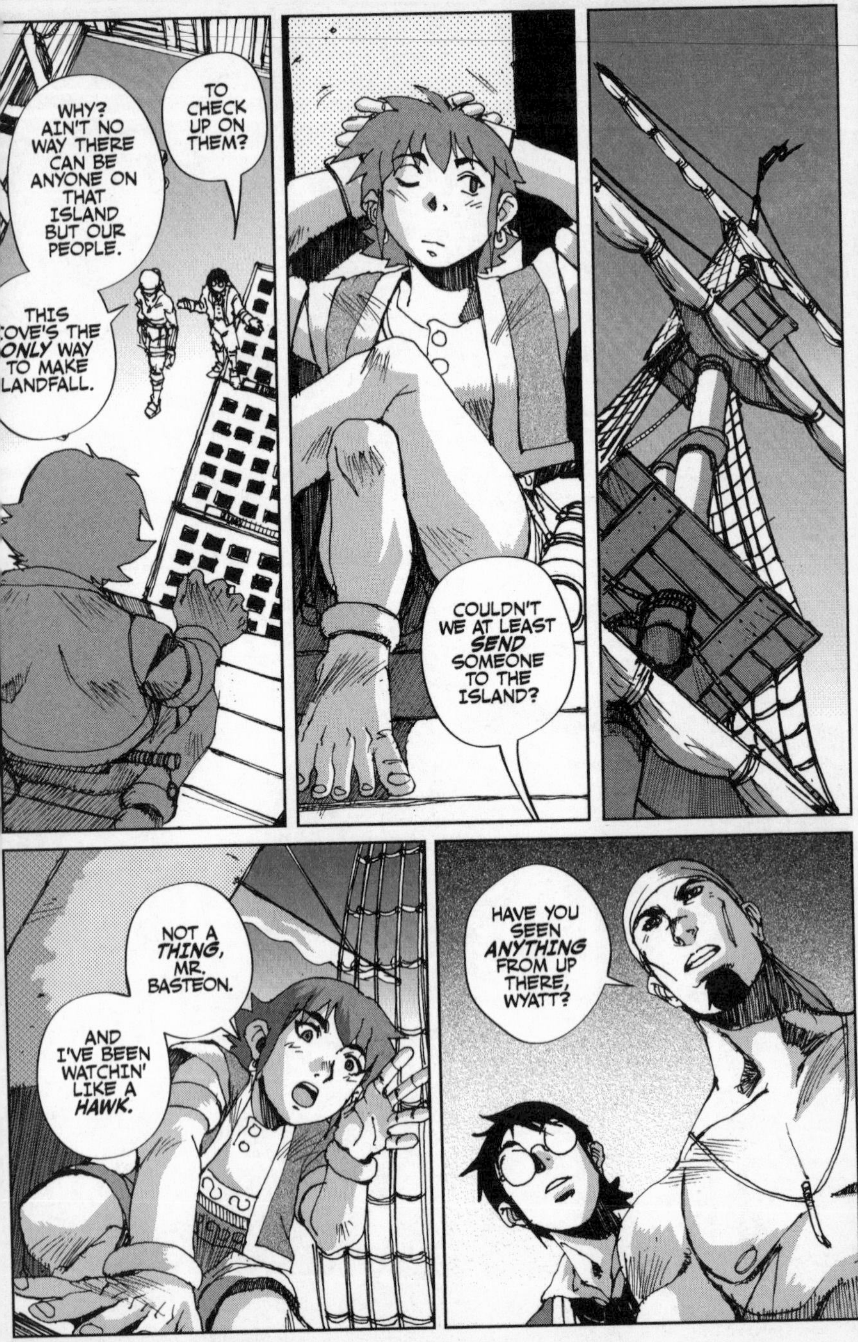
COULDN'T WE AT LEAST *SEND* SOMEONE TO THE ISLAND?
TO CHECK UP ON THEM?
WHY? AIN'T NO WAY THERE CAN BE ANYONE ON THAT ISLAND BUT OUR PEOPLE.
THIS COVE'S THE *ONLY* WAY TO MAKE LANDFALL.
HAVE YOU SEEN *ANYTHING* FROM UP THERE, WYATT?
NOT A *THING*, MR. BASTEON.
AND I'VE BEEN WATCHIN' LIKE A *HAWK*.

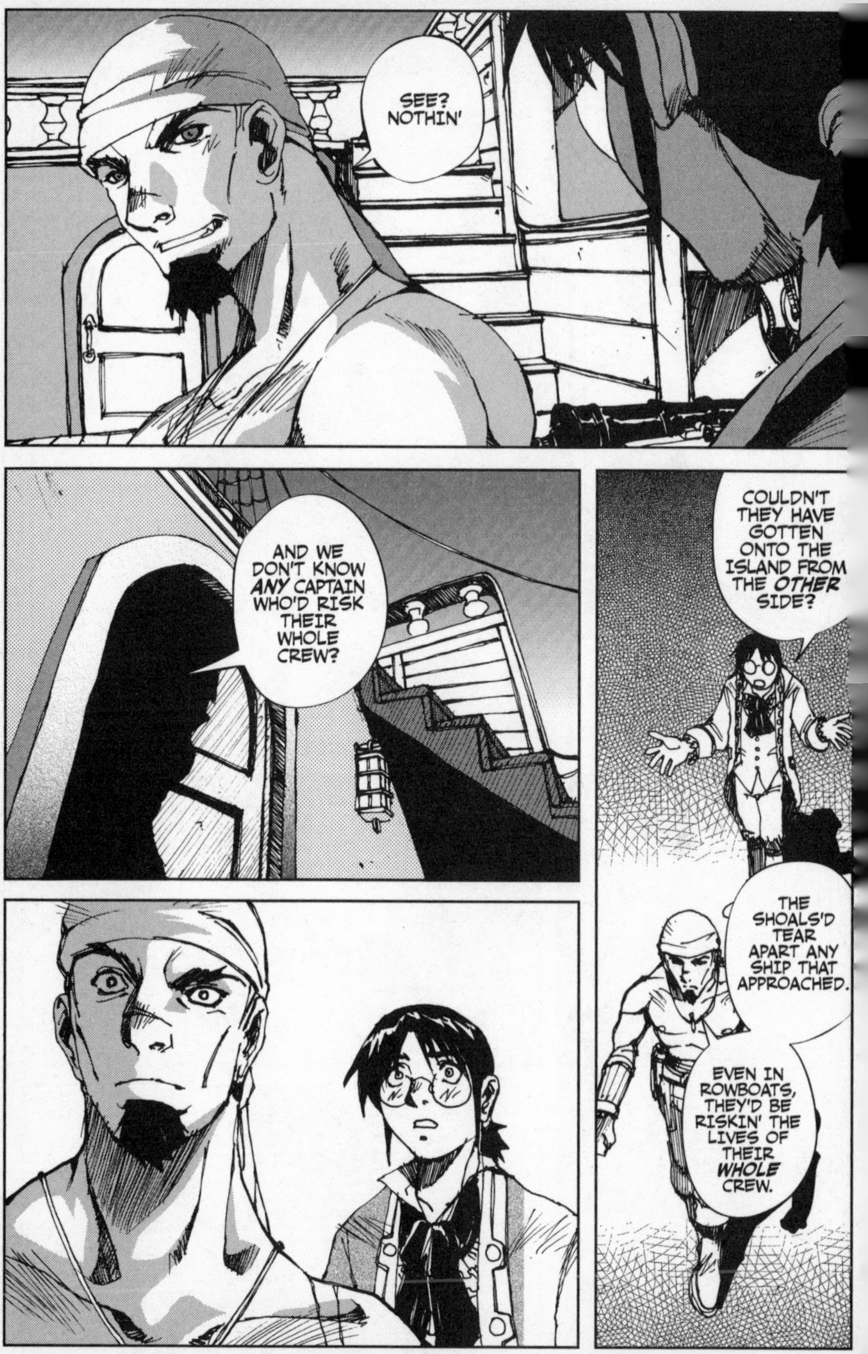
SEE? NOTHIN'
COULDN'T THEY HAVE GOTTEN ONTO THE ISLAND FROM THE *OTHER* SIDE?
AND WE DON'T KNOW *ANY* CAPTAIN WHO'D RISK THEIR WHOLE CREW?
THE SHOALS'D TEAR APART ANY SHIP THAT APPROACHED.
EVEN IN ROWBOATS, THEY'D BE RISKIN' THE LIVES OF THEIR *WHOLE* CREW.

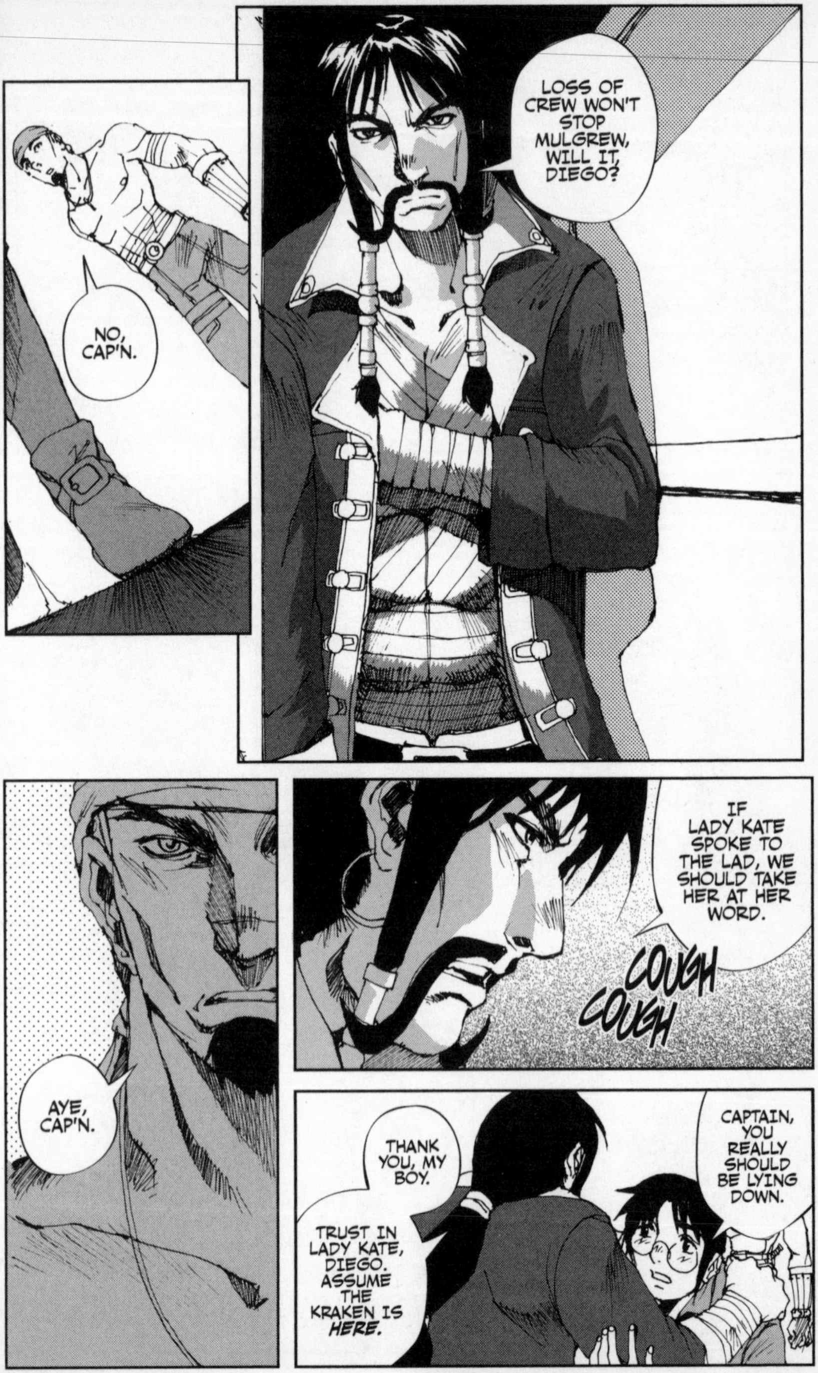
LOSS OF CREW WON'T STOP MULGREW, WILL IT, DIEGO?
NO, CAP'N.
IF LADY KATE SPOKE TO THE LAD, WE SHOULD TAKE HER AT HER WORD.
COUGH COUGH
CAPTAIN, YOU REALLY SHOULD BE LYING DOWN.
THANK YOU, MY BOY.
TRUST IN LADY KATE, DIEGO. ASSUME THE KRAKEN IS *HERE*.
AYE, CAP'N.

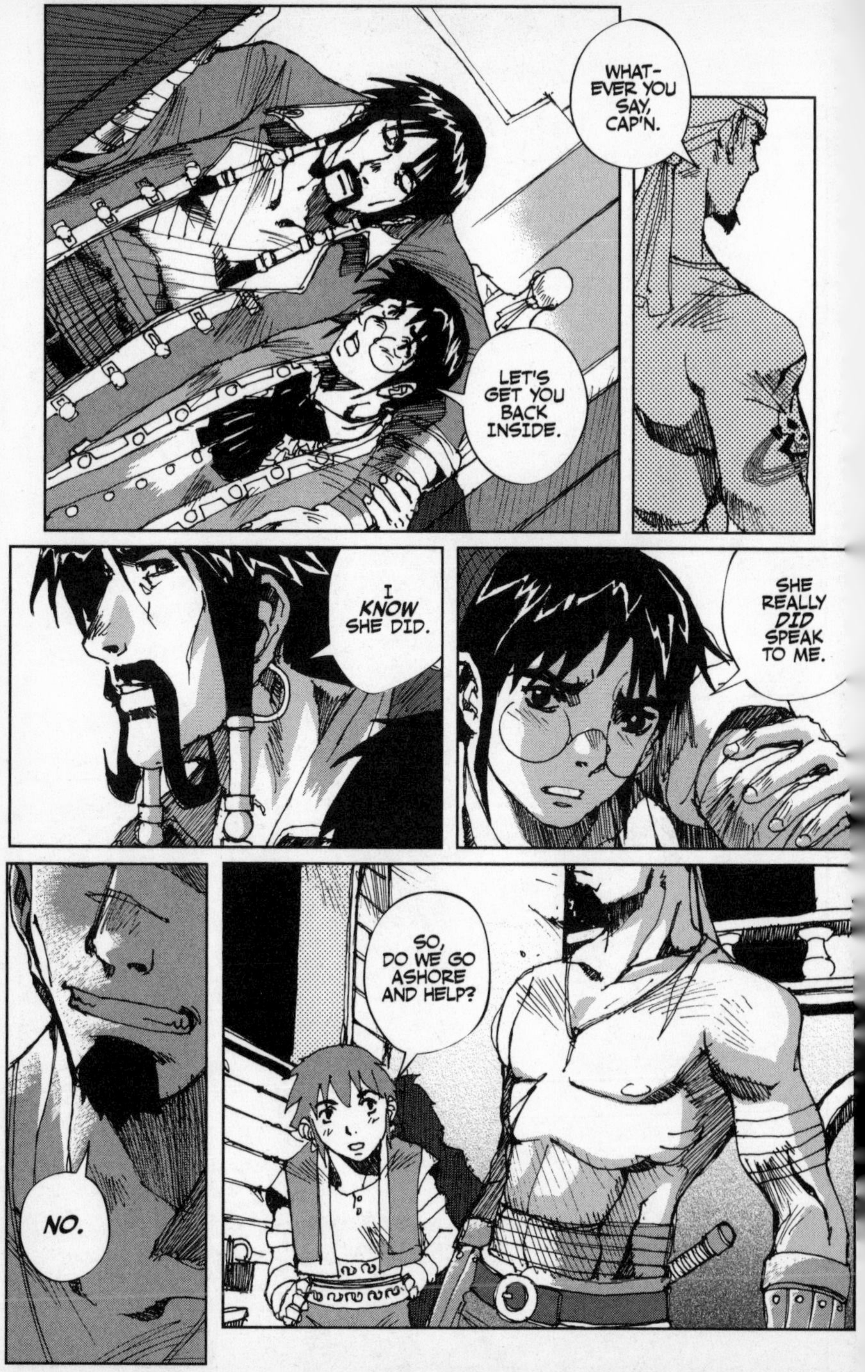
WHAT-EVER YOU SAY, CAP'N.
LET'S GET YOU BACK INSIDE.
SHE REALLY *DID* SPEAK TO ME.
I *KNOW* SHE DID.
SO, DO WE GO ASHORE AND HELP?
NO.

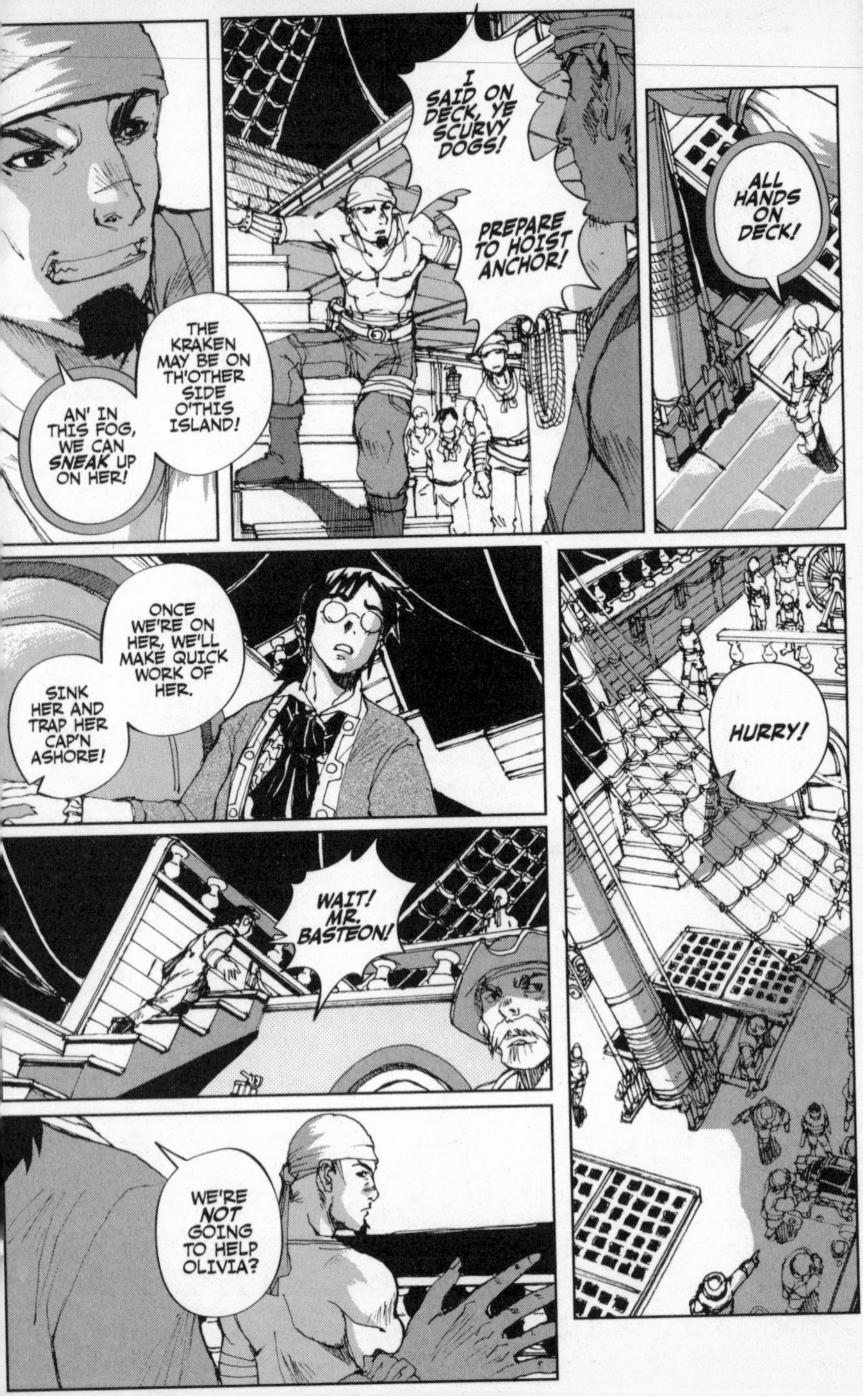
ALL HANDS ON DECK!
I SAID ON DECK, YE SCURVY DOGS!
PREPARE TO HOIST ANCHOR!
THE KRAKEN MAY BE ON TH'OTHER SIDE O'THIS ISLAND!
AN' IN THIS FOG, WE CAN *SNEAK* UP ON HER!
HURRY!
ONCE WE'RE ON HER, WE'LL MAKE QUICK WORK OF HER.
SINK HER AND TRAP HER CAP'N ASHORE!
WAIT! MR. BASTEON!
WE'RE *NOT* GOING TO HELP OLIVIA?

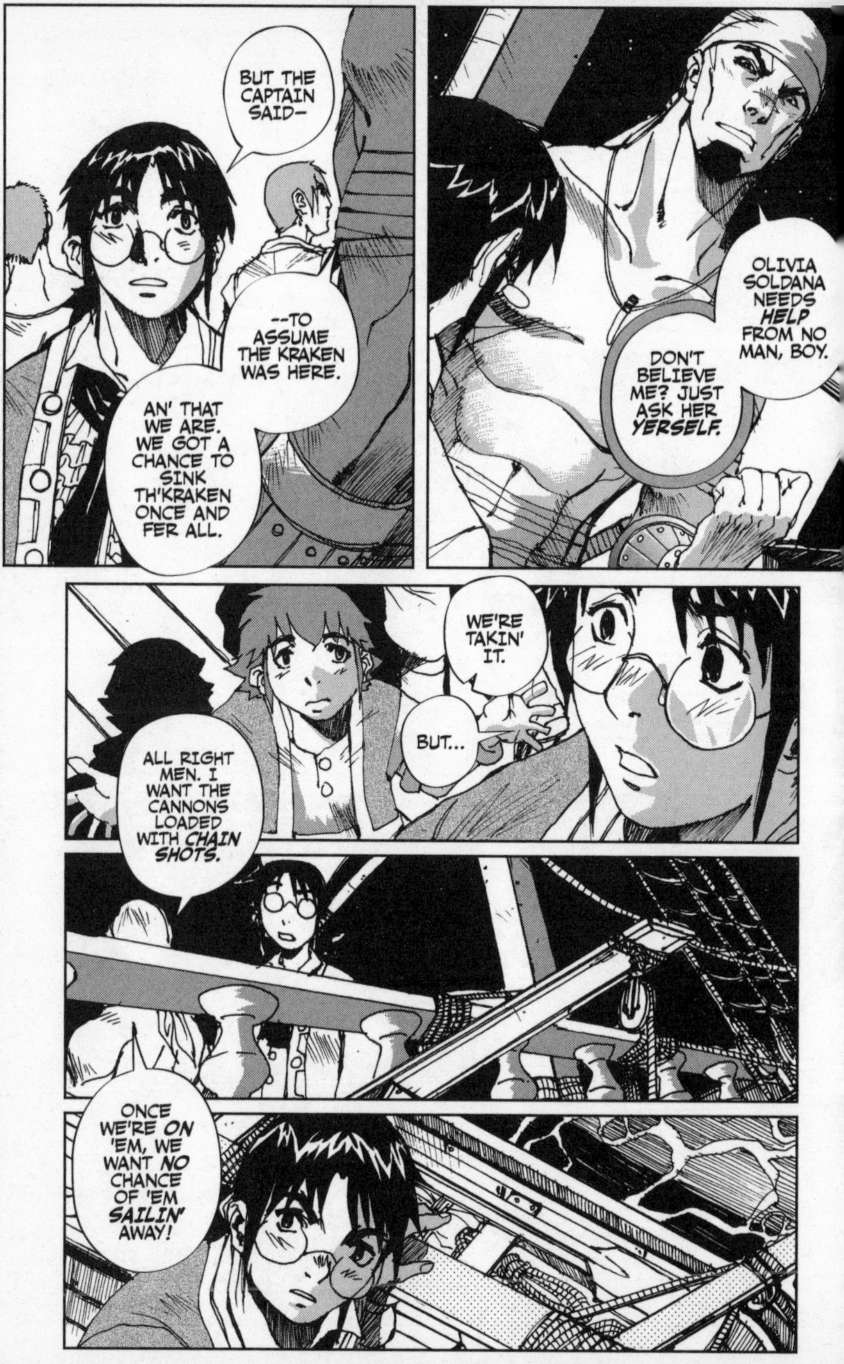
OLIVIA SOLDANA NEEDS *HELP* FROM NO MAN, BOY.
DON'T BELIEVE ME? JUST ASK HER *YERSELF.*
BUT THE CAPTAIN SAID--
--TO ASSUME THE KRAKEN WAS HERE.
AN' THAT WE ARE. WE GOT A CHANCE TO SINK TH'KRAKEN ONCE AND FER ALL.
WE'RE TAKIN' IT.
BUT...
ALL RIGHT MEN. I WANT THE CANNONS LOADED WITH *CHAIN SHOTS.*
ONCE WE'RE *ON* 'EM, WE WANT *NO* CHANCE OF 'EM *SAILIN'* AWAY!

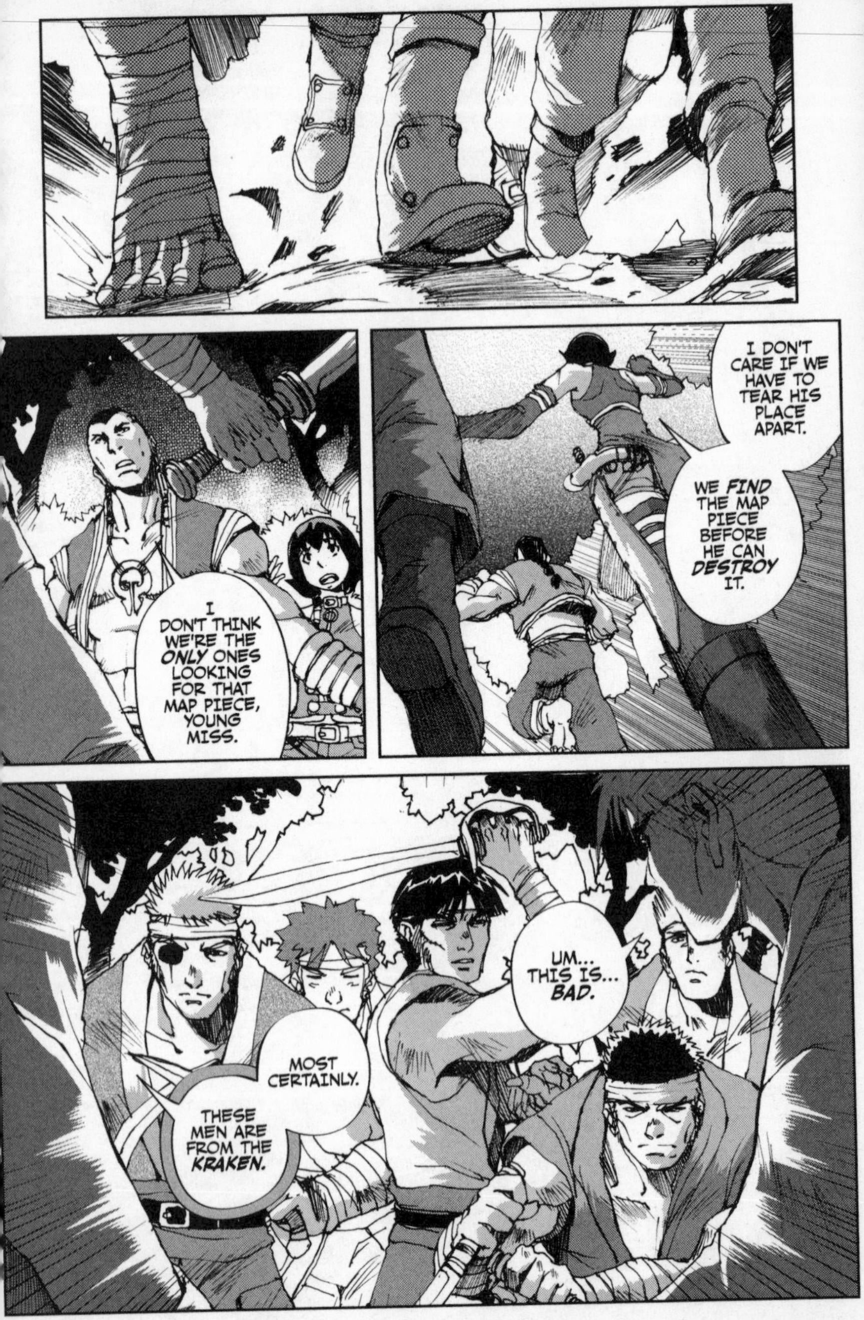
I DON'T CARE IF WE HAVE TO TEAR HIS PLACE APART.
WE *FIND* THE MAP PIECE BEFORE HE CAN *DESTROY* IT.
I DON'T THINK WE'RE THE *ONLY* ONES LOOKING FOR THAT MAP PIECE, YOUNG MISS.
UM... THIS IS... *BAD.*
MOST CERTAINLY.
THESE MEN ARE FROM THE *KRAKEN.*

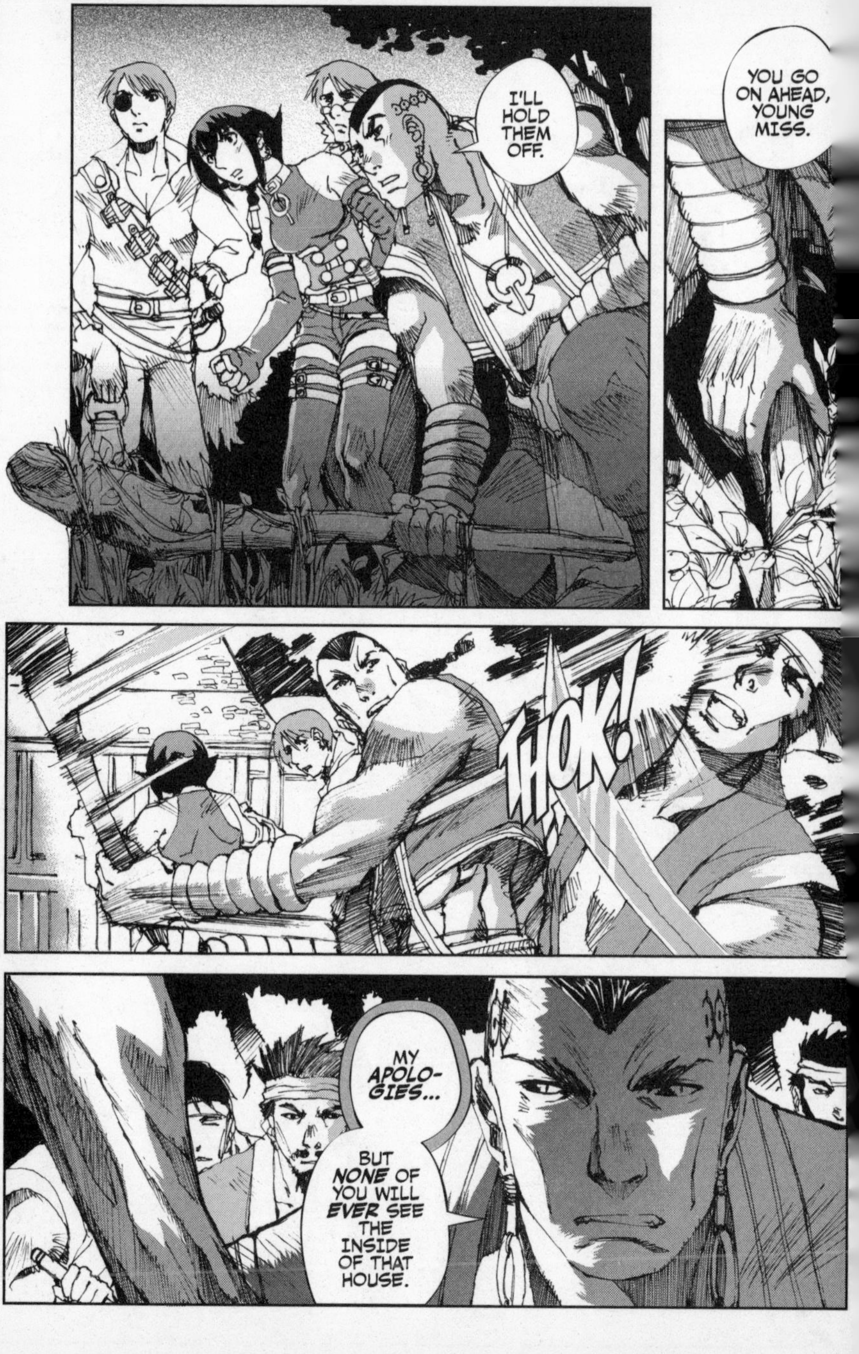
YOU GO ON AHEAD, YOUNG MISS.
I'LL HOLD THEM OFF.
THOK!
MY APOLOGIES...
BUT NONE OF YOU WILL EVER SEE THE INSIDE OF THAT HOUSE.

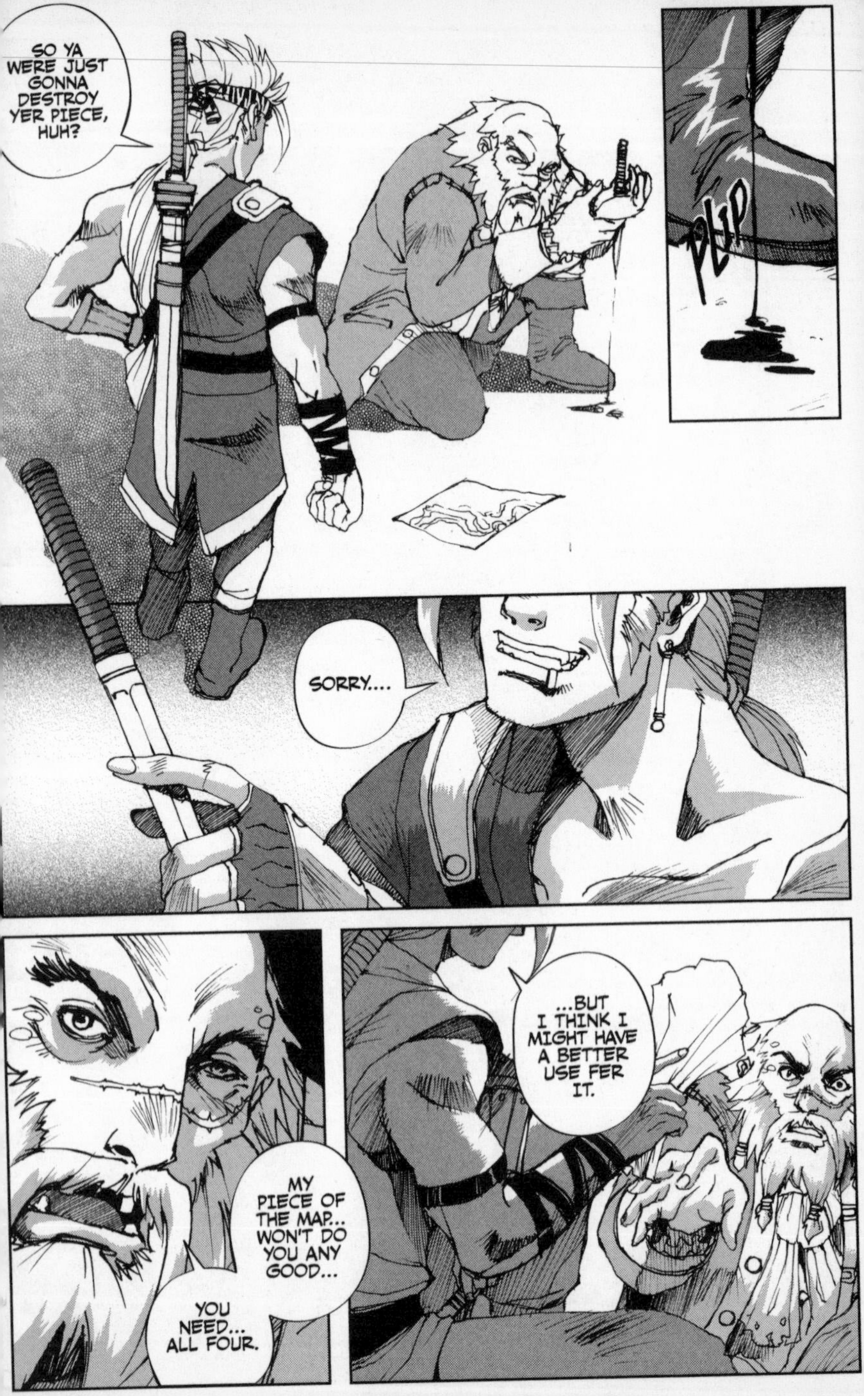
PLIP
SO YA WERE JUST GONNA DESTROY YER PIECE, HUH?
SORRY....
...BUT I THINK I MIGHT HAVE A BETTER USE FER IT.
MY PIECE OF THE MAP... WON'T DO YOU ANY GOOD...
YOU NEED... ALL FOUR.

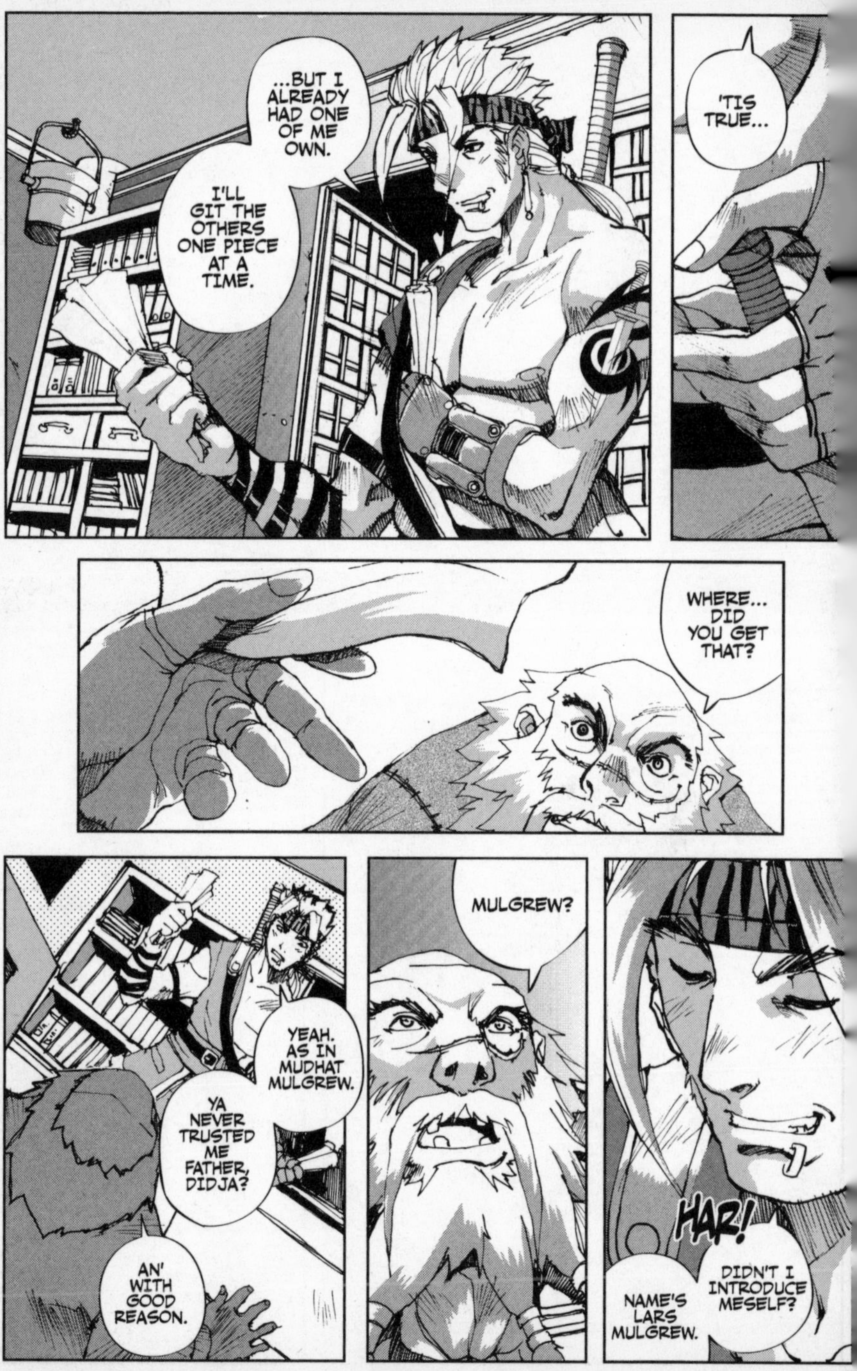
'TIS TRUE...
...BUT I ALREADY HAD ONE OF ME OWN.
I'LL GIT THE OTHERS ONE PIECE AT A TIME.
WHERE... DID YOU GET THAT?
HAR!
DIDN'T I INTRODUCE MESELF?
NAME'S LARS MULGREW.
MULGREW?
YEAH. AS IN MUDHAT MULGREW.
YA NEVER TRUSTED ME FATHER, DIDJA?
AN' WITH GOOD REASON.

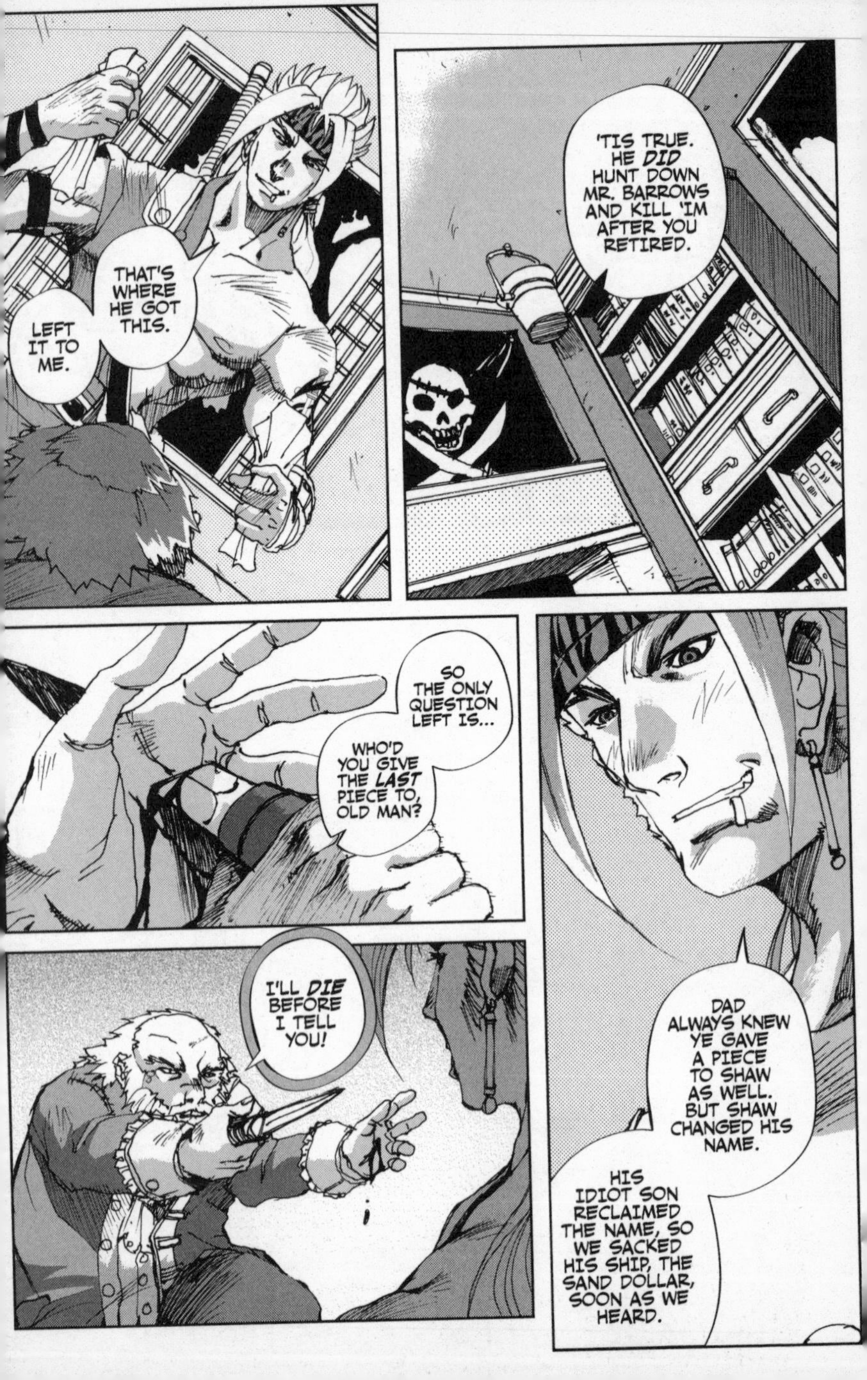
'TIS TRUE. HE *DID* HUNT DOWN MR. BARROWS AND KILL 'IM AFTER YOU RETIRED.
THAT'S WHERE HE GOT THIS.
LEFT IT TO ME.
DAD ALWAYS KNEW YE GAVE A PIECE TO SHAW AS WELL. BUT SHAW CHANGED HIS NAME.
HIS IDIOT SON RECLAIMED THE NAME, SO WE SACKED HIS SHIP, THE SAND DOLLAR, SOON AS WE HEARD.
SO THE ONLY QUESTION LEFT IS...
WHO'D YOU GIVE THE *LAST* PIECE TO, OLD MAN?
I'LL *DIE* BEFORE I TELL YOU!

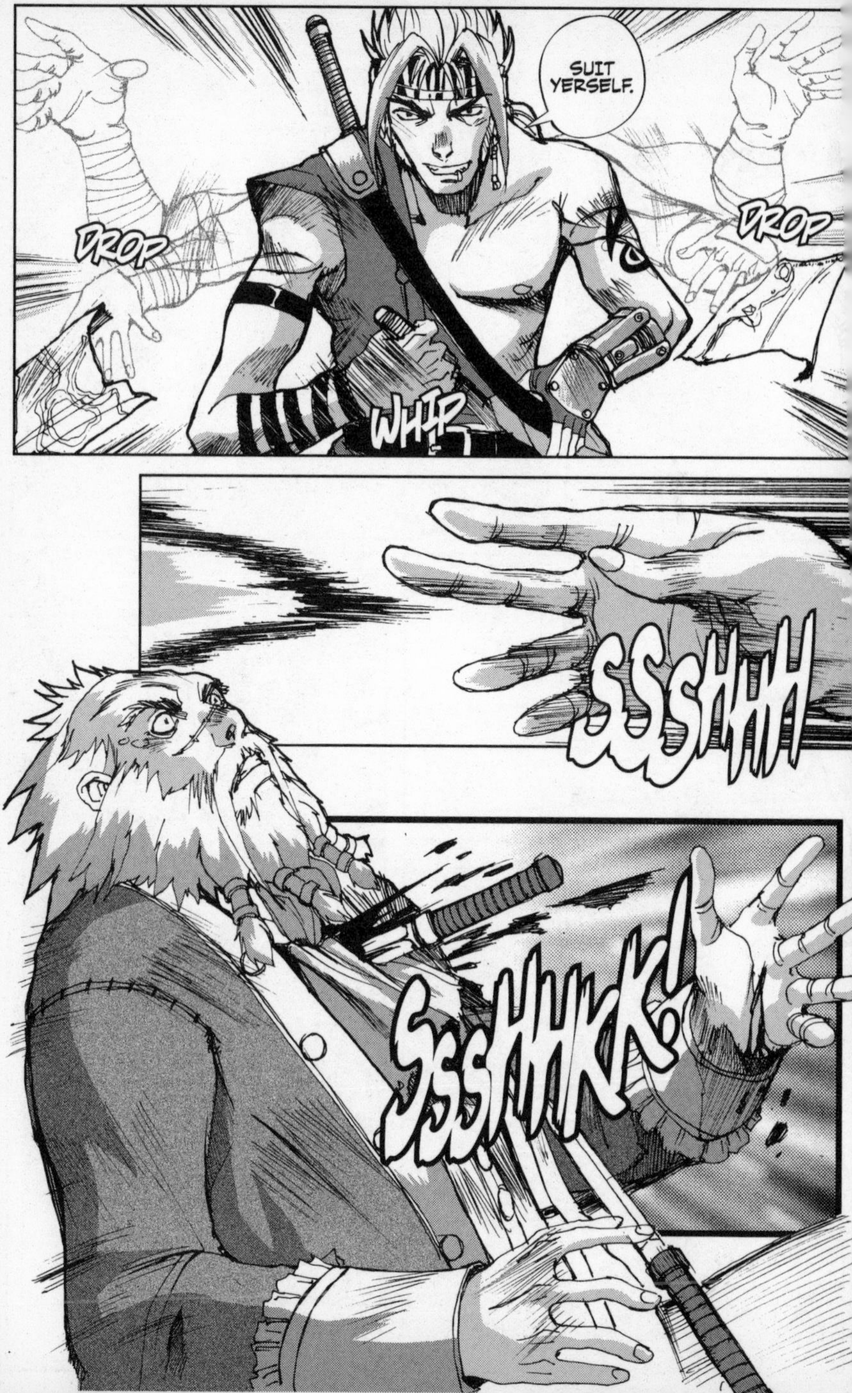
SUIT YERSELF.
DROP
DROP
WHIP
SSSHHH
SSSHHKK!

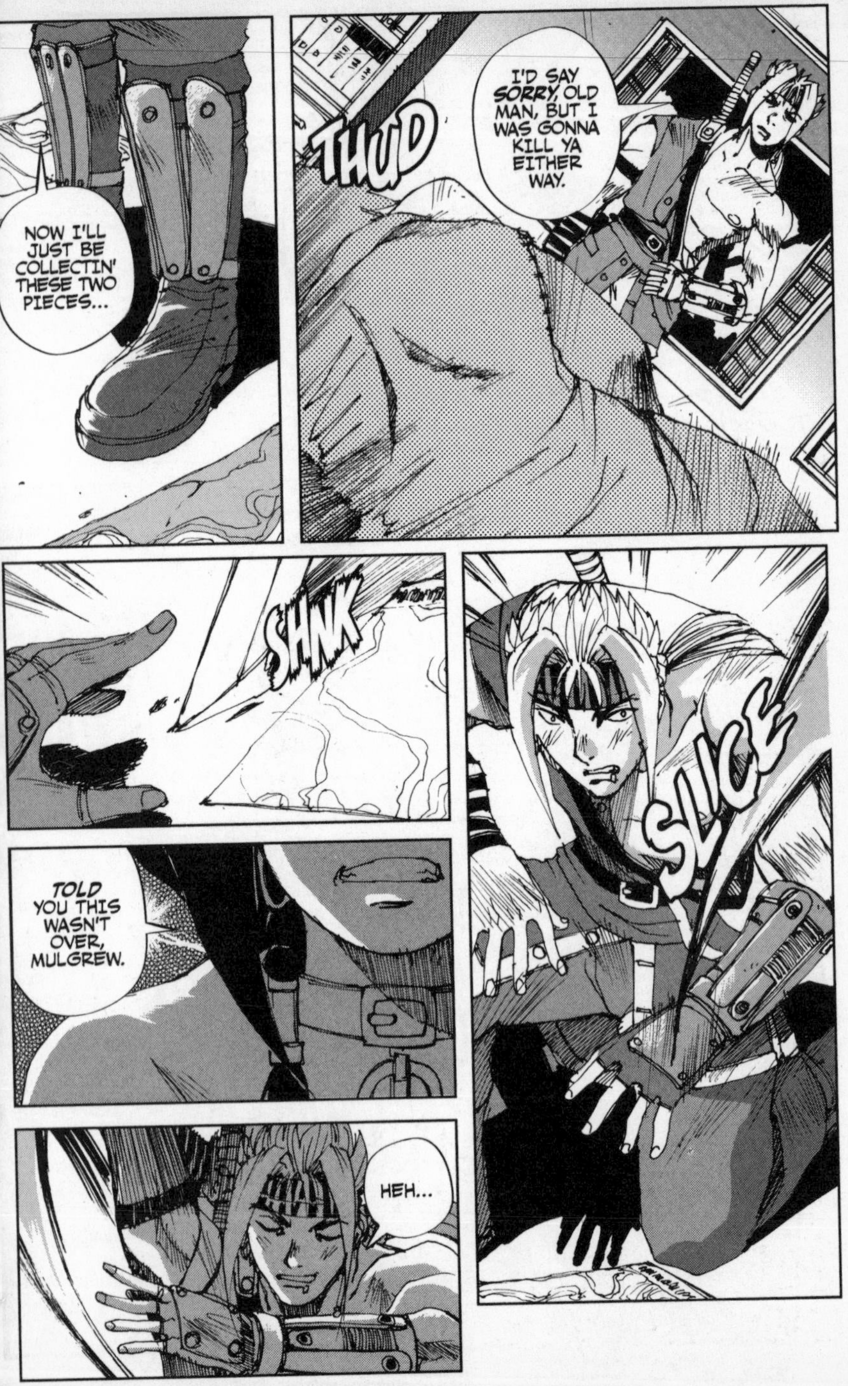
I'D SAY SORRY, OLD MAN, BUT I WAS GONNA KILL YA EITHER WAY.
THUD
NOW I'LL JUST BE COLLECTIN' THESE TWO PIECES...
SLICE
SHNK
TOLD YOU THIS WASN'T OVER, MULGREW.
HEH...

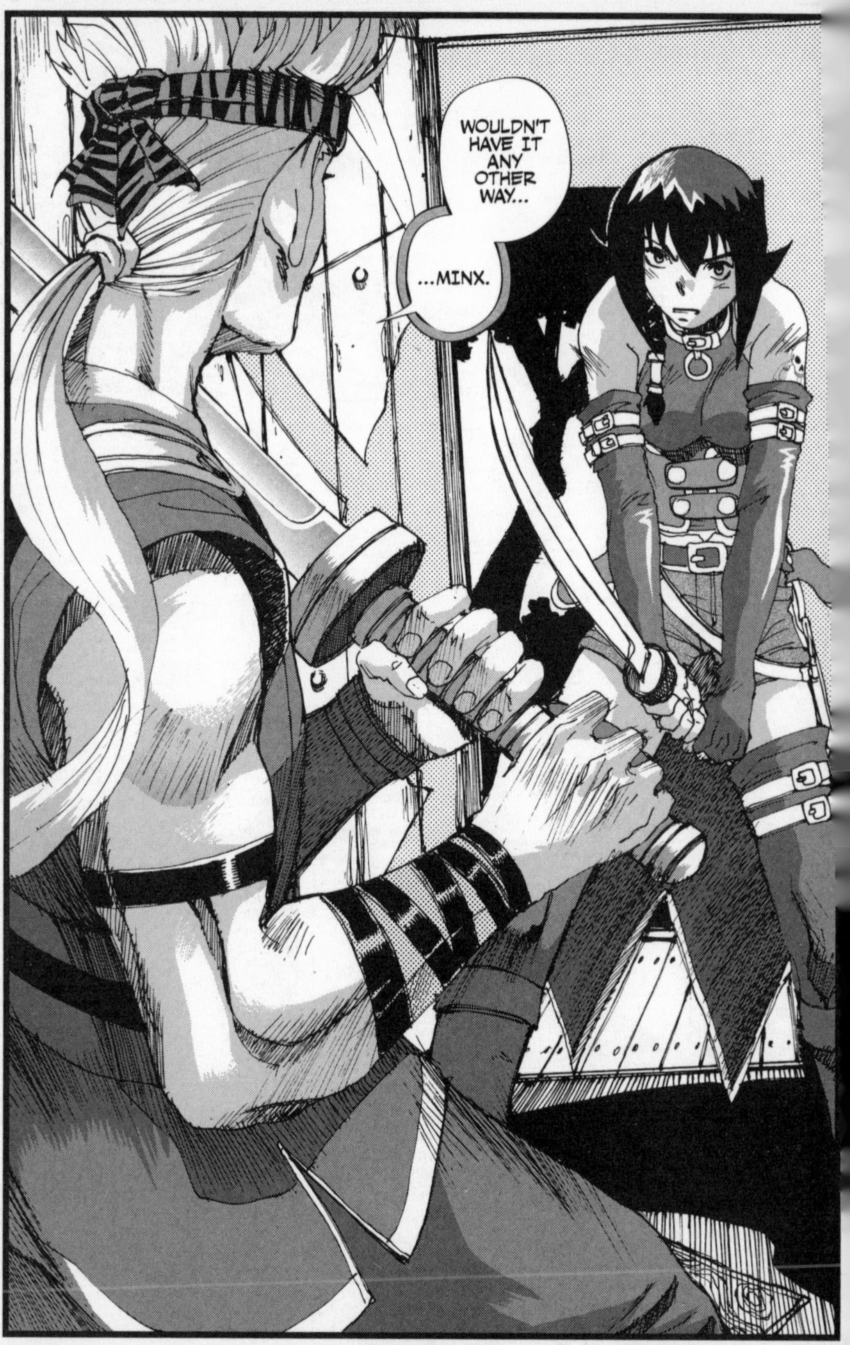
WOULDN'T HAVE IT ANY OTHER WAY...
...MINX.

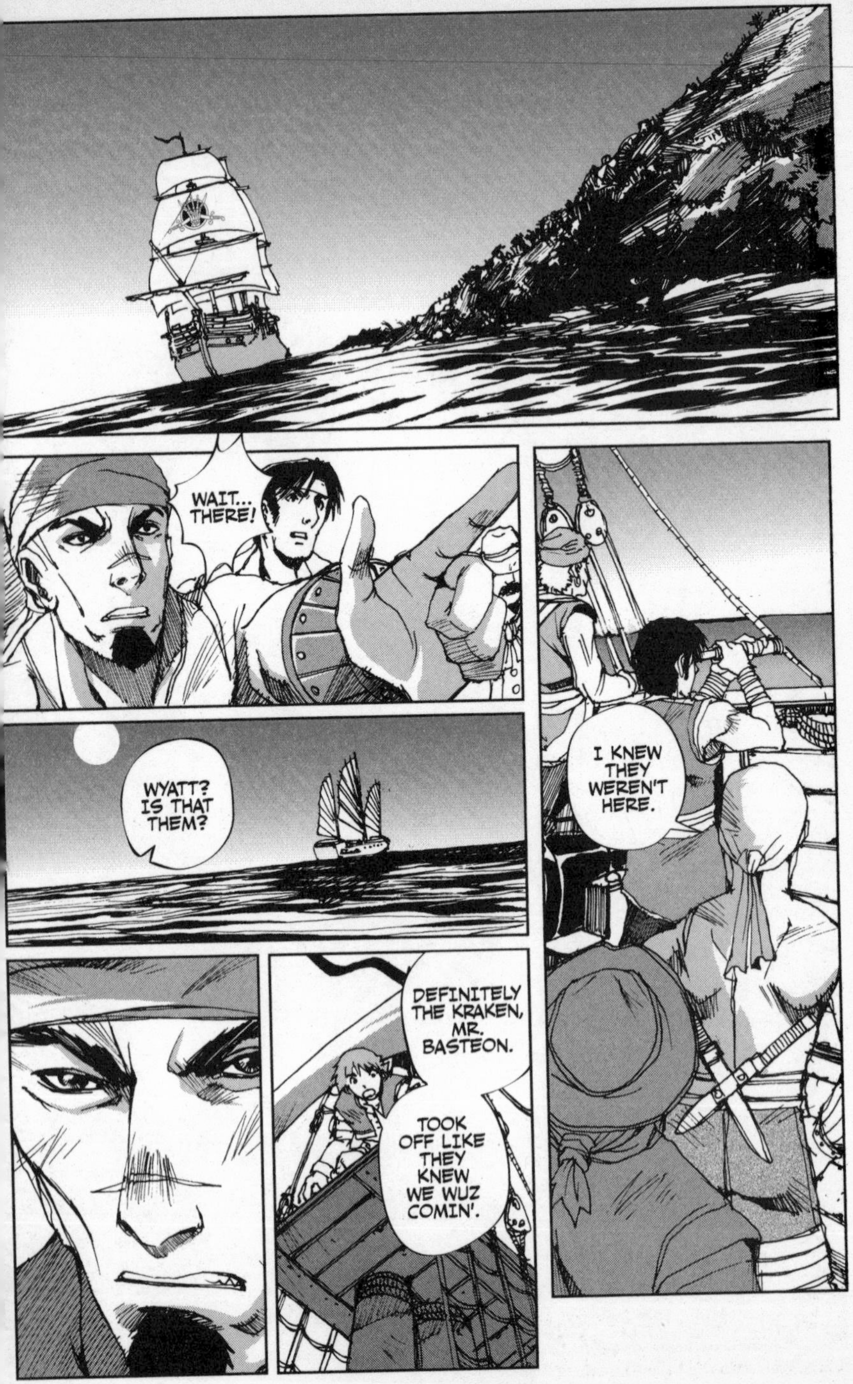
I KNEW THEY WEREN'T HERE.
WAIT... THERE!
WYATT? IS THAT THEM?
DEFINITELY THE KRAKEN, MR. BASTEON.
TOOK OFF LIKE THEY KNEW WE WUZ COMIN'.

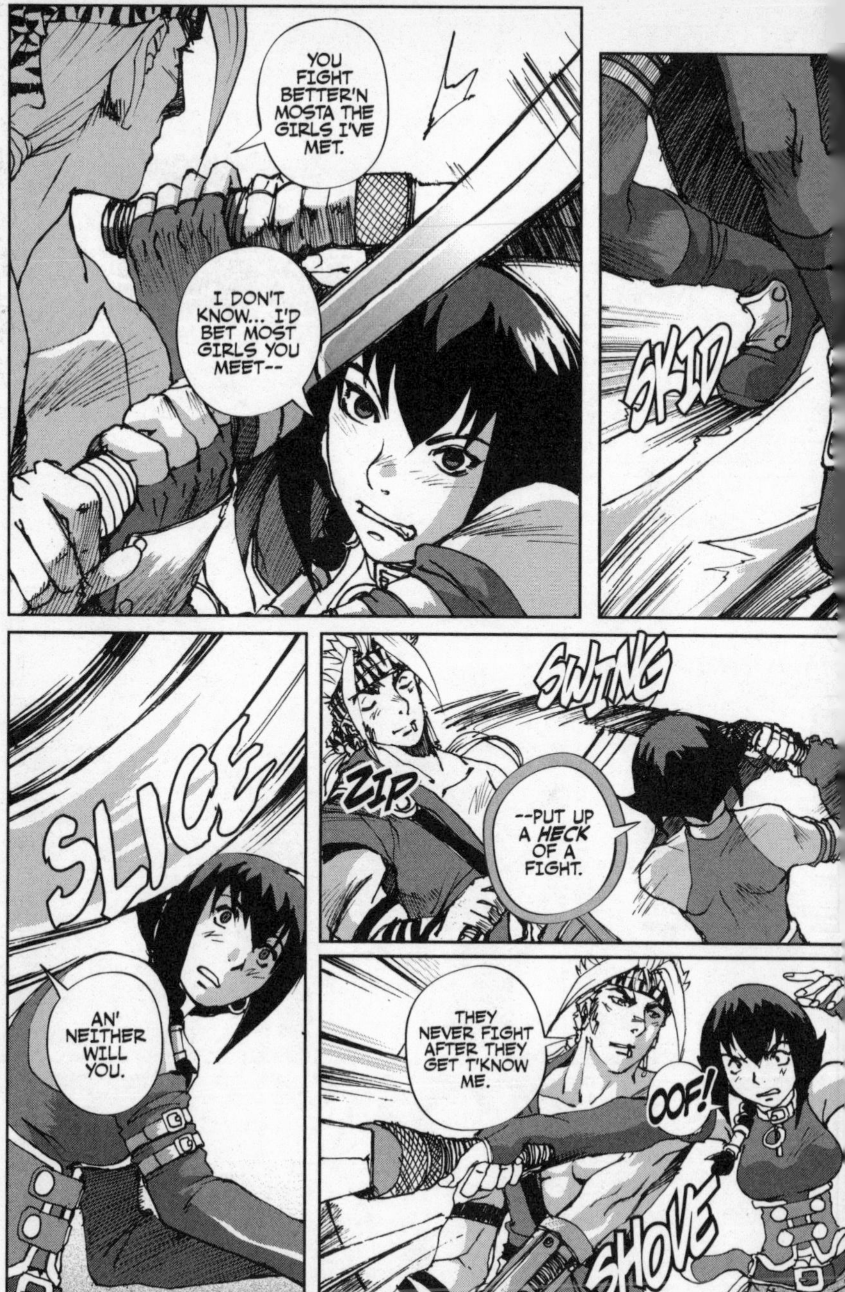
SKID
YOU FIGHT BETTER'N MOSTA THE GIRLS I'VE MET.
I DON'T KNOW... I'D BET MOST GIRLS YOU MEET--
SWING
--PUT UP A *HECK* OF A FIGHT.
ZIP
THEY NEVER FIGHT AFTER THEY GET T'KNOW ME.
OOF!
SHOVE
SLICE
AN' NEITHER WILL YOU.

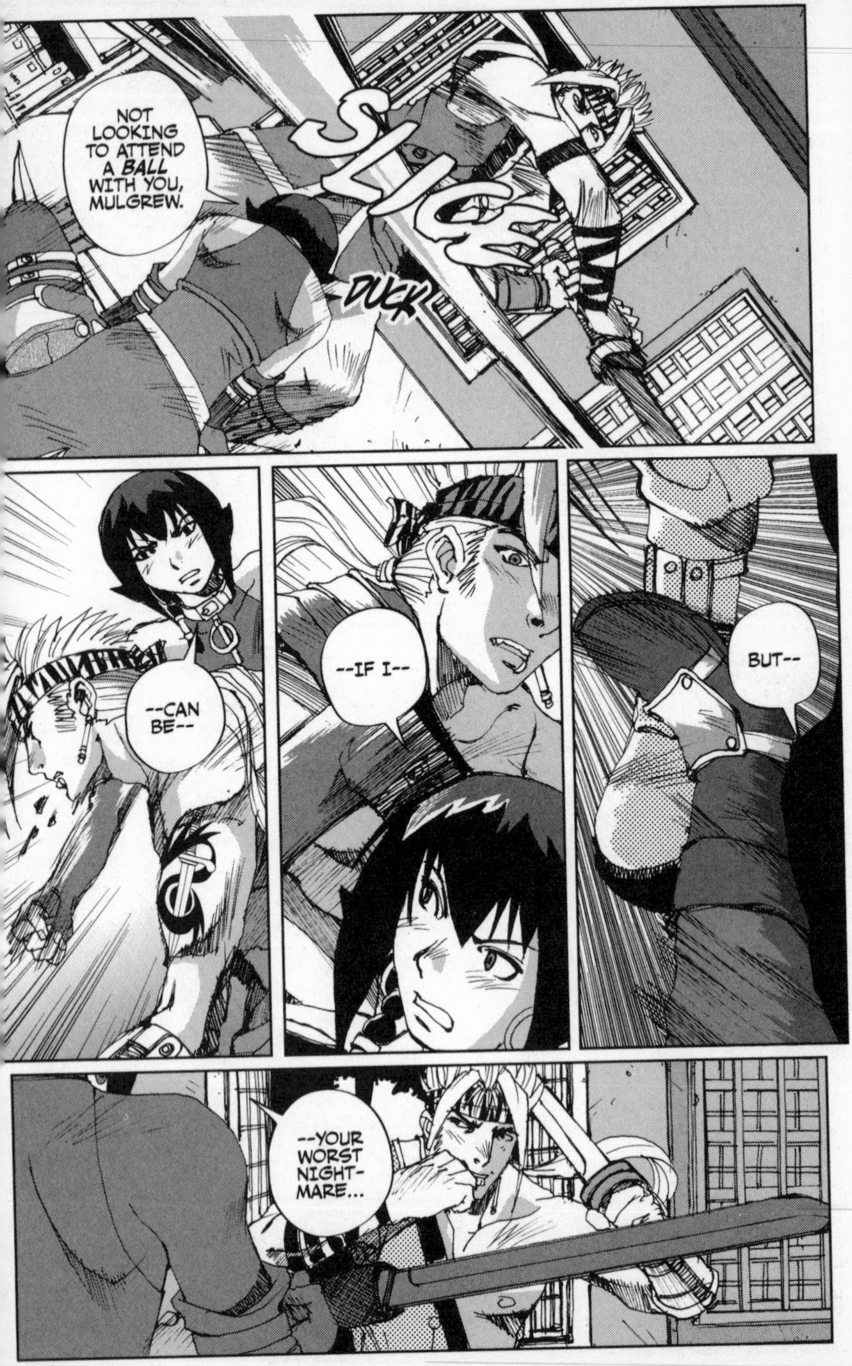
NOT LOOKING TO ATTEND A *BALL* WITH YOU, MULGREW.
DUCK
BUT--
--IF I--
--CAN BE--
--YOUR WORST NIGHT-MARE...

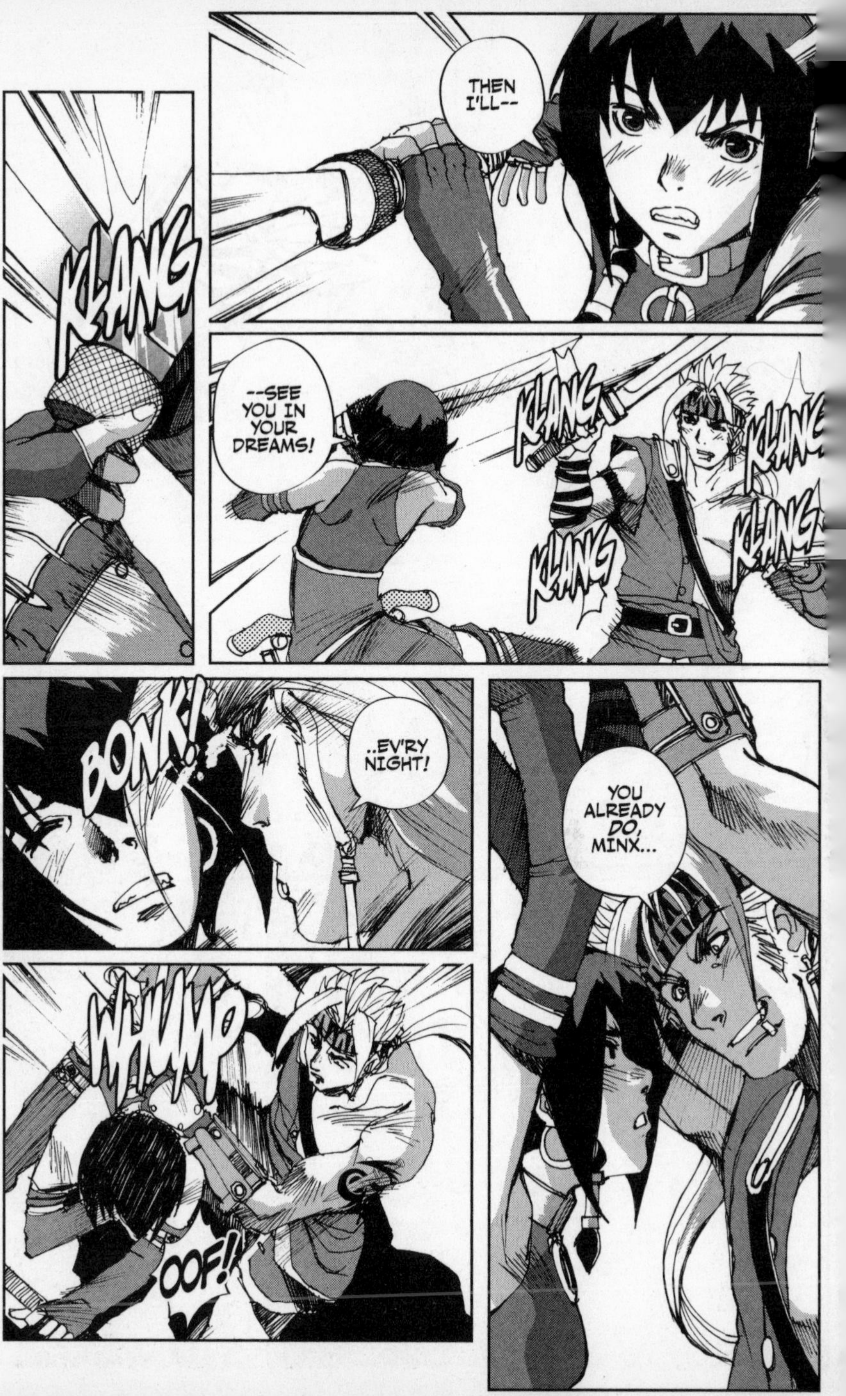
THEN I'LL--
--SEE YOU IN YOUR DREAMS!
KLANG
KLANG
KLANG
KLANG
KLANG
YOU ALREADY DO, MINX...
..EV'RY NIGHT!
BONK!
WHUMP
OOF!!

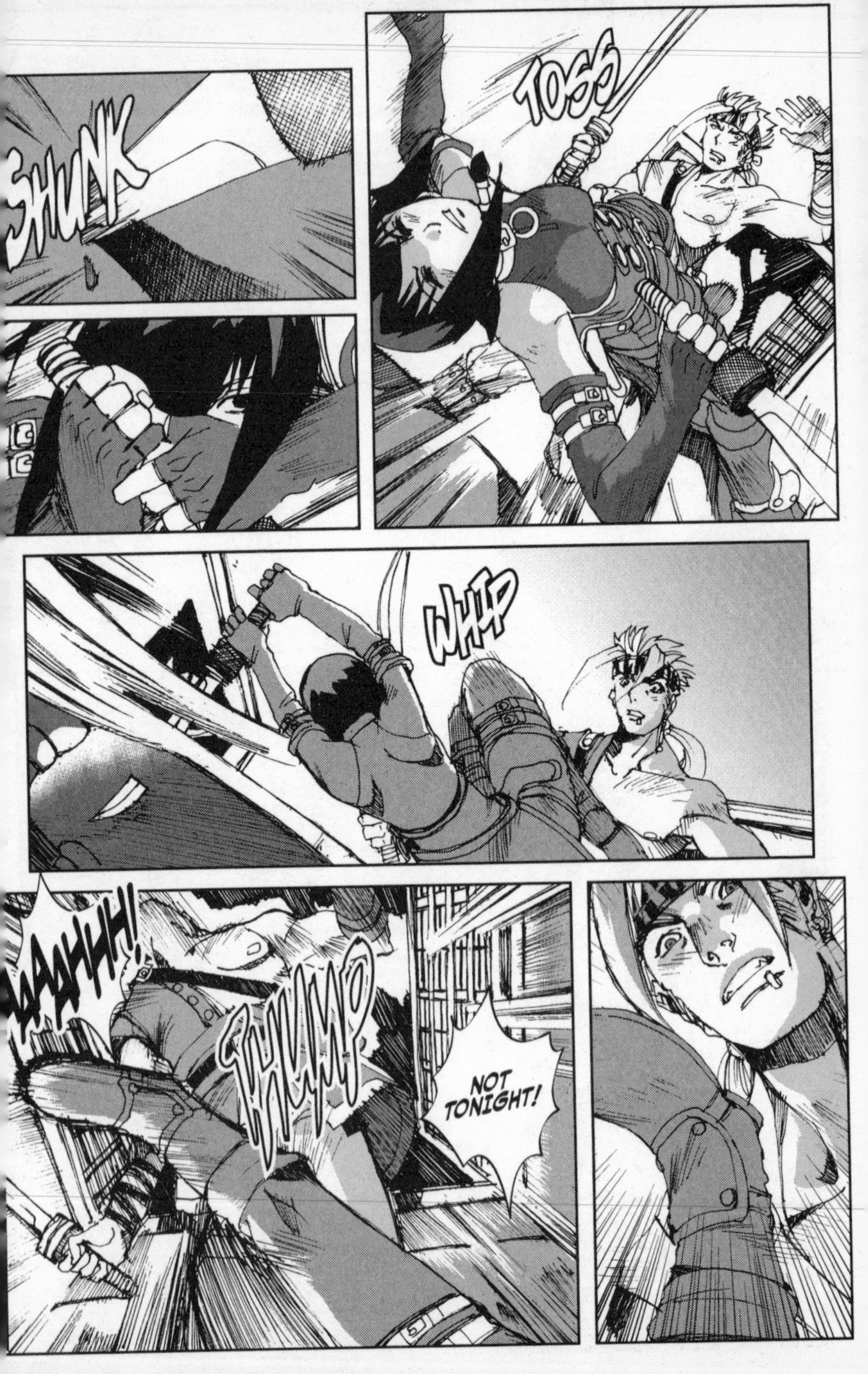
TOSS
SHUNK
WHIP
AAHHH!
THUMP
NOT TONIGHT!

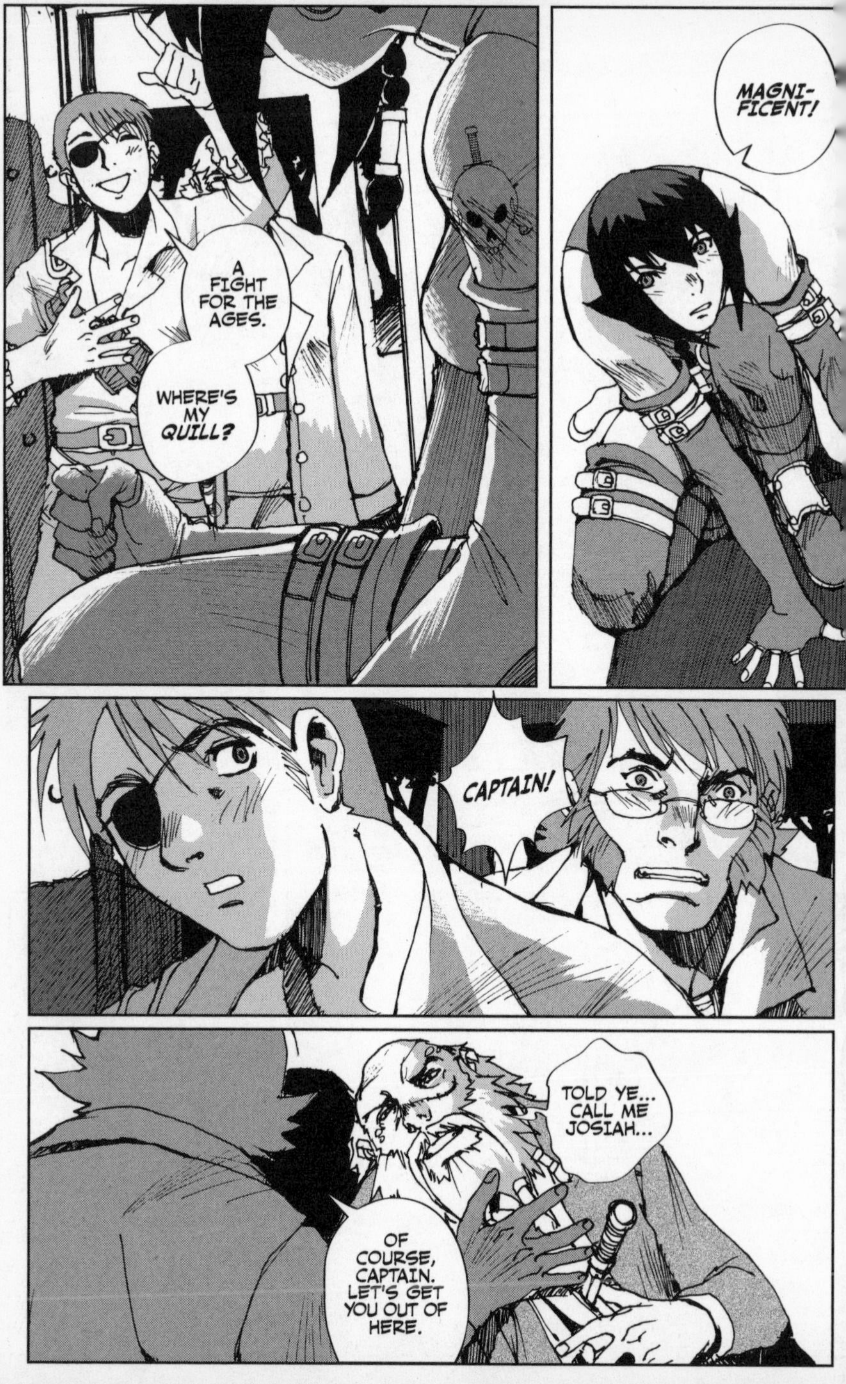
MAGNI-FICENT!
A FIGHT FOR THE AGES.
WHERE'S MY *QUILL?*
CAPTAIN!
TOLD YE... CALL ME JOSIAH...
OF COURSE, CAPTAIN. LET'S GET YOU OUT OF HERE.

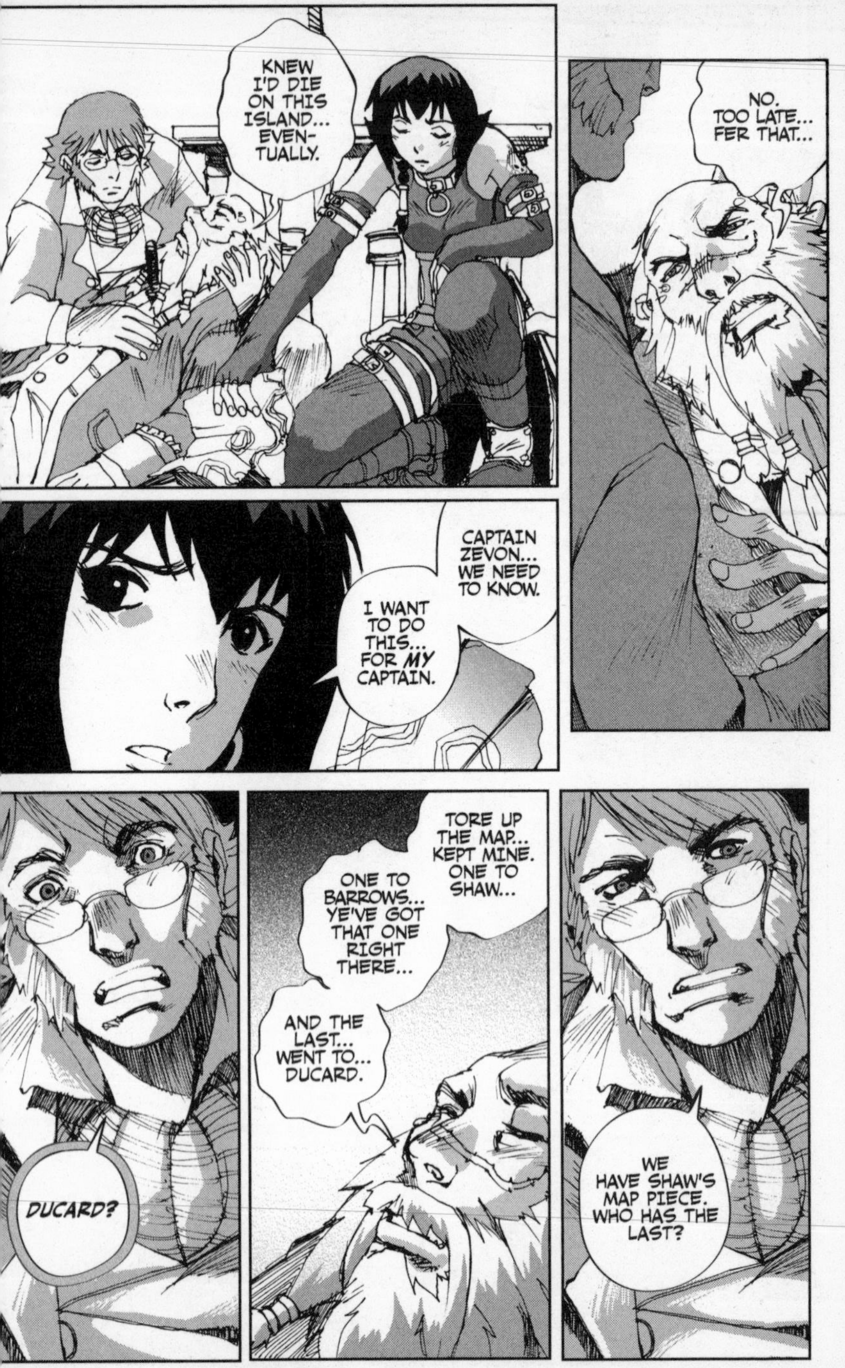
NO. TOO LATE... FER THAT...
KNEW I'D DIE ON THIS ISLAND... EVEN-TUALLY.
CAPTAIN ZEVON... WE NEED TO KNOW.
I WANT TO DO THIS... FOR *MY* CAPTAIN.
WE HAVE SHAW'S MAP PIECE. WHO HAS THE LAST?
TORE UP THE MAP... KEPT MINE. ONE TO SHAW...
ONE TO BARROWS... YE'VE GOT THAT ONE RIGHT THERE...
AND THE LAST... WENT TO... DUCARD.
DUCARD?

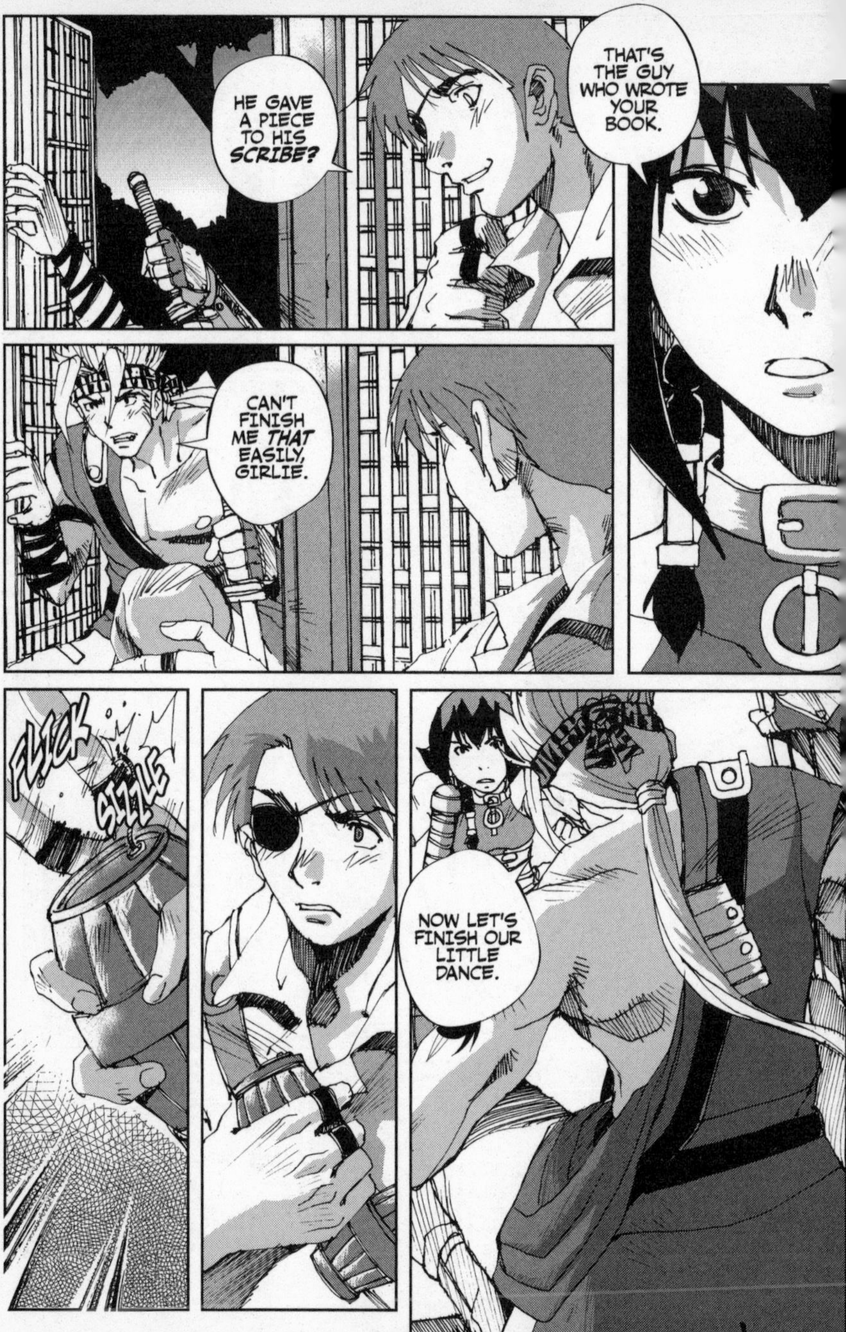
THAT'S THE GUY WHO WROTE YOUR BOOK.
HE GAVE A PIECE TO HIS *SCRIBE?*
CAN'T FINISH ME *THAT* EASILY, GIRLIE.
NOW LET'S FINISH OUR LITTLE DANCE.
FLICK
SIZZLE

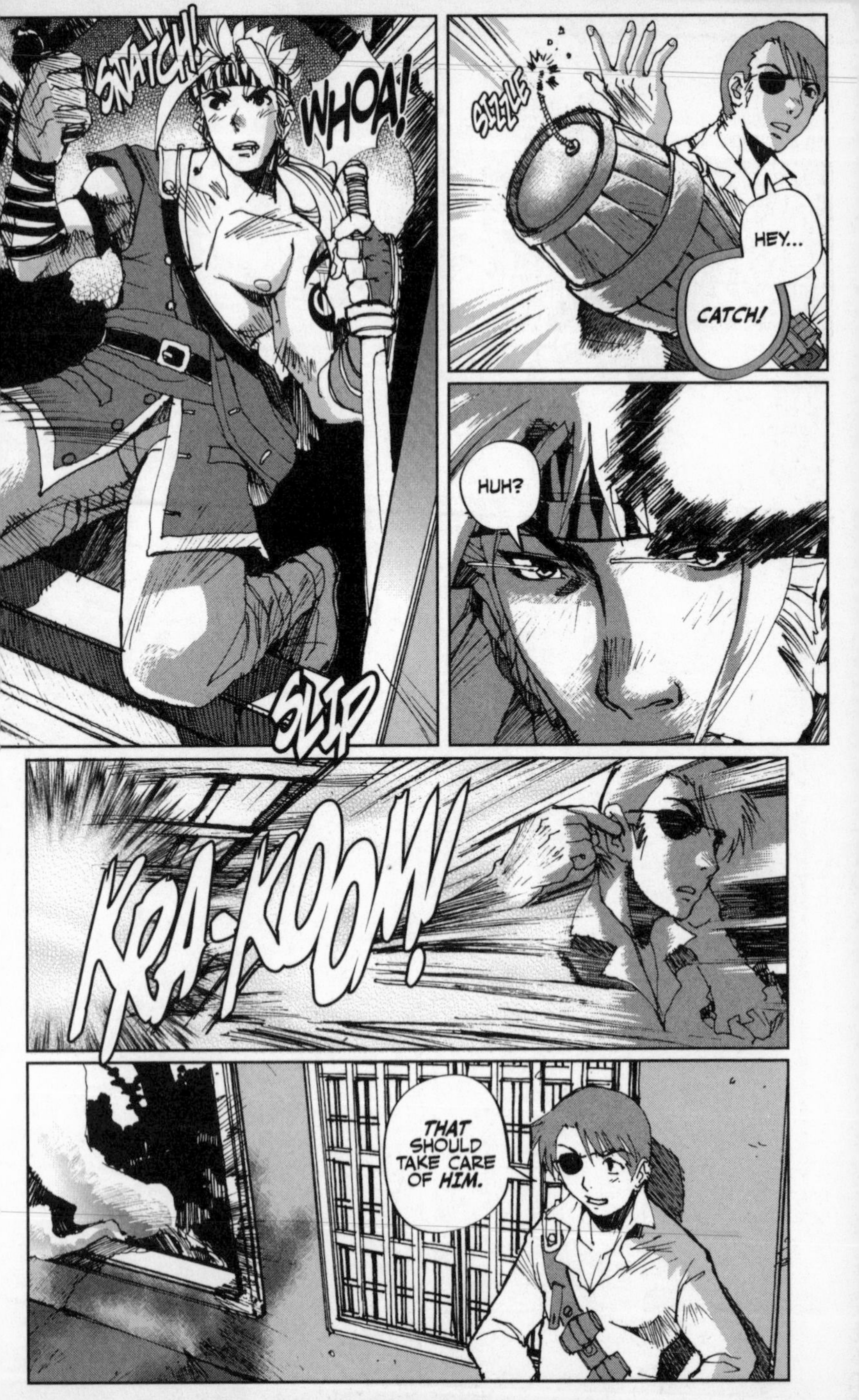
SIZZLE
HEY...
CATCH!
HUH?
SNATCH!
WHOA!
SLIP
KRA-KOOM!
THAT SHOULD TAKE CARE OF HIM.

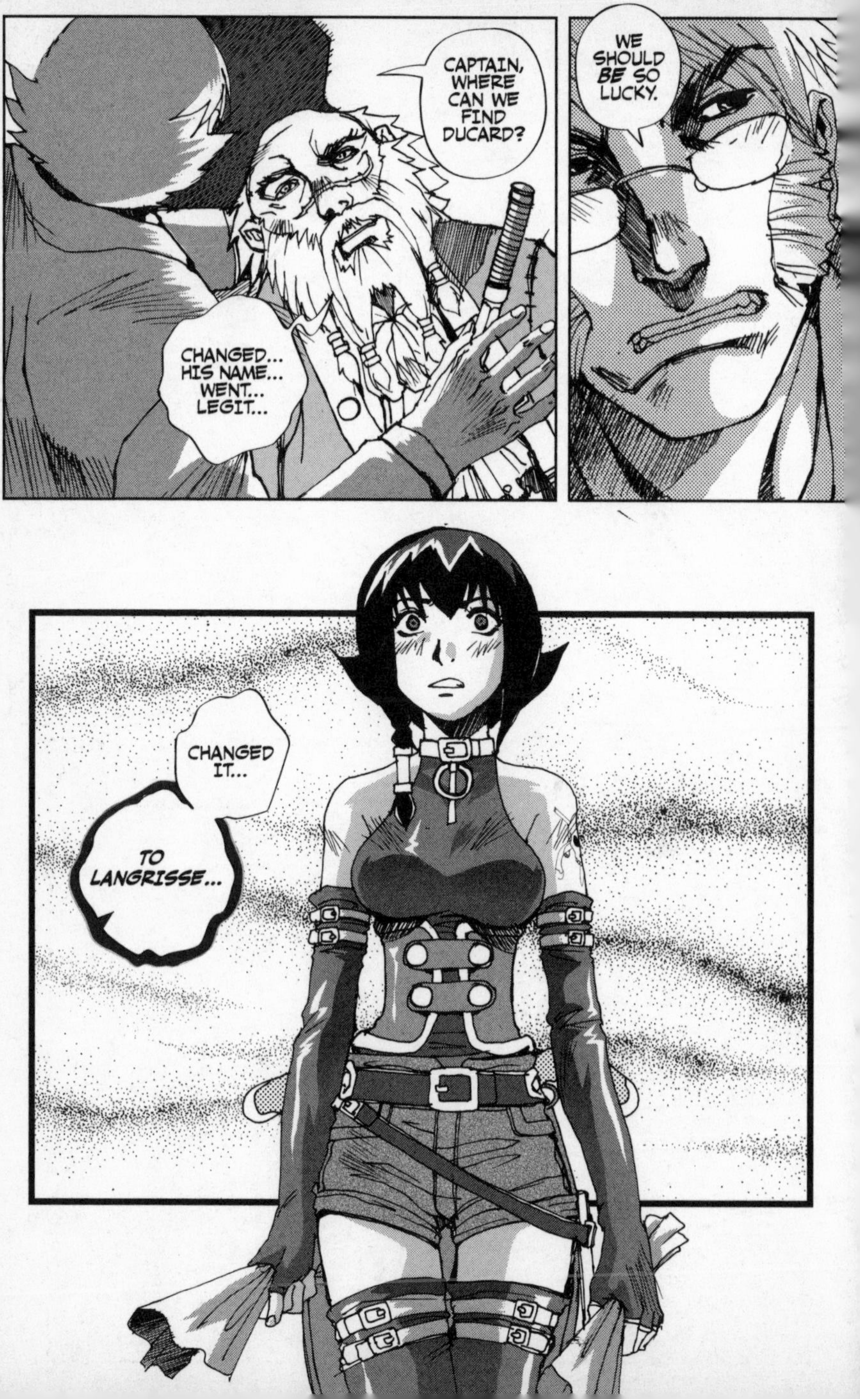
WE SHOULD *BE* SO LUCKY.
CAPTAIN, WHERE CAN WE FIND DUCARD?
CHANGED... HIS NAME... WENT... LEGIT...
CHANGED IT...
TO LANGRISSE...

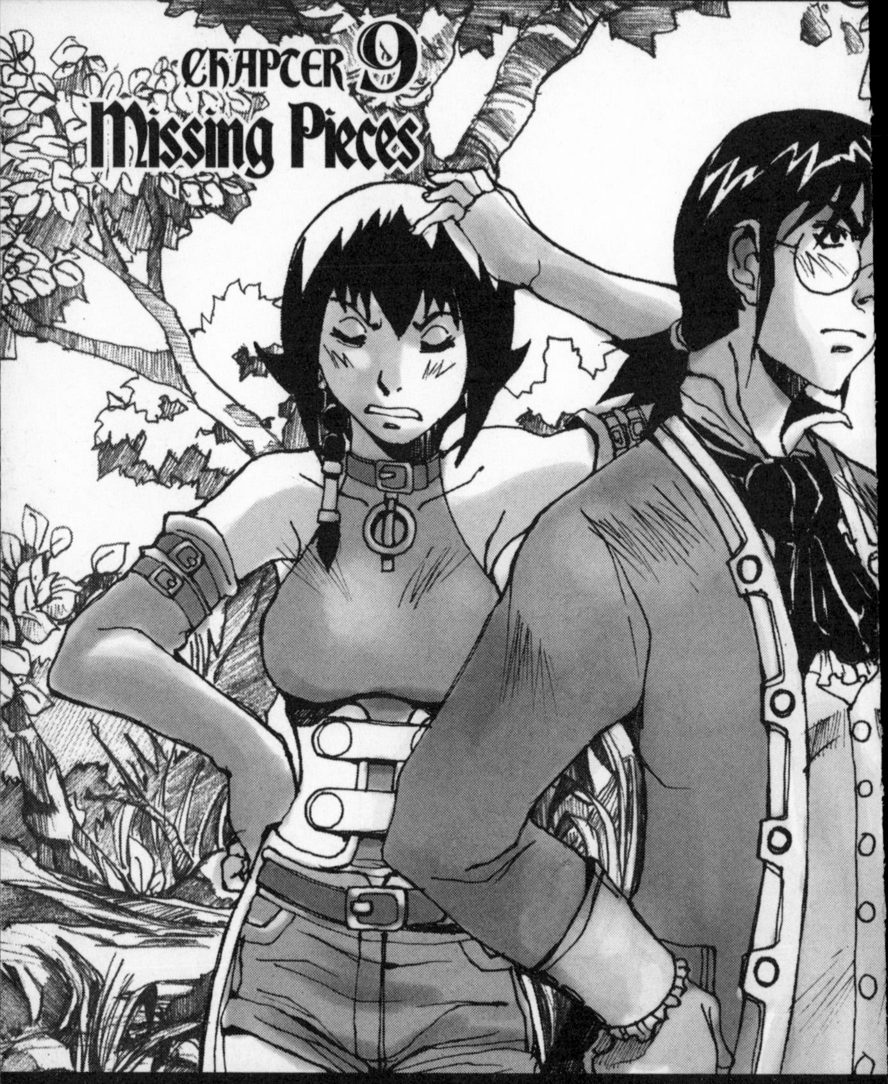
CHAPTER 9
Missing Pieces

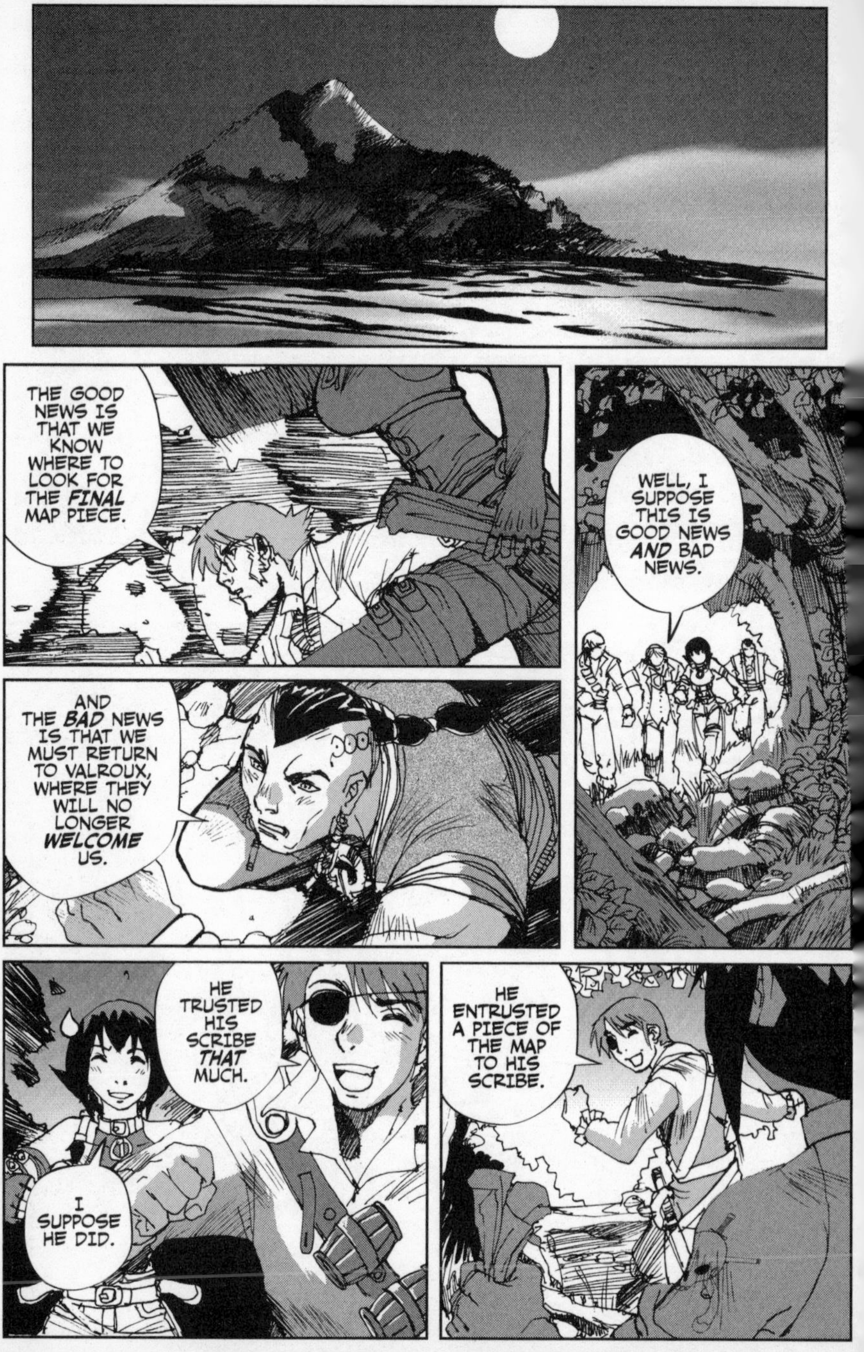
WELL, I SUPPOSE THIS IS GOOD NEWS AND BAD NEWS.
THE GOOD NEWS IS THAT WE KNOW WHERE TO LOOK FOR THE FINAL MAP PIECE.
AND THE BAD NEWS IS THAT WE MUST RETURN TO VALROUX, WHERE THEY WILL NO LONGER WELCOME US.
HE ENTRUSTED A PIECE OF THE MAP TO HIS SCRIBE.
HE TRUSTED HIS SCRIBE THAT MUCH.
I SUPPOSE HE DID.

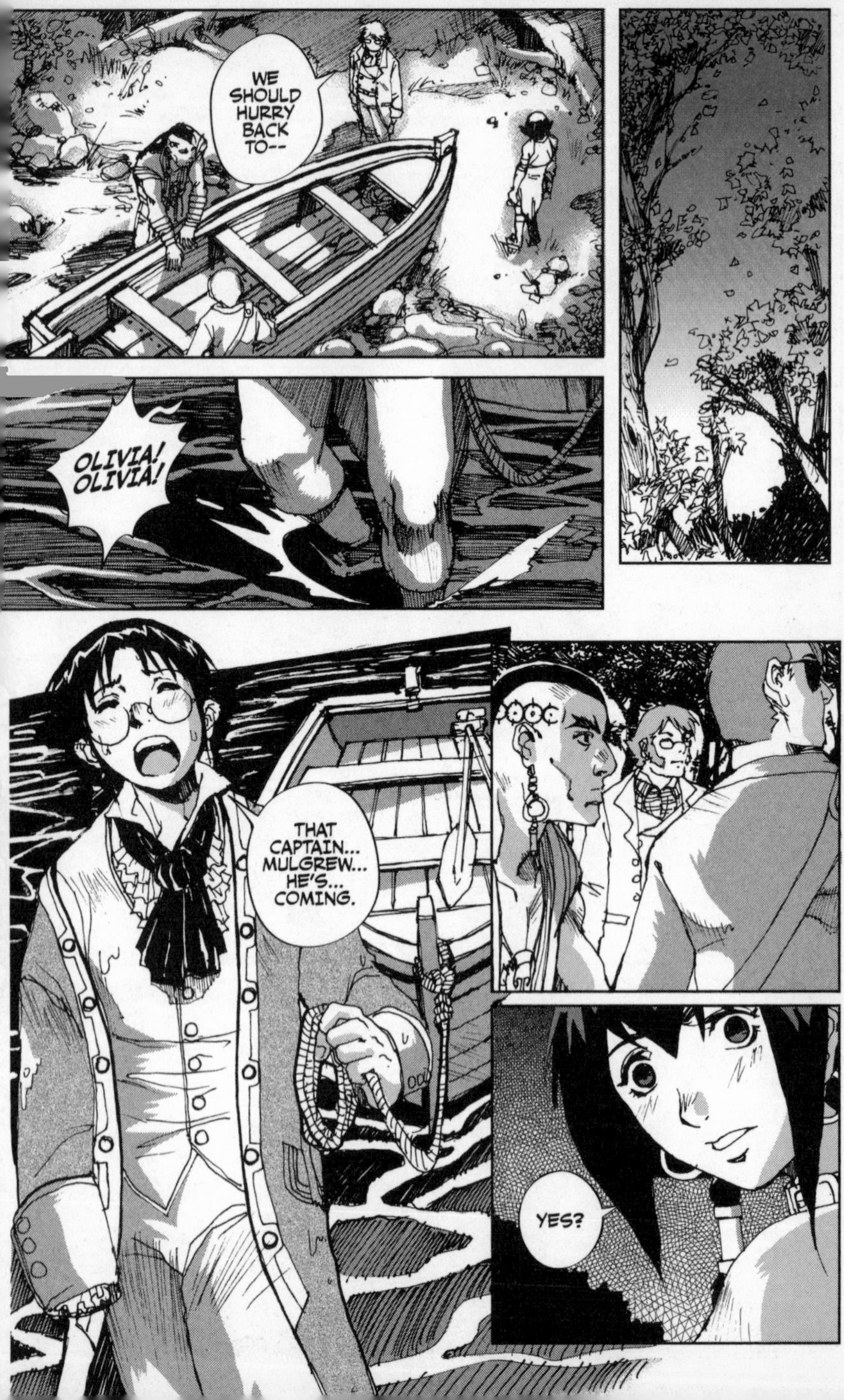
WE SHOULD HURRY BACK TO--
OLIVIA! OLIVIA!
YES?
THAT CAPTAIN... MULGREW... HE'S... COMING.

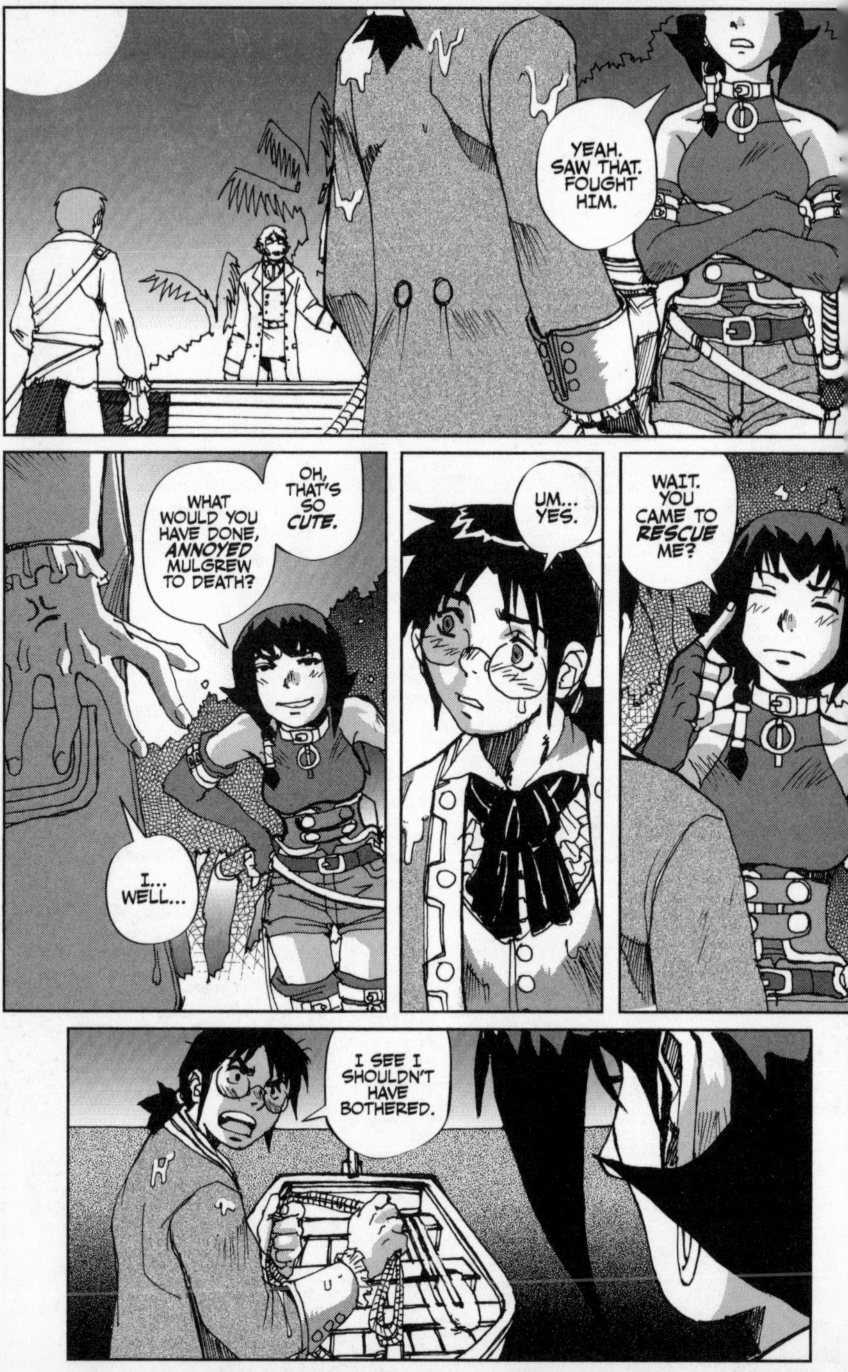
YEAH. SAW THAT. FOUGHT HIM.
WAIT. YOU CAME TO *RESCUE* ME?
UM... YES.
OH, THAT'S SO *CUTE.*
WHAT WOULD YOU HAVE DONE, *ANNOYED* MULGREW TO DEATH?
I... WELL...
I SEE I SHOULDN'T HAVE BOTHERED.

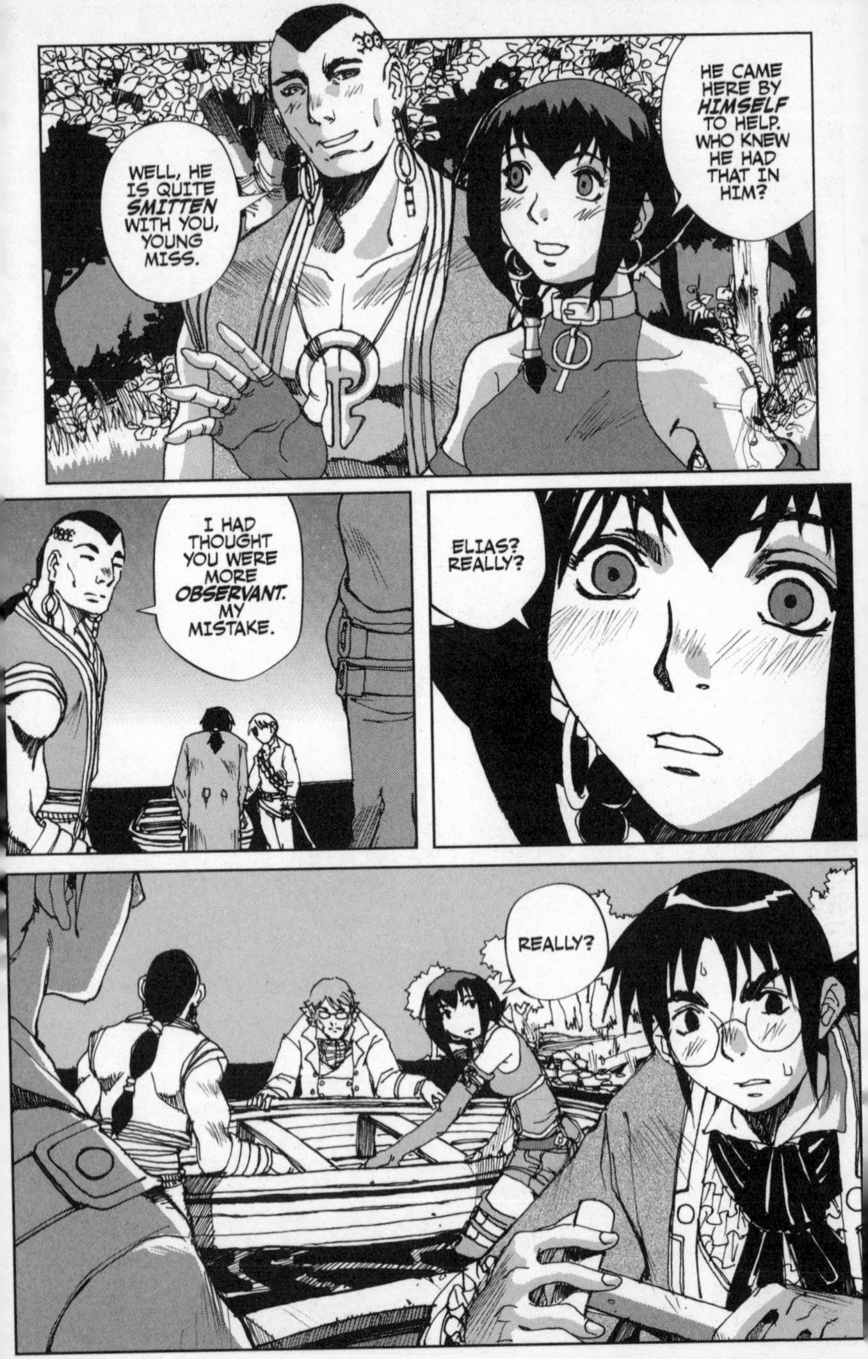
HE CAME HERE BY *HIMSELF* TO HELP. WHO KNEW HE HAD THAT IN HIM?
WELL, HE IS QUITE *SMITTEN* WITH YOU, YOUNG MISS.
ELIAS? REALLY?
I HAD THOUGHT YOU WERE MORE *OBSERVANT*. MY MISTAKE.
REALLY?

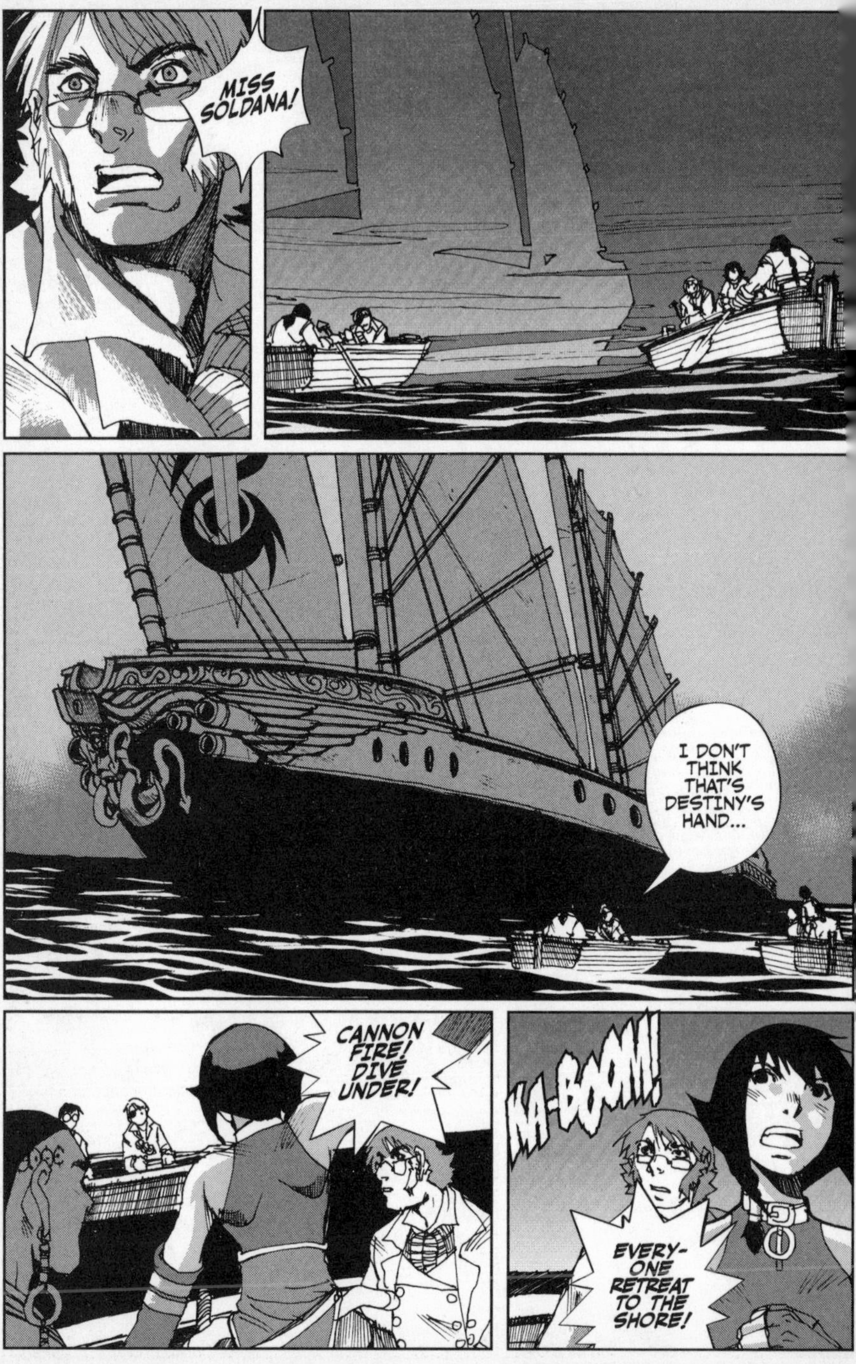
MISS SOLDANA!
I DON'T THINK THAT'S DESTINY'S HAND...
KA-BOOM!
EVERY-ONE RETREAT TO THE SHORE!
CANNON FIRE! DIVE UNDER!

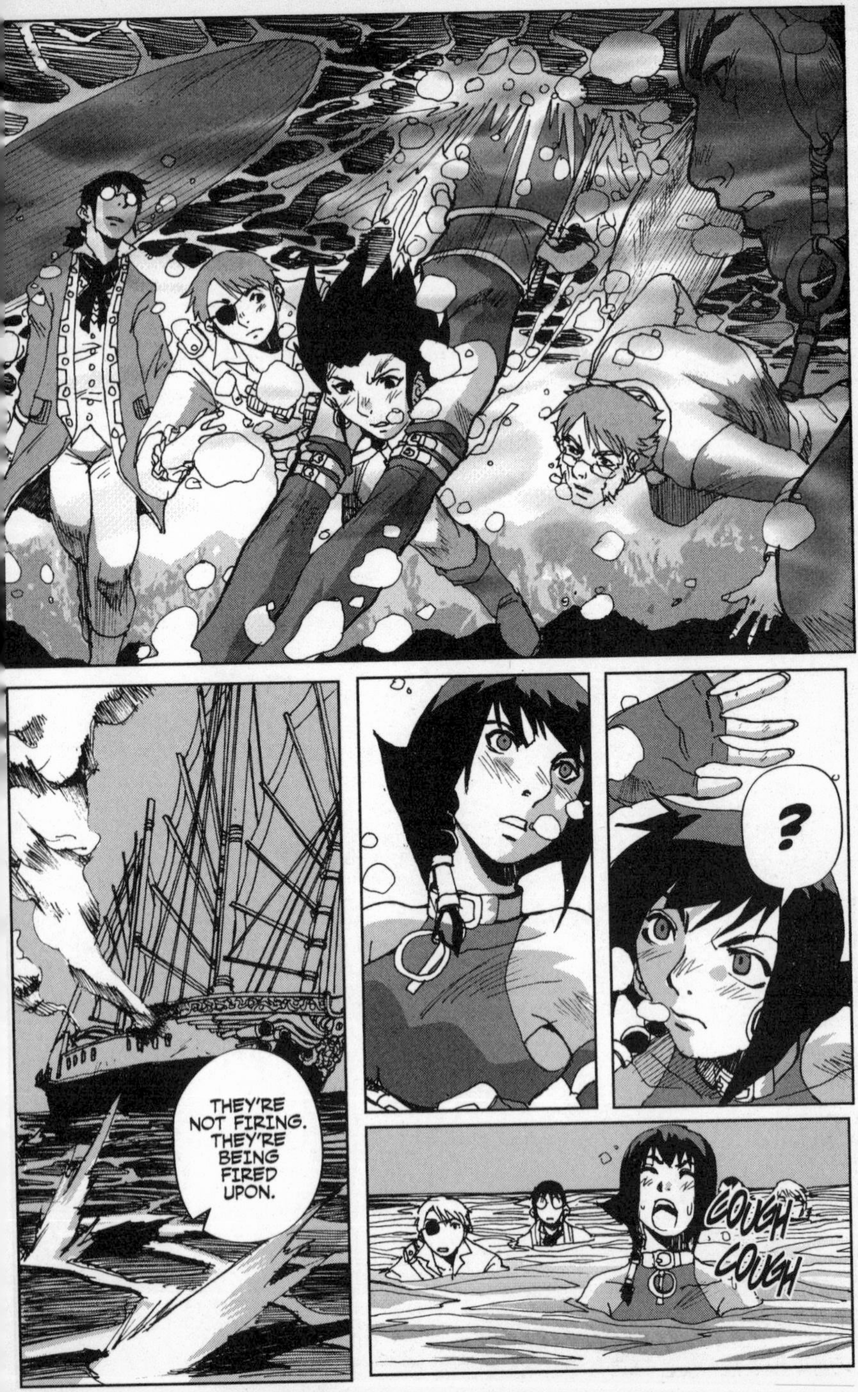
?
COUGH
COUGH
THEY'RE NOT FIRING. THEY'RE BEING FIRED UPON.

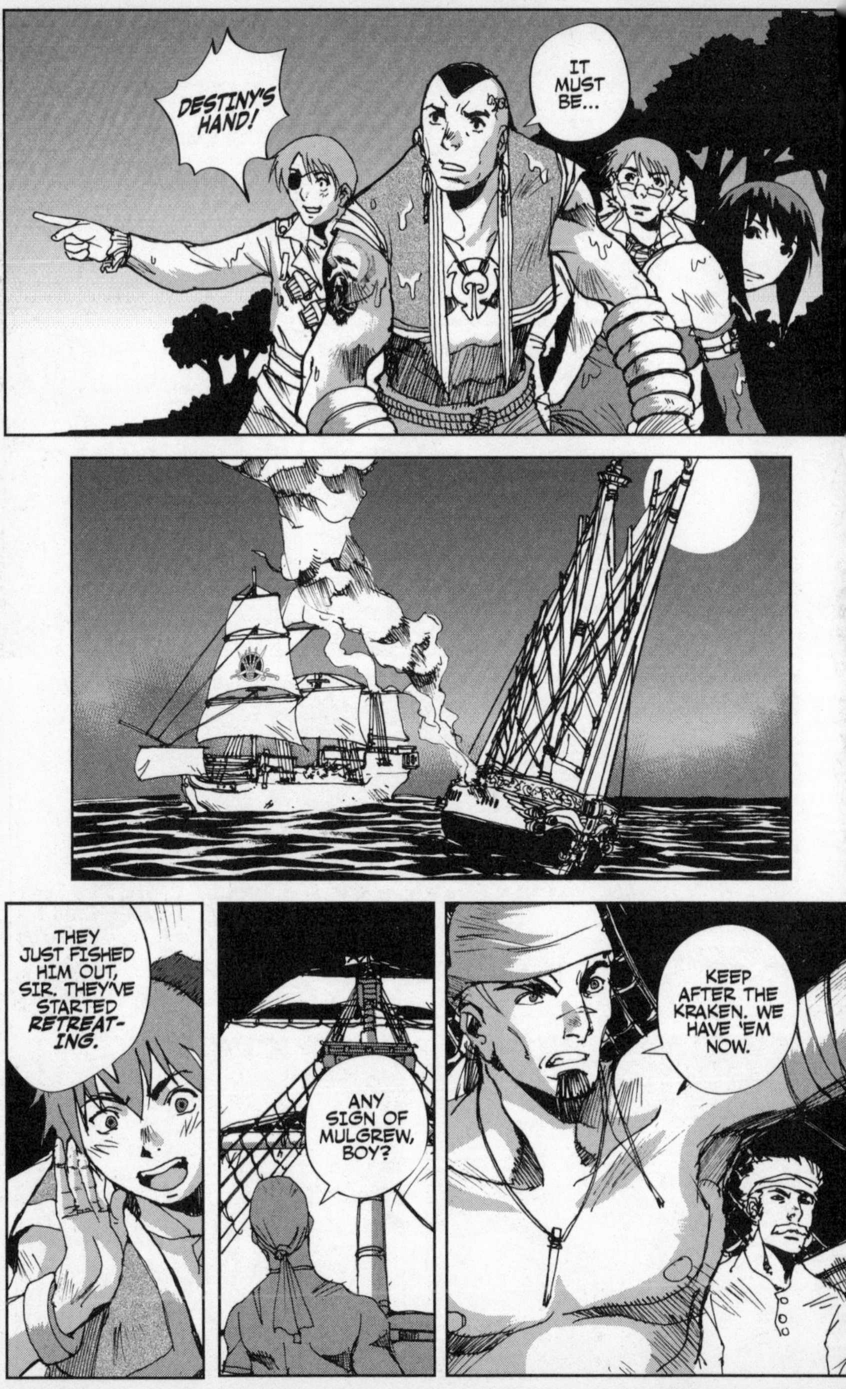
IT MUST BE...
DESTINY'S HAND!
KEEP AFTER THE KRAKEN. WE HAVE 'EM NOW.
ANY SIGN OF MULGREW, BOY?
THEY JUST FISHED HIM OUT, SIR. THEY'VE STARTED RETREATING.

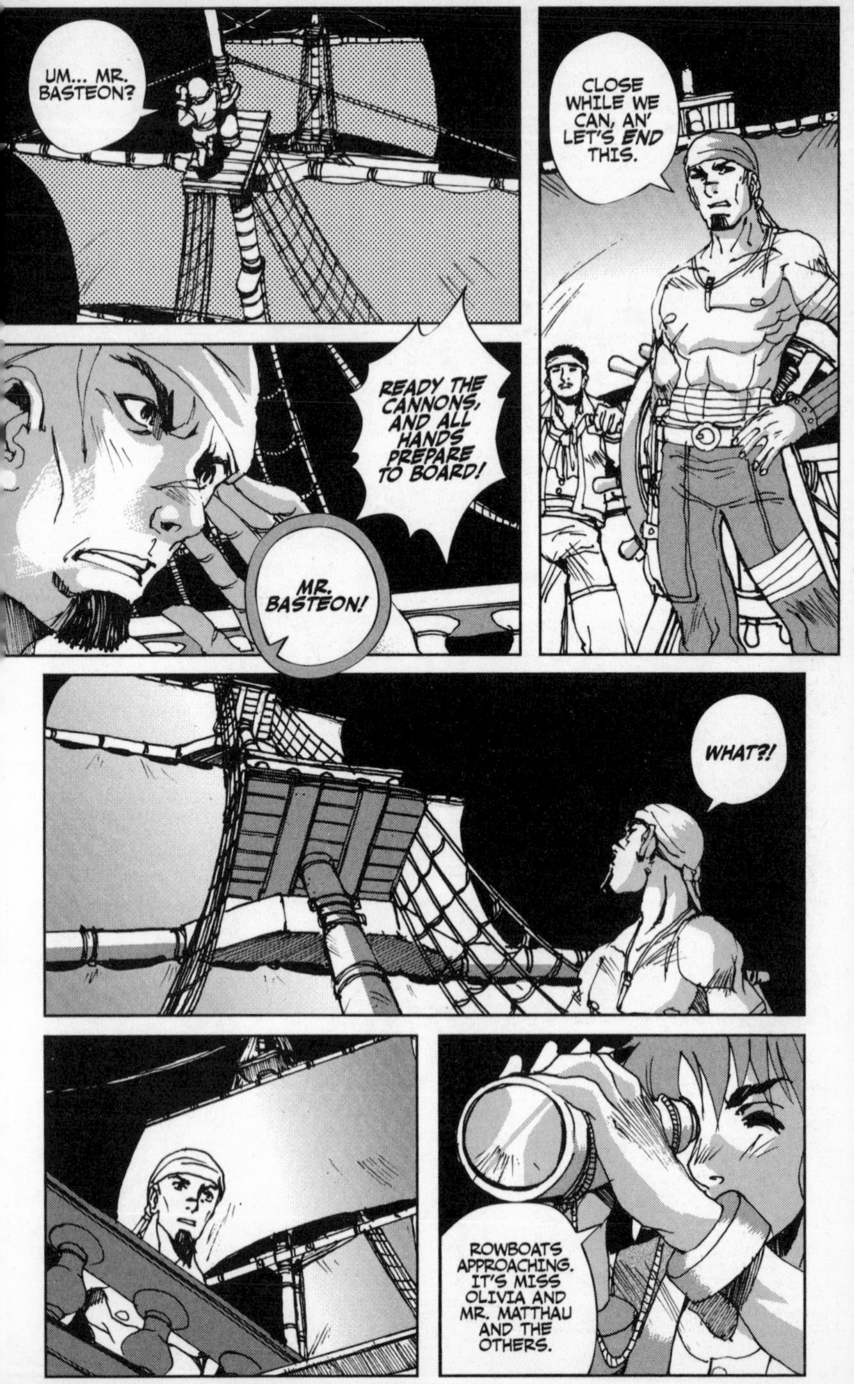
CLOSE WHILE WE CAN, AN' LET'S *END* THIS.
UM... MR. BASTEON?
READY THE CANNONS, AND ALL HANDS PREPARE TO BOARD!
MR. BASTEON!
WHAT?!
ROWBOATS APPROACHING. IT'S MISS OLIVIA AND MR. MATTHAU AND THE OTHERS.

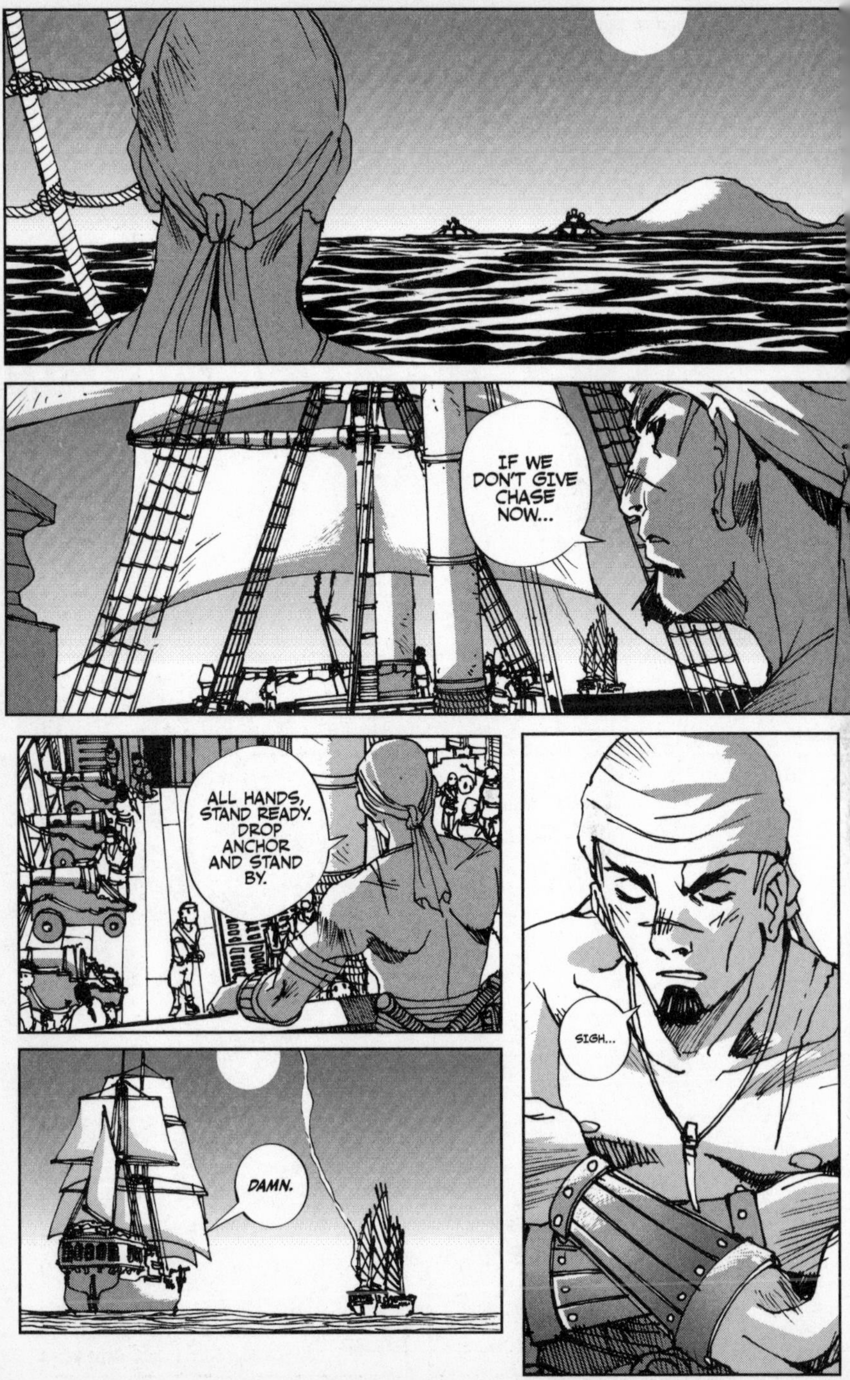
IF WE DON'T GIVE CHASE NOW...
SIGH...
ALL HANDS, STAND READY. DROP ANCHOR AND STAND BY.
DAMN.

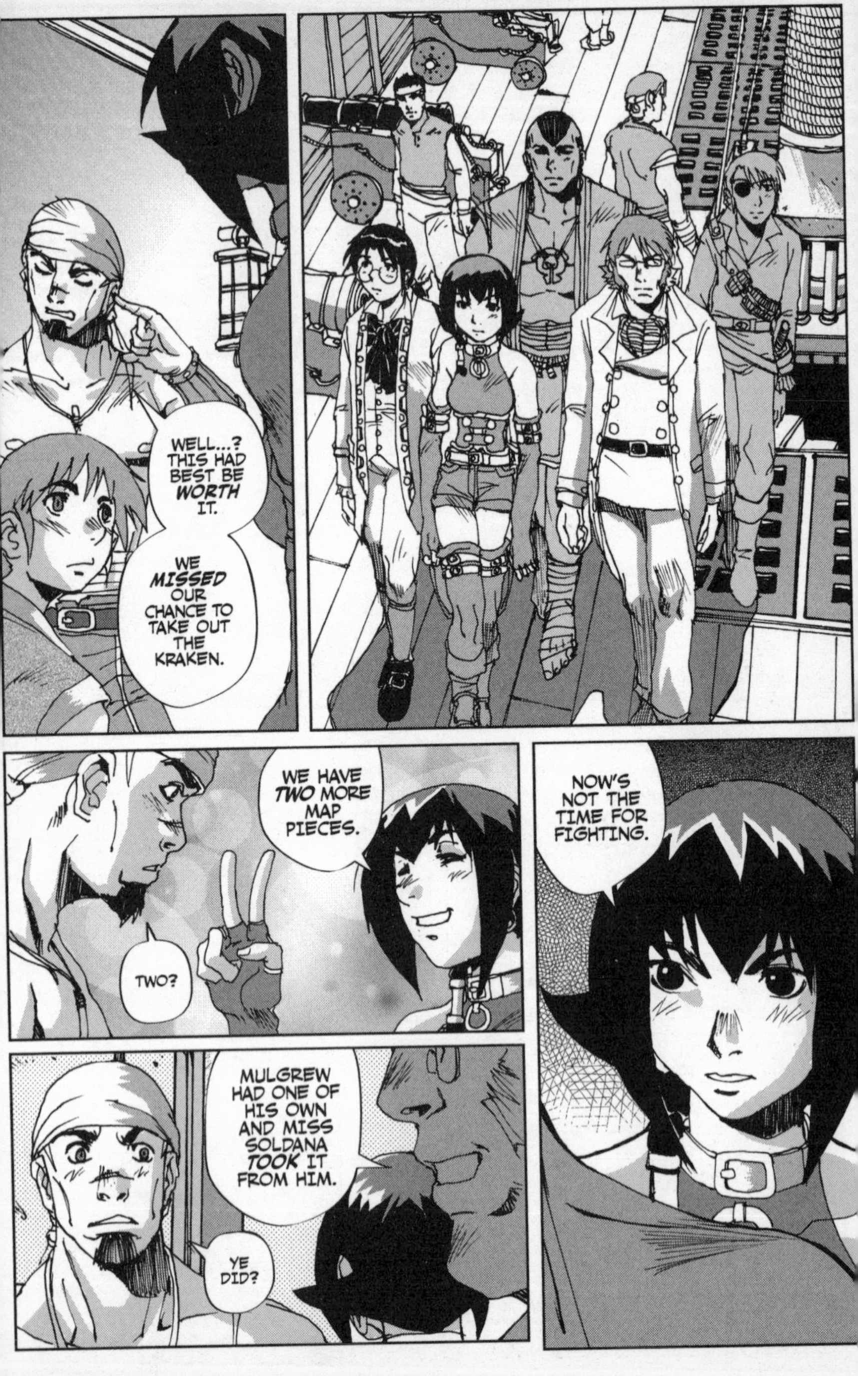
WELL...? THIS HAD BEST BE *WORTH* IT.
WE *MISSED* OUR CHANCE TO TAKE OUT THE KRAKEN.
NOW'S NOT THE TIME FOR FIGHTING.
WE HAVE *TWO* MORE MAP PIECES.
TWO?
MULGREW HAD ONE OF HIS OWN AND MISS SOLDANA *TOOK* IT FROM HIM.
YE DID?

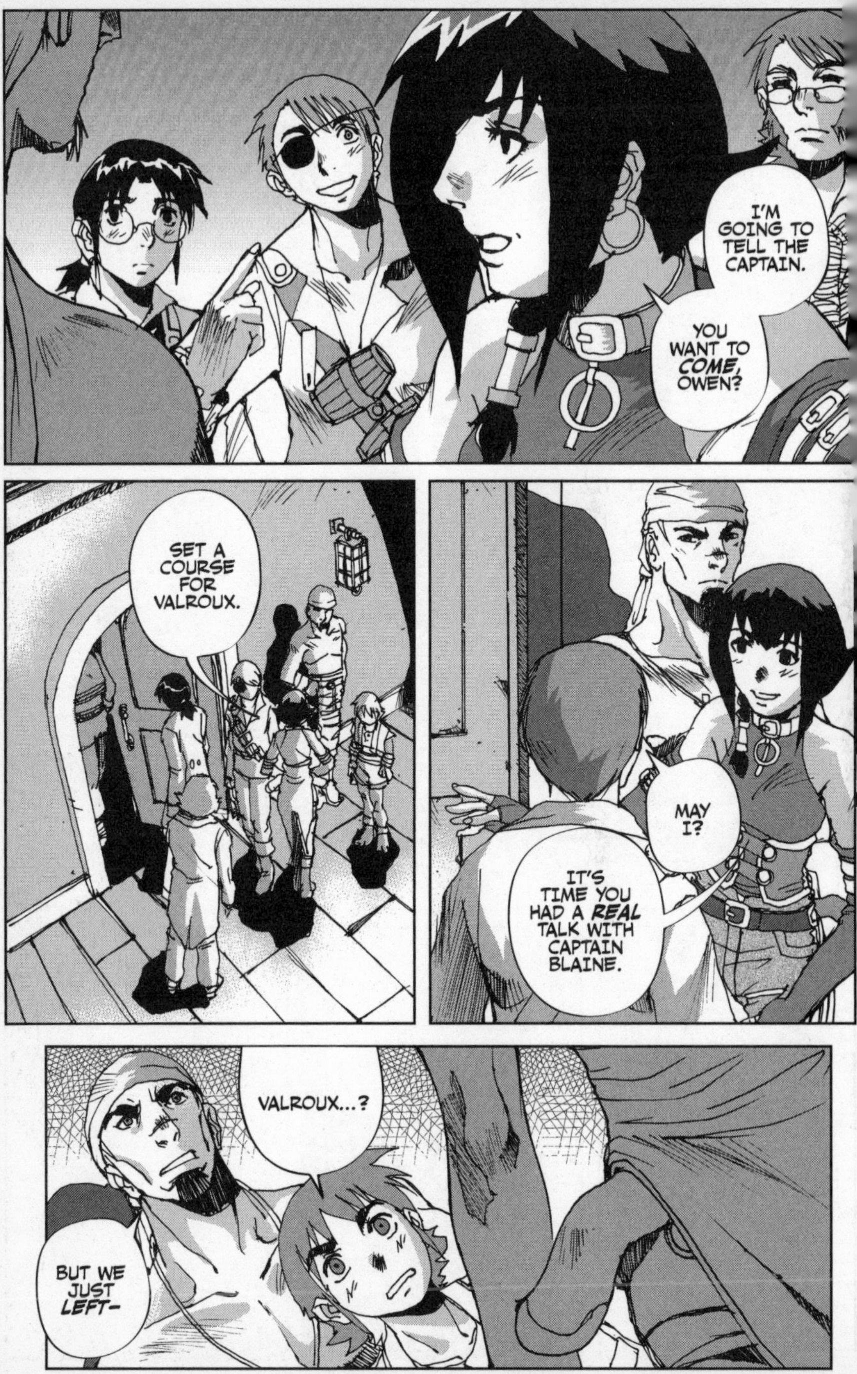
I'M GOING TO TELL THE CAPTAIN.
YOU WANT TO *COME,* OWEN?
MAY I?
IT'S TIME YOU HAD A *REAL* TALK WITH CAPTAIN BLAINE.
SET A COURSE FOR VALROUX.
VALROUX...?
BUT WE JUST *LEFT-*

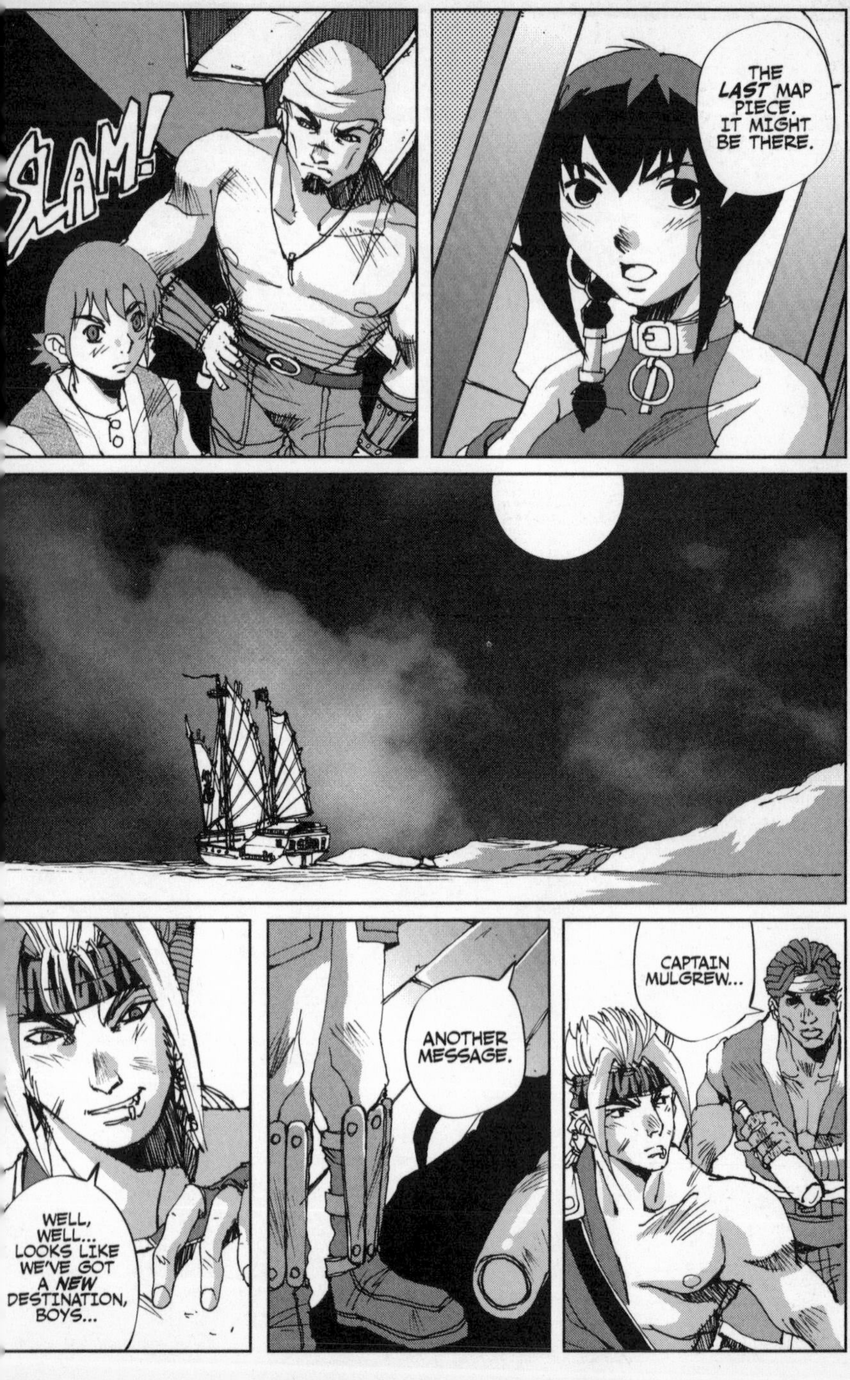
THE *LAST* MAP PIECE. IT MIGHT BE THERE.
SLAM!
CAPTAIN MULGREW...
ANOTHER MESSAGE.
WELL, WELL... LOOKS LIKE WE'VE GOT A *NEW* DESTINATION, BOYS...

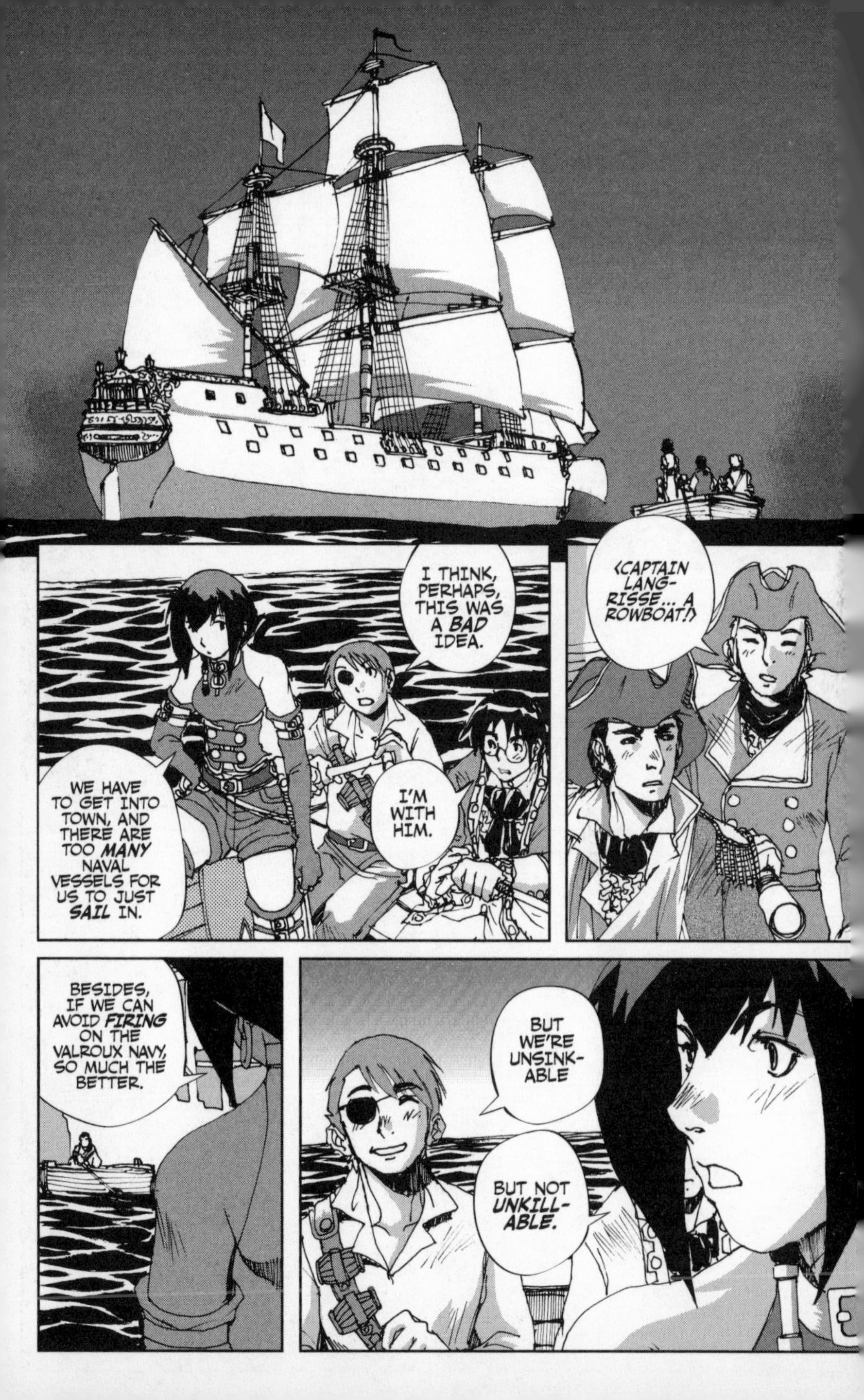
‹CAPTAIN LANG-RISSE... A ROWBOAT!›
I THINK, PERHAPS, THIS WAS A *BAD* IDEA.
I'M WITH HIM.
WE HAVE TO GET INTO TOWN, AND THERE ARE TOO *MANY* NAVAL VESSELS FOR US TO JUST *SAIL* IN.
BUT WE'RE UNSINK-ABLE
BUT NOT *UNKILL-ABLE.*
BESIDES, IF WE CAN AVOID *FIRING* ON THE VALROUX NAVY, SO MUCH THE BETTER.

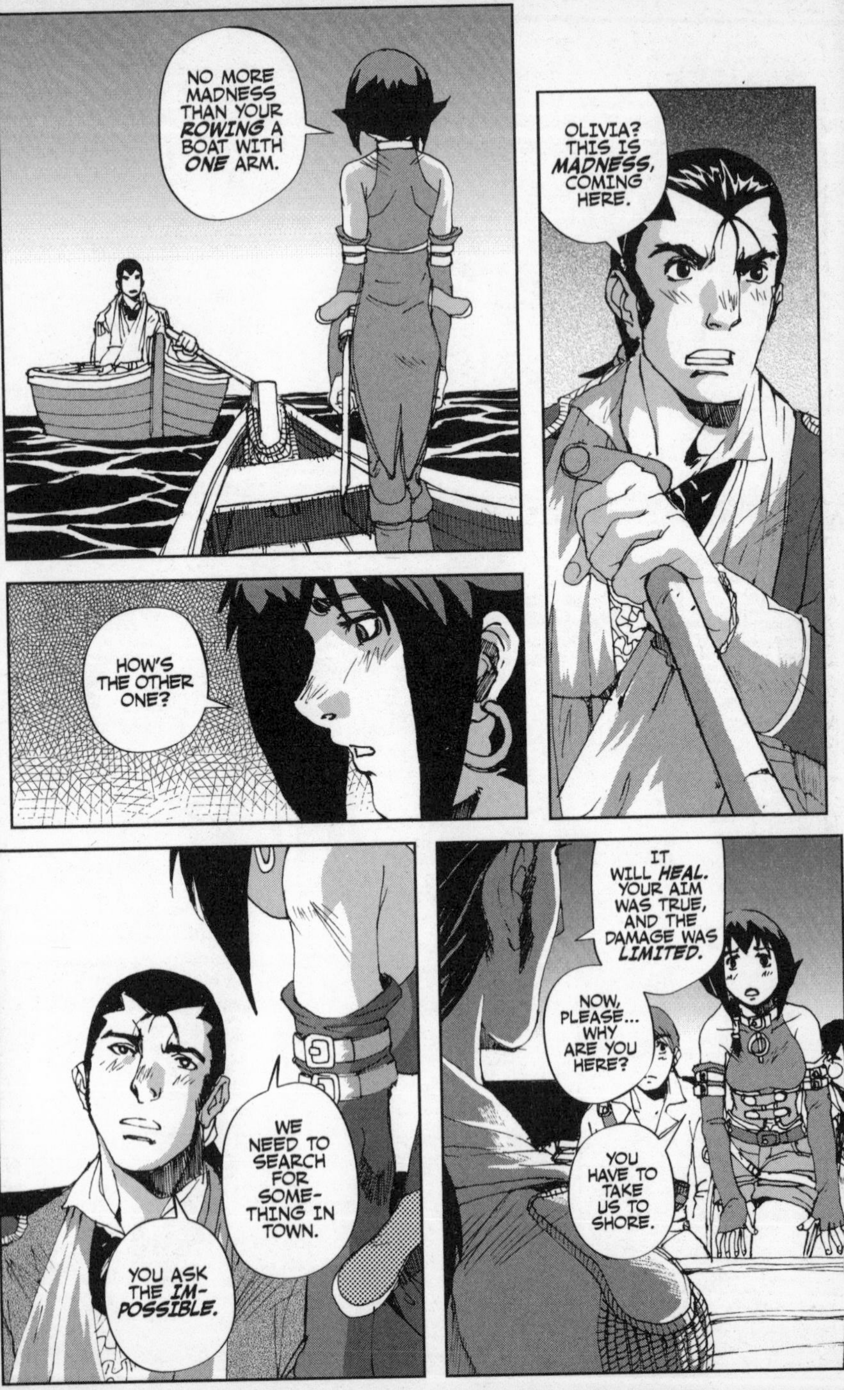
OLIVIA? THIS IS *MADNESS*, COMING HERE.
NO MORE MADNESS THAN YOUR *ROWING* A BOAT WITH *ONE* ARM.
HOW'S THE OTHER ONE?
IT WILL *HEAL*. YOUR AIM WAS TRUE, AND THE DAMAGE WAS *LIMITED*.
NOW, PLEASE... WHY ARE YOU HERE?
YOU HAVE TO TAKE US TO SHORE.
WE NEED TO SEARCH FOR SOME-THING IN TOWN.
YOU ASK THE *IM-POSSIBLE*.

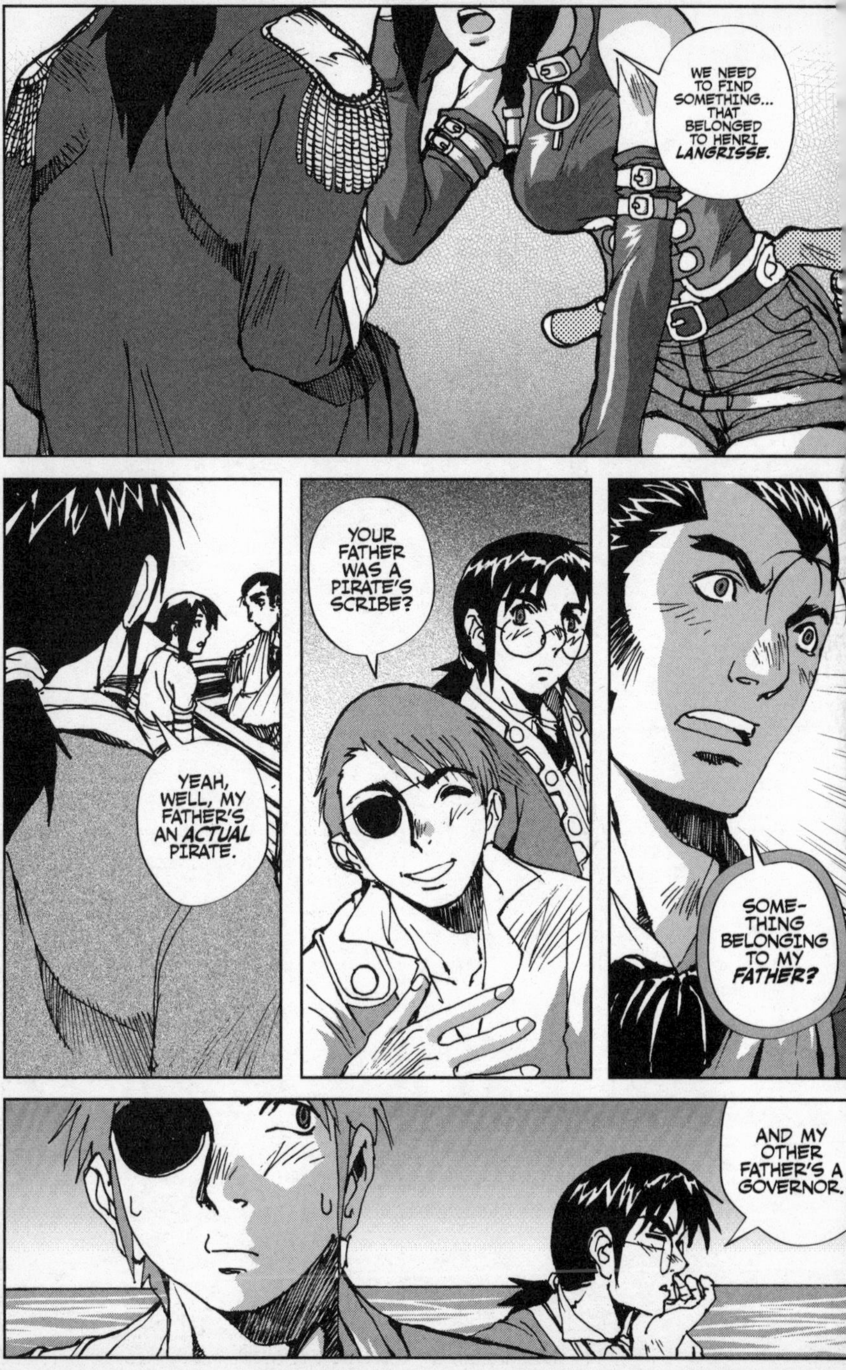
WE NEED TO FIND SOMETHING... THAT BELONGED TO HENRI *LANGRISSE.*
SOME-THING BELONGING TO MY *FATHER?*
YOUR FATHER WAS A PIRATE'S SCRIBE?
YEAH, WELL, MY FATHER'S AN *ACTUAL* PIRATE.
AND MY OTHER FATHER'S A GOVERNOR.

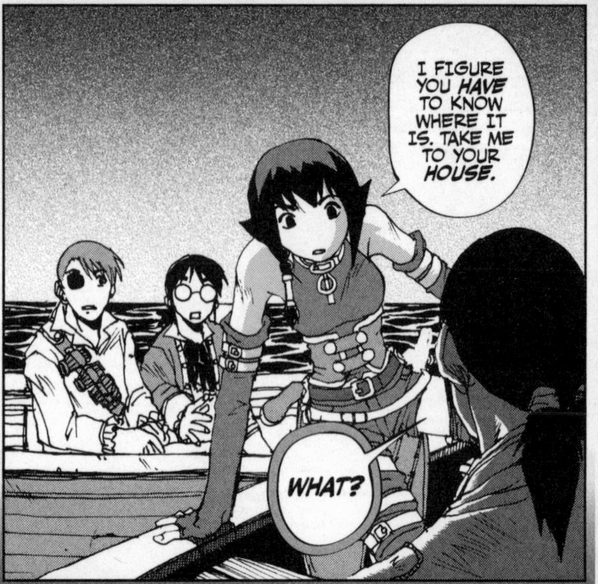
I FIGURE YOU *HAVE* TO KNOW WHERE IT IS. TAKE ME TO YOUR *HOUSE.*
WHAT?

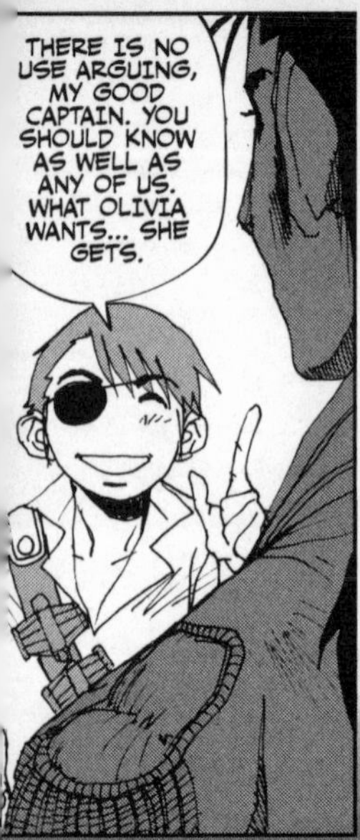
THERE IS NO USE ARGUING, MY GOOD CAPTAIN. YOU SHOULD KNOW AS WELL AS ANY OF US. WHAT OLIVIA WANTS... SHE GETS.

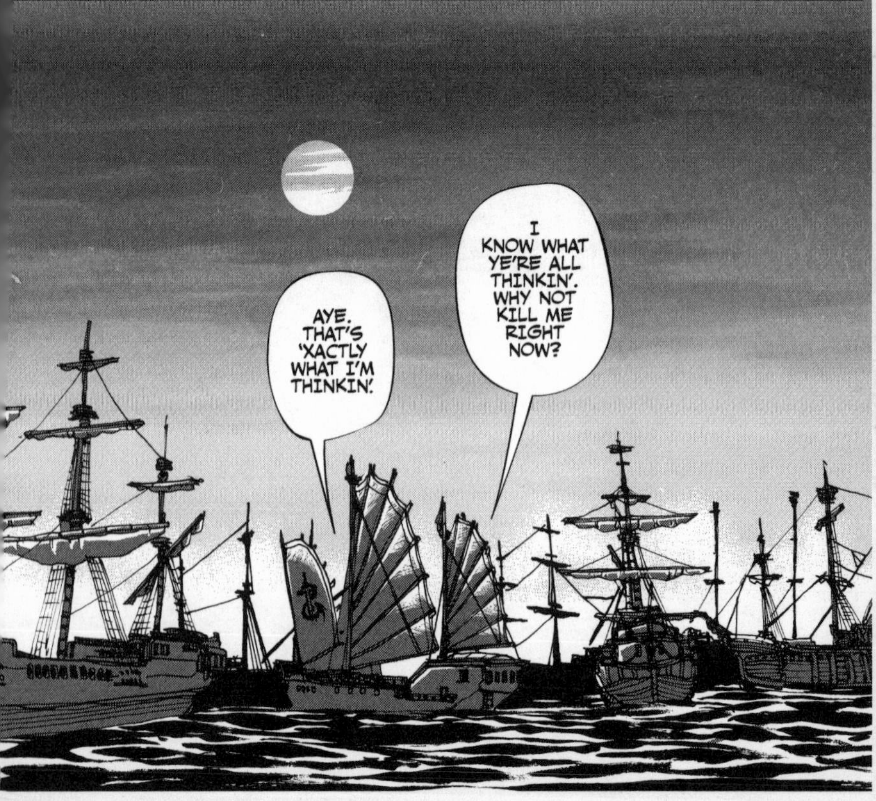
I KNOW WHAT YE'RE ALL THINKIN'. WHY NOT KILL ME RIGHT NOW?
AYE. THAT'S 'XACTLY WHAT I'M THINKIN'.

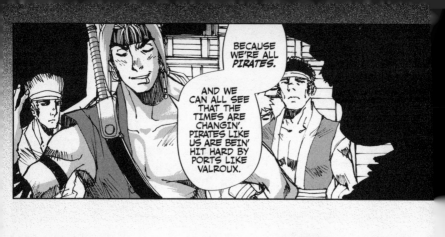

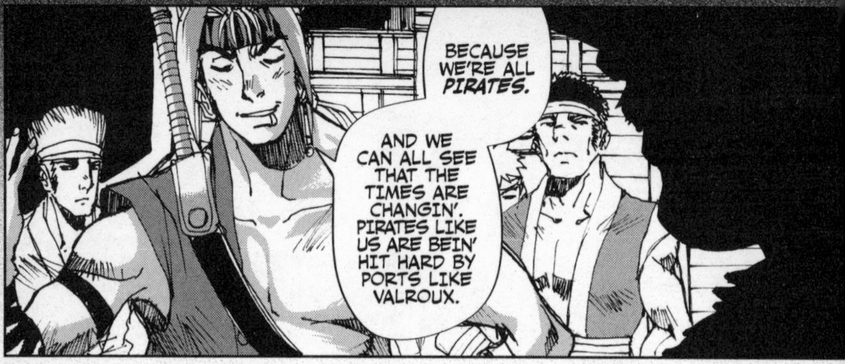
BECAUSE WE'RE ALL *PIRATES.*
AND WE CAN ALL SEE THAT THE TIMES ARE CHANGIN'. PIRATES LIKE US ARE BEIN' HIT HARD BY PORTS LIKE VALROUX.
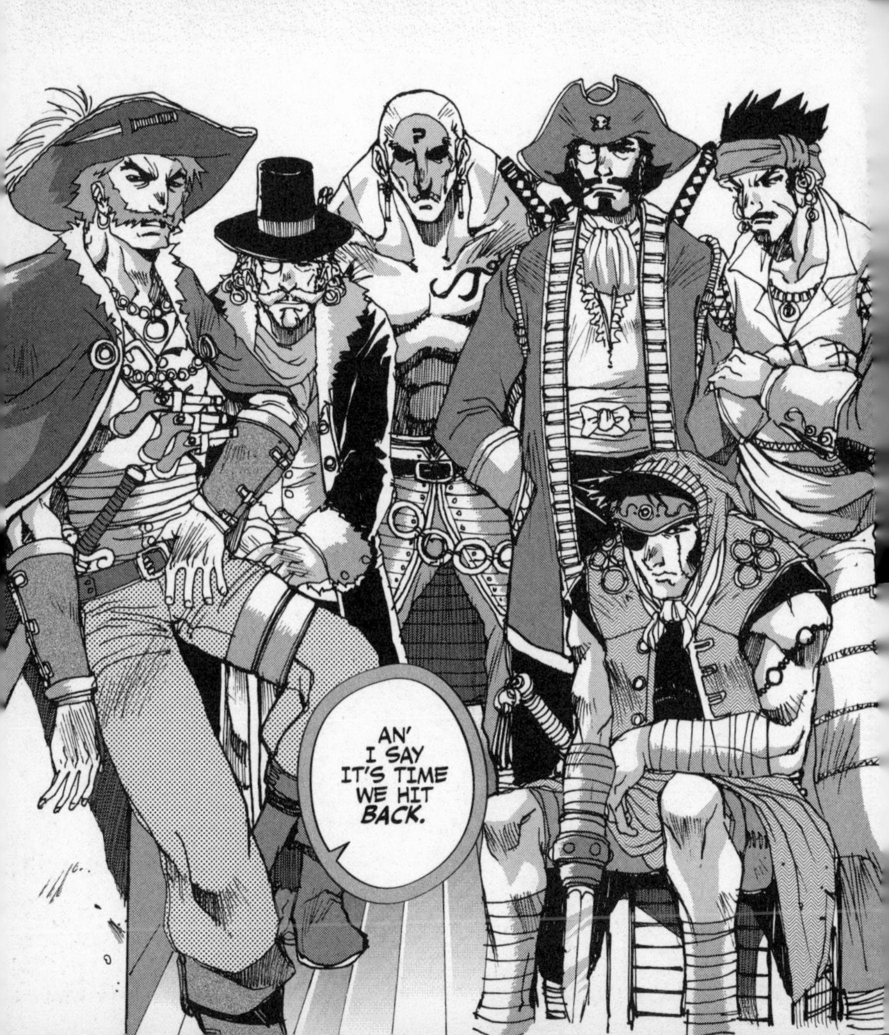
AN' I SAY IT'S TIME WE HIT *BACK.*

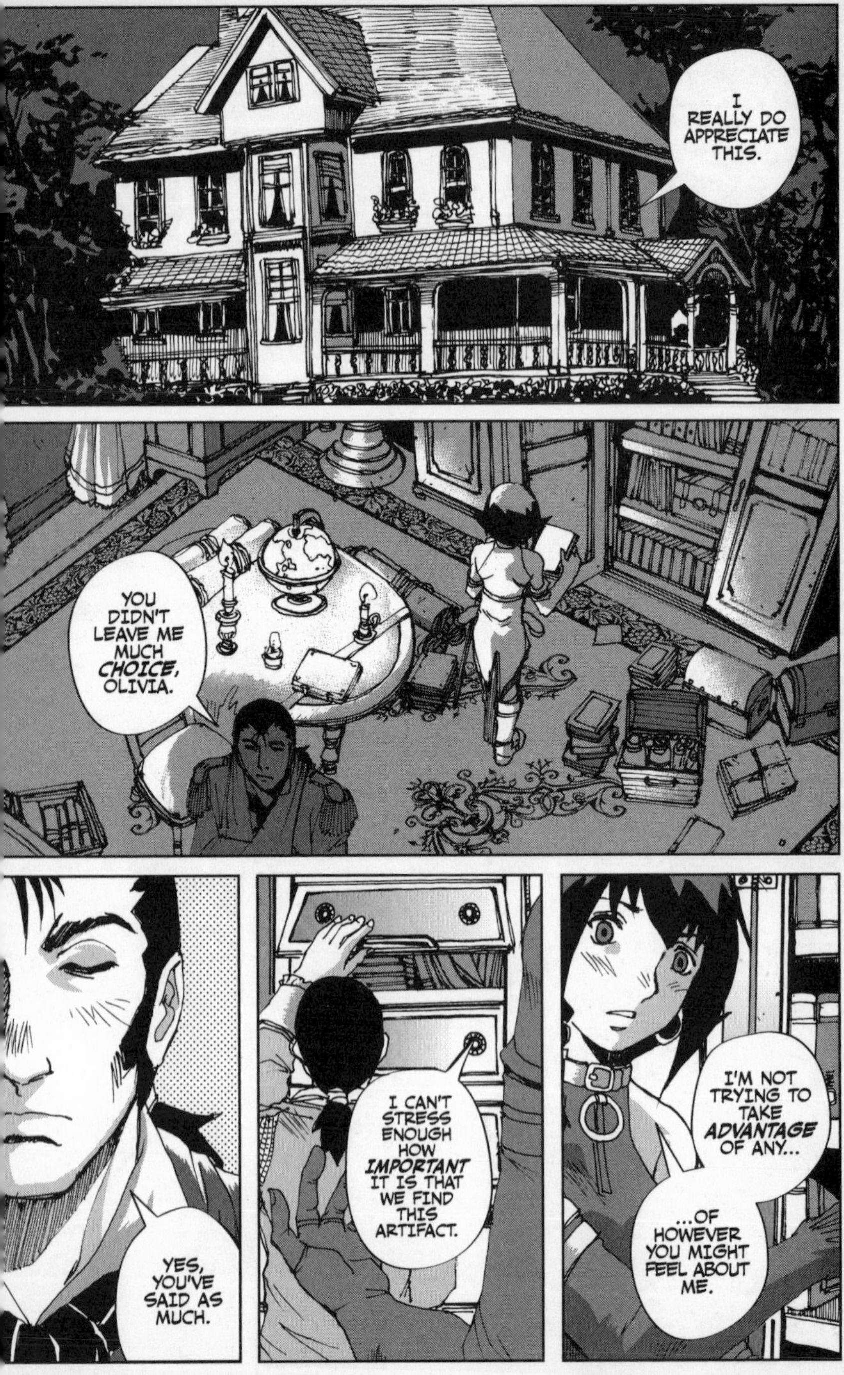
I REALLY DO APPRECIATE THIS.
YOU DIDN'T LEAVE ME MUCH *CHOICE*, OLIVIA.
I'M NOT TRYING TO TAKE *ADVANTAGE* OF ANY...
...OF HOWEVER YOU MIGHT FEEL ABOUT ME.
I CAN'T STRESS ENOUGH HOW *IMPORTANT* IT IS THAT WE FIND THIS ARTIFACT.
YES, YOU'VE SAID AS MUCH.

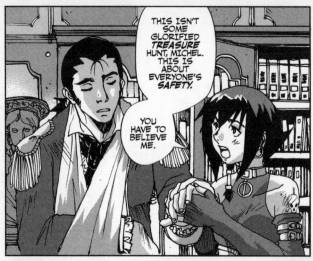

HEY...
THIS ISN'T SOME GLORIFIED *TREASURE* HUNT, MICHEL. THIS IS ABOUT EVERYONE'S *SAFETY.*
YOU HAVE TO BELIEVE ME.
I DO BELIEVE YOU.
MORE IMPORTANTLY, I BELIEVE *IN* YOU.
BUT WE HAVE TO *HURRY.*
MOTHER WILL BE HOME SOON.

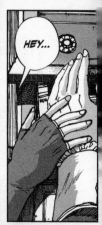

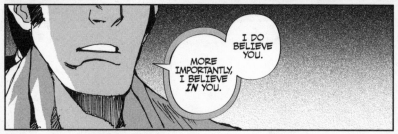

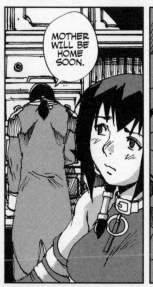

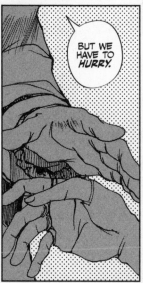

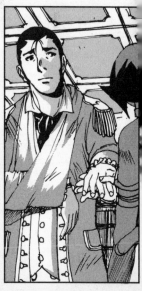

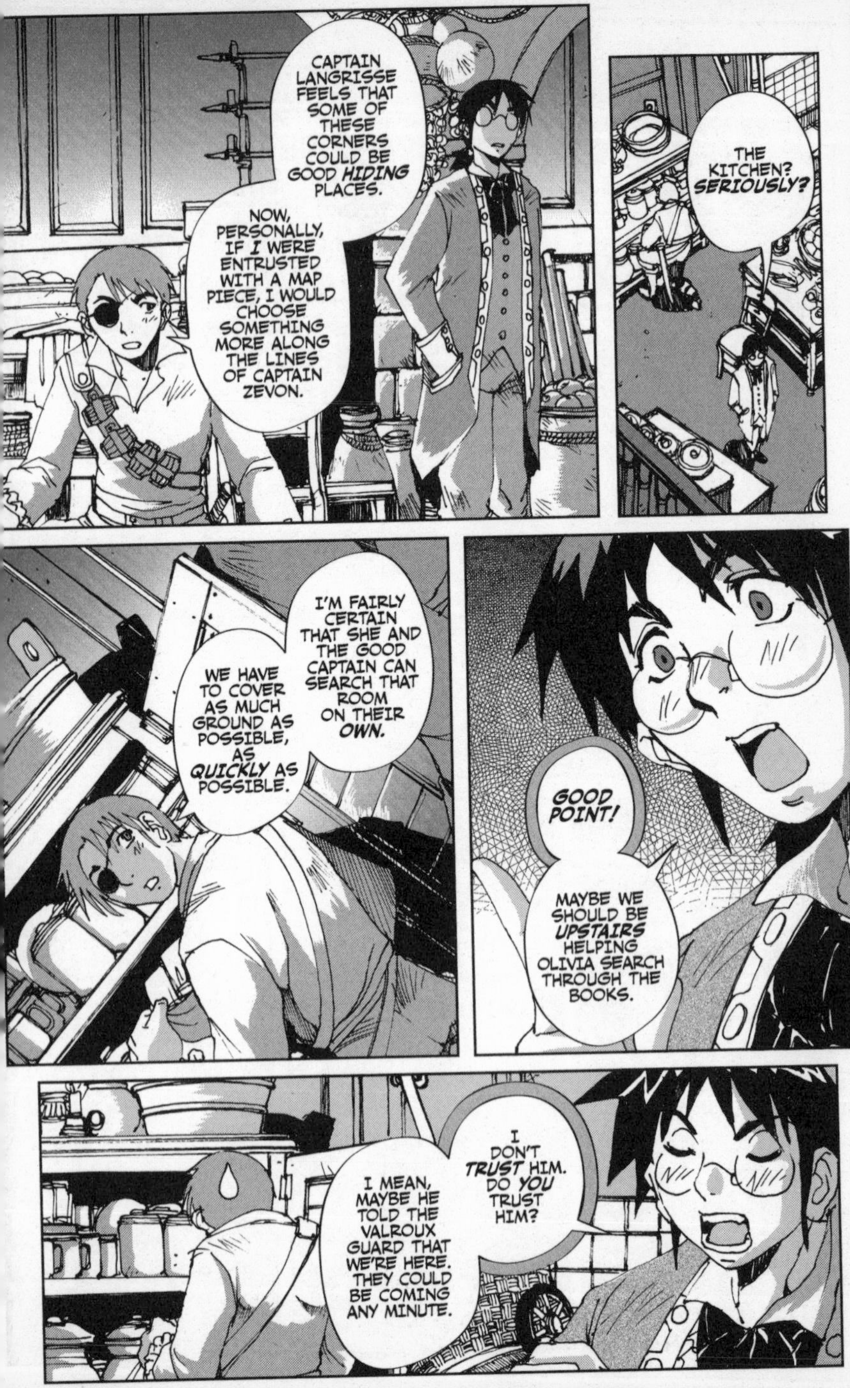
THE KITCHEN? SERIOUSLY?
CAPTAIN LANGRISSE FEELS THAT SOME OF THESE CORNERS COULD BE GOOD HIDING PLACES.
NOW, PERSONALLY, IF I WERE ENTRUSTED WITH A MAP PIECE, I WOULD CHOOSE SOMETHING MORE ALONG THE LINES OF CAPTAIN ZEVON.
GOOD POINT!
MAYBE WE SHOULD BE UPSTAIRS HELPING OLIVIA SEARCH THROUGH THE BOOKS.
I'M FAIRLY CERTAIN THAT SHE AND THE GOOD CAPTAIN CAN SEARCH THAT ROOM ON THEIR OWN.
WE HAVE TO COVER AS MUCH GROUND AS POSSIBLE, AS QUICKLY AS POSSIBLE.
I DON'T TRUST HIM. DO YOU TRUST HIM?
I MEAN, MAYBE HE TOLD THE VALROUX GUARD THAT WE'RE HERE. THEY COULD BE COMING ANY MINUTE.

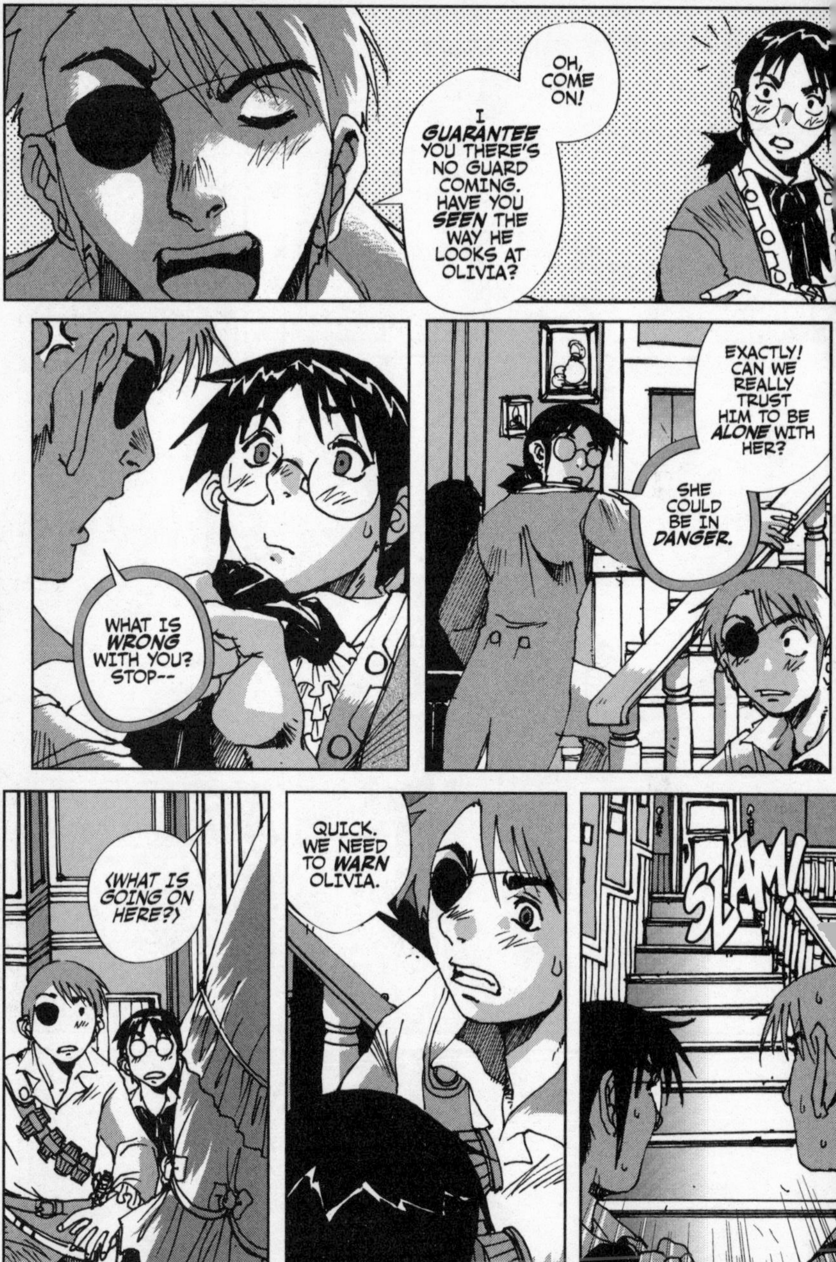
OH, COME ON!
I GUARANTEE YOU THERE'S NO GUARD COMING. HAVE YOU SEEN THE WAY HE LOOKS AT OLIVIA?
EXACTLY! CAN WE REALLY TRUST HIM TO BE ALONE WITH HER?
SHE COULD BE IN DANGER.
WHAT IS WRONG WITH YOU? STOP--
SLAM!
QUICK. WE NEED TO WARN OLIVIA.
<WHAT IS GOING ON HERE?>

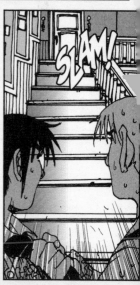

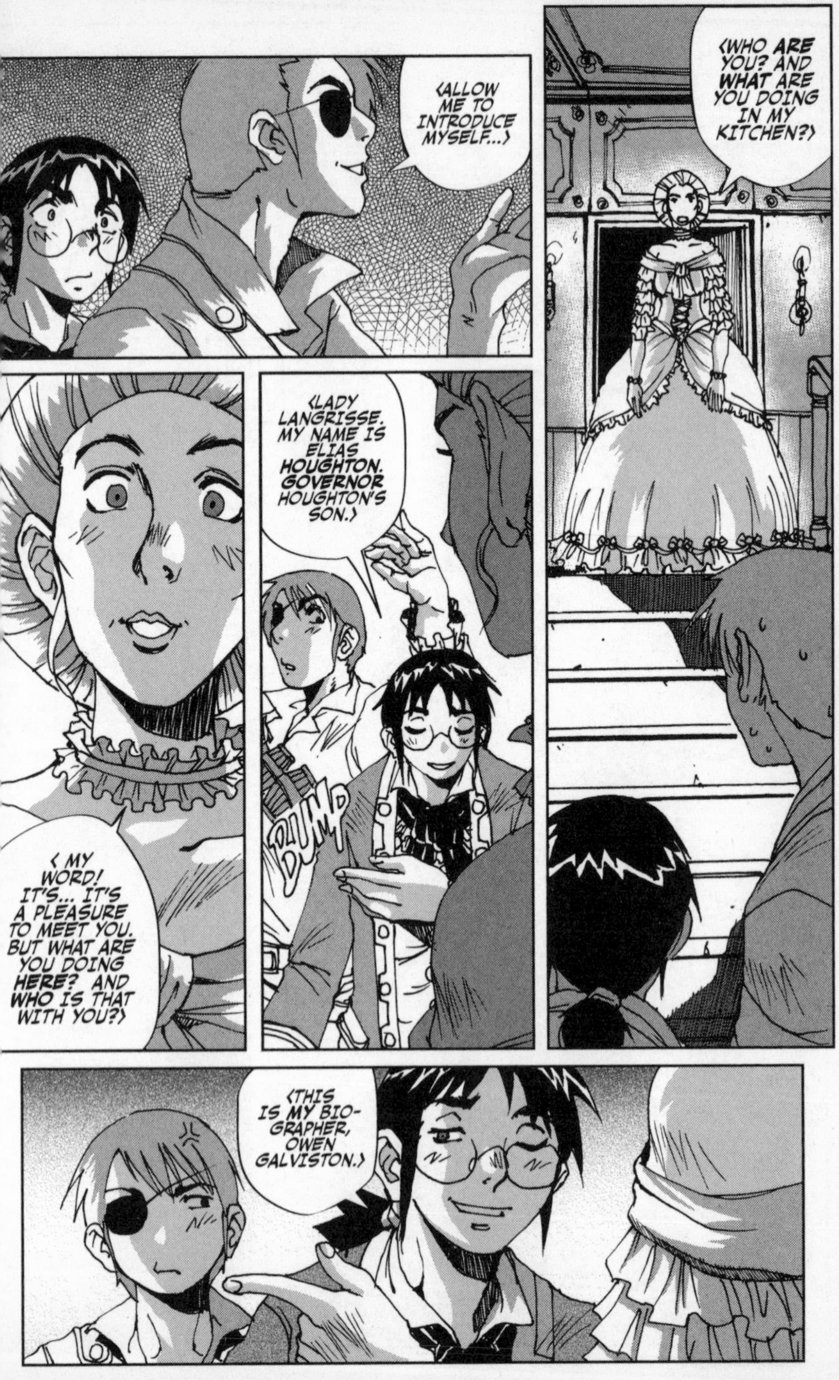

<WHO ARE YOU? AND WHAT ARE YOU DOING IN MY KITCHEN?>
<ALLOW ME TO INTRODUCE MYSELF...>
<LADY LANGRISSE. MY NAME IS ELIAS HOUGHTON. GOVERNOR HOUGHTON'S SON.>
BUMP
< MY WORD! IT'S... IT'S A PLEASURE TO MEET YOU. BUT WHAT ARE YOU DOING HERE? AND WHO IS THAT WITH YOU?>
<THIS IS MY BIO-GRAPHER, OWEN GALVISTON.>

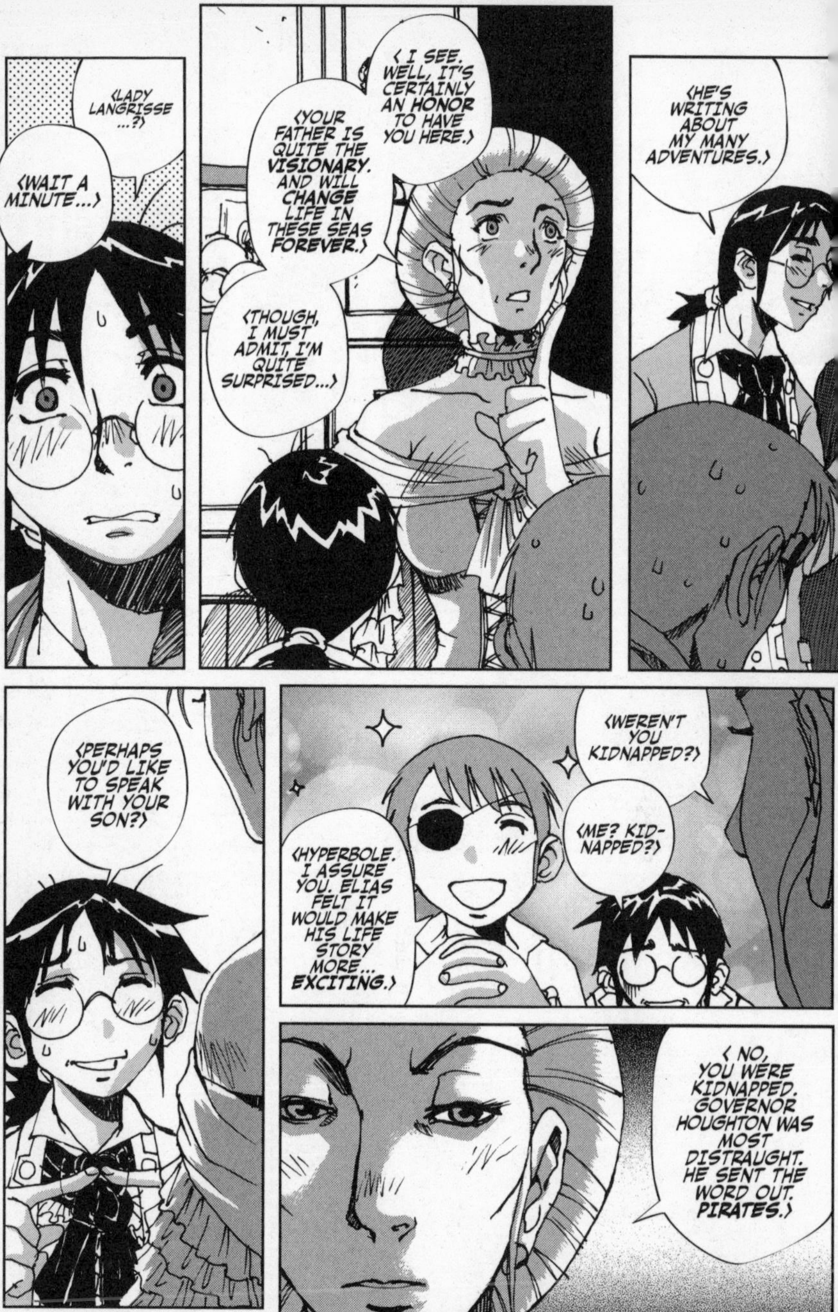
‹HE'S WRITING ABOUT MY MANY ADVENTURES.›
‹ I SEE. WELL, IT'S CERTAINLY AN **HONOR** TO HAVE YOU HERE.›
‹YOUR FATHER IS QUITE THE **VISIONARY.** AND WILL **CHANGE** LIFE IN THESE SEAS **FOREVER.**›
‹THOUGH, I MUST ADMIT, I'M QUITE SURPRISED...›
‹LADY LANGRISSE ...?›
‹WAIT A MINUTE...›
‹WEREN'T YOU KIDNAPPED?›
‹ME? KID-NAPPED?›
‹HYPERBOLE. I ASSURE YOU. ELIAS FELT IT WOULD MAKE HIS LIFE STORY MORE... **EXCITING.**›
‹ NO, YOU WERE KIDNAPPED. GOVERNOR HOUGHTON WAS MOST DISTRAUGHT. HE SENT THE WORD OUT. **PIRATES.**›
‹PERHAPS YOU'D LIKE TO SPEAK WITH YOUR SON?›

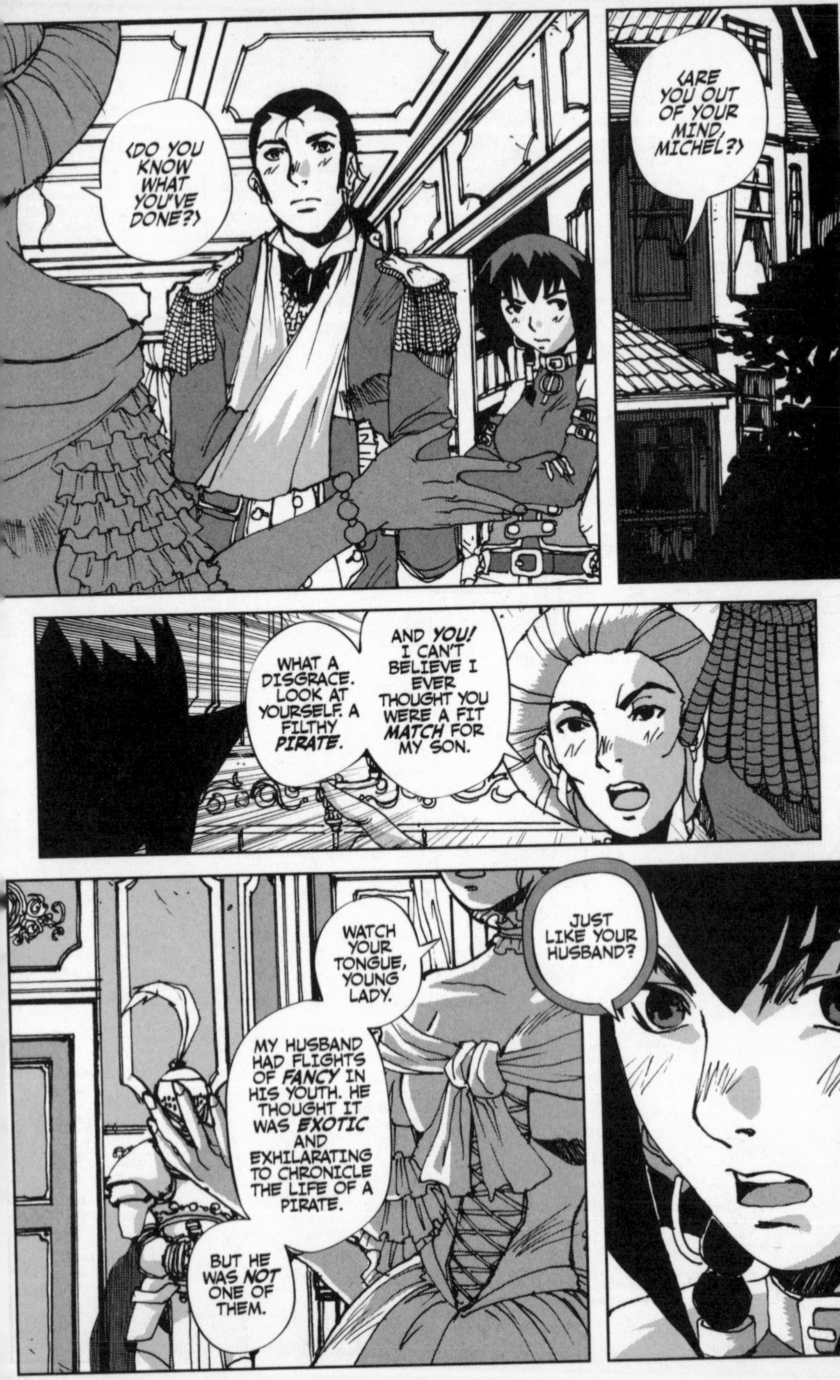
<ARE YOU OUT OF YOUR MIND, MICHEL?>
<DO YOU KNOW WHAT YOU'VE DONE?>
AND *YOU!* I CAN'T BELIEVE I EVER THOUGHT YOU WERE A FIT *MATCH* FOR MY SON.
WHAT A DISGRACE. LOOK AT YOURSELF. A FILTHY *PIRATE*.
JUST LIKE YOUR HUSBAND?
WATCH YOUR TONGUE, YOUNG LADY.
MY HUSBAND HAD FLIGHTS OF *FANCY* IN HIS YOUTH. HE THOUGHT IT WAS *EXOTIC* AND EXHILARATING TO CHRONICLE THE LIFE OF A PIRATE.
BUT HE WAS *NOT* ONE OF THEM.

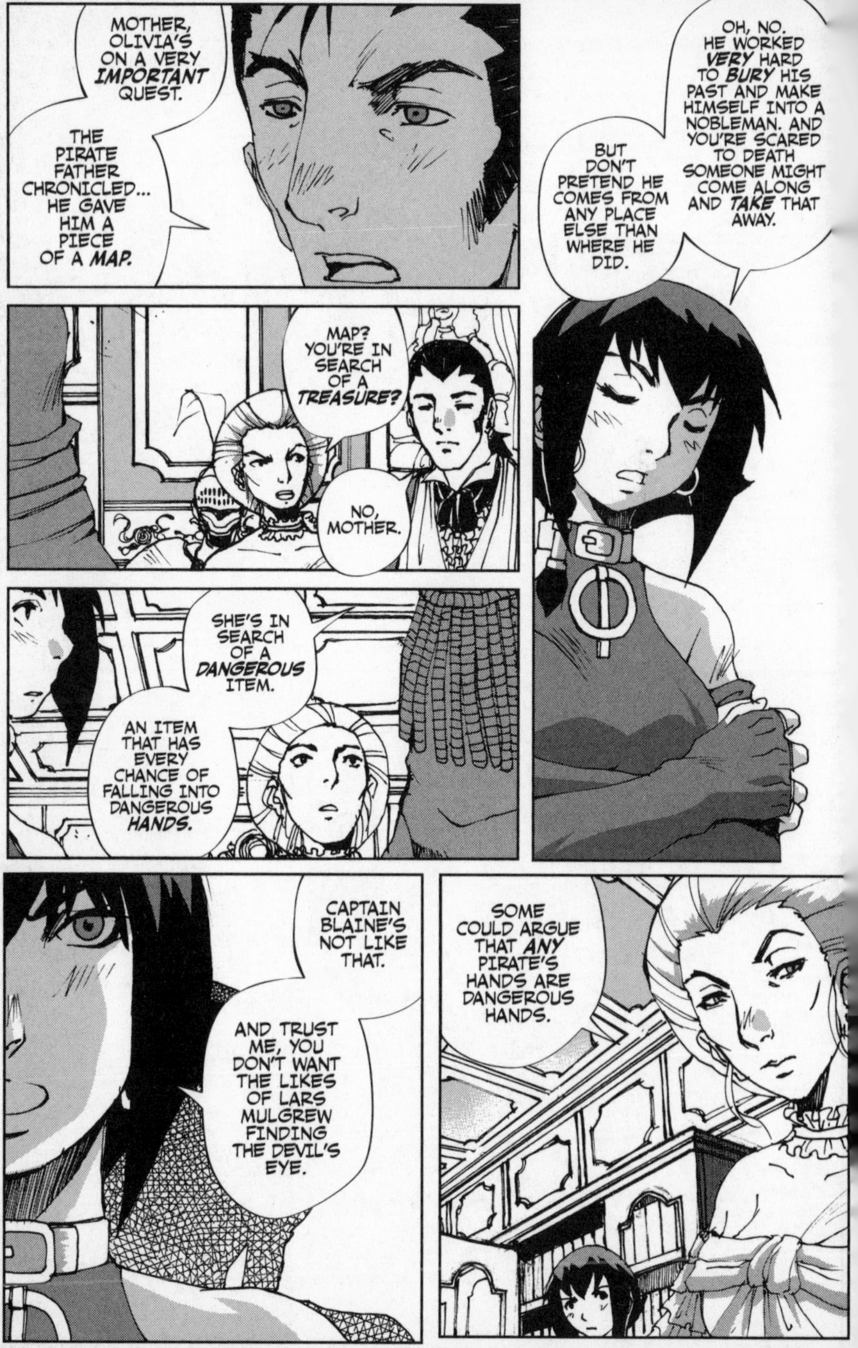
OH, NO. HE WORKED *VERY* HARD TO *BURY* HIS PAST AND MAKE HIMSELF INTO A NOBLEMAN. AND YOU'RE SCARED TO DEATH SOMEONE MIGHT COME ALONG AND *TAKE* THAT AWAY.
BUT DON'T PRETEND HE COMES FROM ANY PLACE ELSE THAN WHERE HE DID.
MOTHER, OLIVIA'S ON A VERY *IMPORTANT* QUEST.
THE PIRATE FATHER CHRONICLED... HE GAVE HIM A PIECE OF A *MAP.*
MAP? YOU'RE IN SEARCH OF A *TREASURE?*
NO, MOTHER.
SHE'S IN SEARCH OF A *DANGEROUS* ITEM.
AN ITEM THAT HAS EVERY CHANCE OF FALLING INTO DANGEROUS *HANDS.*
SOME COULD ARGUE THAT *ANY* PIRATE'S HANDS ARE DANGEROUS HANDS.
CAPTAIN BLAINE'S NOT LIKE THAT.
AND TRUST ME, YOU DON'T WANT THE LIKES OF LARS MULGREW FINDING THE DEVIL'S EYE.

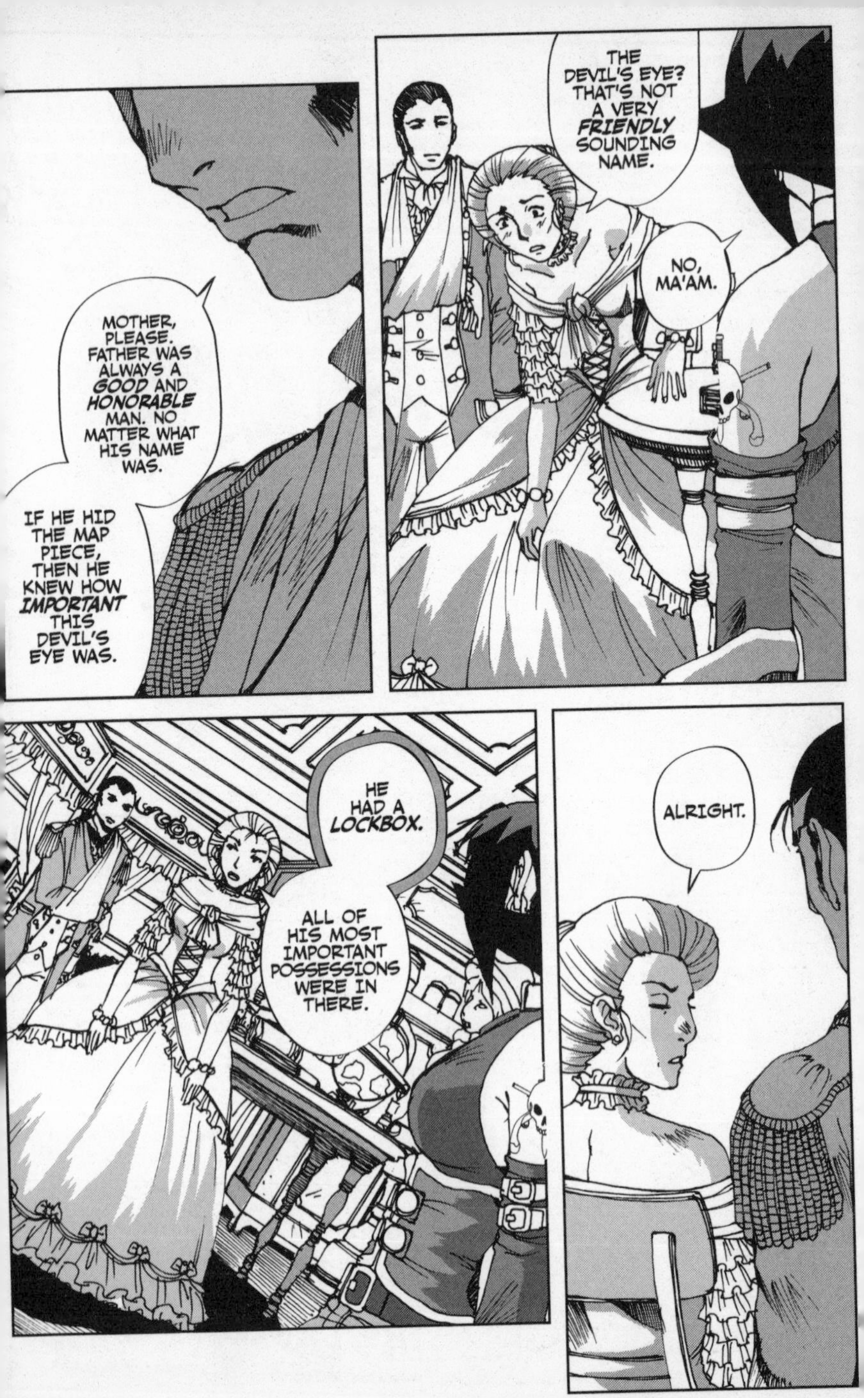
THE DEVIL'S EYE? THAT'S NOT A VERY *FRIENDLY* SOUNDING NAME.
NO, MA'AM.
MOTHER, PLEASE. FATHER WAS ALWAYS A *GOOD* AND *HONORABLE* MAN. NO MATTER WHAT HIS NAME WAS.
IF HE HID THE MAP PIECE, THEN HE KNEW HOW *IMPORTANT* THIS DEVIL'S EYE WAS.
ALRIGHT.
HE HAD A *LOCKBOX.*
ALL OF HIS MOST IMPORTANT POSSESSIONS WERE IN THERE.

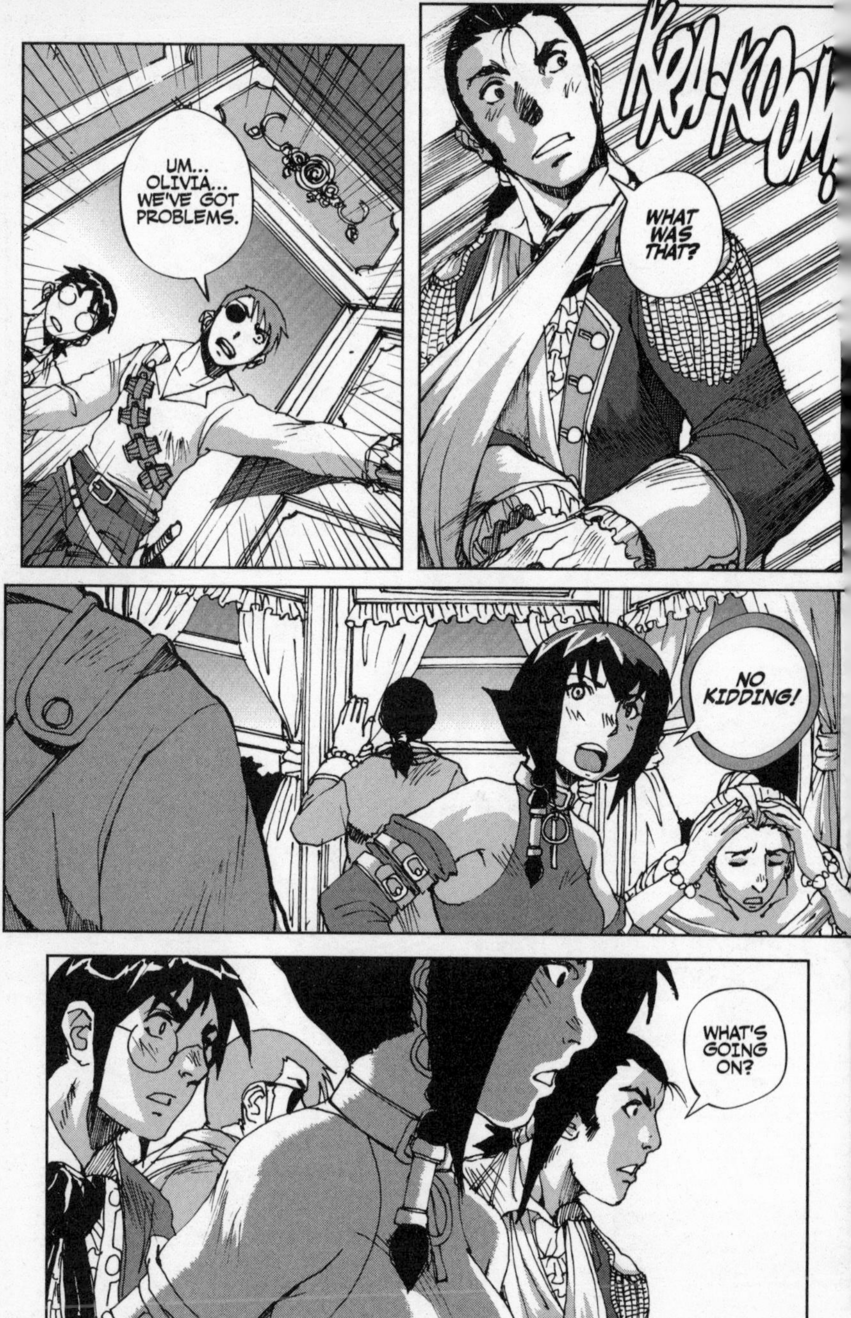
KRA-KOOM
WHAT WAS THAT?
UM... OLIVIA... WE'VE GOT PROBLEMS.
NO KIDDING!
WHAT'S GOING ON?

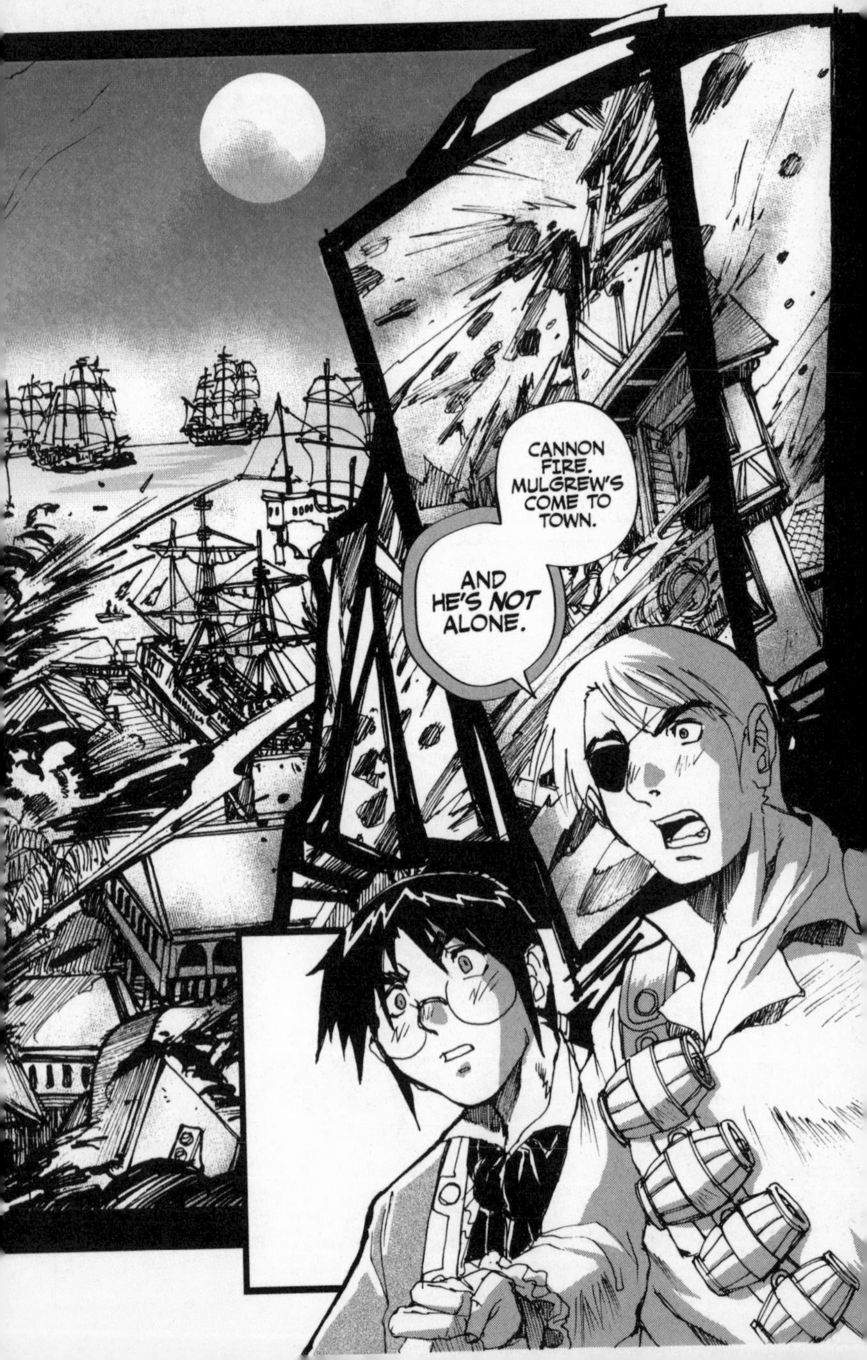
CANNON FIRE. MULGREW'S COME TO TOWN.
AND HE'S *NOT* ALONE.

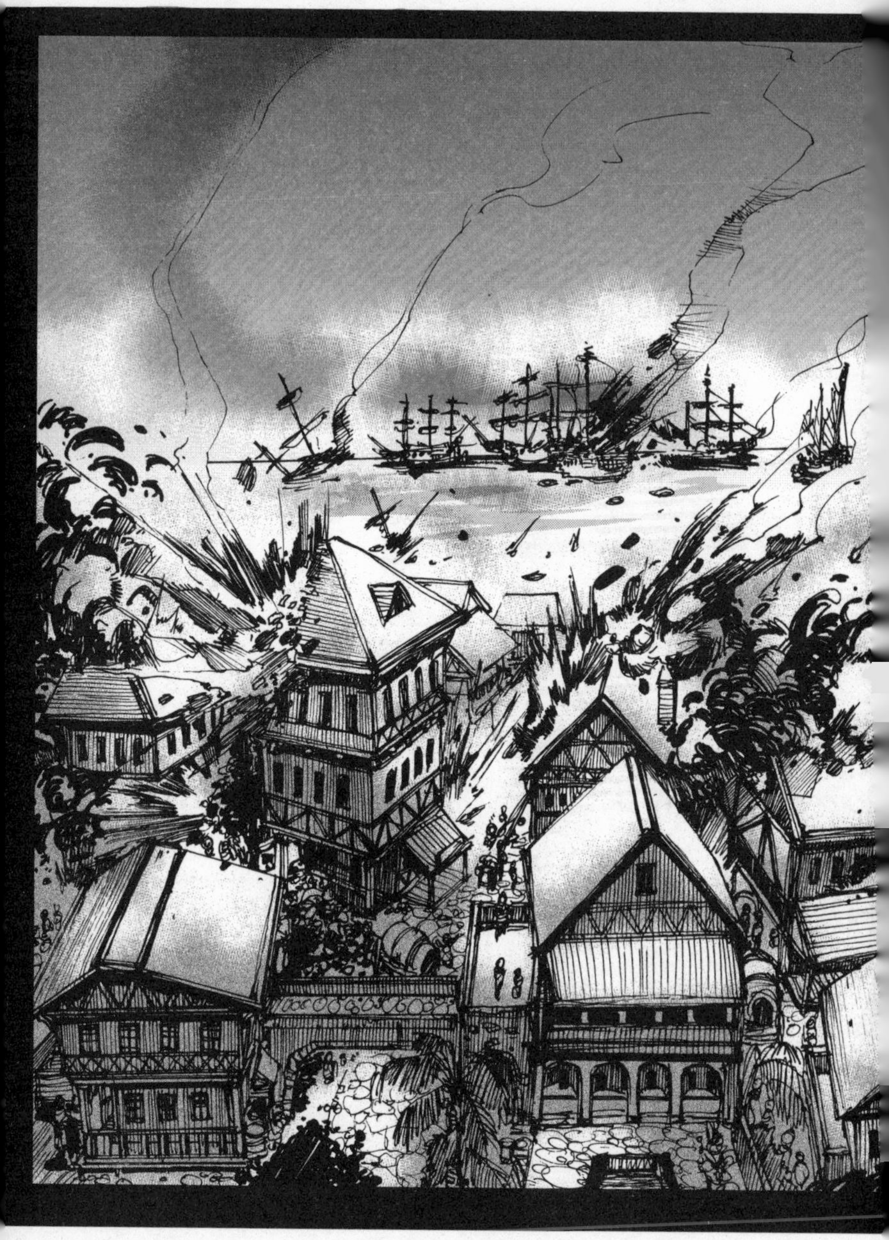

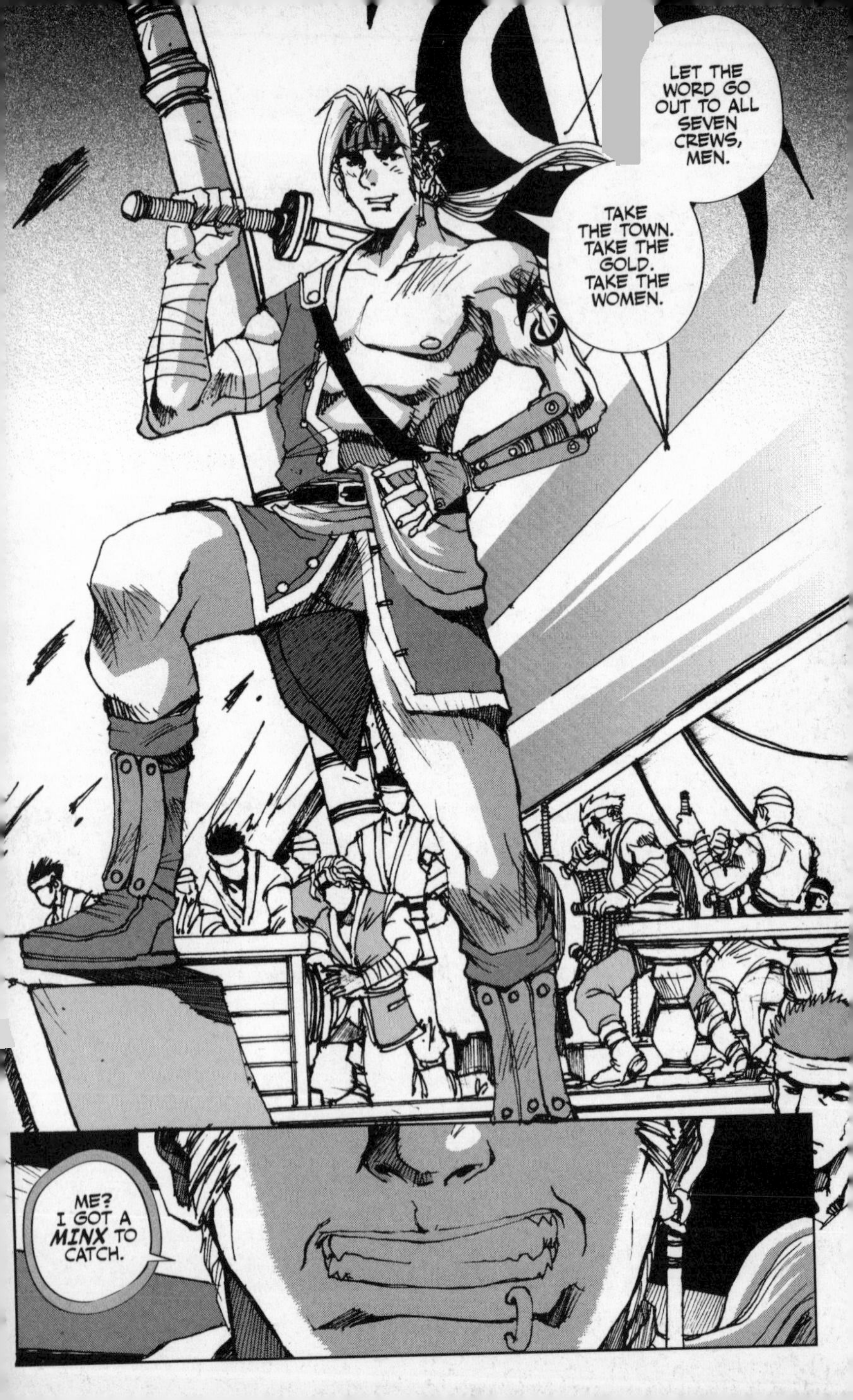
LET THE WORD GO OUT TO ALL SEVEN CREWS, MEN.
TAKE THE TOWN. TAKE THE GOLD. TAKE THE WOMEN.
ME? I GOT A MINX TO CATCH.

CHAPTER 10
Last Stand

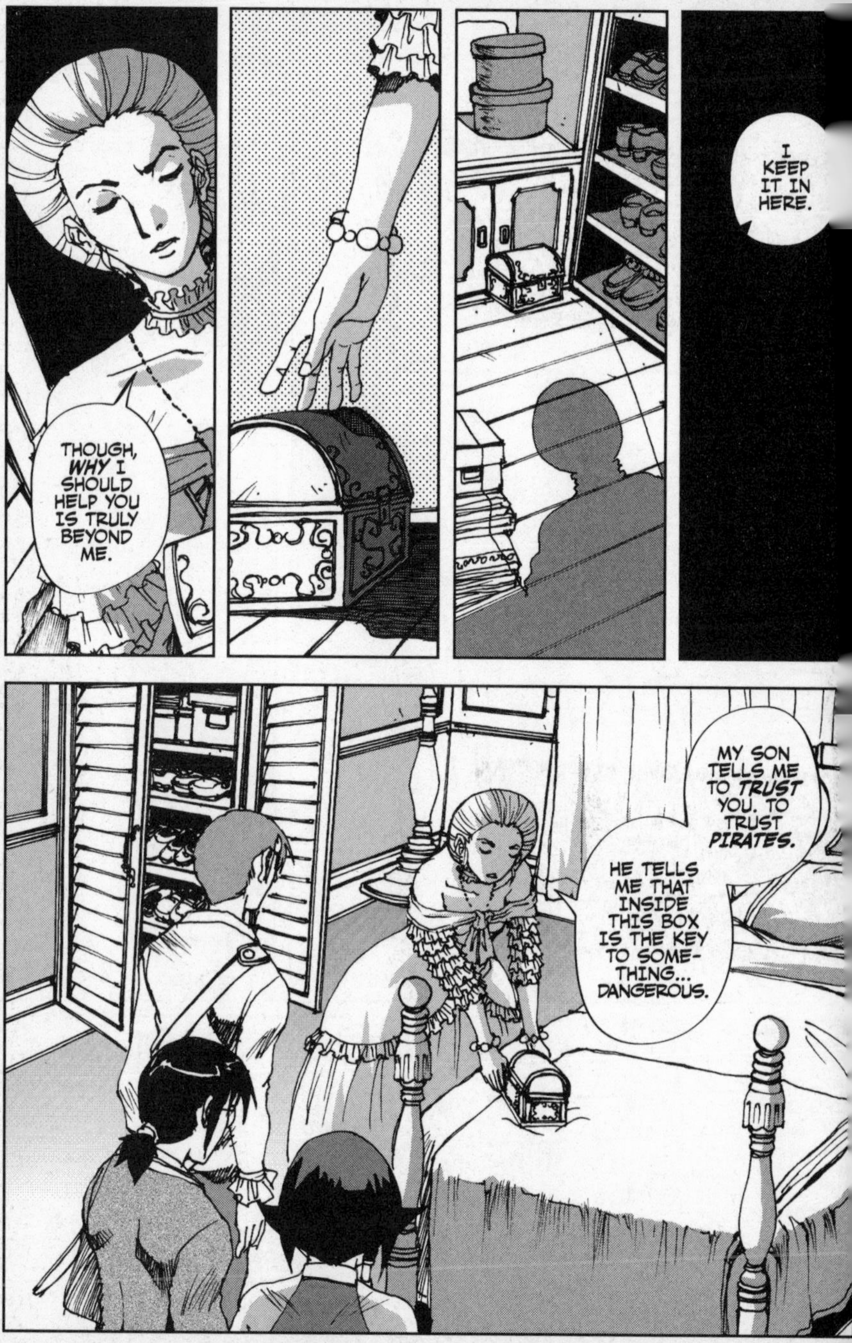
I KEEP IT IN HERE.
THOUGH, *WHY* I SHOULD HELP YOU IS TRULY BEYOND ME.
MY SON TELLS ME TO *TRUST* YOU. TO TRUST *PIRATES.*
HE TELLS ME THAT INSIDE THIS BOX IS THE KEY TO SOMETHING... DANGEROUS.

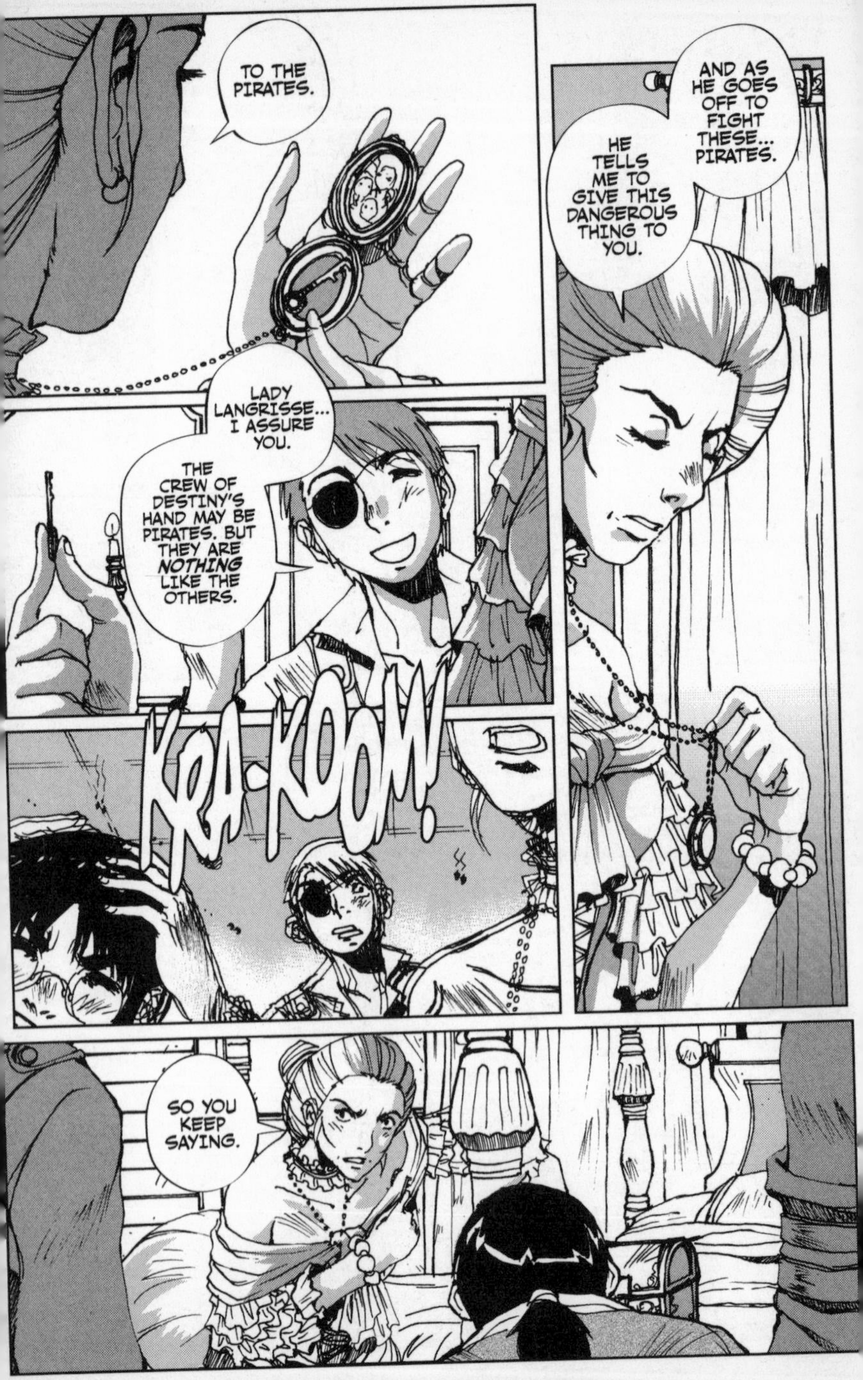
AND AS HE GOES OFF TO FIGHT THESE... PIRATES.
HE TELLS ME TO GIVE THIS DANGEROUS THING TO YOU.
TO THE PIRATES.
LADY LANGRISSE... I ASSURE YOU.
THE CREW OF DESTINY'S HAND MAY BE PIRATES. BUT THEY ARE *NOTHING* LIKE THE OTHERS.
KRA-KOOM!
SO YOU KEEP SAYING.

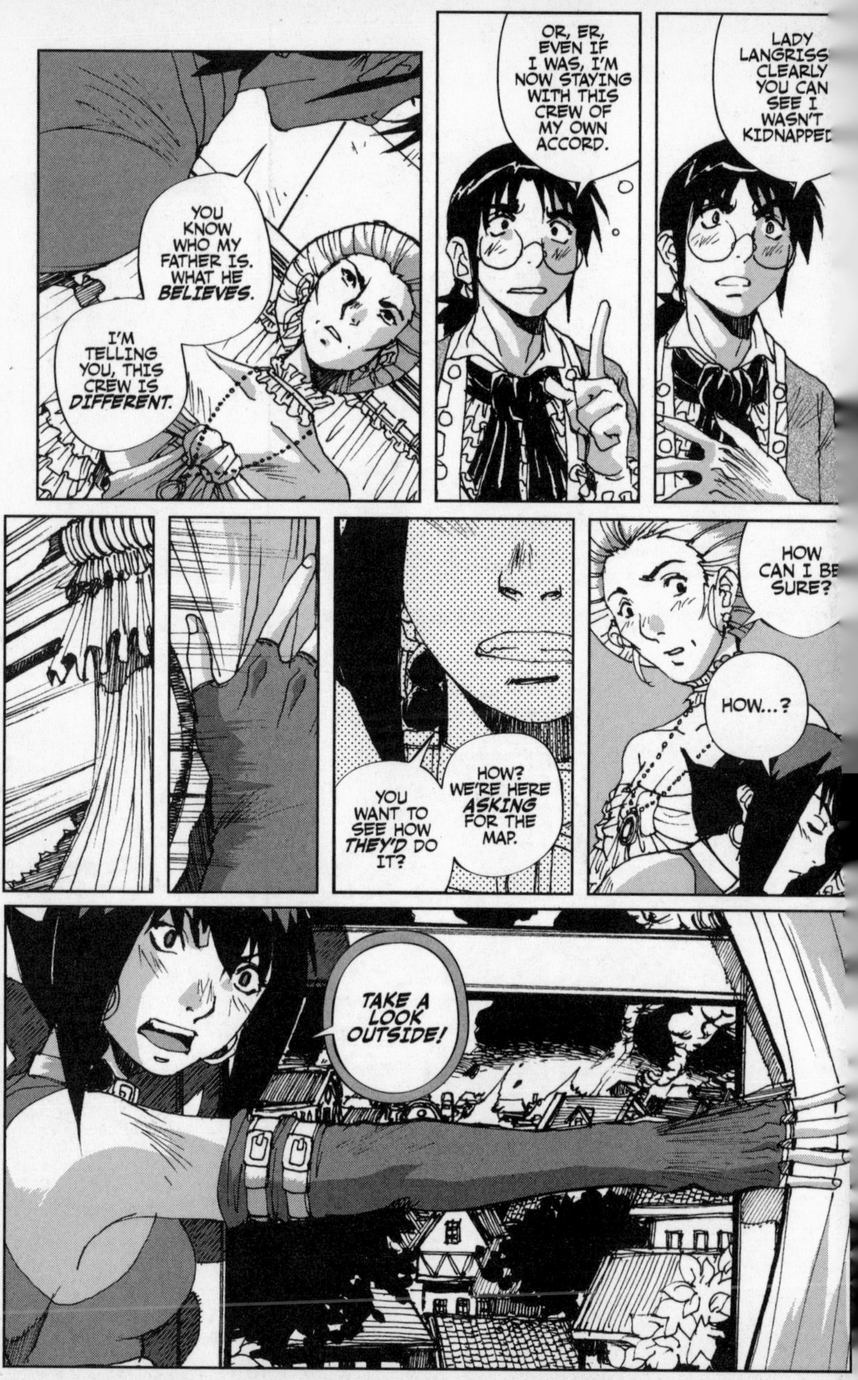
LADY LANGRISS CLEARLY YOU CAN SEE I WASN'T KIDNAPPED
OR, ER, EVEN IF I WAS, I'M NOW STAYING WITH THIS CREW OF MY OWN ACCORD.
YOU KNOW WHO MY FATHER IS. WHAT HE *BELIEVES*.
I'M TELLING YOU, THIS CREW IS *DIFFERENT*.
HOW CAN I BE SURE?
HOW...?
HOW? WE'RE HERE *ASKING* FOR THE MAP.
YOU WANT TO SEE HOW *THEY'D* DO IT?
TAKE A LOOK OUTSIDE!

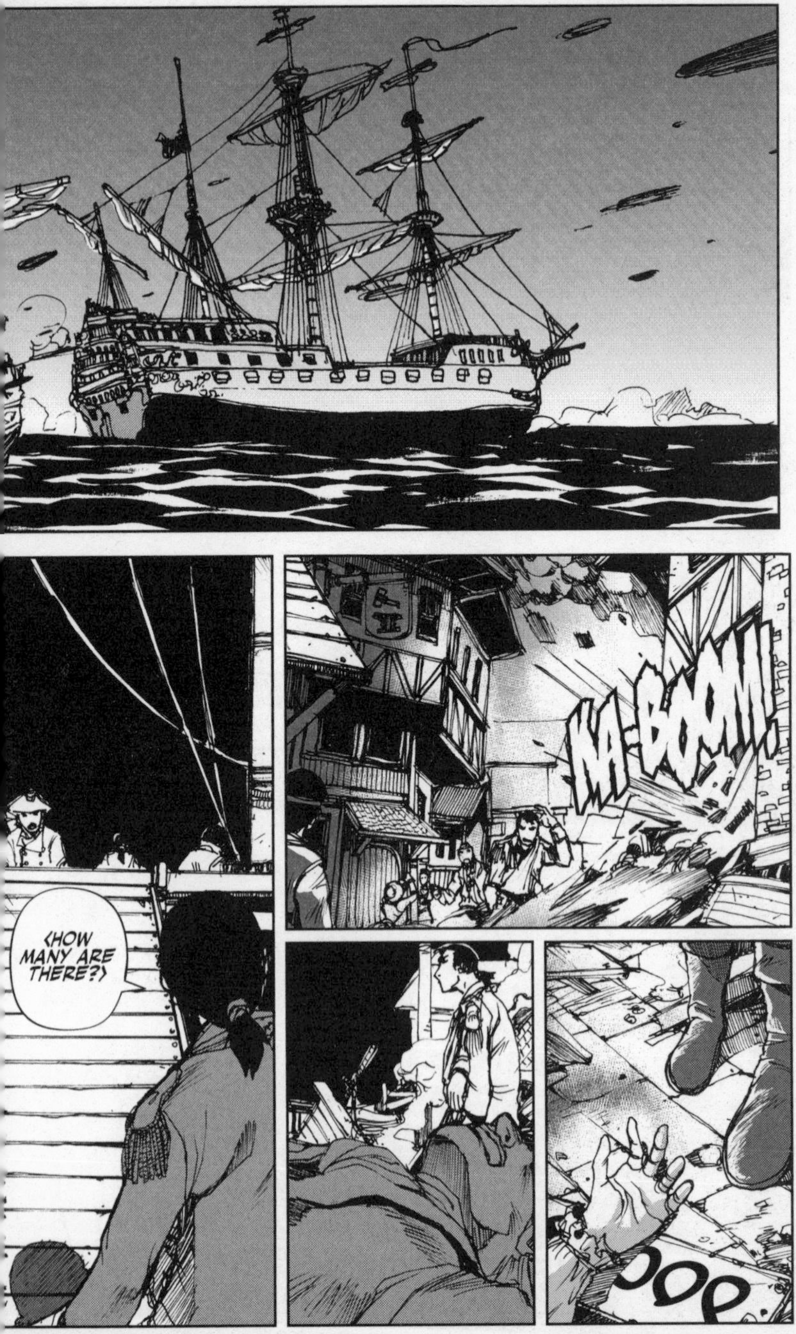
KA-BOOM!
<HOW MANY ARE THERE?>

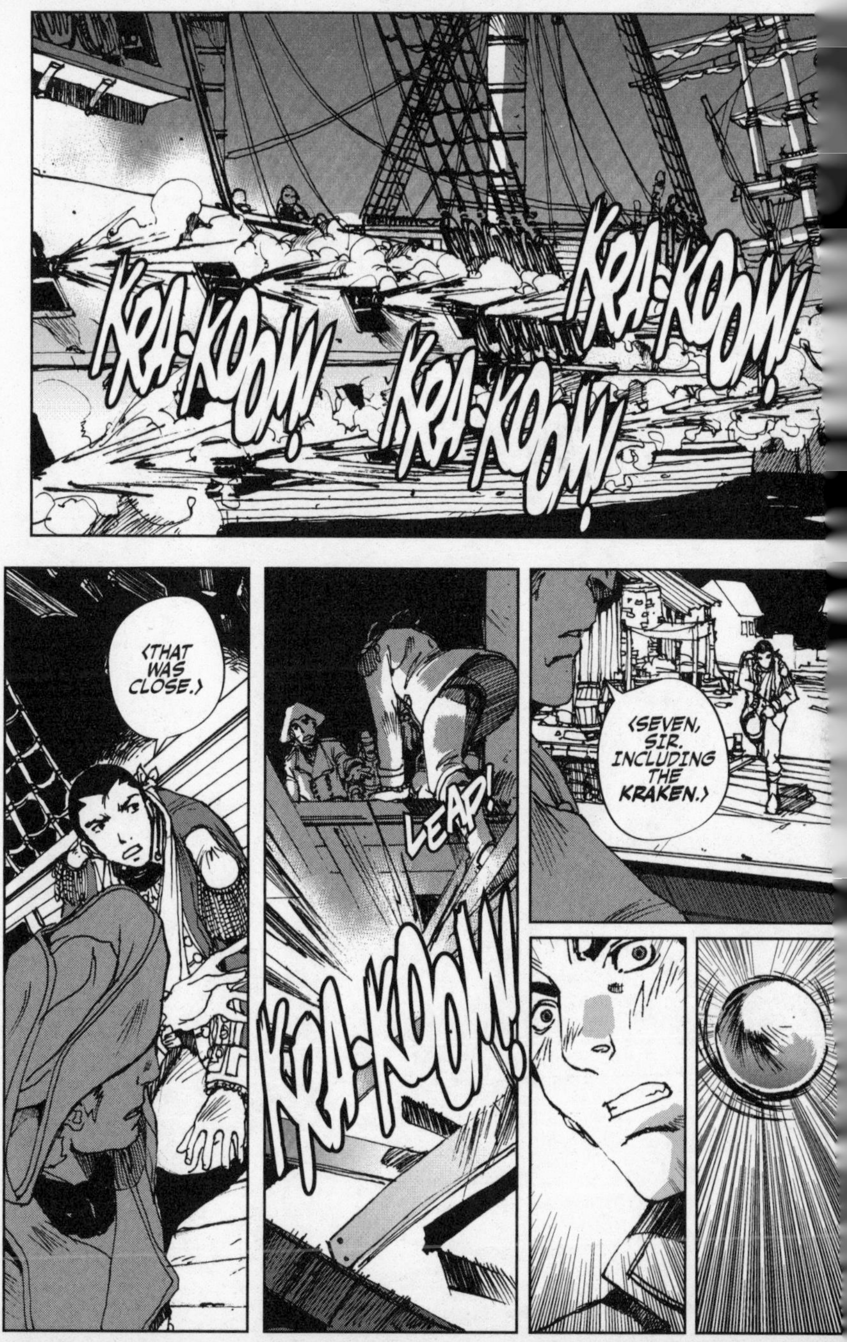
KRA-KOOM!
KRA-KOOM!
KRA-KOOM!
<SEVEN, SIR. INCLUDING THE KRAKEN.>
LEAP!
KRA-KOOM!
<THAT WAS CLOSE.>

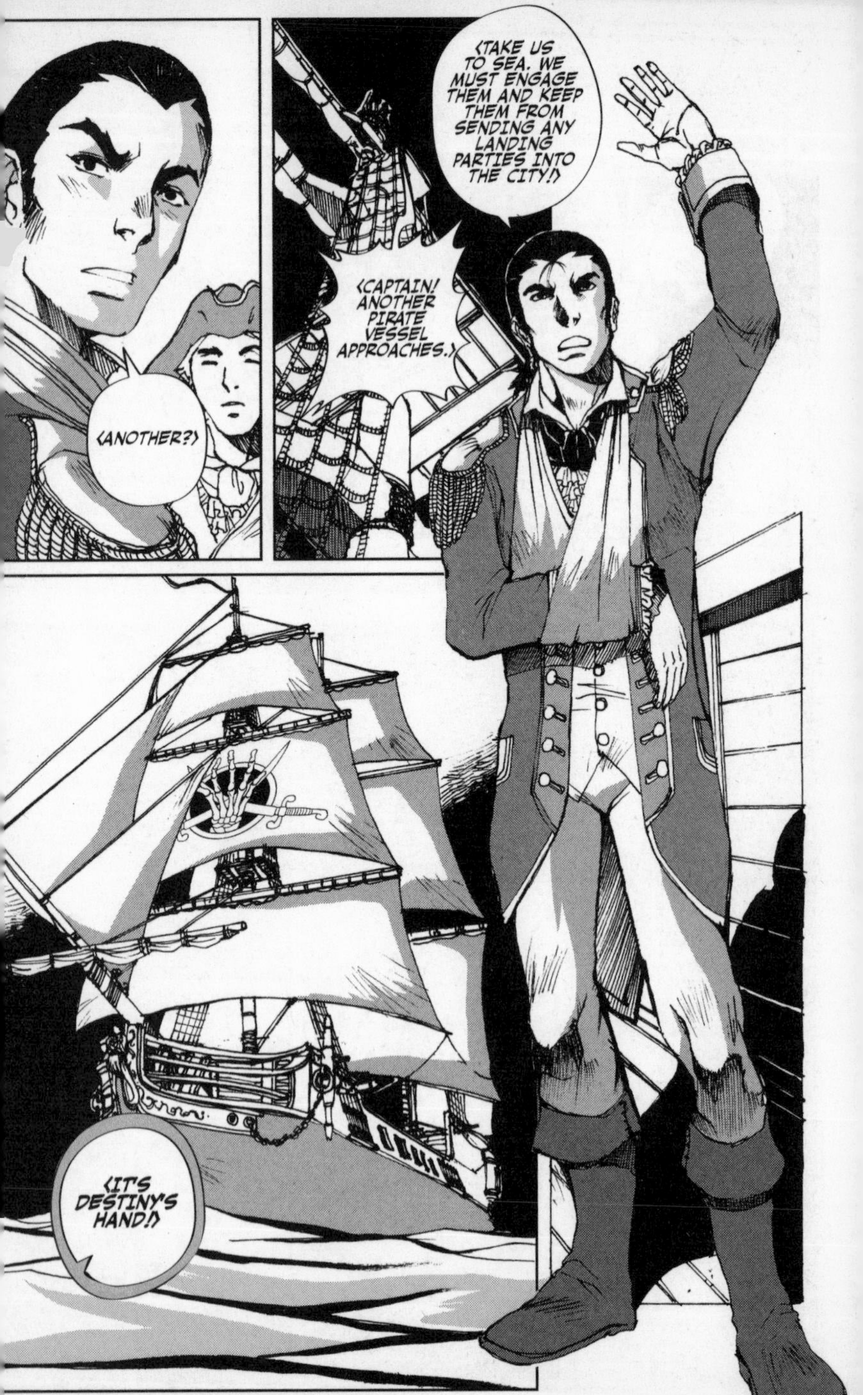
‹CAPTAIN! ANOTHER PIRATE VESSEL APPROACHES.›
‹ANOTHER?›
‹TAKE US TO SEA. WE MUST ENGAGE THEM AND KEEP THEM FROM SENDING ANY LANDING PARTIES INTO THE CITY!›
‹IT'S DESTINY'S HAND!›

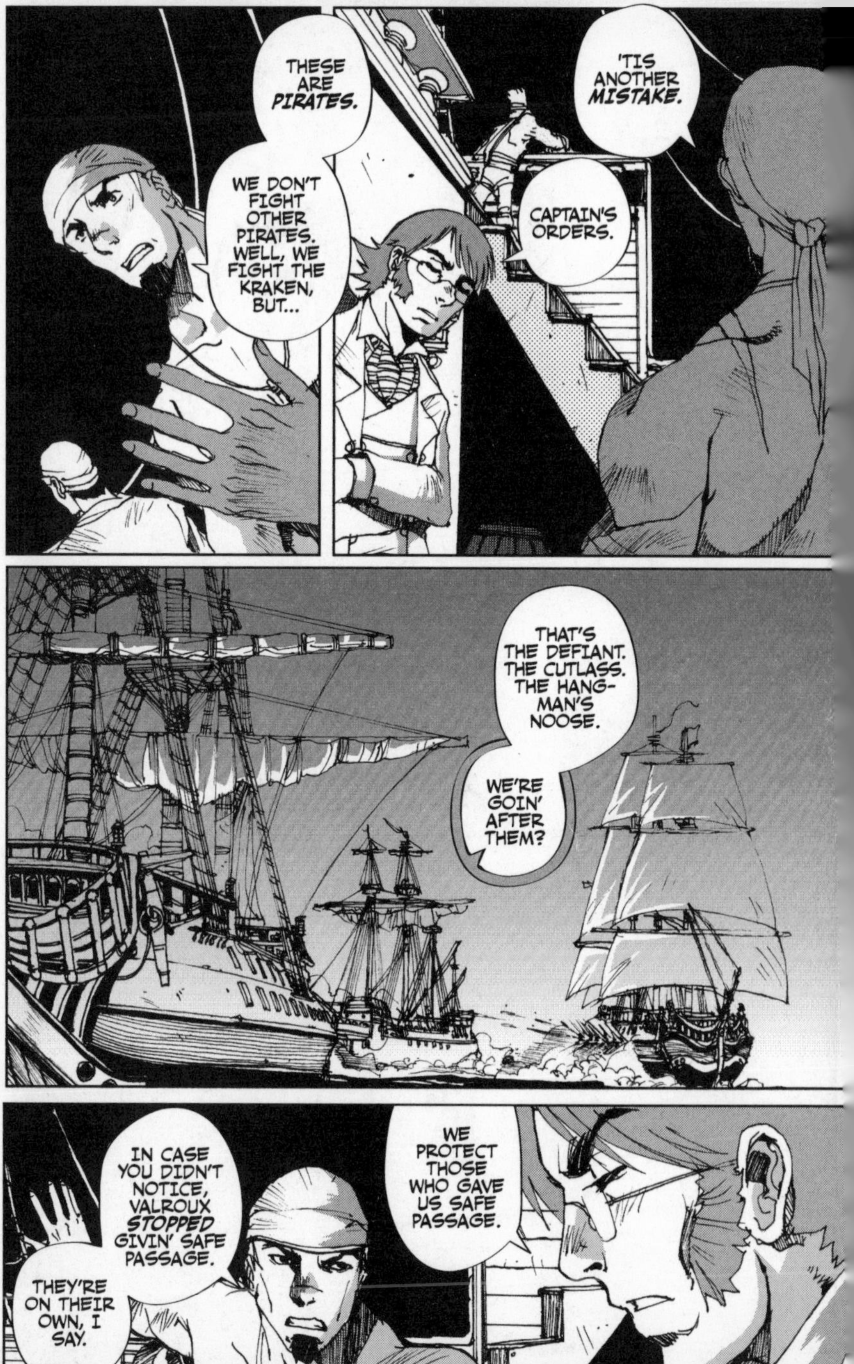
'TIS ANOTHER *MISTAKE.*
CAPTAIN'S ORDERS.
THESE ARE *PIRATES.*
WE DON'T FIGHT OTHER PIRATES. WELL, WE FIGHT THE KRAKEN, BUT...
THAT'S THE DEFIANT. THE CUTLASS. THE HANG-MAN'S NOOSE.
WE'RE GOIN' AFTER THEM?
WE PROTECT THOSE WHO GAVE US SAFE PASSAGE.
IN CASE YOU DIDN'T NOTICE, VALROUX *STOPPED* GIVIN' SAFE PASSAGE.
THEY'RE ON THEIR OWN, I SAY.

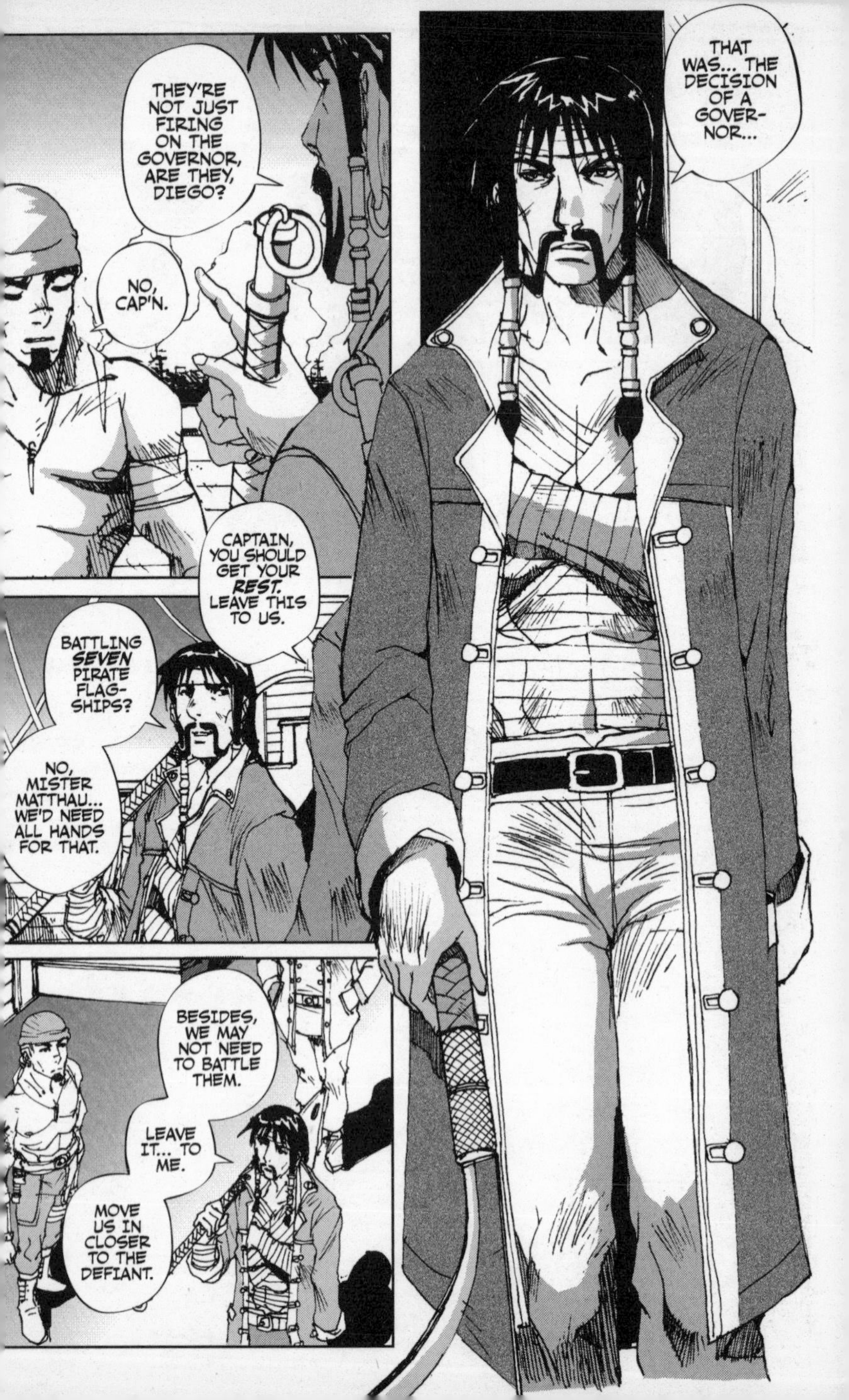
THAT WAS... THE DECISION OF A GOVERNOR...
THEY'RE NOT JUST FIRING ON THE GOVERNOR, ARE THEY, DIEGO?
NO, CAP'N.
CAPTAIN, YOU SHOULD GET YOUR *REST.* LEAVE THIS TO US.
BATTLING *SEVEN* PIRATE FLAGSHIPS?
NO, MISTER MATTHAU... WE'D NEED ALL HANDS FOR THAT.
BESIDES, WE MAY NOT NEED TO BATTLE THEM.
LEAVE IT... TO ME.
MOVE US IN CLOSER TO THE DEFIANT.

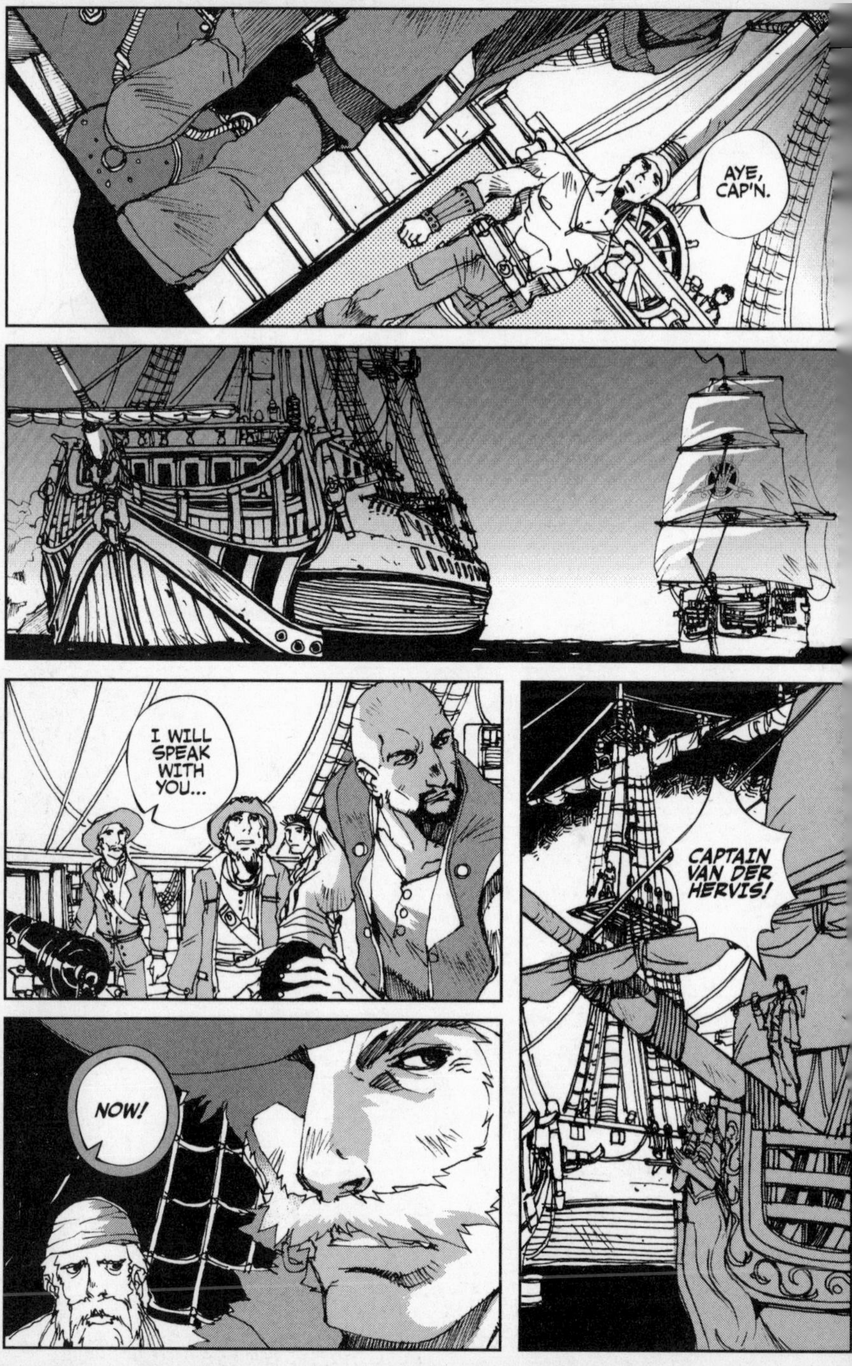
AYE, CAP'N.
CAPTAIN VAN DER HERVIS!
I WILL SPEAK WITH YOU...
NOW!

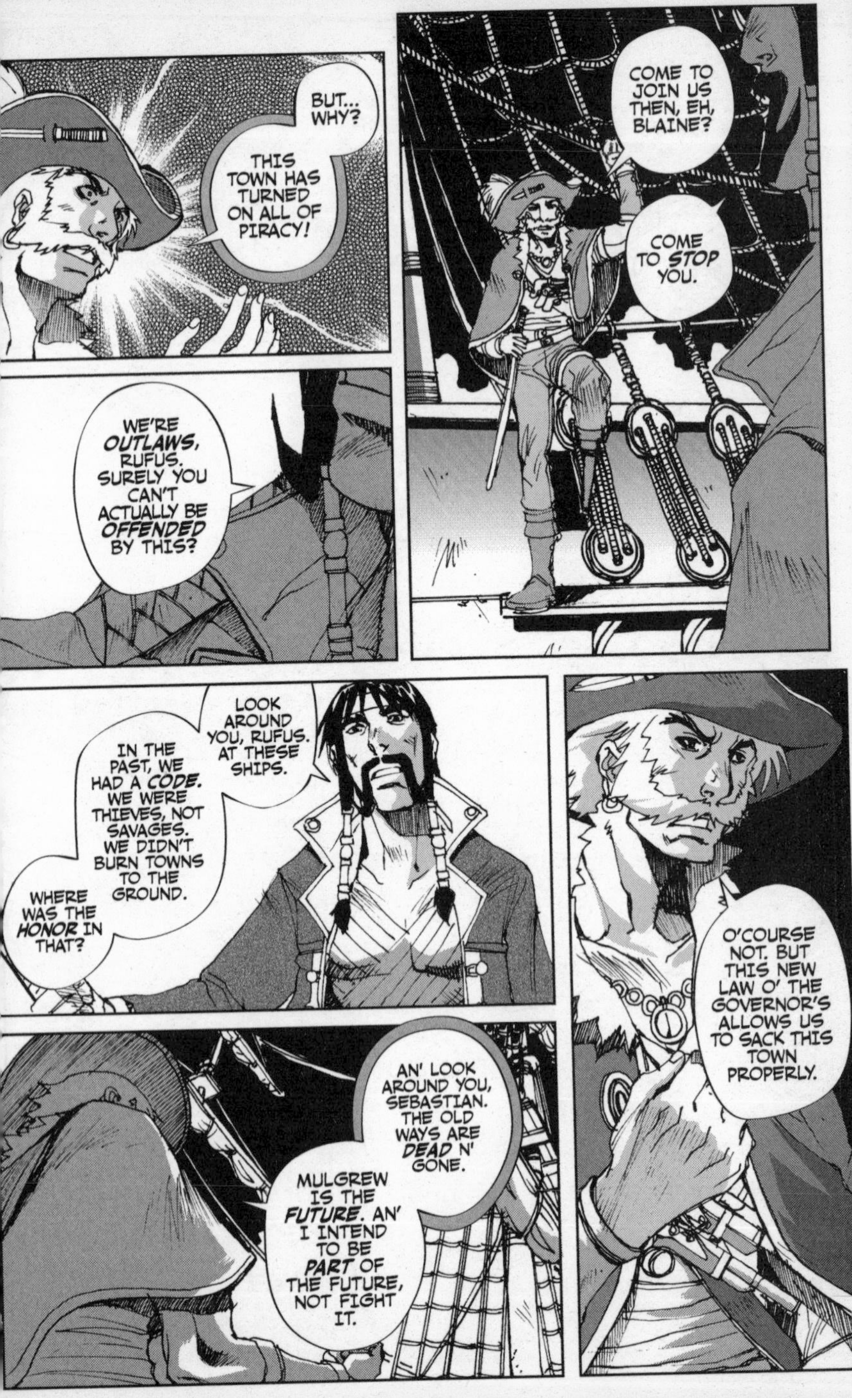
COME TO JOIN US THEN, EH, BLAINE?
COME TO STOP YOU.
BUT... WHY?
THIS TOWN HAS TURNED ON ALL OF PIRACY!
WE'RE OUTLAWS, RUFUS. SURELY YOU CAN'T ACTUALLY BE OFFENDED BY THIS?
O'COURSE NOT. BUT THIS NEW LAW O' THE GOVERNOR'S ALLOWS US TO SACK THIS TOWN PROPERLY.
LOOK AROUND YOU, RUFUS. AT THESE SHIPS.
IN THE PAST, WE HAD A CODE. WE WERE THIEVES, NOT SAVAGES. WE DIDN'T BURN TOWNS TO THE GROUND.
WHERE WAS THE HONOR IN THAT?
AN' LOOK AROUND YOU, SEBASTIAN. THE OLD WAYS ARE DEAD N' GONE.
MULGREW IS THE FUTURE. AN' I INTEND TO BE PART OF THE FUTURE, NOT FIGHT IT.

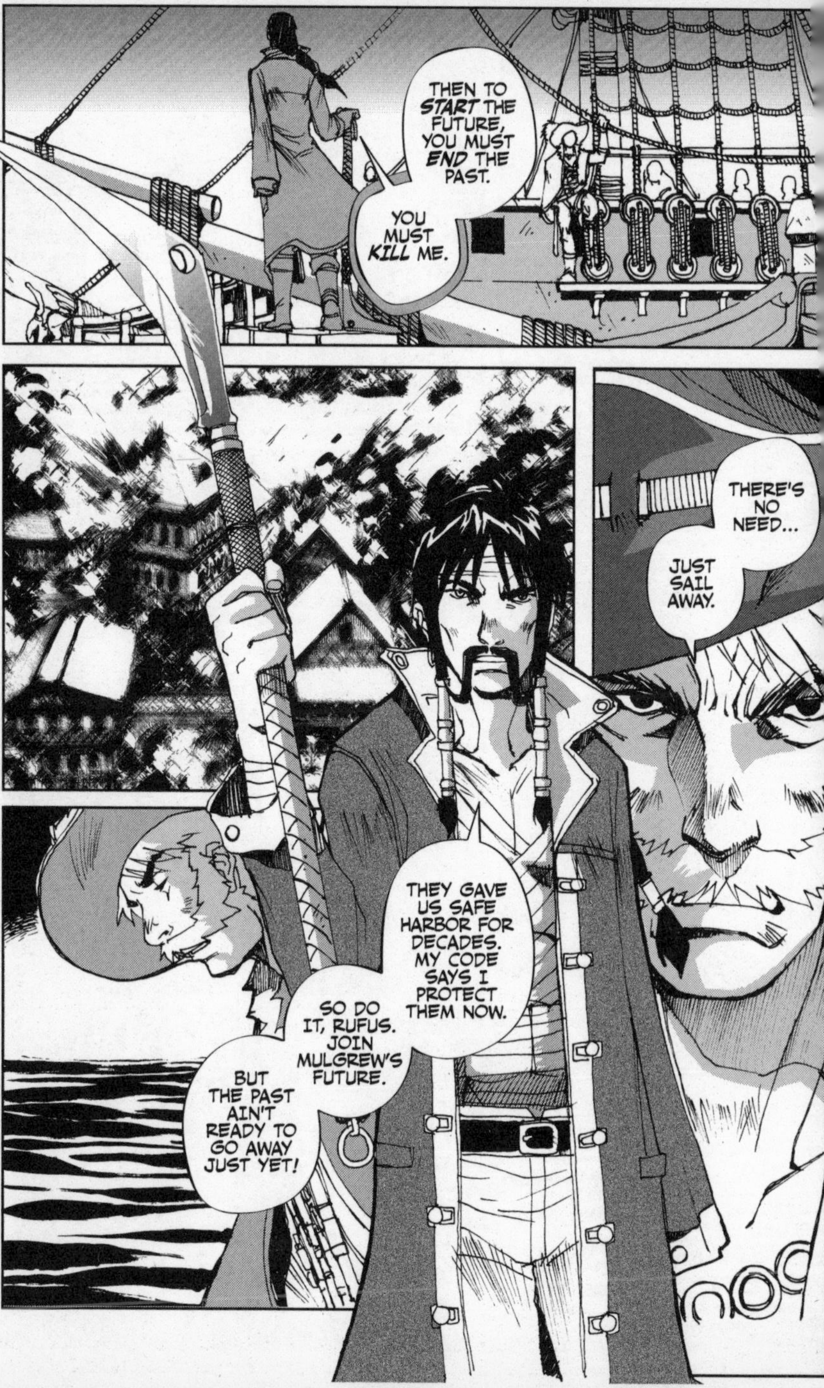
THEN TO START THE FUTURE, YOU MUST END THE PAST.
YOU MUST KILL ME.
THERE'S NO NEED...
JUST SAIL AWAY.
THEY GAVE US SAFE HARBOR FOR DECADES. MY CODE SAYS I PROTECT THEM NOW.
SO DO IT, RUFUS. JOIN MULGREW'S FUTURE.
BUT THE PAST AIN'T READY TO GO AWAY JUST YET!

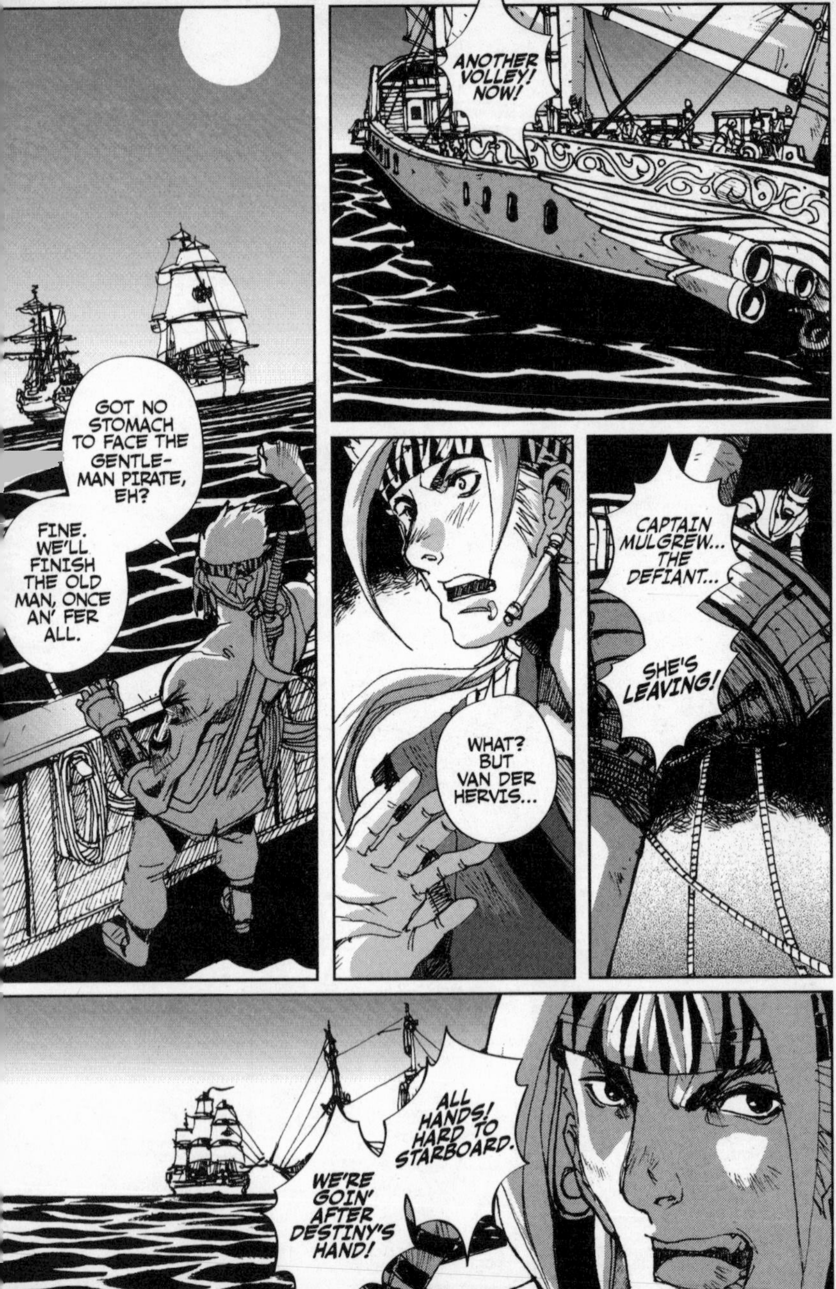
ANOTHER VOLLEY! NOW!
CAPTAIN MULGREW... THE DEFIANT...
SHE'S LEAVING!
WHAT? BUT VAN DER HERVIS...
GOT NO STOMACH TO FACE THE GENTLE-MAN PIRATE, EH?
FINE. WE'LL FINISH THE OLD MAN, ONCE AN' FER ALL.
ALL HANDS! HARD TO STARBOARD.
WE'RE GOIN' AFTER DESTINY'S HAND!

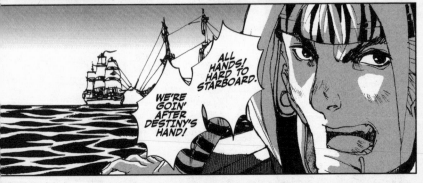

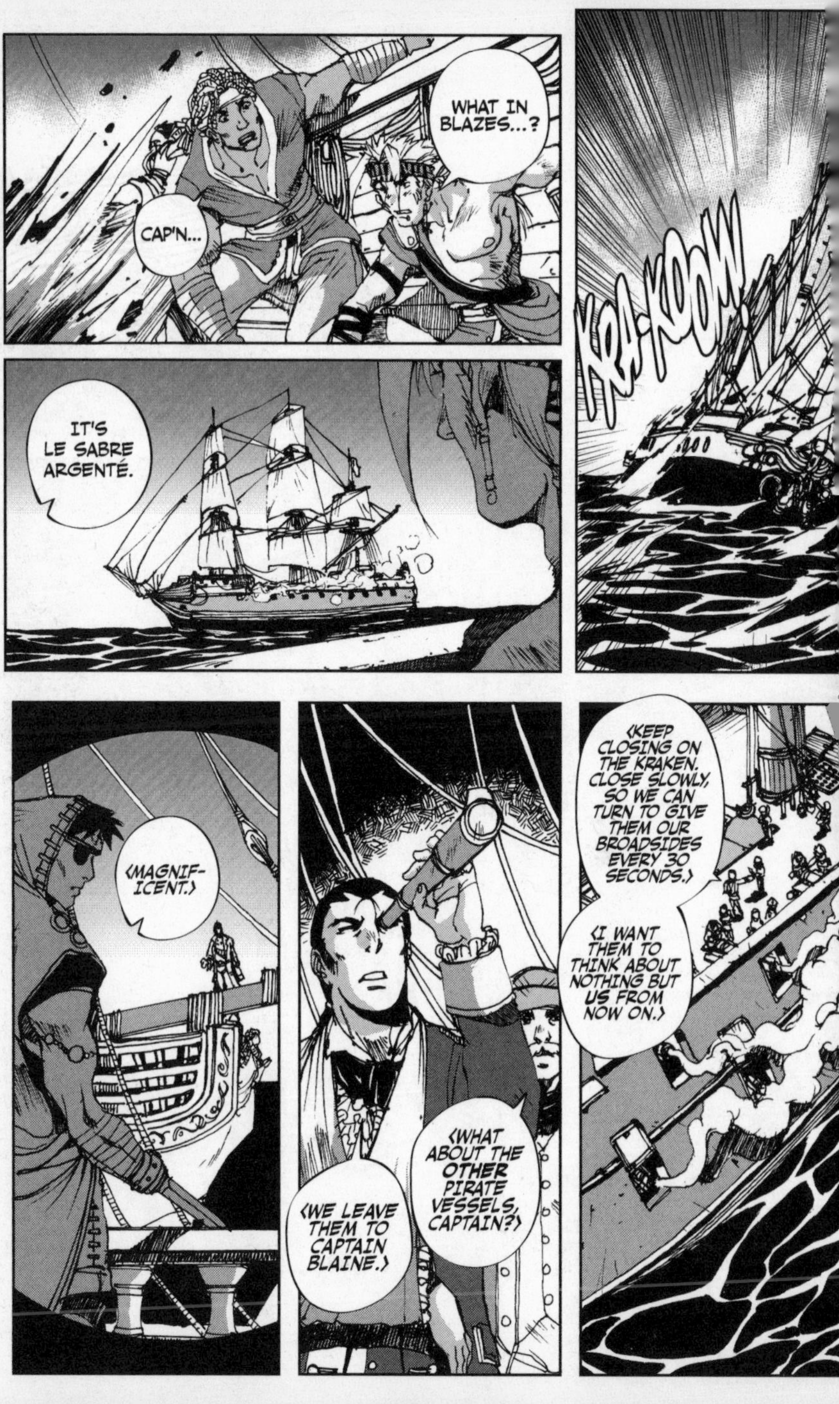
KRA-KOOM
WHAT IN BLAZES...?
CAP'N...
IT'S LE SABRE ARGENTÉ.
‹KEEP CLOSING ON THE KRAKEN. CLOSE SLOWLY, SO WE CAN TURN TO GIVE THEM OUR BROADSIDES EVERY 30 SECONDS.›
‹I WANT THEM TO THINK ABOUT NOTHING BUT US FROM NOW ON.›
‹WHAT ABOUT THE OTHER PIRATE VESSELS, CAPTAIN?›
‹WE LEAVE THEM TO CAPTAIN BLAINE.›
‹MAGNIFICENT.›

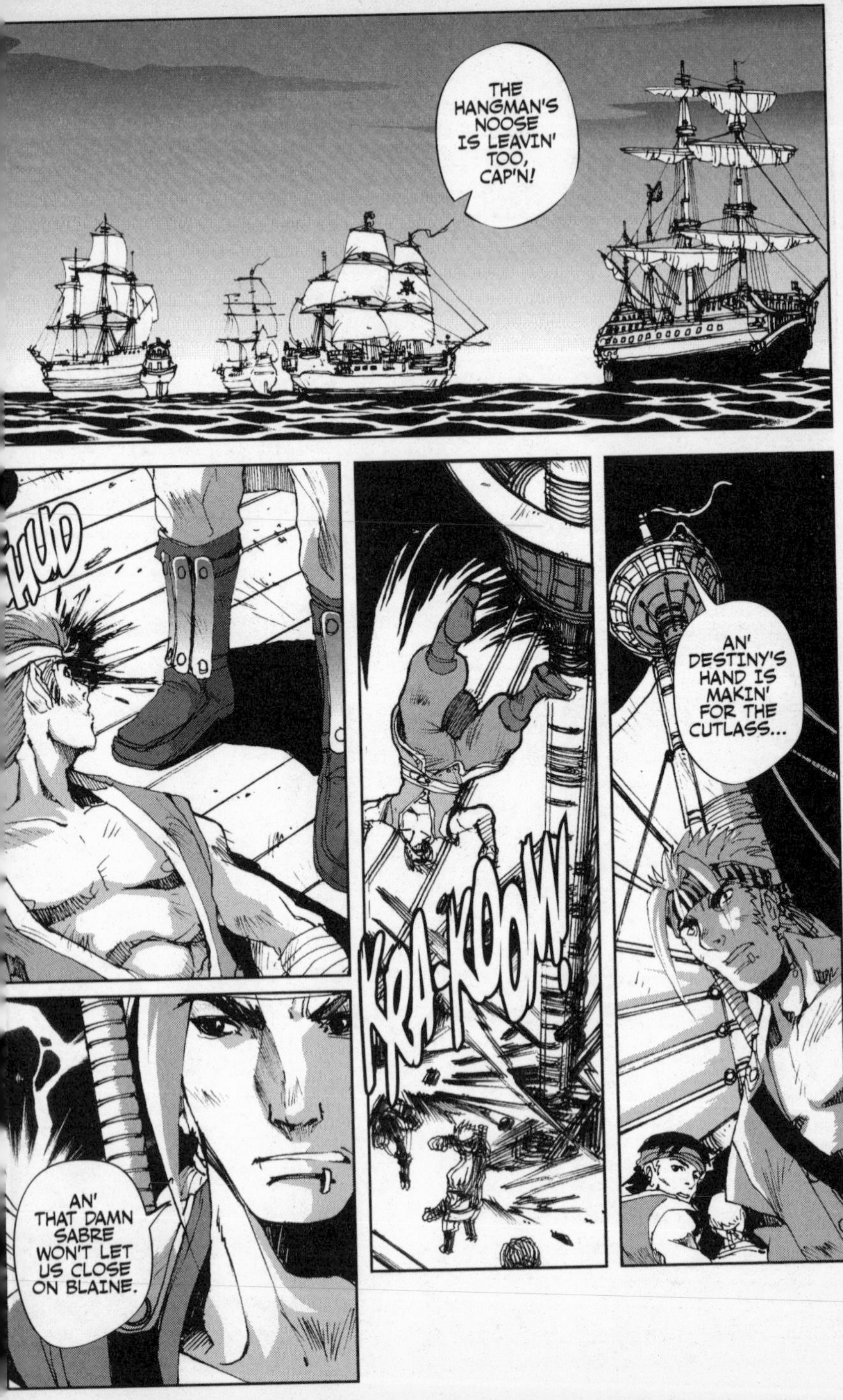

THE HANGMAN'S NOOSE IS LEAVIN' TOO, CAP'N!
AN' DESTINY'S HAND IS MAKIN' FOR THE CUTLASS...
KRA-KOOM!!
AN' THAT DAMN SABRE WON'T LET US CLOSE ON BLAINE.

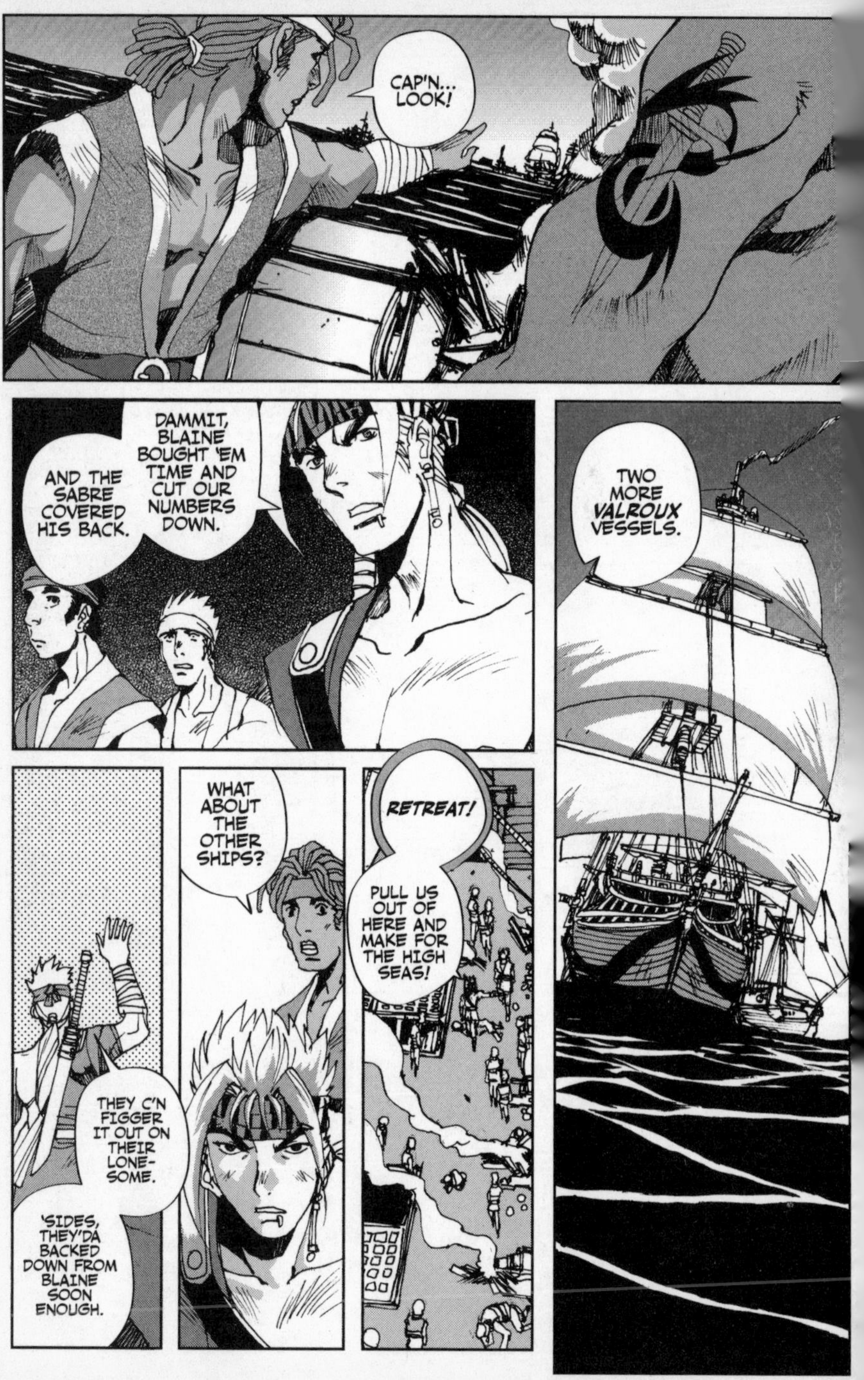
CAP'N... LOOK!
TWO MORE VALROUX VESSELS.
DAMMIT, BLAINE BOUGHT 'EM TIME AND CUT OUR NUMBERS DOWN.
AND THE SABRE COVERED HIS BACK.
RETREAT!
PULL US OUT OF HERE AND MAKE FOR THE HIGH SEAS!
WHAT ABOUT THE OTHER SHIPS?
THEY C'N FIGGER IT OUT ON THEIR LONE-SOME.
'SIDES, THEY'DA BACKED DOWN FROM BLAINE SOON ENOUGH.

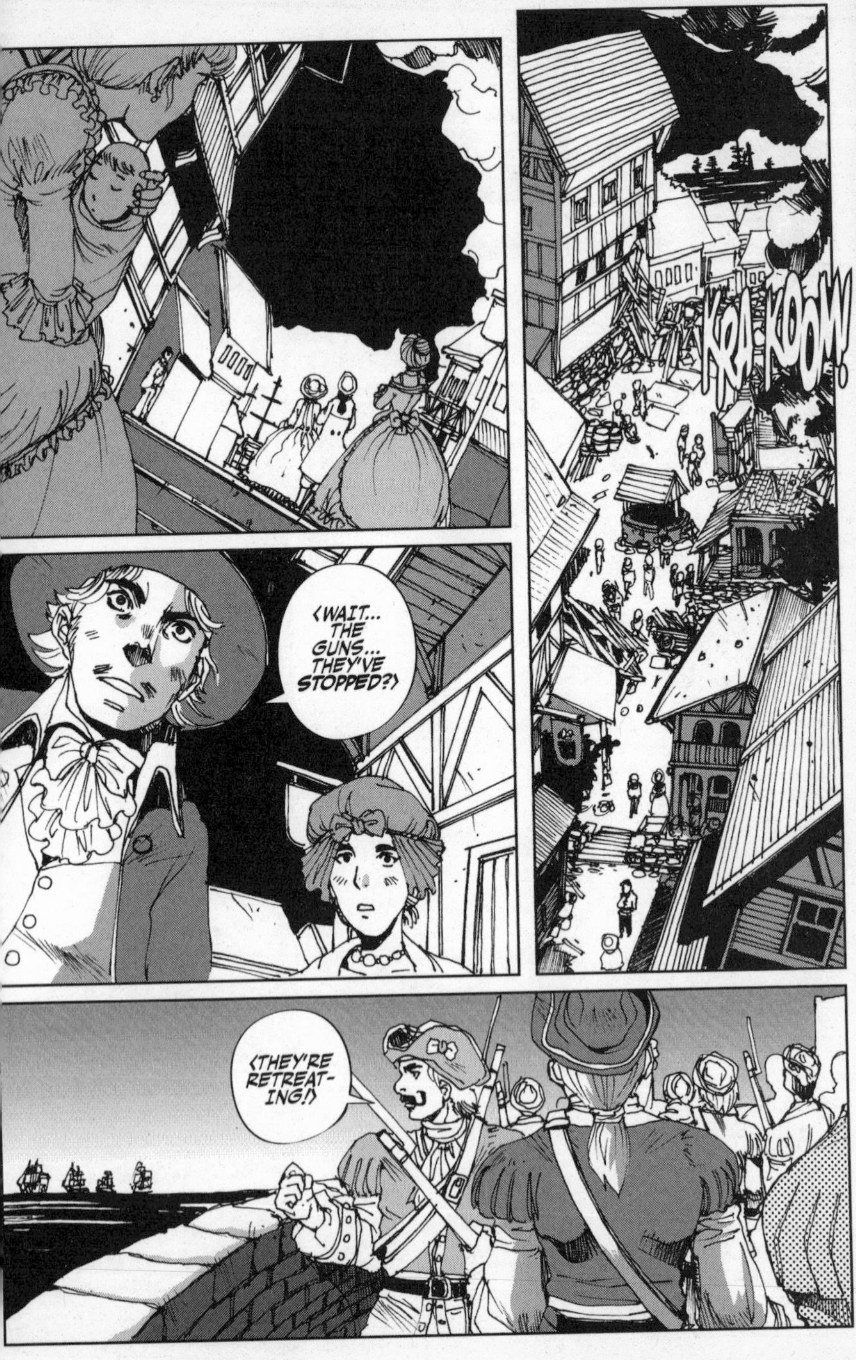
KRA-KOOM!
‹WAIT... THE GUNS... THEY'VE STOPPED?›
‹THEY'RE RETREAT-ING!›

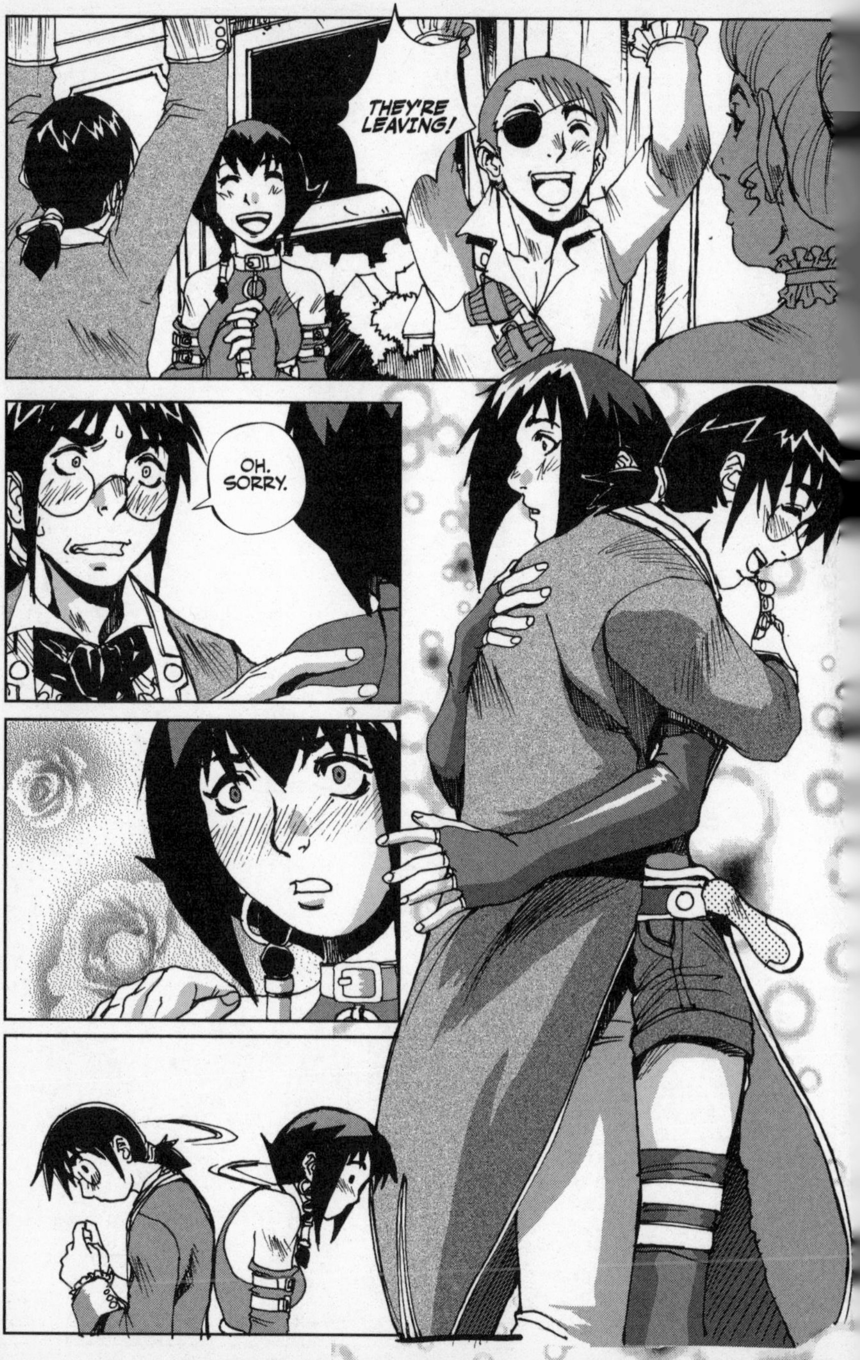
THEY'RE LEAVING!
OH. SORRY.

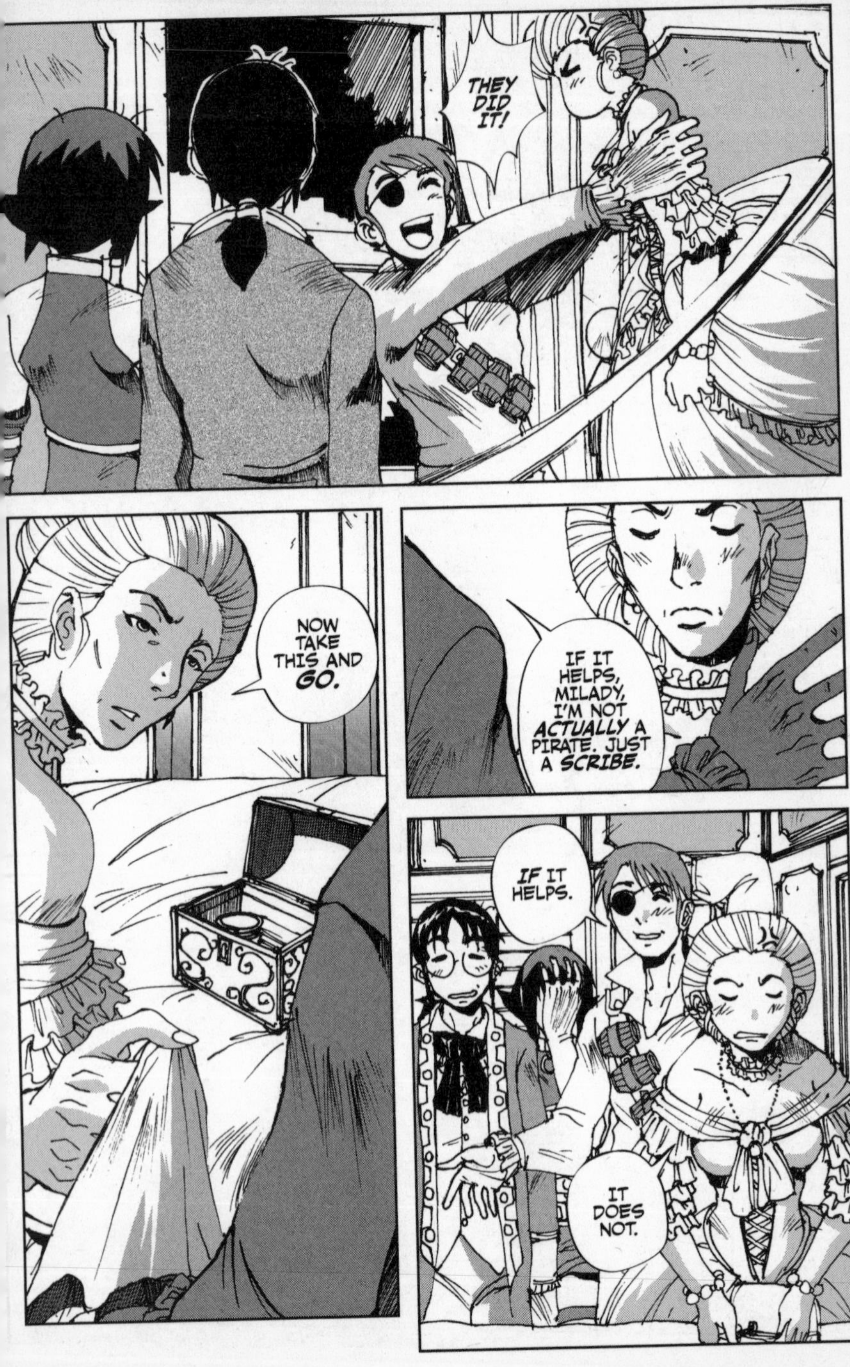
THEY DID IT!
IF IT HELPS, MILADY, I'M NOT *ACTUALLY* A PIRATE. JUST A *SCRIBE.*
IF IT HELPS.
IT DOES NOT.
NOW TAKE THIS AND *GO.*

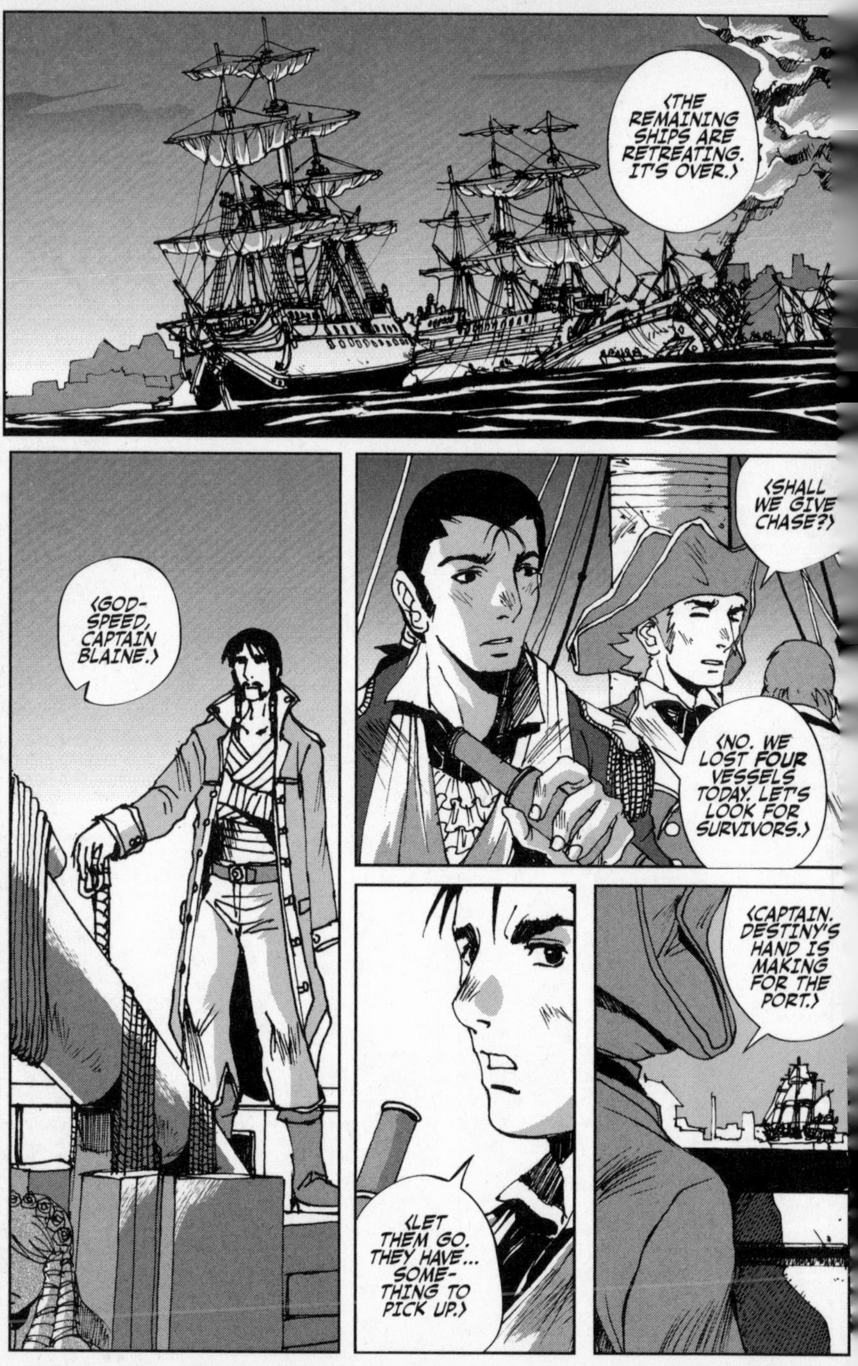
‹THE REMAINING SHIPS ARE RETREATING. IT'S OVER.›
‹SHALL WE GIVE CHASE?›
‹NO. WE LOST **FOUR** VESSELS TODAY. LET'S LOOK FOR SURVIVORS.›
‹CAPTAIN. DESTINY'S HAND IS MAKING FOR THE PORT.›
‹LET THEM GO. THEY HAVE... SOME-THING TO PICK UP.›
‹GOD-SPEED, CAPTAIN BLAINE.›

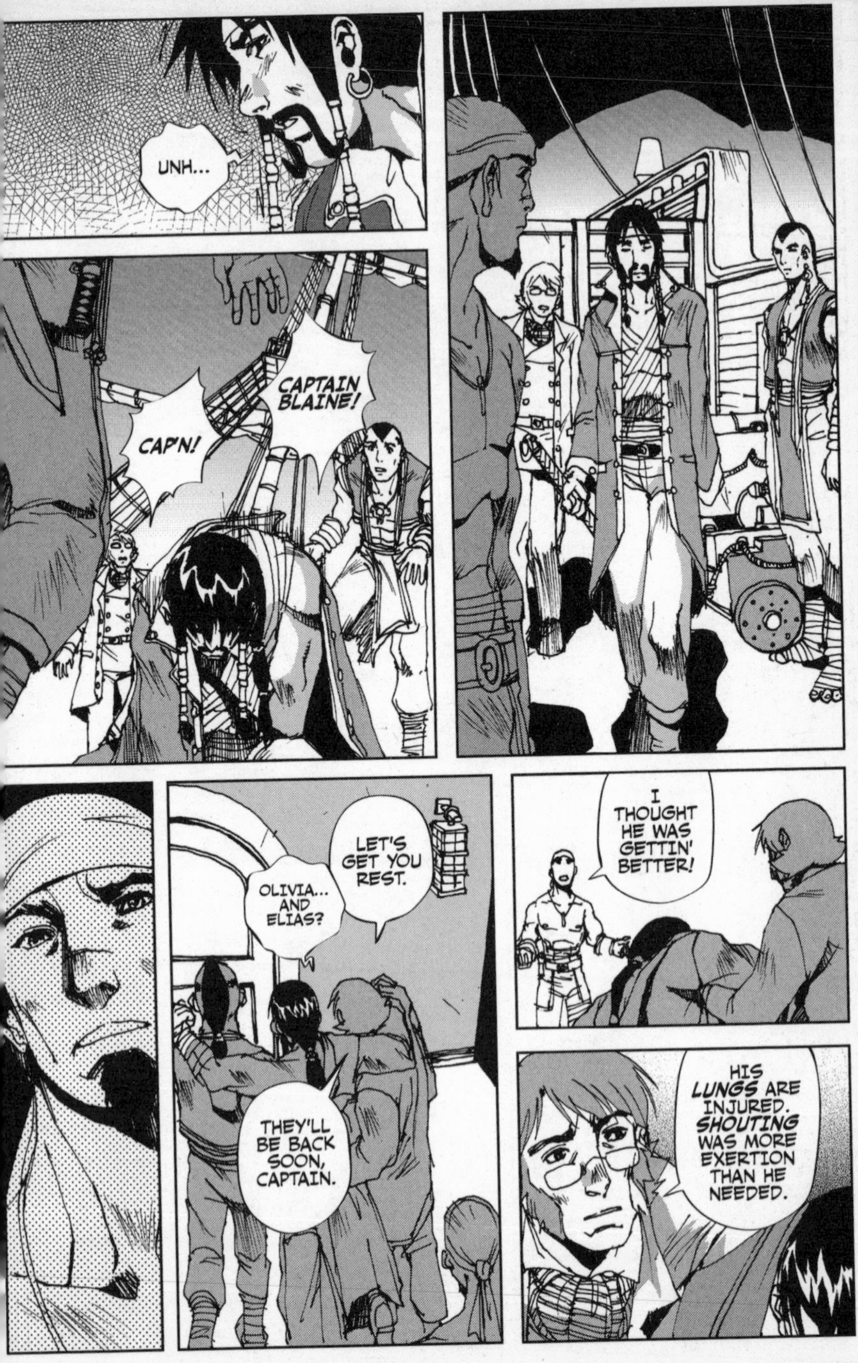
UNH...
CAPTAIN BLAINE!
CAP'N!
I THOUGHT HE WAS GETTIN' BETTER!
HIS LUNGS ARE INJURED. SHOUTING WAS MORE EXERTION THAN HE NEEDED.
LET'S GET YOU REST.
OLIVIA... AND ELIAS?
THEY'LL BE BACK SOON, CAPTAIN.

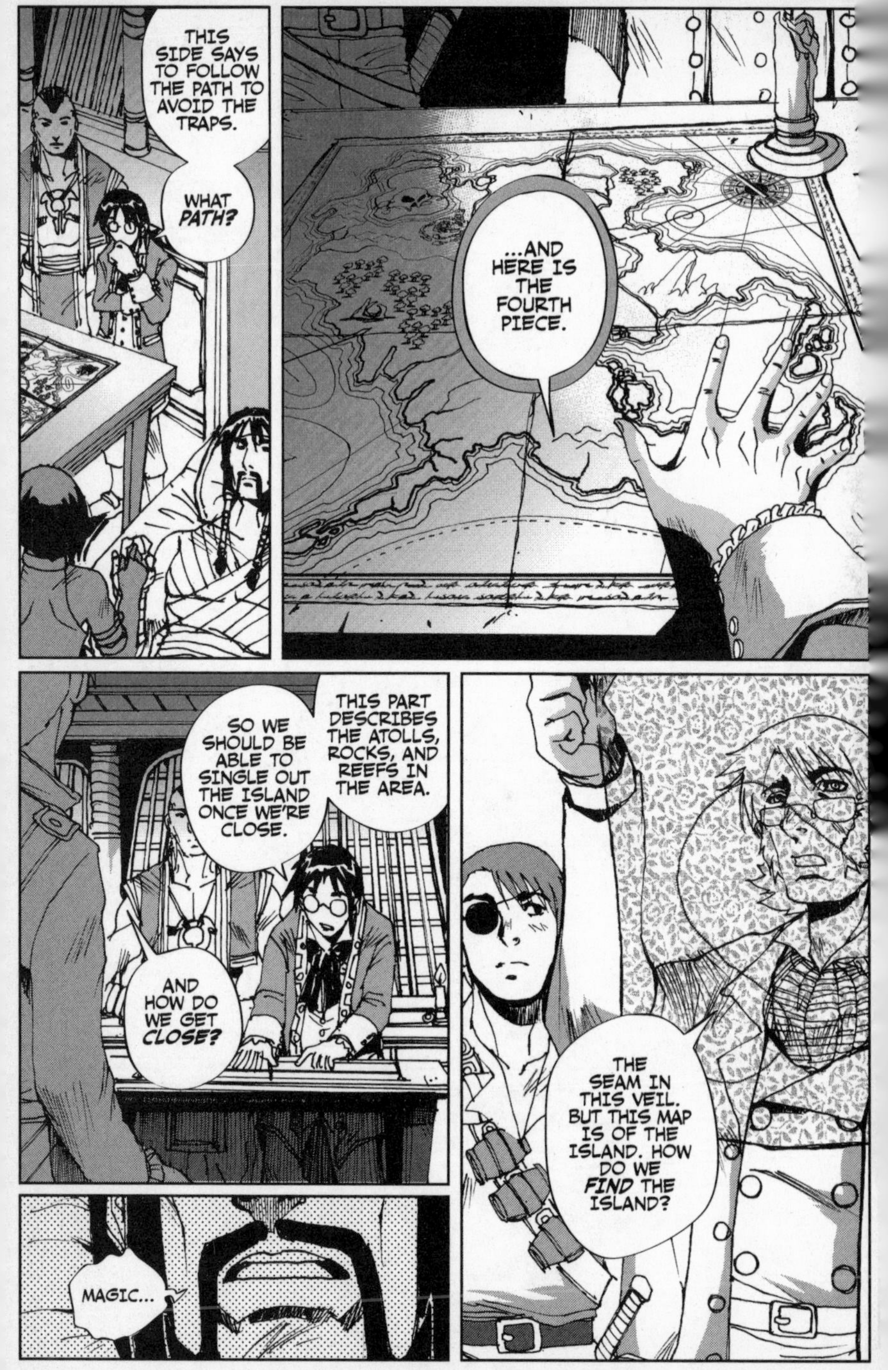
...AND HERE IS THE FOURTH PIECE.
THIS SIDE SAYS TO FOLLOW THE PATH TO AVOID THE TRAPS.
WHAT *PATH?*
THE SEAM IN THIS VEIL. BUT THIS MAP IS OF THE ISLAND. HOW DO WE *FIND* THE ISLAND?
THIS PART DESCRIBES THE ATOLLS, ROCKS, AND REEFS IN THE AREA.
SO WE SHOULD BE ABLE TO SINGLE OUT THE ISLAND ONCE WE'RE CLOSE.
AND HOW DO WE GET *CLOSE?*
MAGIC...

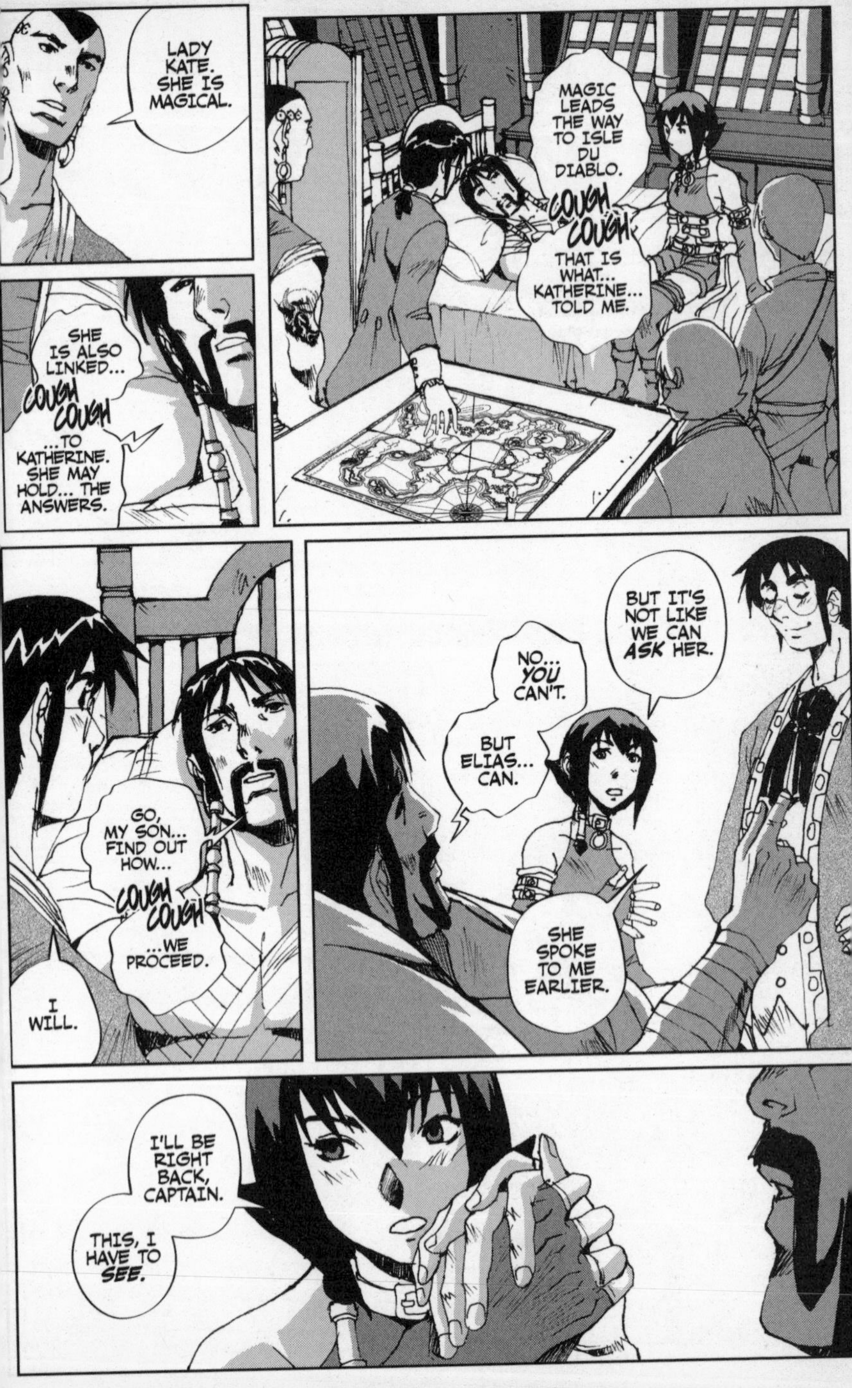
MAGIC LEADS THE WAY TO ISLE DU DIABLO.
COUGH COUGH
THAT IS WHAT... KATHERINE... TOLD ME.
LADY KATE. SHE IS MAGICAL.
SHE IS ALSO LINKED...
COUGH COUGH
...TO KATHERINE. SHE MAY HOLD... THE ANSWERS.
BUT IT'S NOT LIKE WE CAN *ASK* HER.
NO... *YOU* CAN'T.
BUT ELIAS... CAN.
SHE SPOKE TO ME EARLIER.
GO, MY SON... FIND OUT HOW...
COUGH COUGH
...WE PROCEED.
I WILL.
I'LL BE RIGHT BACK, CAPTAIN.
THIS, I HAVE TO *SEE*.

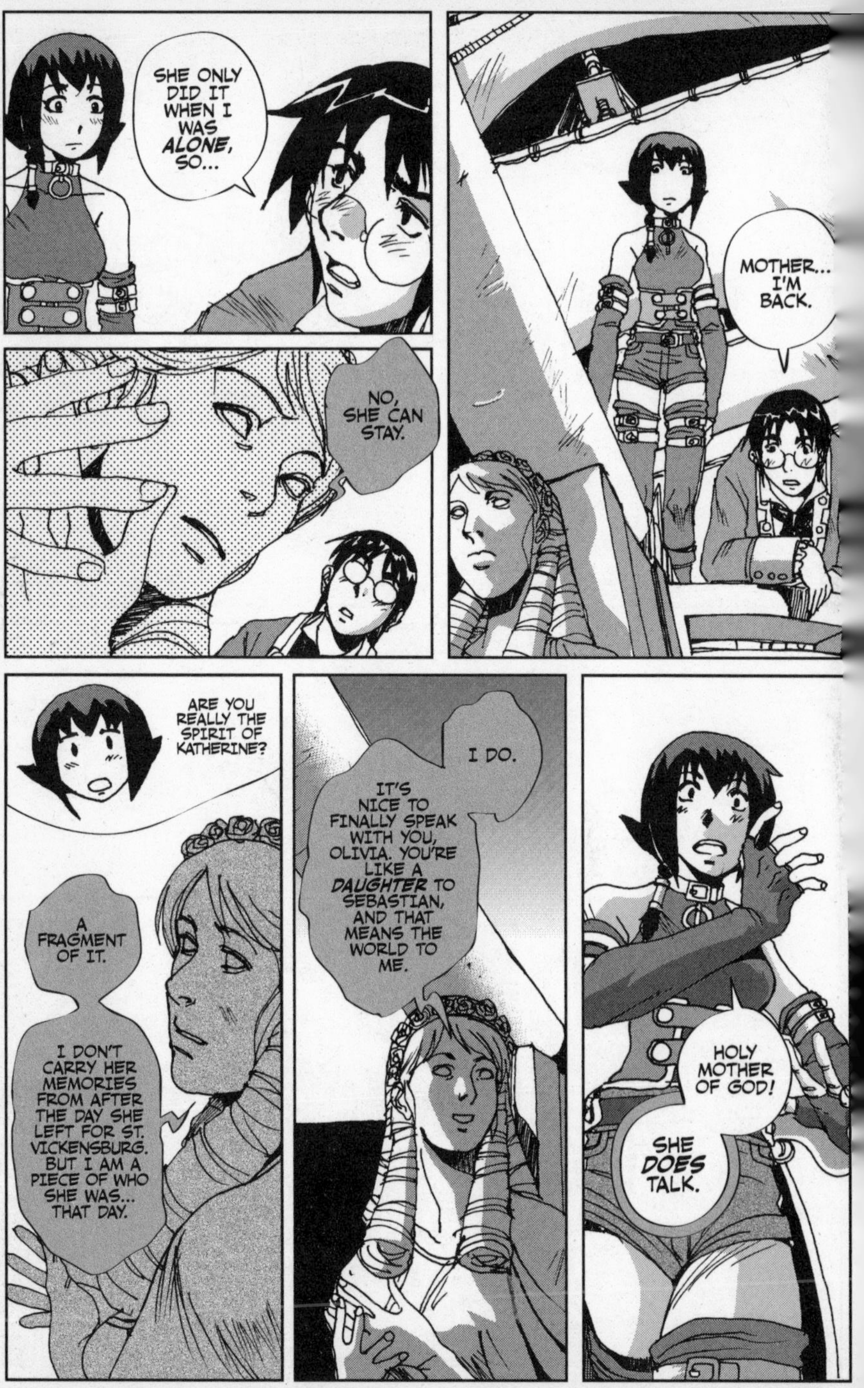
MOTHER... I'M BACK.
SHE ONLY DID IT WHEN I WAS *ALONE*, SO...
NO, SHE CAN STAY.
HOLY MOTHER OF GOD!
SHE *DOES* TALK.
I DO.
IT'S NICE TO FINALLY SPEAK WITH YOU, OLIVIA. YOU'RE LIKE A *DAUGHTER* TO SEBASTIAN, AND THAT MEANS THE WORLD TO ME.
ARE YOU REALLY THE SPIRIT OF KATHERINE?
A FRAGMENT OF IT.
I DON'T CARRY HER MEMORIES FROM AFTER THE DAY SHE LEFT FOR ST. VICKENSBURG. BUT I AM A PIECE OF WHO SHE WAS... THAT DAY.

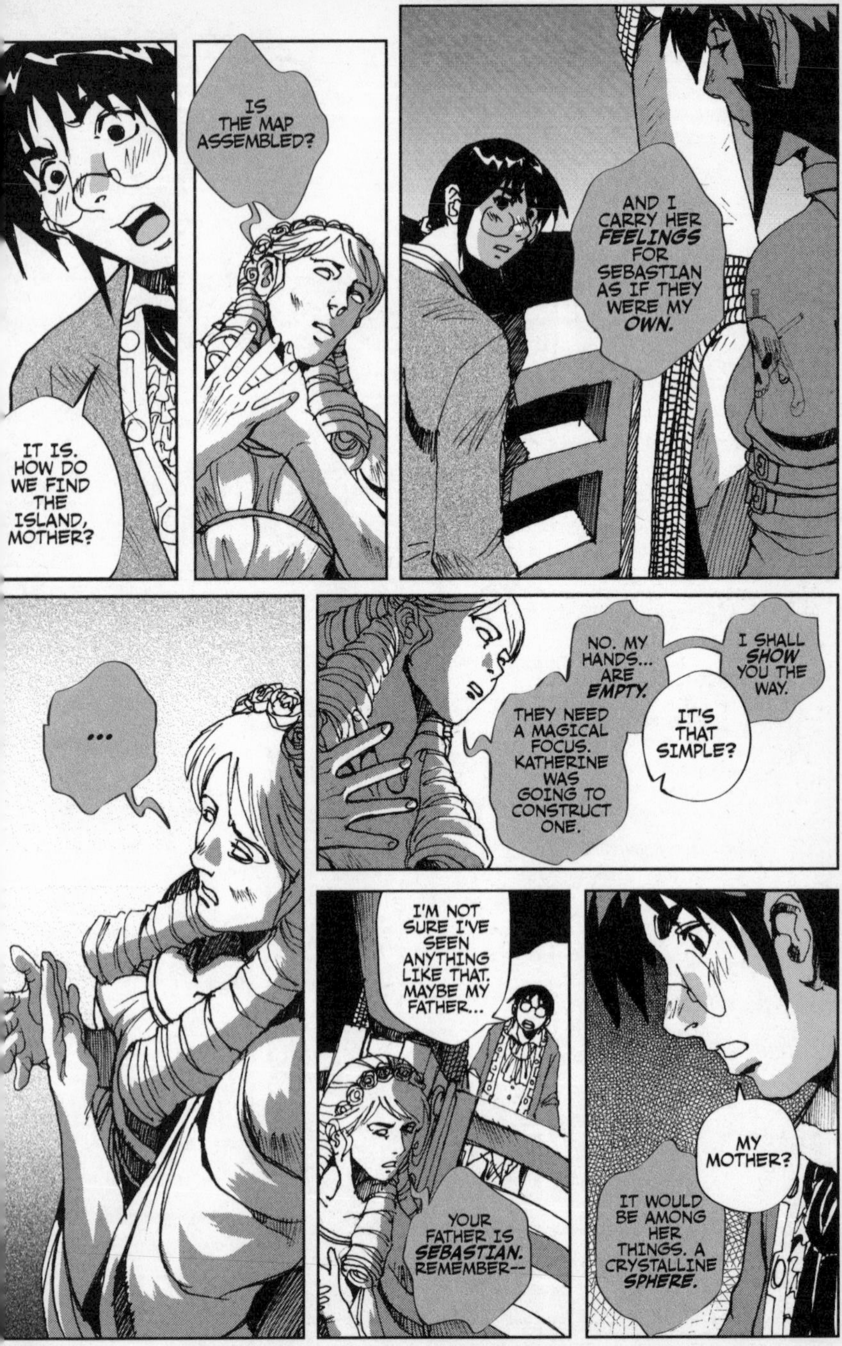
AND I CARRY HER *FEELINGS* FOR SEBASTIAN AS IF THEY WERE MY *OWN.*
IS THE MAP ASSEMBLED?
IT IS. HOW DO WE FIND THE ISLAND, MOTHER?
I SHALL *SHOW* YOU THE WAY.
IT'S THAT SIMPLE?
NO. MY HANDS... ARE *EMPTY.*
THEY NEED A MAGICAL FOCUS. KATHERINE WAS GOING TO CONSTRUCT ONE.
MY MOTHER?
IT WOULD BE AMONG HER THINGS. A CRYSTALLINE *SPHERE.*
I'M NOT SURE I'VE SEEN ANYTHING LIKE THAT. MAYBE MY FATHER...
YOUR FATHER IS *SEBASTIAN.* REMEMBER--
...

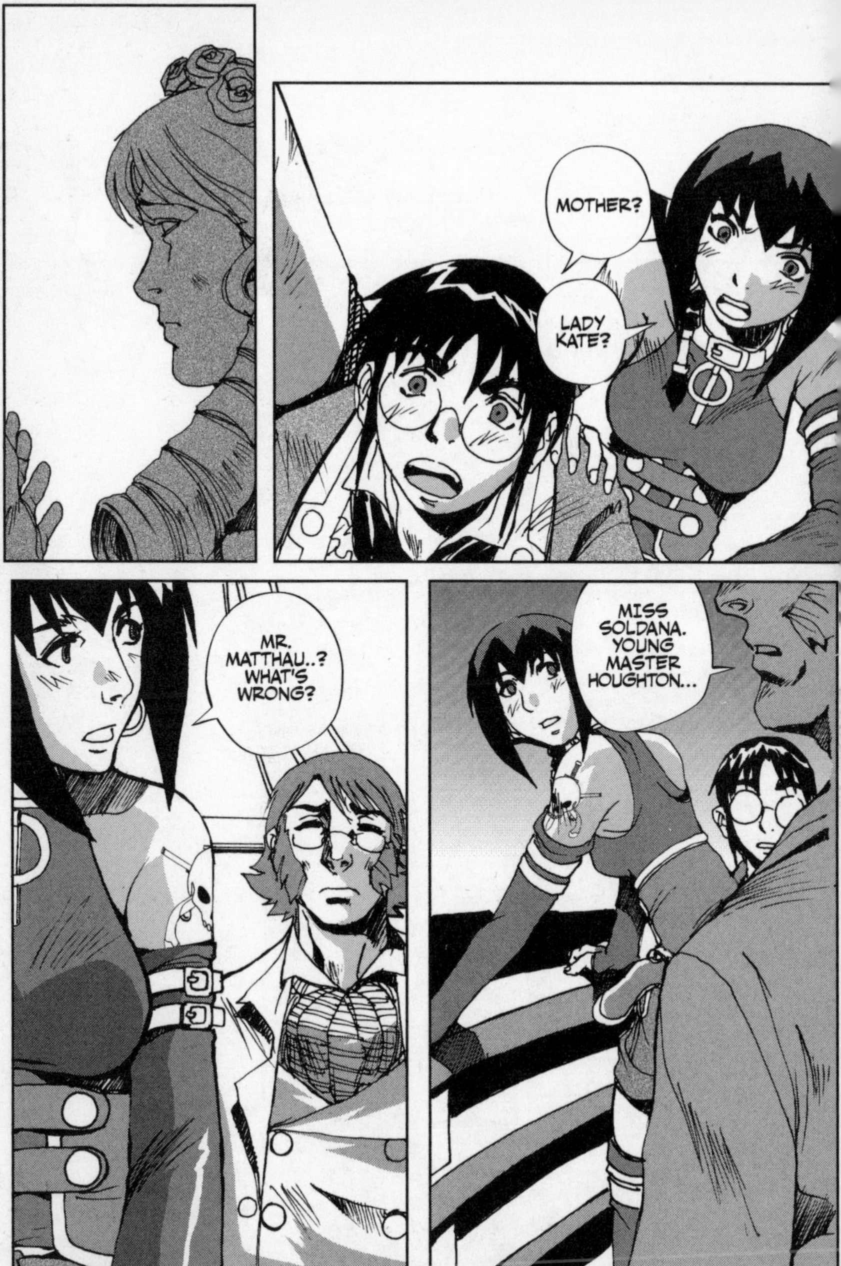
MOTHER?
LADY KATE?
MISS SOLDANA. YOUNG MASTER HOUGHTON...
MR. MATTHAU..? WHAT'S WRONG?

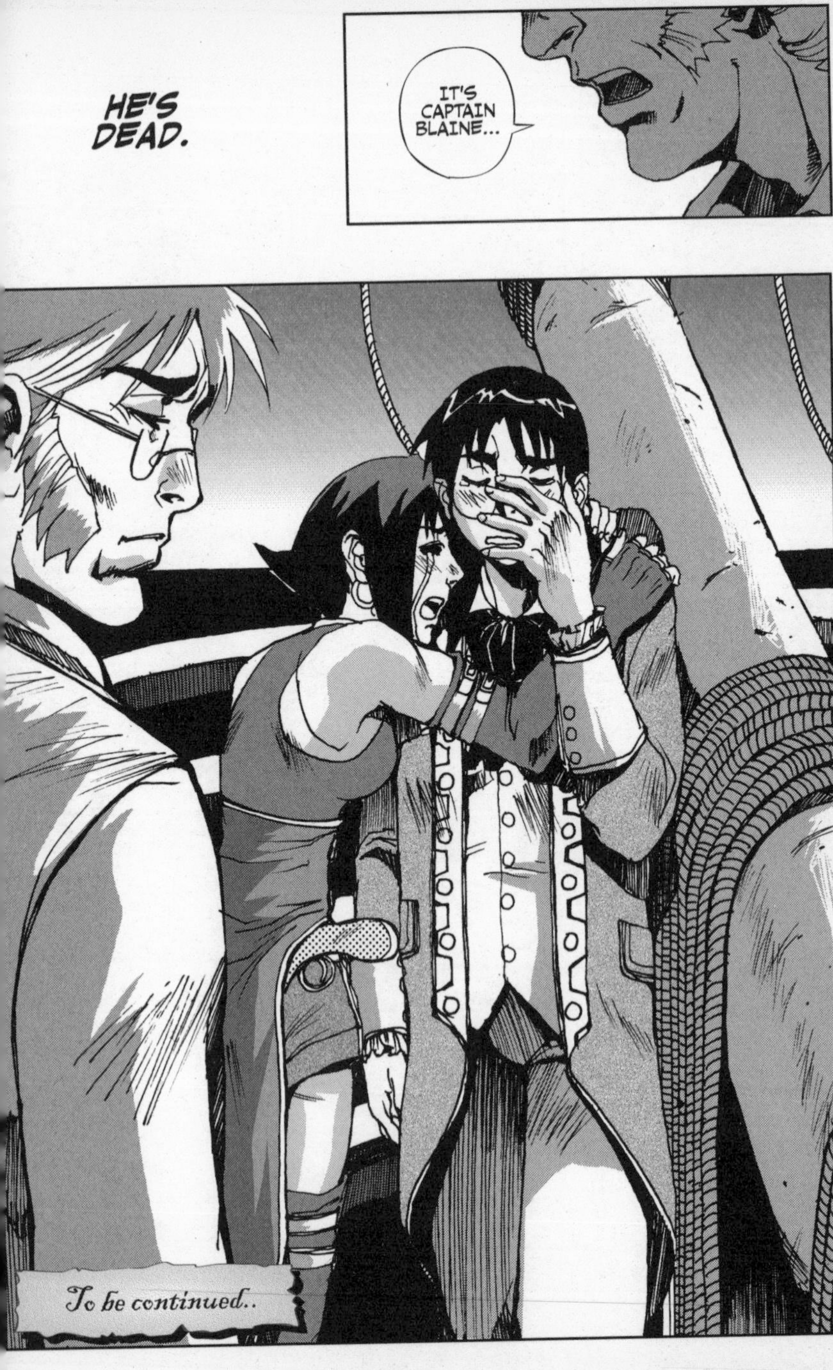
IT'S CAPTAIN BLAINE...
HE'S DEAD.
To be continued..

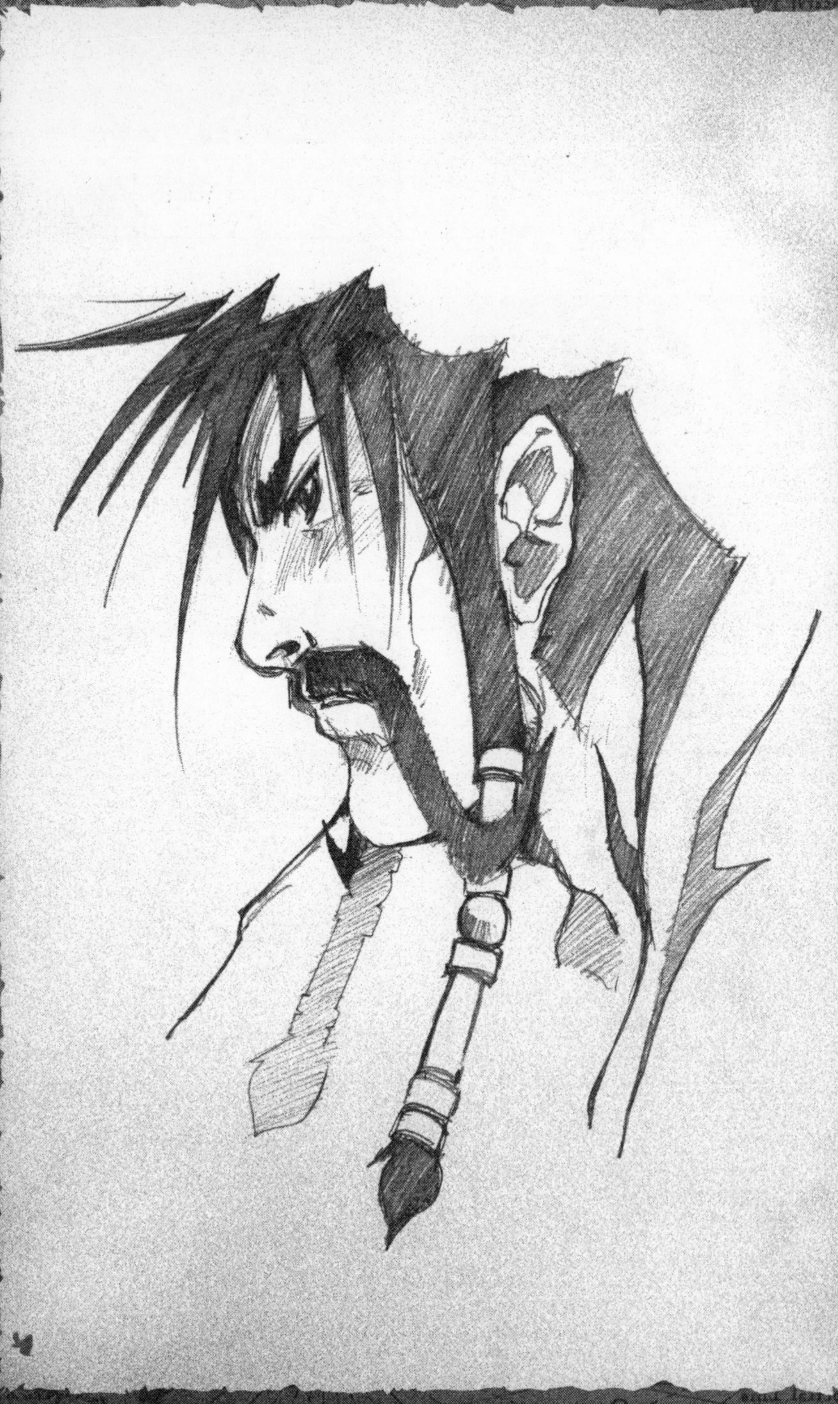

LET'S MEET MR. DIEGO BASTEON

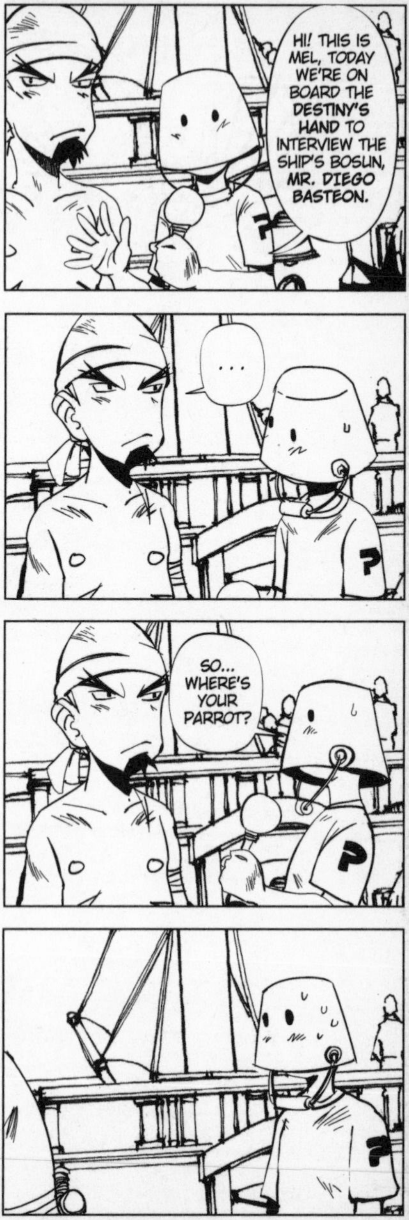
HI! THIS IS MEL, TODAY WE'RE ON BOARD THE DESTINY'S HAND TO INTERVIEW THE SHIP'S BOSUN, MR. DIEGO BASTEON.
...
SO... WHERE'S YOUR PARROT?

MANGA ELVES

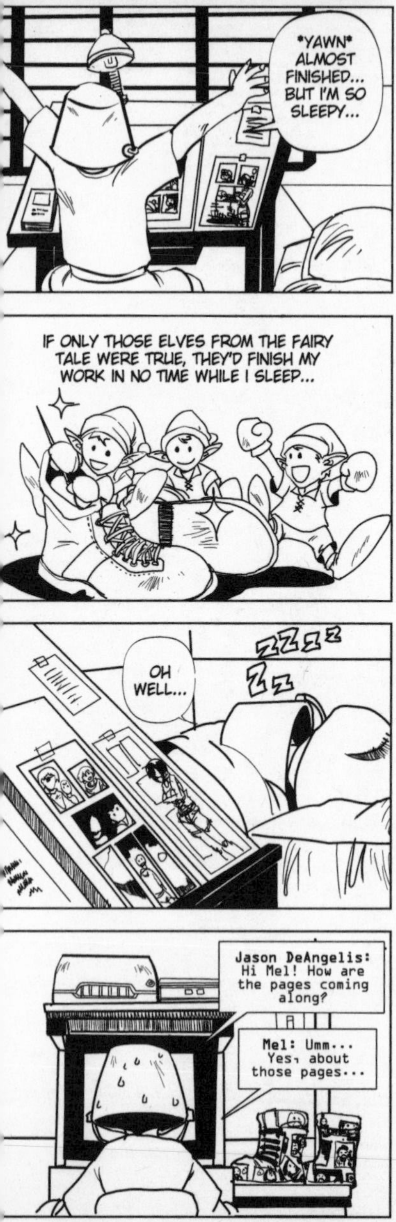
YAWN ALMOST FINISHED... BUT I'M SO SLEEPY...
IF ONLY THOSE ELVES FROM THE FAIRY TALE WERE TRUE, THEY'D FINISH MY WORK IN NO TIME WHILE I SLEEP...
OH WELL...
ZZZZZ
Jason DeAngelis: Hi Mel! How are the pages coming along?
Mel: Umm... Yes, about those pages...

The Kraken

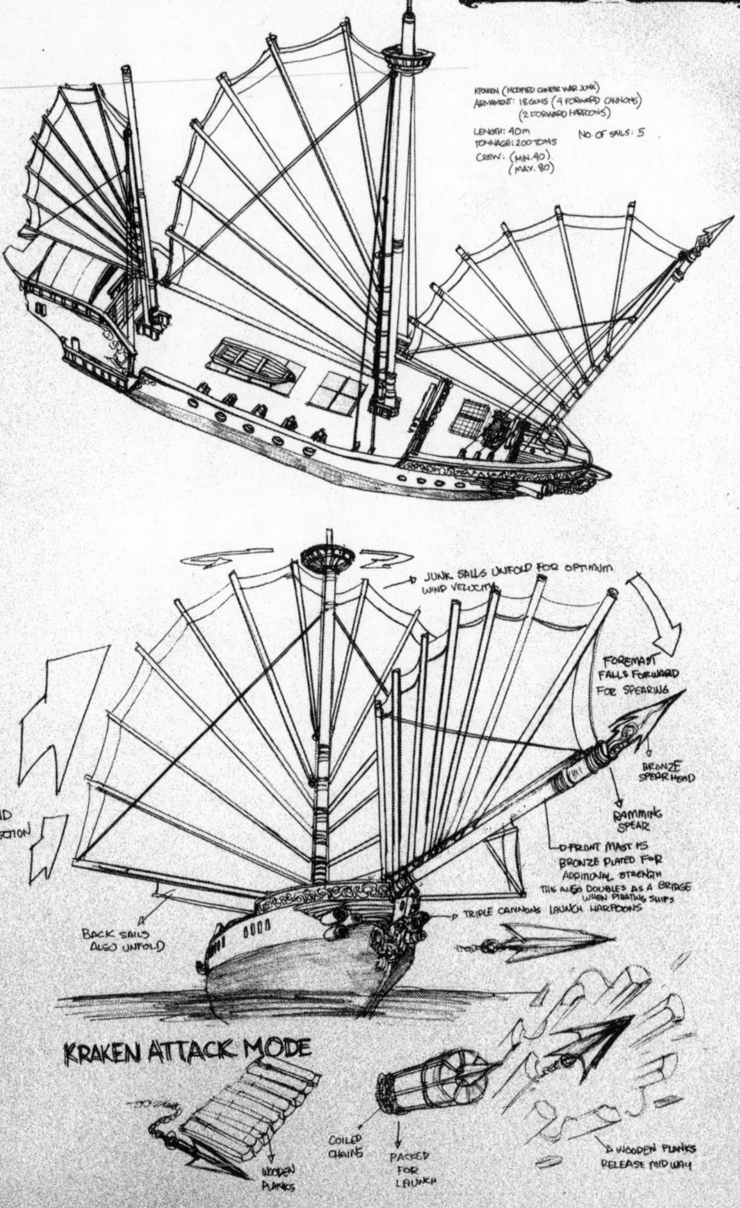
KRAKEN (MODIFIED CHINESE WAR JUNK)
ARMAMENT: 18 GUNS (4 FORWARD CANNONS)
(2 FORWARD HARPOONS)
LENGTH: 40m
TONNAGE: 200 TONS
CREW: (MIN. 40)
(MAX. 80)
NO. OF SAILS: 5
JUNK SAILS UNFOLD FOR OPTIMUM WIND VELOCITY
FOREMAST FALLS FORWARD FOR SPEARING
BRONZE SPEAR HEAD
RAMMING SPEAR
FRONT MAST IS BRONZE PLATED FOR ADDITIONAL STRENGTH
THIS ALSO DOUBLES AS A BRIDGE WHEN PIRATING SHIPS
WIND DIRECTION
TRIPLE CANNONS LAUNCH HARPOONS
BACK SAILS ALSO UNFOLD
KRAKEN ATTACK MODE
WOODEN PLANKS
COILED CHAINS
PACKED FOR LAUNCH
WOODEN PLANKS RELEASE MID WAY

Le Sabre Argenté

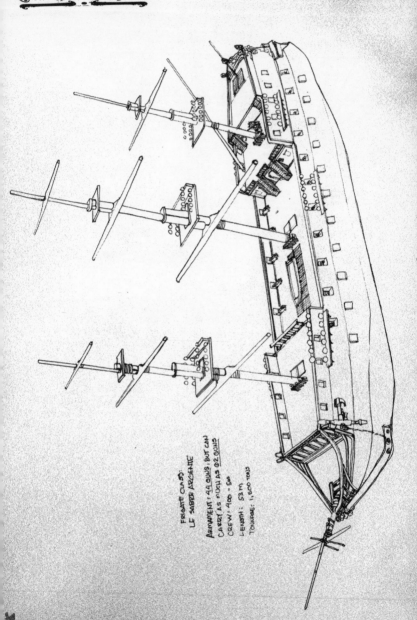

FRIGATE CLASS:
LE SABRE ARGENTÉ

ARMAMENT: 44 GUNS; BUT CAN
CARRY AS MUCH AS 02 GUNS
CREW: 900 - 500
LENGTH: 53 M
TONNAGE: 1,500 TONS

Destiny's Hand

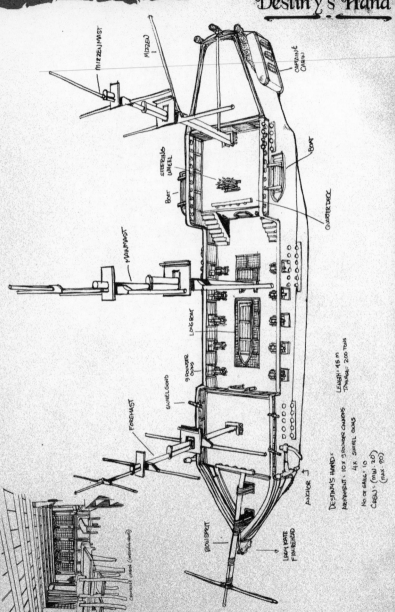

MIZZENMAST

MIZZEN

CAPTAIN'S CABIN

STEERING WHEEL

BOAT

BOAT

QUARTER DECK

MAINMAST

LONG BOAT

9 POUNDER GUNS

SWIVEL GUNS

FOREMAST

ANCHOR

BOWSPRIT

LION FIGUREHEAD

CAPTAIN'S CABIN (DETAIL VIEW)

DESTINY'S HAND:
ARMAMENT: 10 X 9 POUNDER CANNONS
4 X SWIVEL GUNS
No. OF SAILS: 10
CREW: (MIN.: 20)
(MAX.: 80)
LENGTH: 45 m
TONNAGE: 200 TONS

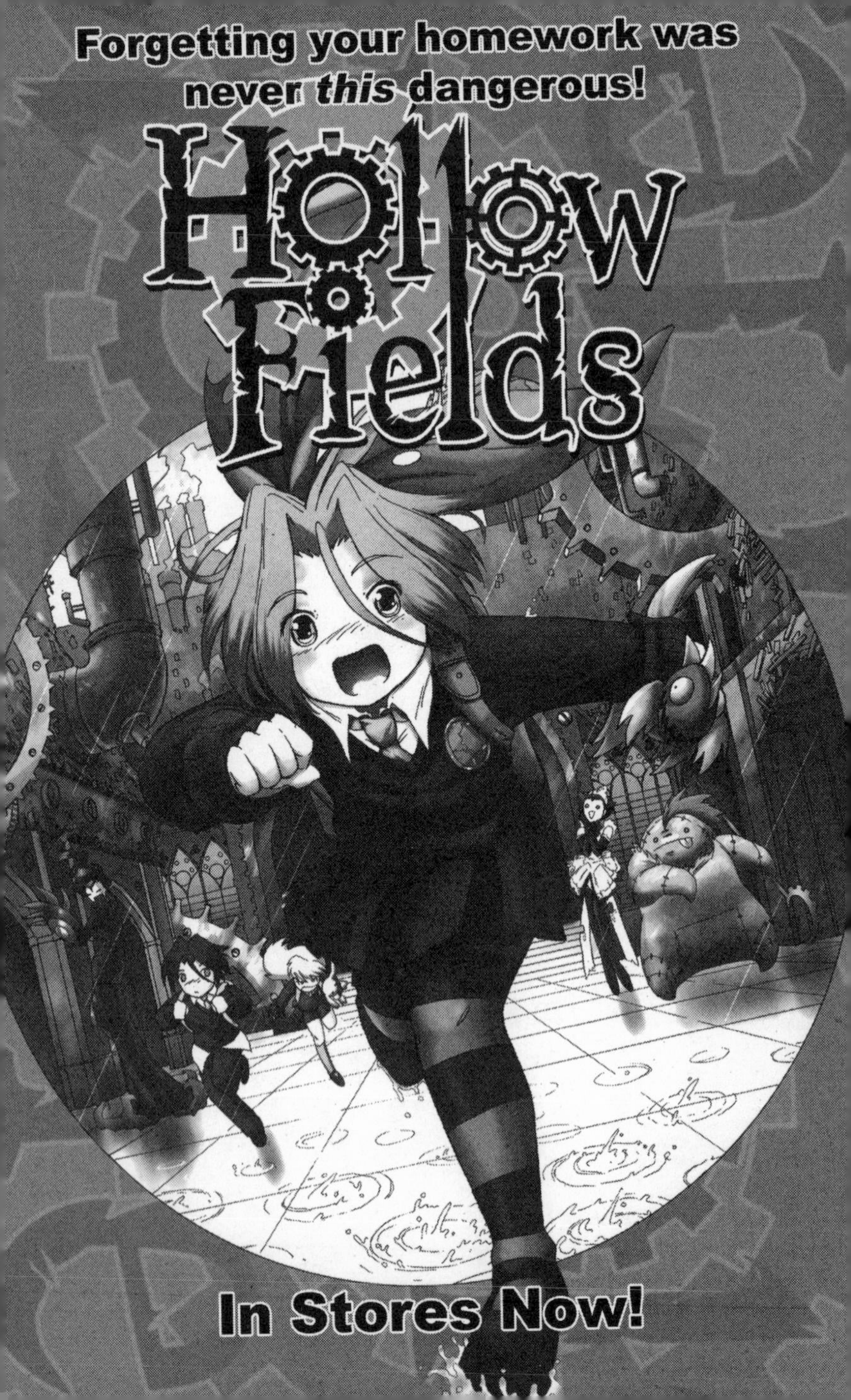
Forgetting your homework was never *this* dangerous!
Hollow Fields
In Stores Now!

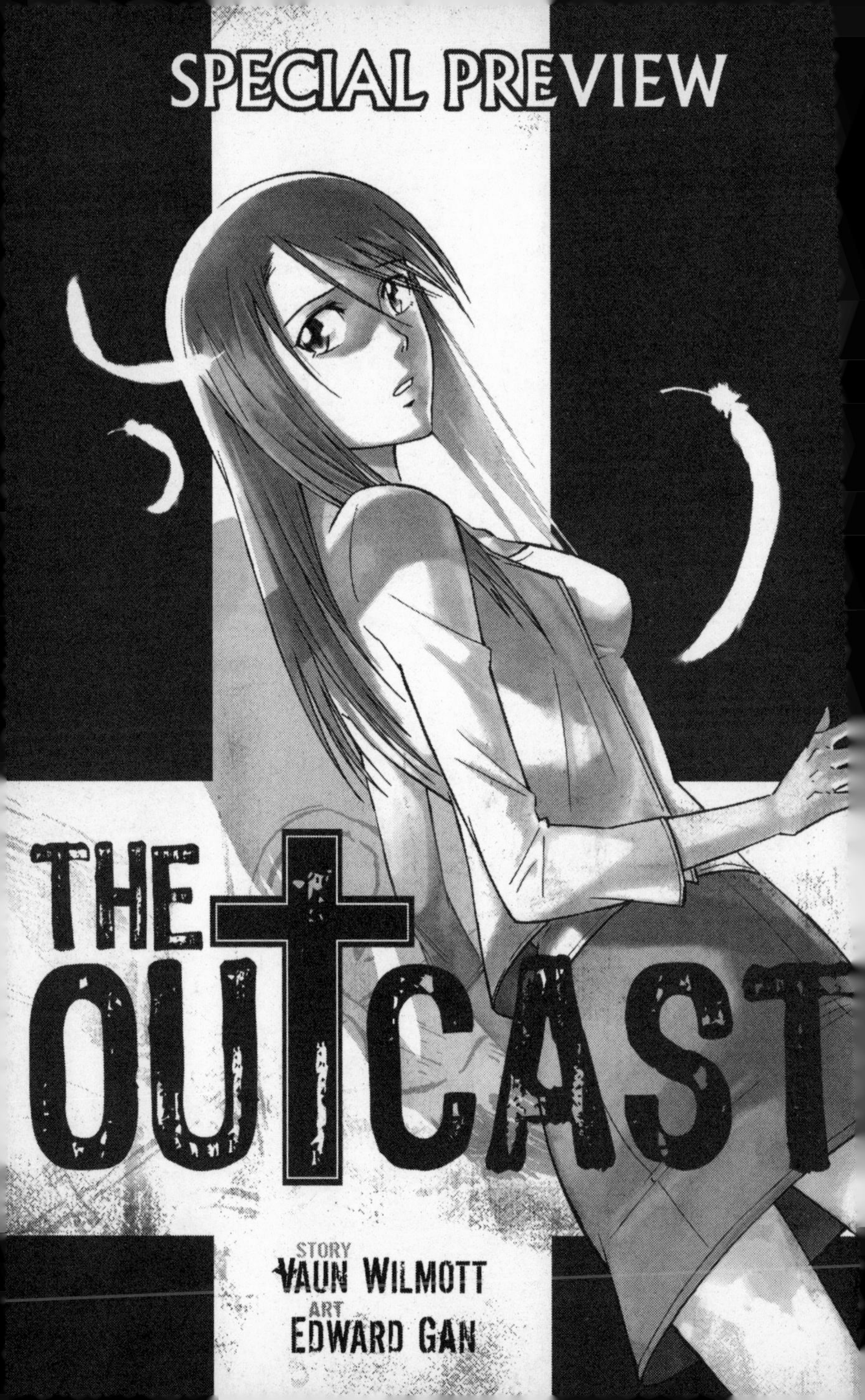
SPECIAL PREVIEW
THE OUTCAST
STORY
VAUN WILMOTT
ART
EDWARD GAN

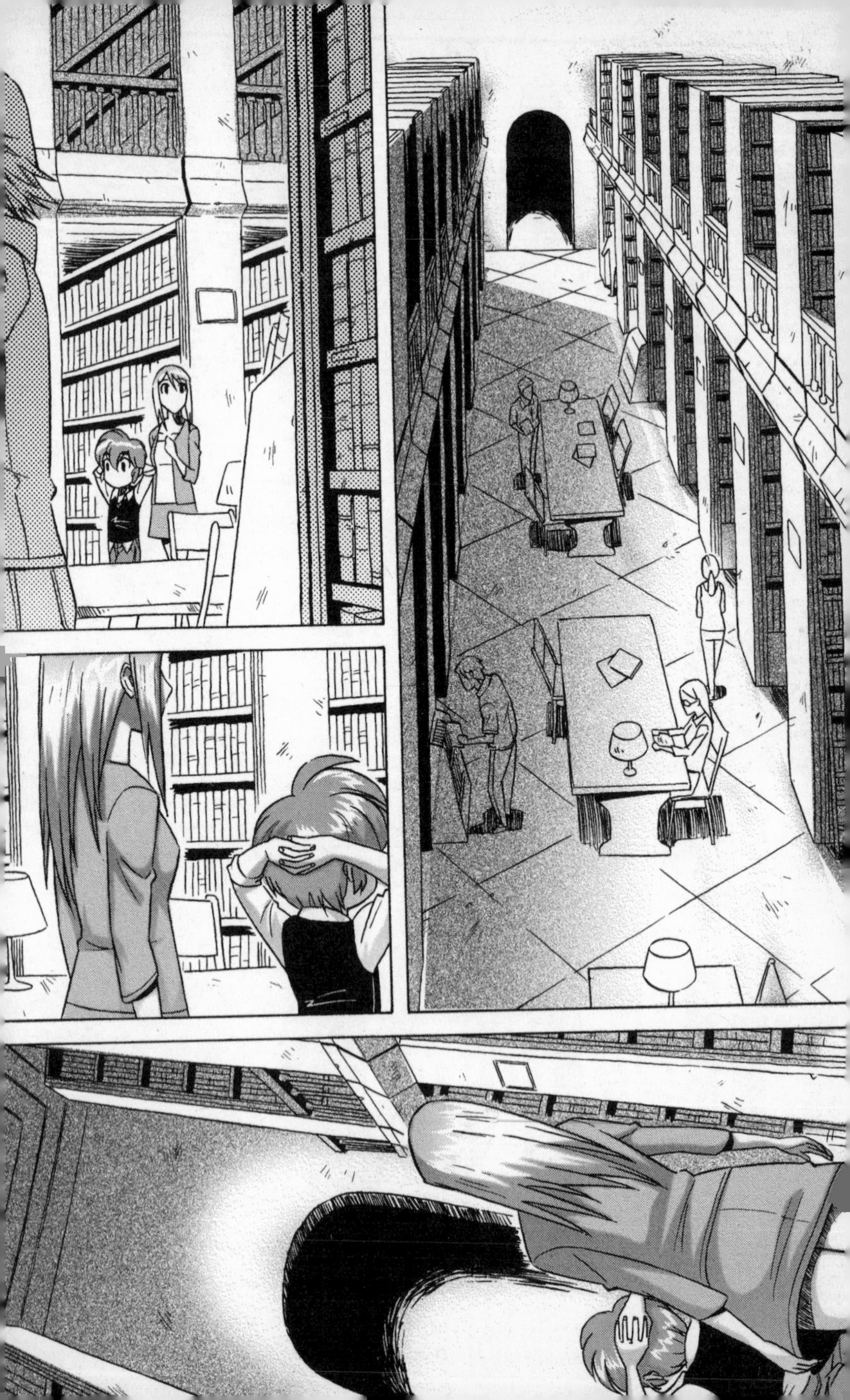

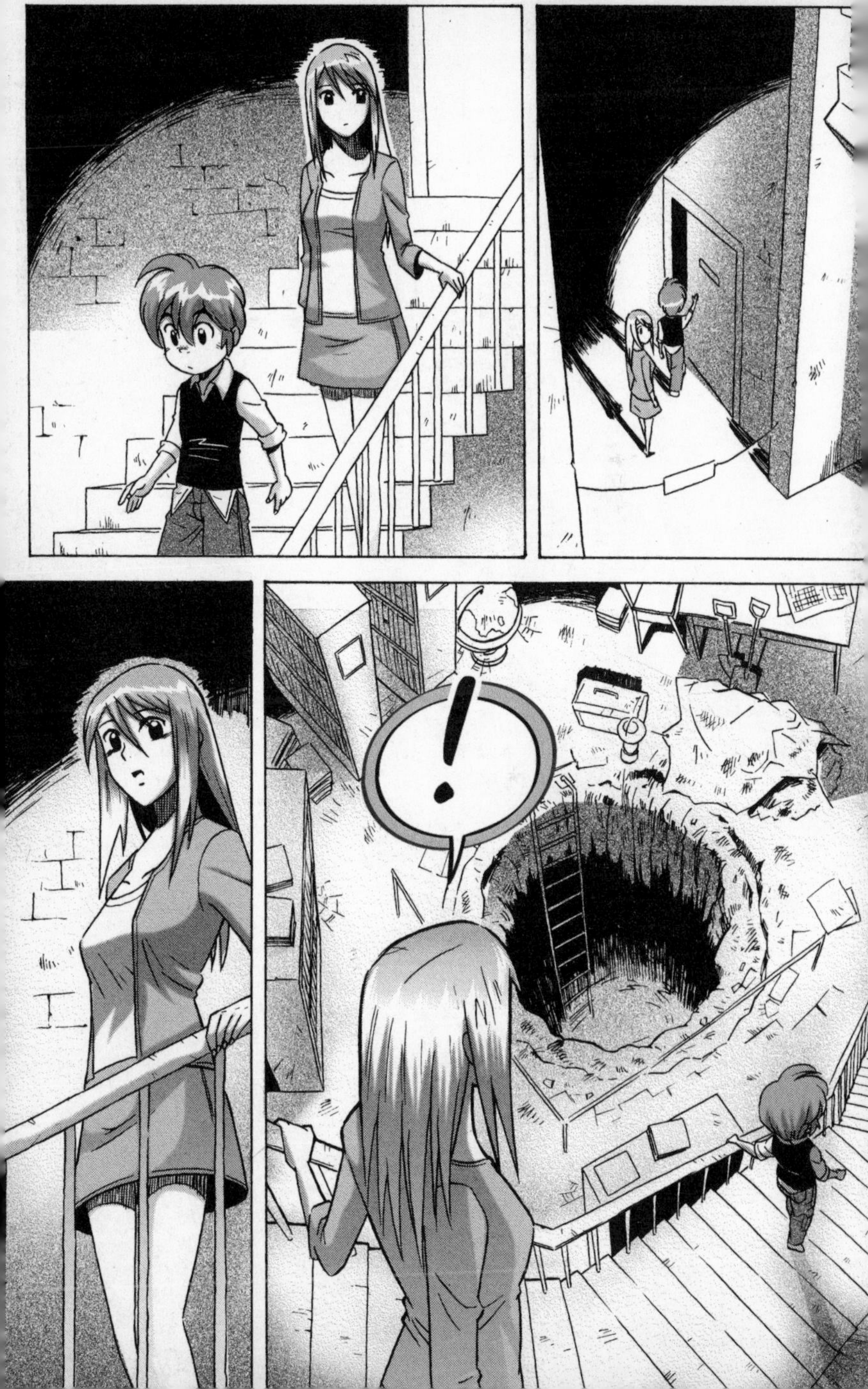
!

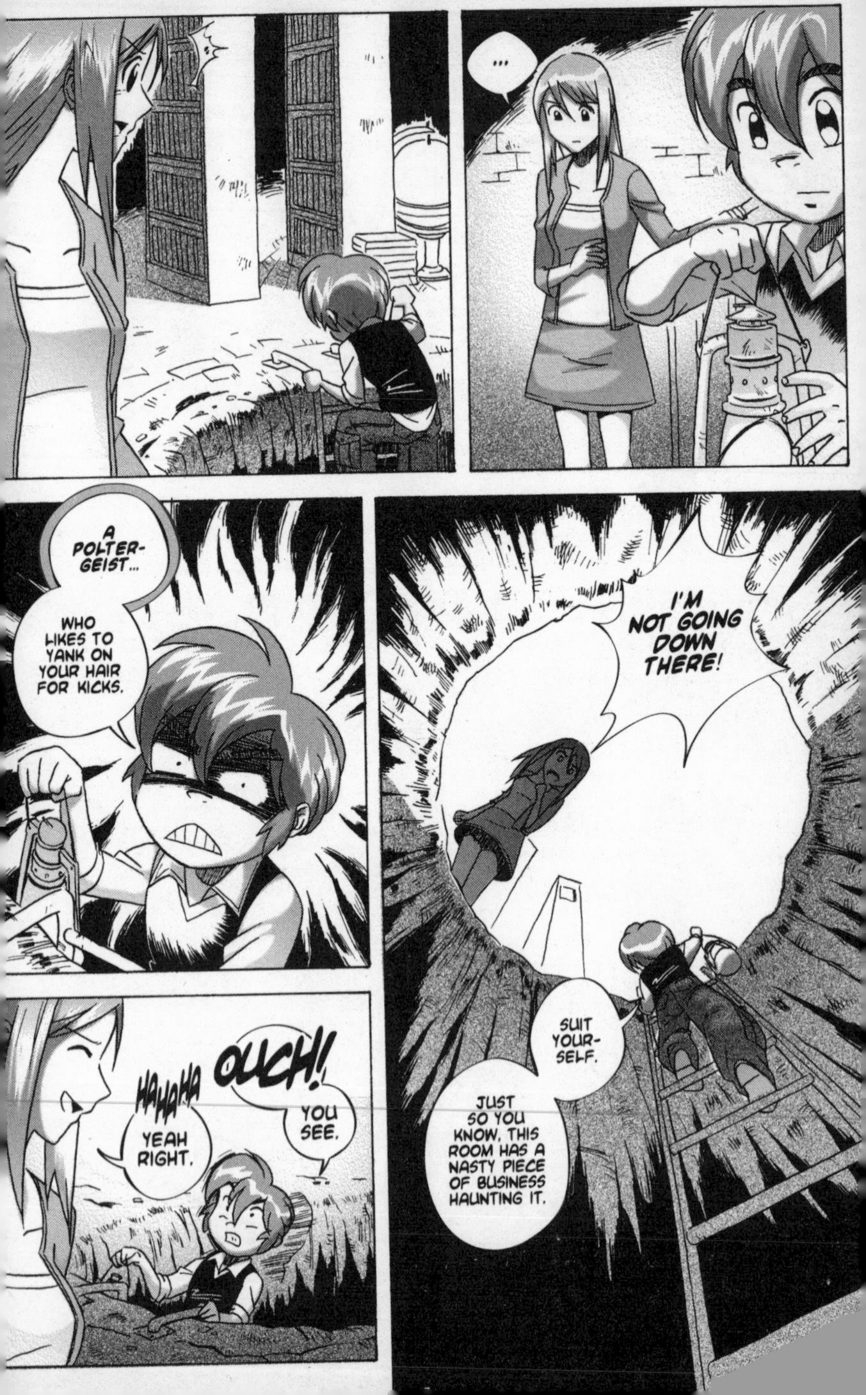
...
I'M NOT GOING DOWN THERE!
SUIT YOURSELF.
JUST SO YOU KNOW, THIS ROOM HAS A NASTY PIECE OF BUSINESS HAUNTING IT.
A POLTERGEIST...
WHO LIKES TO YANK ON YOUR HAIR FOR KICKS.
HAHAHA
YEAH RIGHT.
OUCH!
YOU SEE.

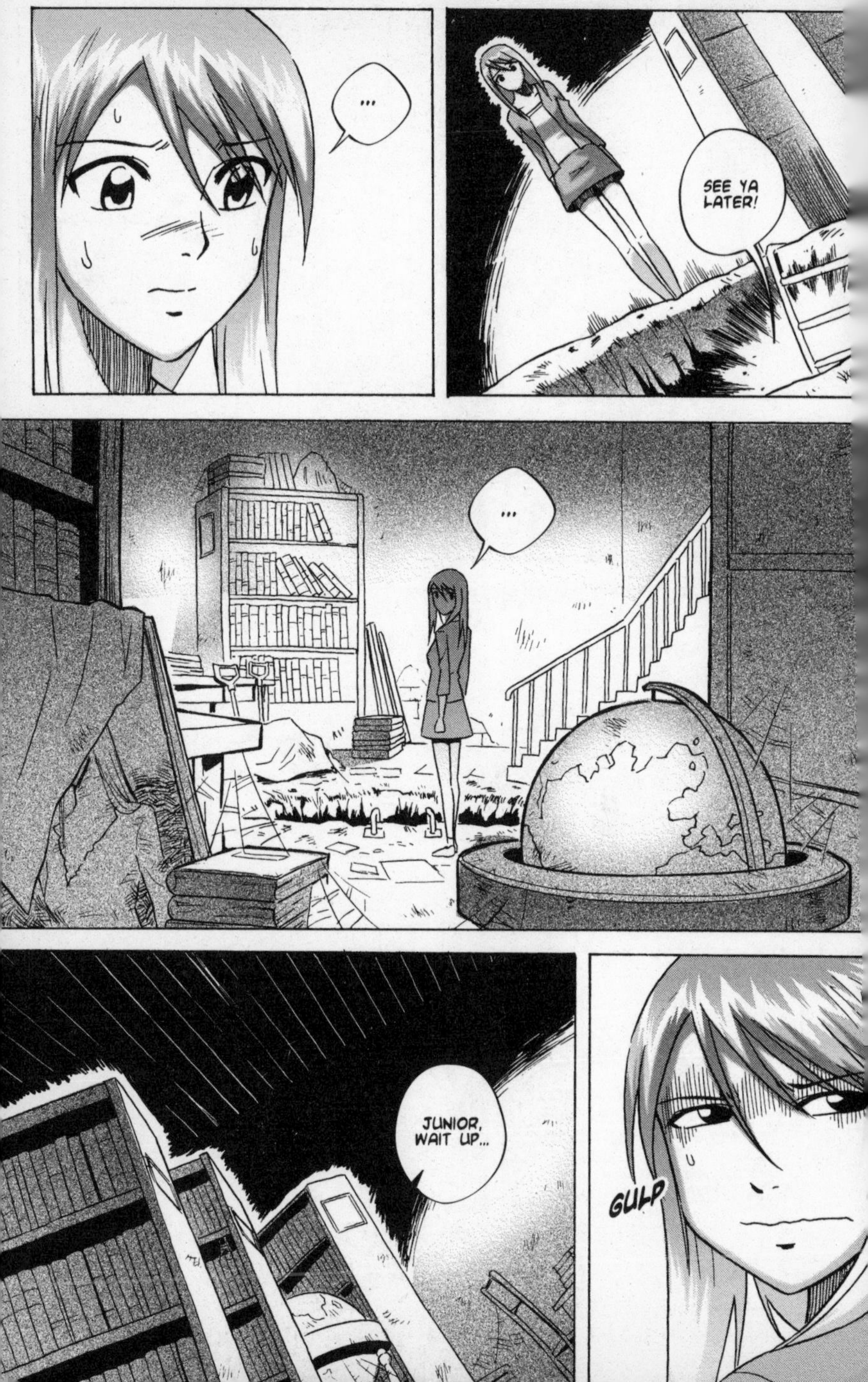
SEE YA LATER!
...
...
GULP
JUNIOR, WAIT UP...

...

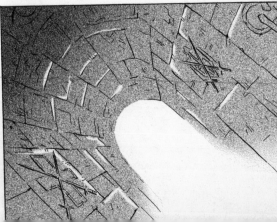

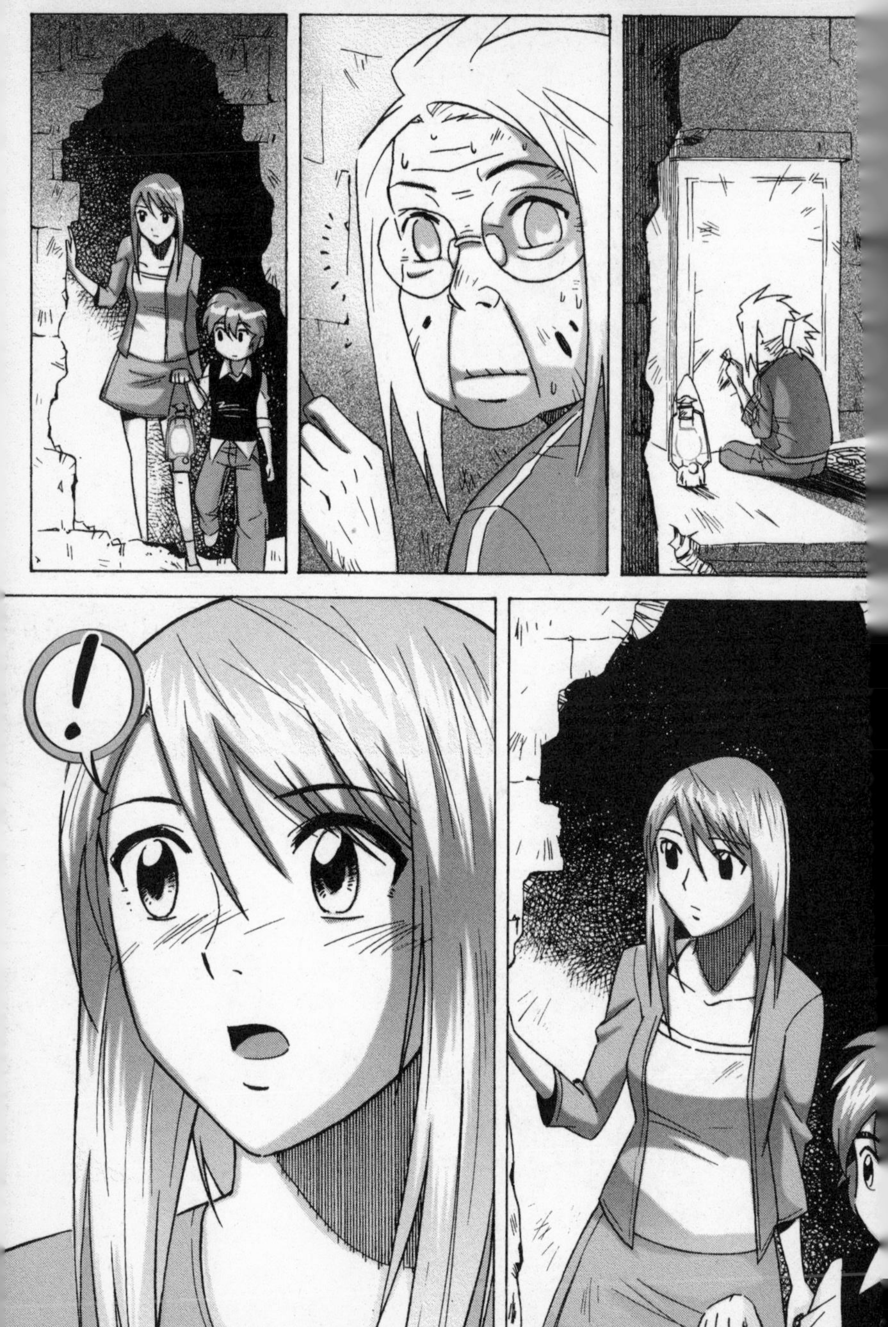
!

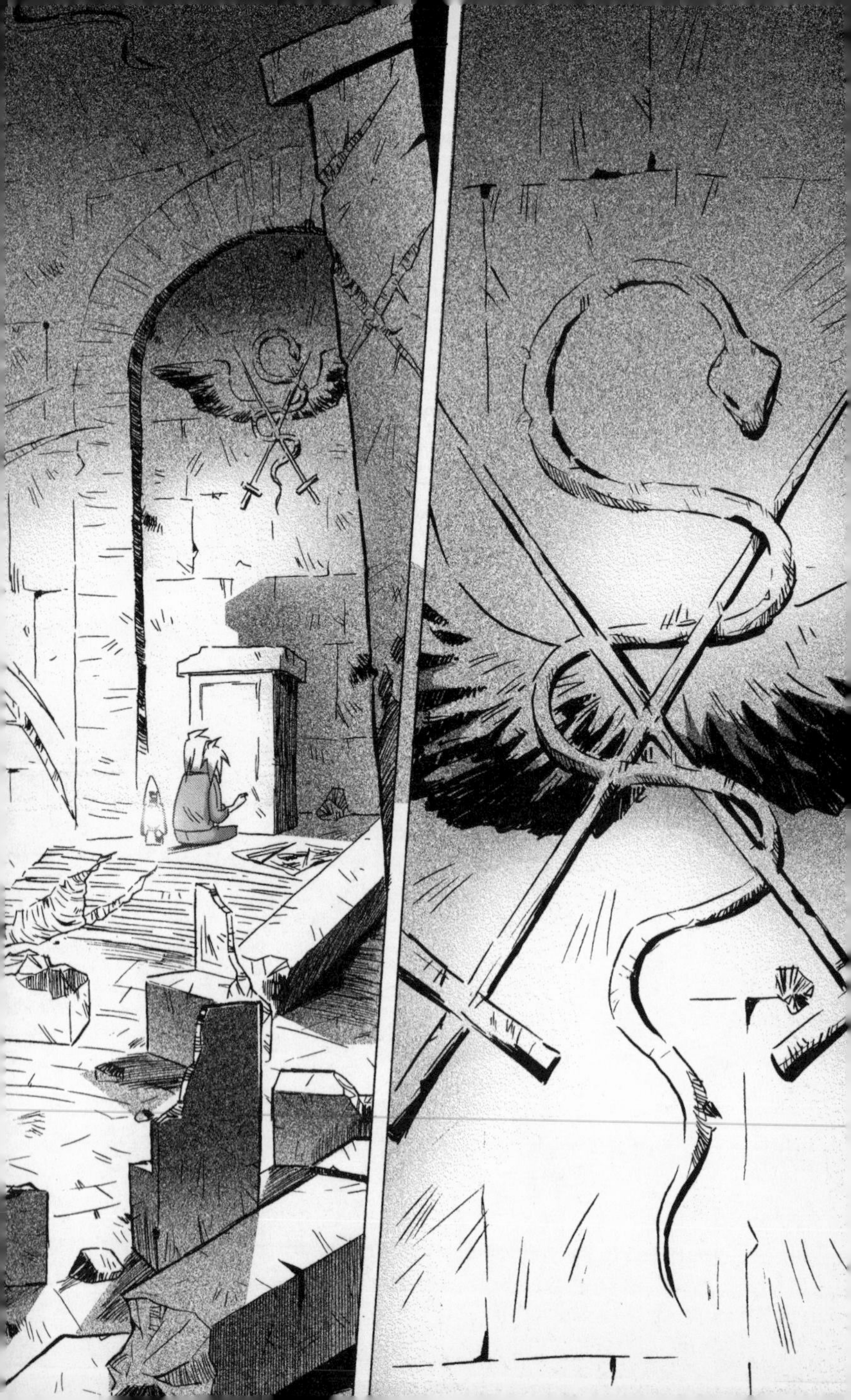

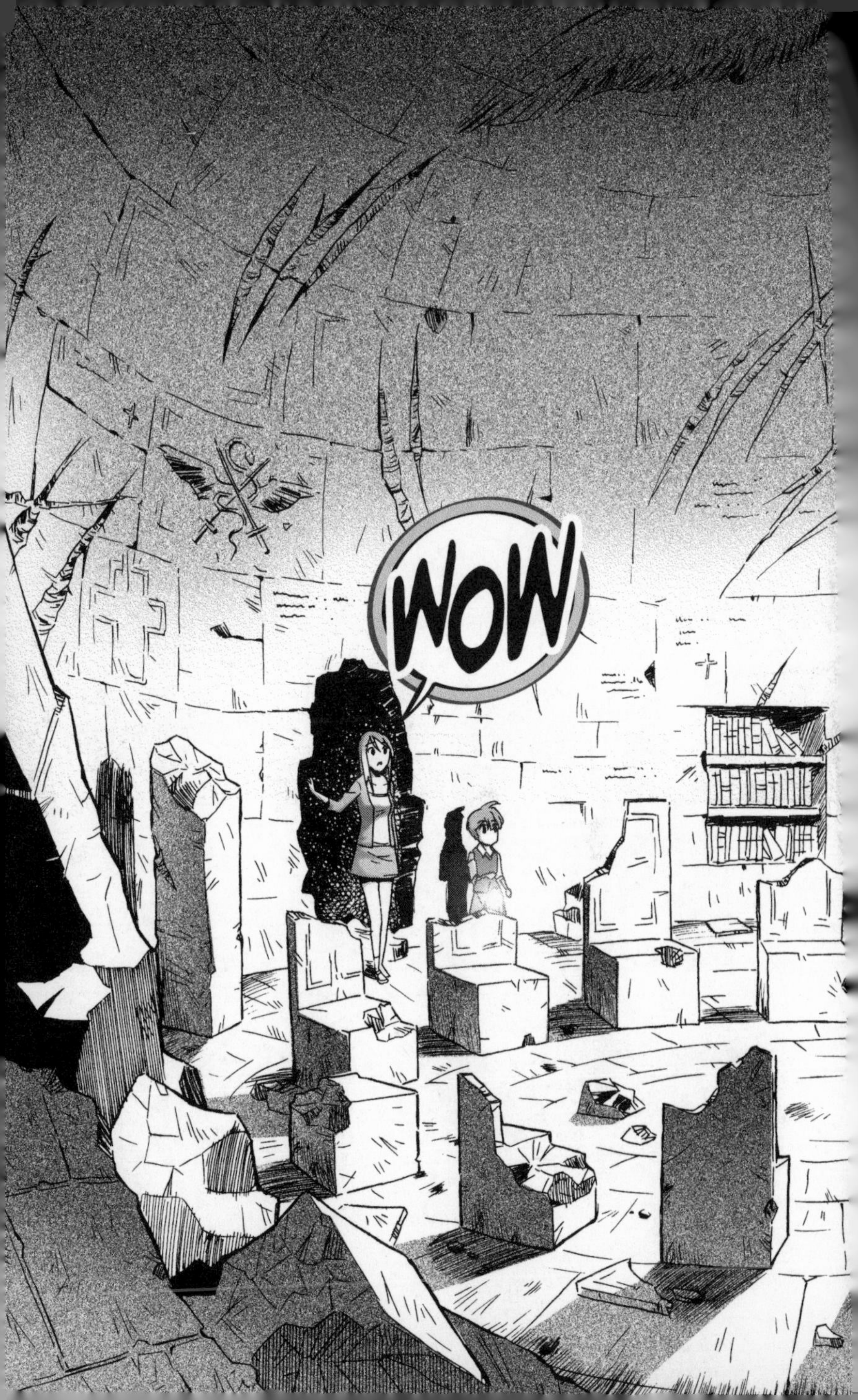
WOW

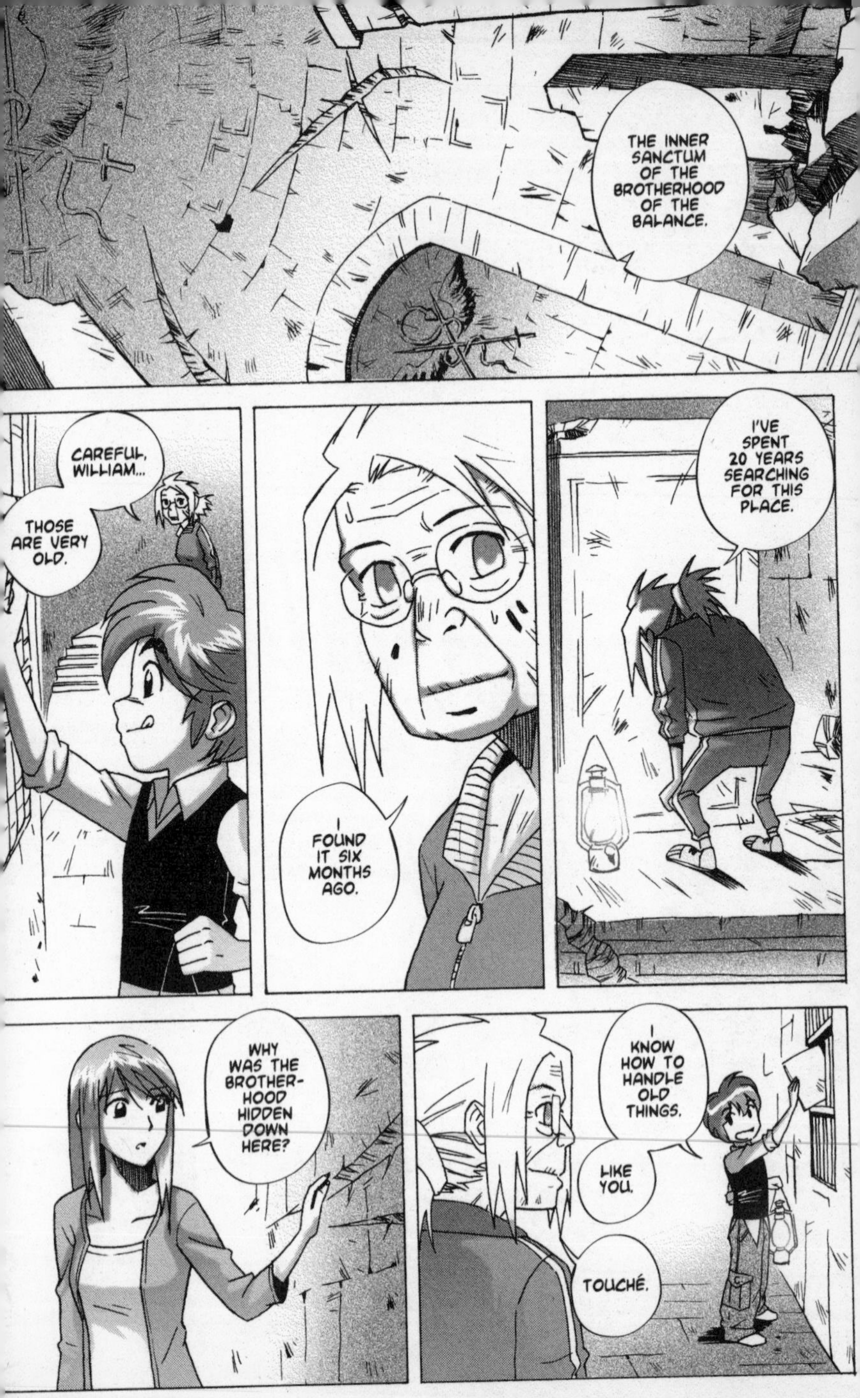
THE INNER SANCTUM OF THE BROTHERHOOD OF THE BALANCE.
I'VE SPENT 20 YEARS SEARCHING FOR THIS PLACE.
I FOUND IT SIX MONTHS AGO.
CAREFUL, WILLIAM...
THOSE ARE VERY OLD.
I KNOW HOW TO HANDLE OLD THINGS.
LIKE YOU.
TOUCHÉ.
WHY WAS THE BROTHER-HOOD HIDDEN DOWN HERE?

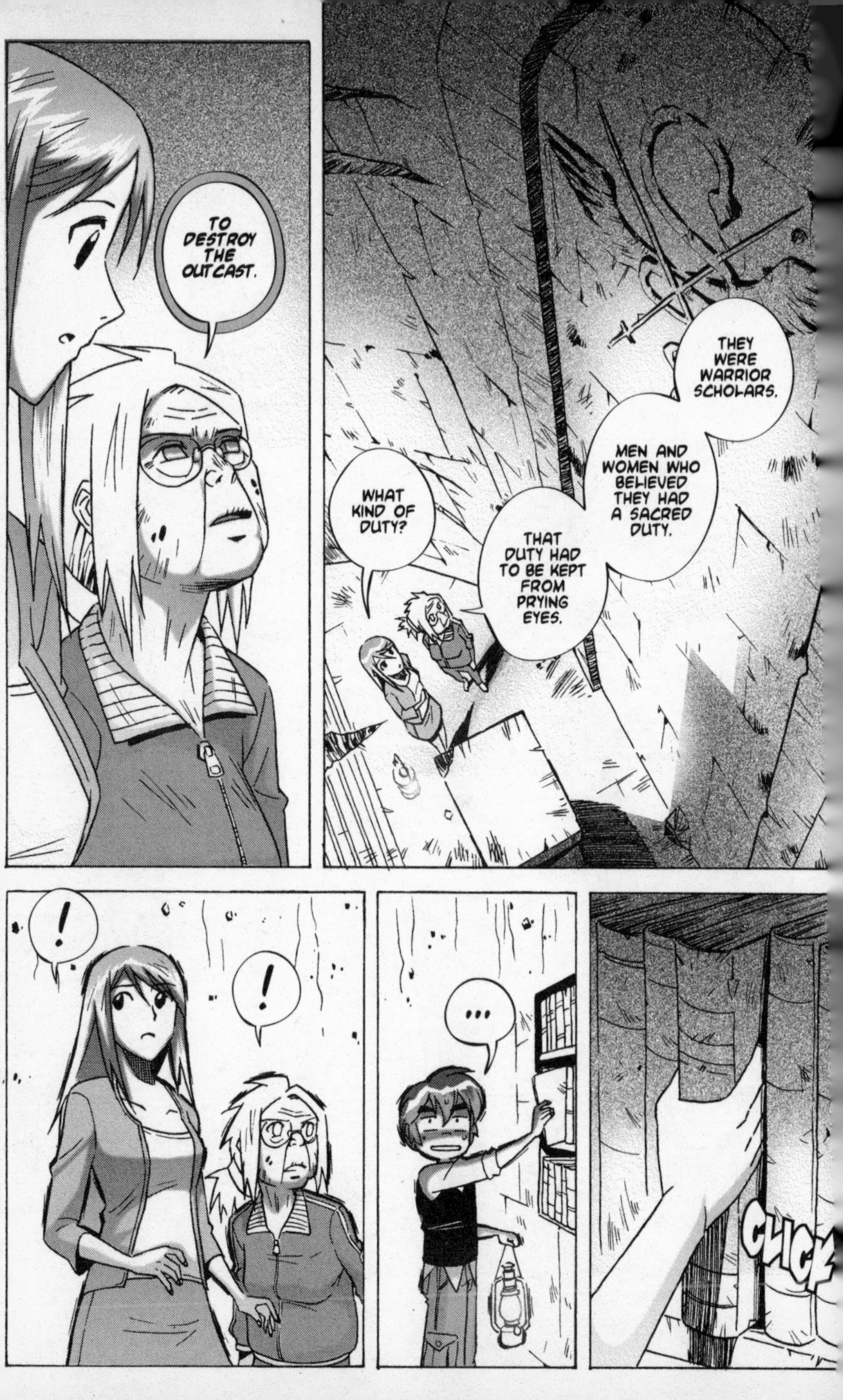
THEY WERE WARRIOR SCHOLARS.
MEN AND WOMEN WHO BELIEVED THEY HAD A SACRED DUTY.
THAT DUTY HAD TO BE KEPT FROM PRYING EYES.
WHAT KIND OF DUTY?
TO DESTROY THE OUTCAST.
CLICK
...
!
!

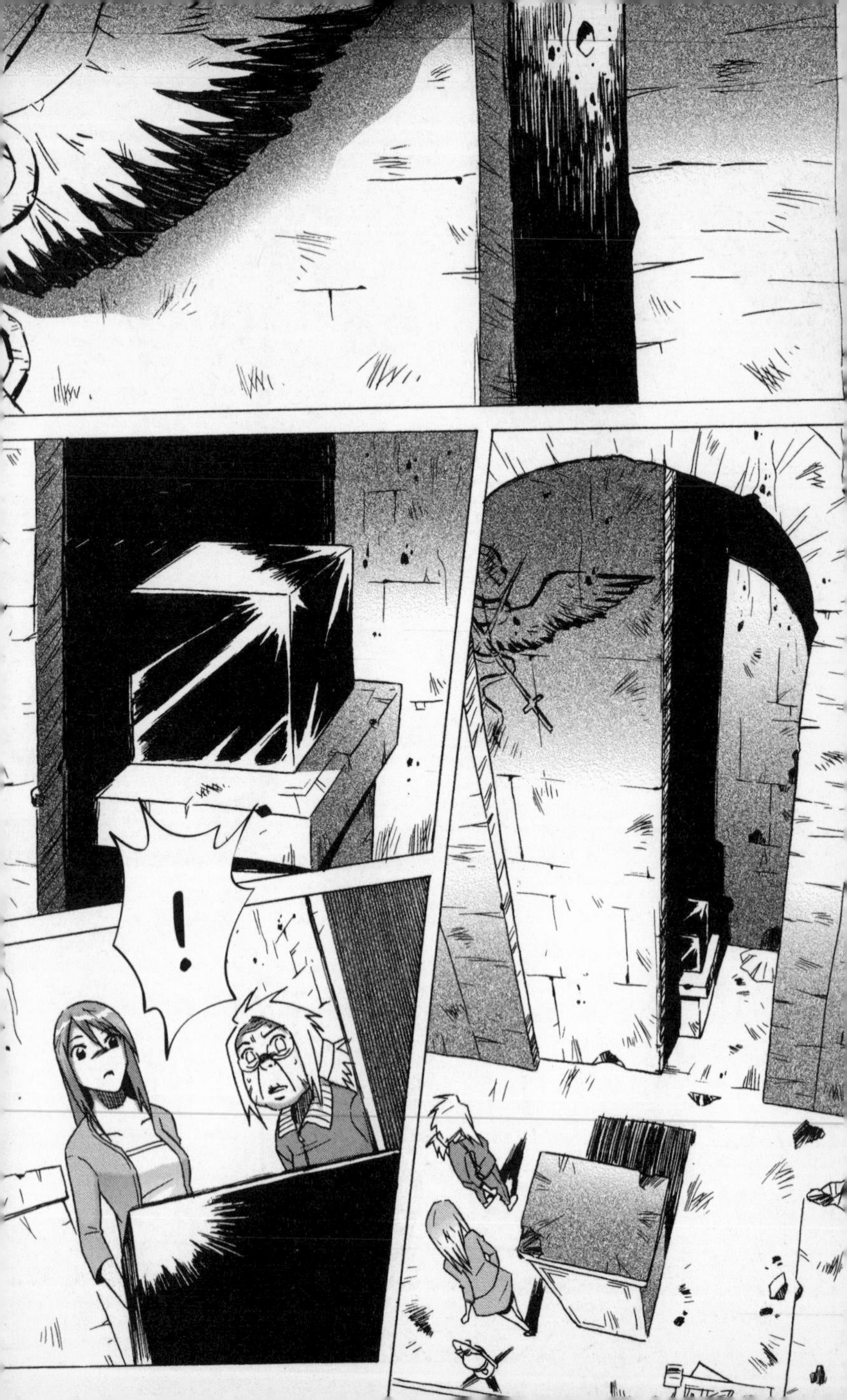
!

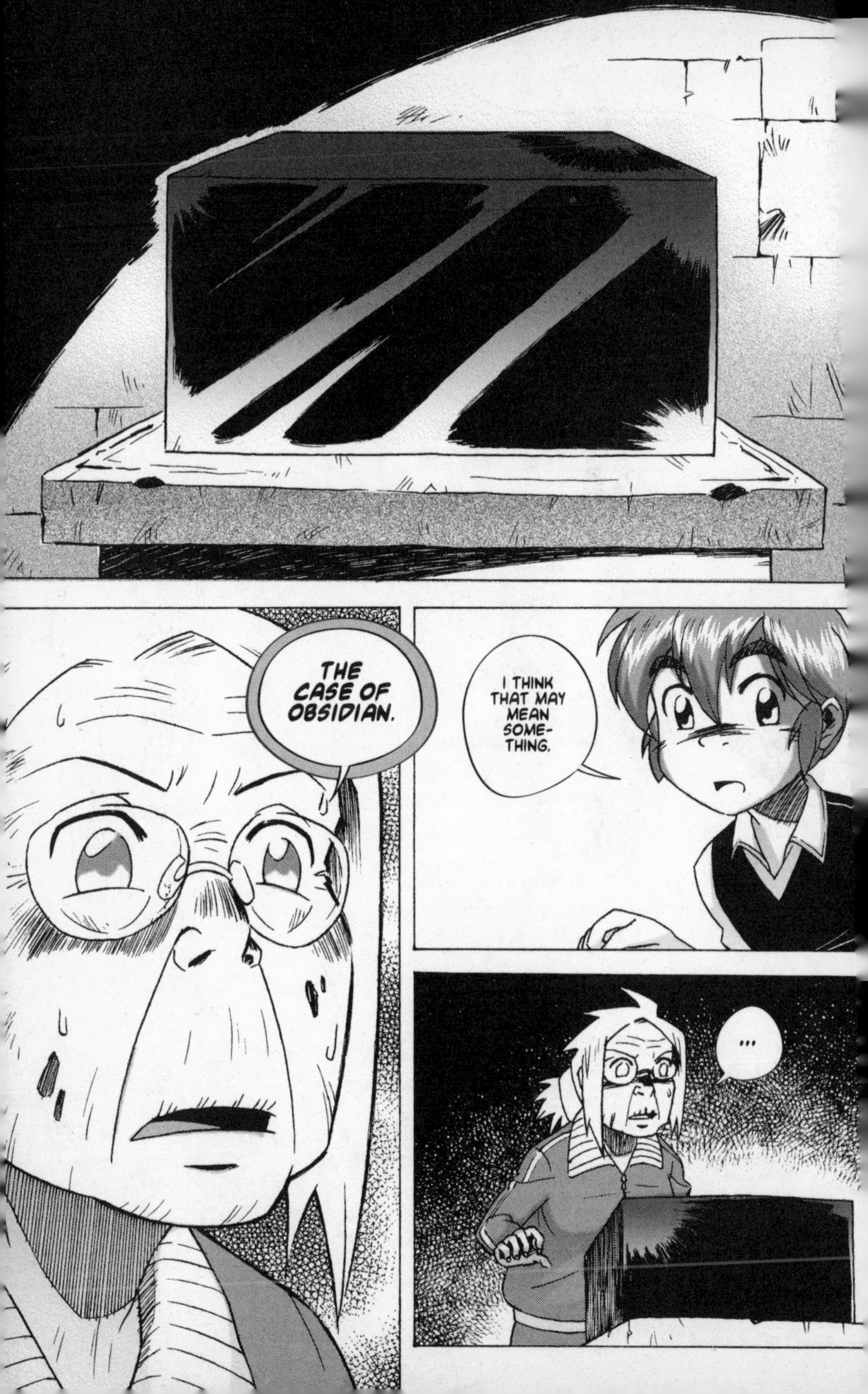
I THINK THAT MAY MEAN SOME-THING.
...
THE CASE OF OBSIDIAN.

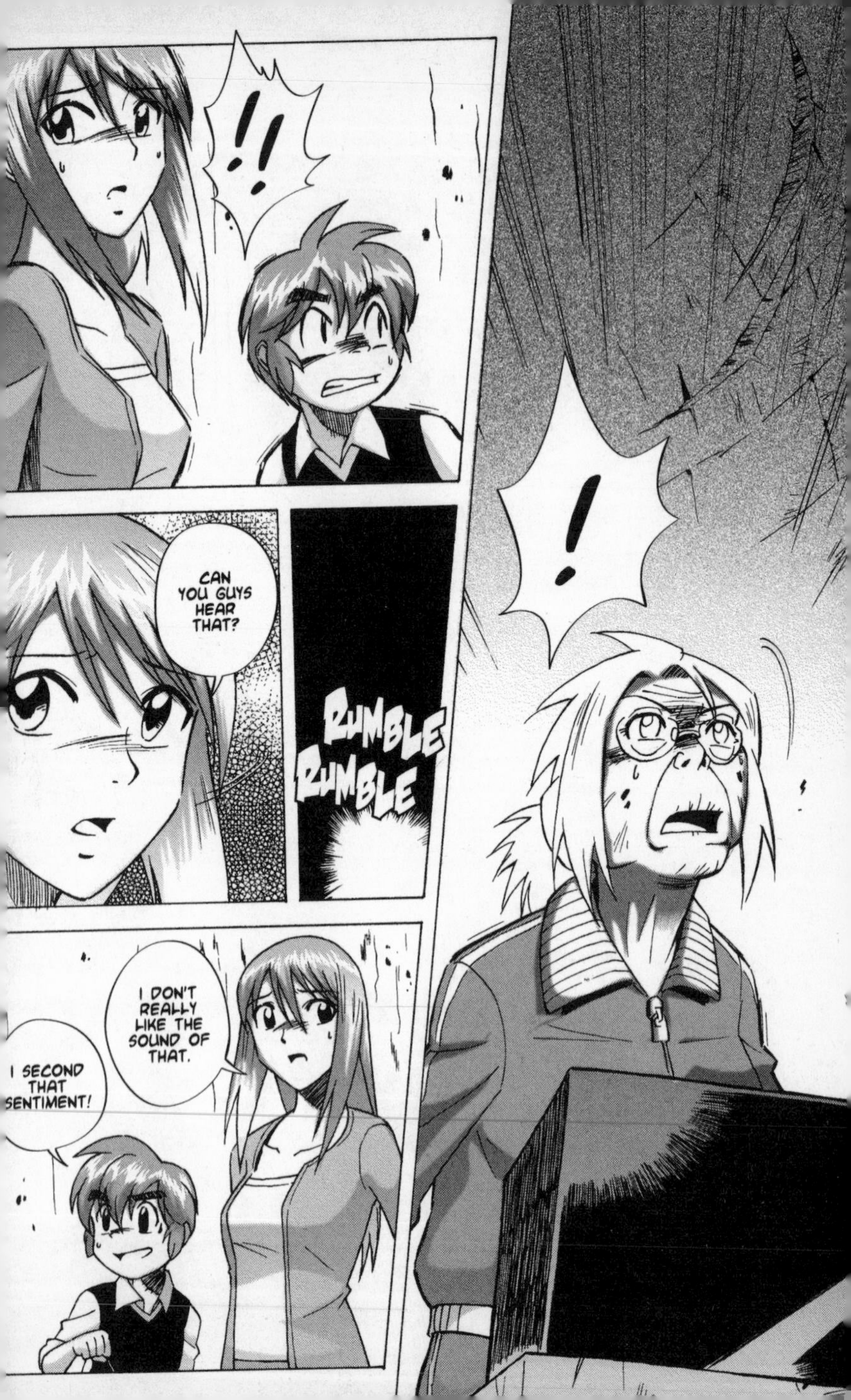
!
!!
RUMBLE RUMBLE
CAN YOU GUYS HEAR THAT?
I DON'T REALLY LIKE THE SOUND OF THAT.
I SECOND THAT SENTIMENT!

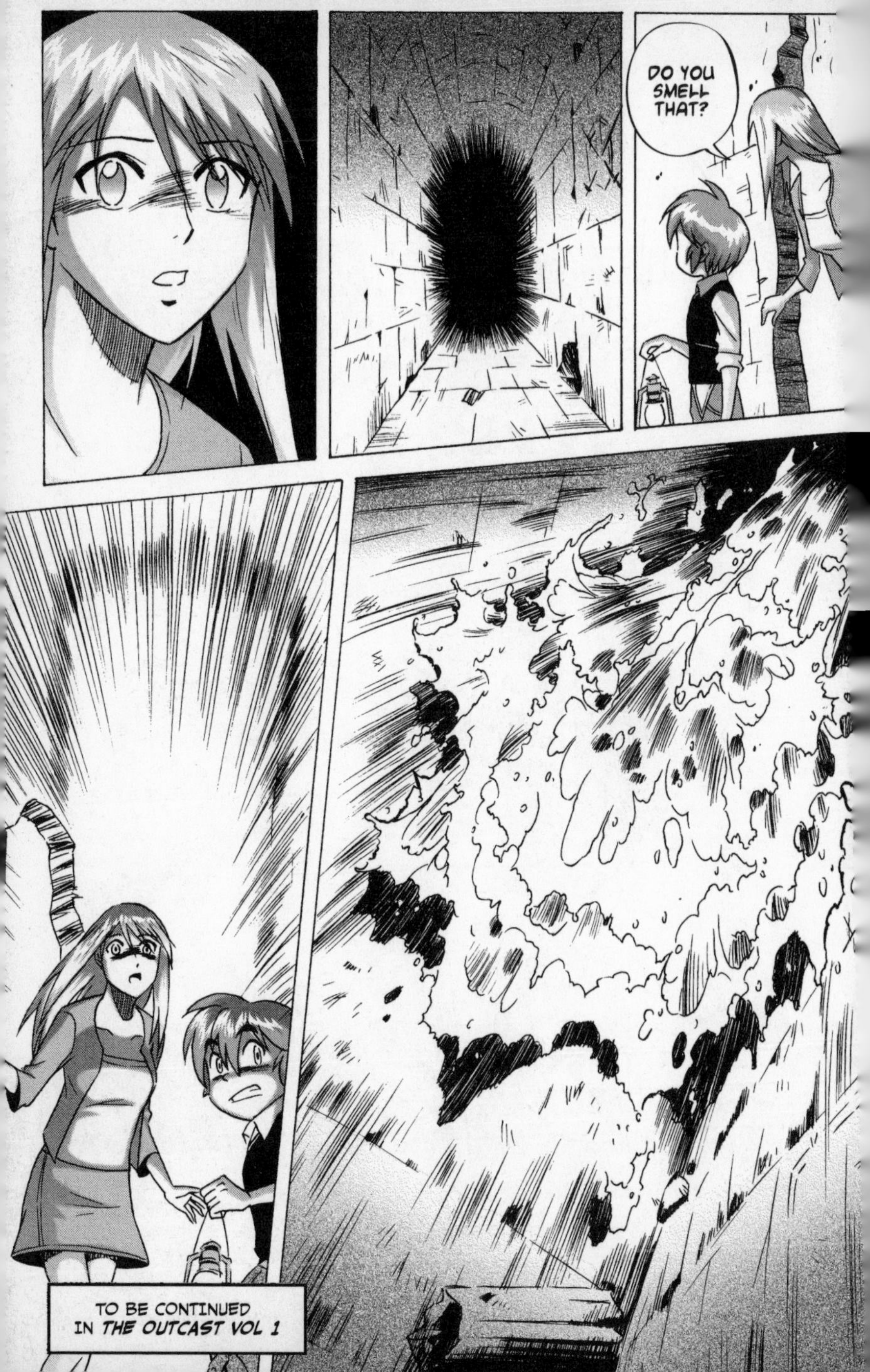
DO YOU SMELL THAT?
TO BE CONTINUED IN THE OUTCAST VOL 1

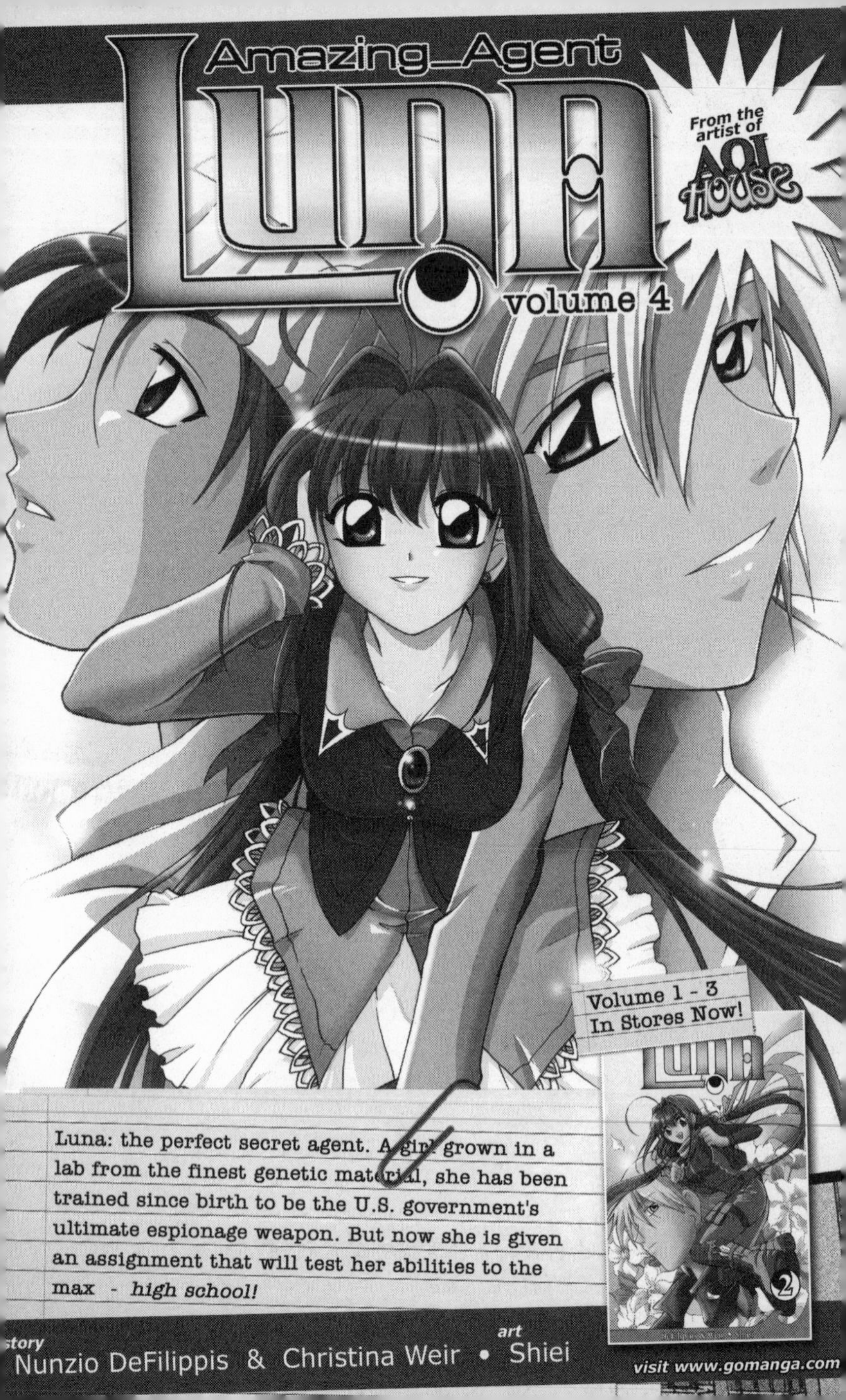

Amazing Agent
LUNA
volume 4
From the artist of AOI HOUSE
Volume 1 - 3
In Stores Now!
LUNA
2
Luna: the perfect secret agent. A girl grown in a lab from the finest genetic material, she has been trained since birth to be the U.S. government's ultimate espionage weapon. But now she is given an assignment that will test her abilities to the max - high school!
story
Nunzio DeFilippis & Christina Weir
art
Shiei
visit www.gomanga.com

THE END

YOU'RE READING THE WRONG WAY

This is the last page of *Destiny's Hand* Volume 2.

This book reads from right to left, Japanese style. To read from the beginning, flip the book over to the other side, start with the top right panel, and take it from there.

If this is your first time reading manga, just follow the diagram. It may seem backwards at first, but you'll get used to it! Have fun!